S0-AFO-071

CHILTON'S
REPAIR & TUNE-UP GUIDE

FORD MERCURY 1968-83

Custom • Custom 500 • Galaxie 500 • XL • LTD through 1982
Crown Victoria • Ranch Wagon • Country Sedan • Country Squire
Marquis through 1982 • Gran Marquis • Colony Park
Park Lane • Monterey • Commuter

Vice President and General Manager JOHN P. KUSHNERICK
Managing Editor KERRY A. FREEMAN, S.A.E.
Senior Editor RICHARD J. RIVELE, S.A.E.
Editor CARL CANFIELD, S.A.E.

CHILTON BOOK COMPANY
Radnor, Pennsylvania
19089

SAFETY NOTICE

Proper service and repair procedures are vital to the safe, reliable operation of all motor vehicles, as well as the personal safety of those performing repairs. This book outlines procedures for servicing and repairing vehicles using safe, effective methods. The procedures contain many NOTES, CAUTIONS and WARNINGS which should be followed along with standard safety procedures to eliminate the possibility of personal injury or improper service which could damage the vehicle or compromise its safety.

It is important to note that repair procedures and techniques, tools and parts for servicing motor vehicles, as well as the skill and experience of the individual performing the work vary widely. It is not possible to anticipate all of the conceivable ways or conditions under which vehicles may be serviced, or to provide cautions as to all of the possible hazards that may result. Standard and accepted safety precautions and equipment should be used when handling toxic or flammable fluids, and safety goggles or other protection should be used during cutting, grinding, chiseling, prying, or any other process that can cause material removal or projectiles.

Some procedures require the use of tools specially designed for a specific purpose. Before substituting another tool or procedure, you must be completely satisfied that neither your personal safety, nor the performance of the vehicle will be endangered.

Although information in this guide is based on industry sources and is as complete as possible at the time of publication, the possibility exists that the manufacturer made later changes which could not be included here. While striving for total accuracy, Chilton Book Company cannot assume responsibility for any errors, changes, or omissions that may occur in the compilation of this data.

PART NUMBERS

Part numbers listed in this reference are not recommendations by Chilton for any product by brand name. They are references that can be used with interchange manuals and aftermarket supplier catalogs to locate each brand supplier's discrete part number.

ACKNOWLEDGMENTS

The Chilton Book Company expresses its appreciation to the Ford Motor Company, Dearborn, Michigan, for their generous assistance.

Copyright © 1983 by Chilton Book Company
All Rights Reserved
Published in Radnor, Pennsylvania 19089 by Chilton Book Company

Manufactured in the United States of America
1234567890   2109876543

Chilton's Repair & Tune-Up Guide: Ford and Mercury 1968–83
ISBN 0-8019-7318-X pbk.
Library of Congress Catalog Card No. 82-72940

CONTENTS

Quick Reference Specifications For Your Vehicle

Fill in this chart with the most commonly used specifications for your vehicle. Specifications can be found in Chapters 1 through 3 or on the tune-up decal under the hood of the vehicle.

 Tune-Up

Firing Order_____

Spark Plugs:

    Type_____

    Gap (in.)_____

Point Gap (in.)_____

Dwell Angle (°)_____

Ignition Timing (°)_____

    Vacuum (Connected/Disconnected)_____

Valve Clearance (in.)

    Intake_____   Exhaust_____

Capacities

Engine Oil (qts)

    With Filter Change_____

    Without Filter Change_____

Cooling System (qts)_____

Manual Transmission (pts)_____

    Type_____

Automatic Transmission (pts)_____

    Type_____

Front Differential (pts)_____

    Type_____

Rear Differential (pts)_____

    Type_____

Transfer Case (pts)_____

    Type_____

FREQUENTLY REPLACED PARTS

Use these spaces to record the part numbers of frequently replaced parts.

PCV VALVE

Manufacturer_____

Part No._____

OIL FILTER

Manufacturer_____

Part No._____

AIR FILTER

Manufacturer_____

Part No._____

General Information and Maintenance

HOW TO USE THIS BOOK

This book has been written to help the Ford or Mercury owner perform maintenance, tune-ups and repairs on his automobile. It is intended for both the novice and for those more familiar with auto repairs. Since this book contains information on very simple operations (Chapters 1 and 2) and the more involved ones (Chapters 3–9), the user will not outgrow the book as he masters simple repairs and is ready to progress to more difficult operations. Chapter 10 contains helpful Troubleshooting information for all systems on the car.

Several things were assumed of you while the repair procedures were being written. They are mentioned here so that you will be aware of them. It was assumed that you own, or are willing to purchase, a basic set of hand tools and equipment. A skeletal listing of tools and equipment has been drawn up for you.

For many repair operations, the factory has suggested a special tool to perform the repairs. If it was at all possible, a conventional tool was substituted for the special tool in these cases. However, there are some operations which cannot be done without the use of these tools. To perform these jobs correctly, it will be necessary to order the tool through your local Ford or Mercury dealer's parts department.

Two basic rules of automobile mechanics deserve mentioning here. Whenever the left-side of the car is referred to, it is meant to specify the driver's side. Likewise, the right-side of the car means the passenger's side. Also, most screws, nuts, and bolts are removed by turning counterclockwise and tightened by turning clockwise.

Before performing any repairs, read the entire section of the book that deals with that job. In many places a description of the system is provided. By reading this first, and then reading the entire repair procedure, you will understand the function of the system you will be working on and what will be involved in the repair operation, prior to starting the job. This will enable you to avoid problems and also to help you learn about your car while you are working on it.

While every effort was made to make the book as simple, yet as detailed as possible, there is no substitute for personal experience. You can gain the confidence and feel for mechanical things needed to make auto repairs only by doing them yourself. If you take your time and cnncentrate on what you are doing, you will be amazed at how fast you can learn.

TOOLS AND EQUIPMENT

Now that you have purchased this book and committed yourself to maintaining your car, a small set of basic tools and equipment will prove handy. The first group of items should be adequate for most maintenance and light repair procedures:

• Sliding T-bar handle or ratchet wrench; ⅜ in. drive socket wrench set (with 12 in. breaker bar);
  • Universal adapter for socket wrench set;
  • Flat blade and phillips head screwdrivers;
  • Pliers;
  • Adjustable wrench;
  • Locking pliers;
  • Open-end wrench set;
  • Feeler gauge set;
  • Oil filter strap wrench;
  • Brake adjusting spoon;
  • Drift pin;
  • Torque wrench;
  • A hammer.

Along with the above mentioned tools, the following equipment should be on hand:
• Scissors jack or hydraulic jack of sufficient capacity;

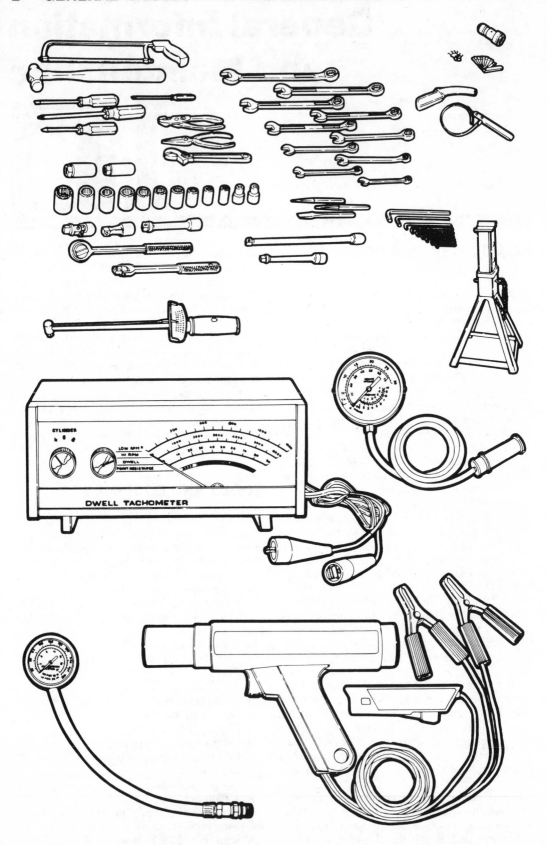

The tools and equipment shown here will handle the majority of the maintenance on a car

- Jackstands of sufficient capacity;
- Wheel blocks;
- Grease gun (hand-operated type);
- Drip pan (low and wide);
- Drop light;
- Tire pressure gauge;
- Penetrating oil (spray lubricant);
- Waterless hand cleaner.

In this age of emission controls and high priced gasoline, it is important to keep your car in proper tune. The following items, though they will represent an investment equal or greater to that of the first group, will tell you everything you might need to know about a car's state of tune:

- 12-volt test light;
- Compression gauge;
- Manifold vacuum gauge;
- Power timing light;
- A dwell-tachometer.

Special Tools

Some repair procedures in this book call for the use of special factory tools. Although every effort is made to explain the repair job using your regular set of tools, sometimes the use of a special tool cannot be avoided. These tools are obtainable from your local Ford dealer or can be ordered directly through the Owatonna Tool Company, Owatonna, Minnesota, 55060.

SERVICING YOUR VEHICLE SAFELY

It is virtually impossible to anticipate all of the hazards involved with automotive maintenance and service but care and common sense will prevent most accidents.

The rules of safety for mechanics range from "don't smoke around gasoline," to "use the proper tool for the job." The trick to avoiding injuries is to develop safe work habits and take every possible precaution.

Do's

- Do keep a fire extinguisher and first aid kit within easy reach.
- Do wear safety glasses or goggles when cutting, drilling, grinding or prying. If you wear glasses for the sake of vision, then they should be made of hardened glass that can serve also as safety glasses, or wear safety goggles over your regular glasses.
- Do shield your eyes whenever you work around the battery. Batteries contain sul-

phuric acid; in case of contact with the eyes or skin, flush the area with water or a mixture of water and baking soda and get medical attention immediately.

- Do use safety stands dor any under-car service. Jacks are for raising vehicles; safety stands are for making sure the vehicle stays raised until you want it to come down. Whenever the vehicle is raised, block the wheels remaining on the ground and set the parking brake.
- Do use adequate ventilation when working with any chemicals. Asbestos dust resulting from brake lining wear can cause cancer.
- Do disconnect the negative battery cable when working on the electrical system. The primary ignition system can contain up to 40,000 volts.
- Do follow manufacturer's directions whenever working with potentially hazardous materials. Both brake fluid and antifreeze are poisonous if taken internally.
- Do properly maintain your tools. Loose hammerheads, mushroomed punches and chisels, frayed or poorly grounded electrical cords, excessively worn screwdrivers, spread wrenches (open end), cracked sockets, slipping ratchest, or faulty droplight sockets can cause accidents.
- Do use the proper size and type of tool for the job being done.
- Do when possible, pull on a wrench handle rather than push on it, and adjust your stance to prevent a fall.
- Do be sure that adjustable wrenches are tightly adjusted on the nut or bolt and pulled so that the face is on the side of the fixed jaw.
- Do select a wrench or socket that fits the nut or bolt. The wrench or socket should sit straight, not cocked.
- Do strike squarely with a hammer; avoid glancing blows.
- Do set the parking brake and block the drive wheels if the work requires that the engine be running.

Dont's

- Don't run an engine in a garage or anywhere else without proper ventilation— EVER! Carbon monoxide is poisonous; it is absorbed by the body 400 times faster than oxygen; it takes a long time to leave the human body and you can build up a deadly supply of it in your system by simply breathing in a little every day. You may not realize you are slowly poisoning yourself. Always use power vents, windows, fans or open the garage doors.
- Don't work around moving parts while wearing a necktie or other loose clothing. Short

sleeves are much safer than long, loose sleeves. Hard-toed shoes with neoprene soles protect your toes and give a better grip on slippery surfaces. Jewelry such as watches, fancy belt buckles, beads or body adornment of any kind is not safe working around a car. Long hair should be hidden under a hat or cap.

• Don't use pockets for toolboxes. A fall or bump can drive a screwdriver deep into your body. Even a wiping cloth hanging from the back pocket can wrap around a spinning shaft or fan.

• Don't smoke when working around gasoline, cleaning solvent or other flammable material.

• Don't smoke when working around the battery. When the battery is being charged, it gives off explosive hydrogen gas.

• Don't use gasoline to wash your hands; there are excellent soaps available. Gasoline may contain lead, and lead can enter the body through a cut, accumulating in the body until you are very ill. Gasoline also removes all the natural oils from the skin so that bone dry hands will suck up oil and grease.

• Don't service the air conditioning system unless you are equipped with the necessary tools and training. The refrigerant, R-12, is extremely cold and when exposed to the air, will instantly freeze any surface it comes in contact with, including your eyes. Although the refrigerant is normally non-toxic, R-12 becomes a deadly poisonous gas in the presence of an open flame. One good whiff of the vapors from burning refrigerant can be fatal.

SERIAL NUMBER IDENTIFICATION

Vehicle Identification Number

1968–80

The official vehicle identification number for title and registration purposes is stamped on a metal tag, which is fastened to the top of the instrument panel. The tag is located on the driver's side, visible through the windshield. The first digit in the vehicle identification number is the model year of the car (0—1970, 4—1974, etc.). The second digit is the assembly plant code for the plant in which the vehicle was built. The third and fourth digits are the body serial code designations (2-dr sdn, 4-dr sdn). The fifth digit is the engine code which identifies the type of engine originally installed in the vehicle (see "Engine Codes" chart). The last six digits are the consecutive unit numbers which start at 100,001 for the

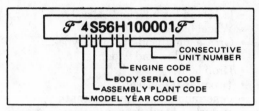

Vehicle identification number tag

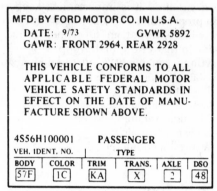

Vehicle certification label—1973–80

first car of a model year built at each assembly plant.

From 1981

Beginning in 1981, the serial number contains seventeen or more digits or letters. The first three give the "world" manufacturer code; the fourth—the type of restraint system; the fifth will remain the letter "P"; the sixth and seventh—the car line, series and body type; the eighth—the engine type; the ninth—a check digit; the tenth—the model year; the eleventh—the assembly plant; the remaining numbers are the production sequence.

Vehicle Certification Label

The vehicle certification label is attached to the left door lock pillar on 2-door models and on the rear face of the driver's door on 4-door models. The top half of the label contains the name of the vehicle manufacturer, date of manufacture and the manufacturer's certification statement. On 1973 and later models, the top half of the label also contains the gross vehicle weight rating and the front and rear gross vehicle axle ratings. The gross vehicle weight rating is useful in determining the load carrying capacity of your car. Merely subtract the curb weight from the posted gross weight and what is left over is how much you can haul around. The bottom half of the vehicle certification label contains the vehicle identification number (as previously described), the body type code, the exterior paint color code, the

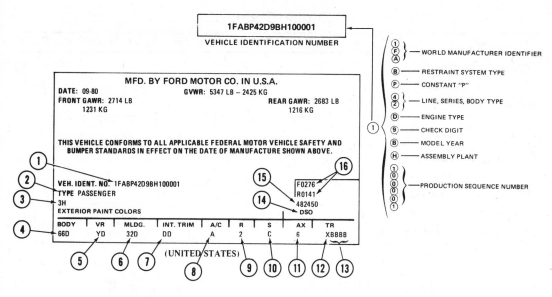

1FABP42D9BH100001

VEHICLE IDENTIFICATION NUMBER

MFD. BY FORD MOTOR CO. IN U.S.A.

DATE: 09-80   GVWR: 5347 LB – 2425 KG
FRONT GAWR: 2714 LB   REAR GAWR: 2683 LB
        1231 KG   1216 KG

THIS VEHICLE CONFORMS TO ALL APPLICABLE FEDERAL MOTOR VEHICLE SAFETY AND
BUMPER STANDARDS IN EFFECT ON THE DATE OF MANUFACTURE SHOWN ABOVE.

VEH. IDENT. NO. 1FABP42D9BH100001
TYPE PASSENGER
3H
EXTERIOR PAINT COLORS

BODY	VR	MLDG.	INT. TRIM	A/C	R	S	AX	TR
66D	YD	32D	DD	A	2	C	6	XBBBB

(UNITED STATES)

F0276
R0141
482450
DSO

- (1) (F) (A) } WORLD MANUFACTURER IDENTIFIER
- (B) — RESTRAINT SYSTEM TYPE
- (P) — CONSTANT "P"
- (4) (2) } LINE, SERIES, BODY TYPE
- (D) — ENGINE TYPE
- (9) — CHECK DIGIT
- (B) — MODEL YEAR
- (H) — ASSEMBLY PLANT
- (1)(0)(0)(0)(0)(1) } PRODUCTION SEQUENCE NUMBER

2. Vehicle type
3. Paint
4. Body type code
5. Vinyl roof
6. Body side moulding
7. Trim code—(First code letter = fabric and seat type. Second code = color)
8. Air conditioning
9. Radio
10. Sun/moon roof
11. Axle ratio
12. Transmission
13. Springs—Front l. and r., rear l. and r. (4 codes)
14. District sales office
15. PTO/SPL order number
16. Accessory reserve load

Vehicle identification—from 1981

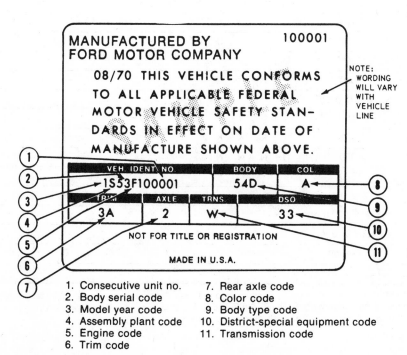

MANUFACTURED BY
FORD MOTOR COMPANY   100001

08/70 THIS VEHICLE CONFORMS
TO ALL APPLICABLE FEDERAL
MOTOR VEHICLE SAFETY STAN-
DARDS IN EFFECT ON DATE OF
MANUFACTURE SHOWN ABOVE.

NOTE:
WORDING
WILL VARY
WITH
VEHICLE
LINE

VEH. IDENT. NO.	BODY	COL.
1S53F100001	54D	A

TRIM	AXLE	TRNS.	DSO
3A	2	W	33

NOT FOR TITLE OR REGISTRATION

MADE IN U.S.A.

1. Consecutive unit no.
2. Body serial code
3. Model year code
4. Assembly plant code
5. Engine code
6. Trim code
7. Rear axle code
8. Color code
9. Body type code
10. District-special equipment code
11. Transmission code

Vehicle certification label—1970–72

Engine Codes

6-Cylinder Models

Disp	Bbl	Hp	'68	'69	'70	'71	'72	'73	'74	'75	'76	'77	'78	'79	'80	'81	'82	'83
240	1	103 (net)					V											
240	1	140				V												
240	1	150	V	V	V													

8-Cylinder Models

Disp	Bbl	Hp	'68	'69	'70	'71	'72	'73	'74	'75	'76	'77	'78	'79	'80	'81	'82	'83
255	2	255, 120 (net)															D	D
302	2①	140, 130 (net)					F		——			F		F	F	F	F	F
302	2	210	F	F	F	F												
351W	2	153, 162, 145 (net)*					H	H	H			H	H	G	G	G	G	
351C	2	163 (net)					H	H	H									
351M	2	148 (net)								H								
351M	2	152 (net)									H	H	H	H				
351	2	240				H												
351	2	250			H													
390	2	255				Y												
390	2	265		Y	Y													
390	2	270	Y	Y														
390	2	280	X															
390	4	315	Z															
400	2	158 (net)								S		S	S					
400	2	170 (net)							S									
400	2	172 (net)					S	S										
400	2	180 (net)									S	S						
400	2	260				S												
428	4	340	Q															
428PI	4	360	P	P	P													
429	4	208, 212 (net)*					N	N										
429PI	4	NA					P											
429	4	320		K	K	K												
429	4	360	N	N	N	N												
429PI	4	370				P												
460	4	202 (net)										A	A	A				
460	4	195, 218, 220 (net)*							A	A								
460	4	200, 208, 212 (net)*					A	A										
460PI	4	226 (net)										C	C	C				
460PI	4	267, 274, 275 (net)*						C	C									

PI Police Interceptor
* Net horsepower rating varies with model application
① 1982–83 U.S. models are equipped with electronic Fuel injection

Rear Axle Ratio Codes

Ratio	'68	'69	'70	'71	'72	'73	'74	'75	'76	'77	'78	'79	'80	'81	'82	'83
2.26:1	—	—	—	—	—	—	—	—	—	—	—	G	G	—	—	—
2.47:1	—	—	—	—	—	—	—	—	—	—	B	—	—	—	—	—
2.50:1	—	—	—	—	—	—	—	—	—	1(J)	—	—	—	—	—	
2.73:1	—	—	—	—	—	—	—	—	—	—	—	8(H)	8	8(M)	8(M)	8(M)
2.75:1	1(A)	2(K)	2(K)	2(K)	2(K)	2(K)	2(K)	2(K)	2(K)	2(K)	2(K)	—	—	—	—	—
2.80:1	3(C)	4(M)	4(M)	—	—	—	—	—	—	—	—	—	—	—	—	—
3.00:1	5(E)	6(O)	6(O)	6(O)	6(O)	6(O)	6(O)	6(O)	6(O)	6(O)	6(O)	—	—	—	—	—
3.07:1	—	—	B	B	—	—	5(E)	5(E)	—	—	—	—	—	—	—	—
3.08:1	—	—	—	—	—	—	—	—	—	—	—	Y	Y(Z)	Y(Z)	Y(Z)	Y(Z)
3.10:1	9	7(P)	—	—	—	—	—	—	—	—	—	—	—	—	—	—
3.25:1	7(G)	9(R)	9(R)	9(R)	9(R)	9(R)	9(R)	9(R)	9(R)	9(R)	—	—	—	—	—	—
3.42:1	—	—	—	—	—	—	—	—	—	—	—	—	—	—	4(D)	4(D)
3.50:1	8	—	—	—	—	—	—	—	—	—	—	—	—	—	—	—

NOTE: *Figures in Parentheses indicate locking differential.*

Transmission Codes

Type	Year	Code
3 speed manual	68–71	1
4 speed manual	68	5
4 speed manual	69	6
C4 automatic	68–74	W
C4 automatic	78–80	W
AOD*	80–83	T
FMX automatic	68–80	X
CW automatic	74–75	Y
C6 automatic	68–80	U
C6 automatic (towing)	68–79	Z

*Automatic Overdrive

interior trim color and material code, the rear axle code (see "Rear Axle Codes" chart), the transmission code (see "Transmission Codes" chart) and the district and special order codes.

The vehicle certification label is constructed of special material to guard against its alteration. If it is tampered with or removed, it will be destroyed or the word "VOID" will appear.

ROUTINE MAINTENANCE

Maintenance Interval Chart

The numerals in the maintenance chart represent the suggested intervals between service in thousands of miles or number of months, whichever occurs first.

4,000 miles or 4 mmnths	4
6,000 miles or 6 months	6
8,000 miles or 8 months	8
12,000 miles or 12 months	12
18,000 miles or 18 months	18
24,000 miles or 24 months	24
30,000 miles or 30 months	30
36,000 miles or 36 months	36
As Needed	A/N
Does not apply	—

Air Filter Replacement

At the recommended intervals in the maintenance chart, the air filter element must be replaced. If the vehicle is operated under severely dusty conditions, the element should be changed sooner. On all six and 8 cylinder models, the air filter cover is retained with a single wing nut on top of and in the center of the cover. To replace the element, unscrew the wing nut, lift off the cover and discard the old element.

When the air cleaner is removed, check the choke plate and external linkage for freedom of movement. Brush away all dirt and spray the plate corners and linkage with a small amount of penetrating cleaner/lubricant such as CRC®.

Wipe the air fliter housing clean with a solvent-moistened rag and install the new element with the word "FRONT" facing the front of the car. Install the cover and wing nut finger-tight.

Positive Crankcase Ventilation (PCV) Valve

See "Emission Controls Component Service" in Chapter 4.

Evaporative Control System Canister

See "Emission Control Component Service" in Chapter 4.

Crankcase Ventilation Filter (in Air Cleaner) Replacement

At the recommended intervals in the maintenance chart, or sooner if the car is operated in dusty areas, at low rpm, for trailer towing, or if the car is used for short runs preventing the engine from reaching operating temperature, the crankcase ventilation filter in the air cleaner must be replaced. Do not attempt to clean this filter.

To replace the filter, simply remove the air filter cover and pull the old crankcase filter out of its housing. Push a new crankcase filter into the housing and install the air filter cover.

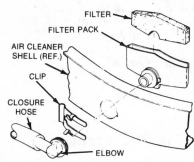

FILTER
FILTER PACK
AIR CLEANER SHELL (REF.)
CLIP
CLOSURE HOSE
ELBOW

Crankcase ventilation filter

Crankcase Filler Cap Cleaning

At the recommended intervals in the maintenance chart, the oil filler cap must be cleaned. Disconnect the positive crankcase ventilation hose from the cap and lift the cap from the rocker cover. Soak the cap in kerosene or mineral spirits to clean the internal element of sludge and blow-by material. After agitating the cap in the solution, shake the cap dry. Reinstall the cap and connect the hose.

Exhaust Gas Recirculation System Component Cleaning

See "Emission Controls Component Service" in Chapter 4.

Exhaust Control Valve (Heat Riser)

1968–71

Some models are equipped with exhaust control (heat riser) valves located near the head pipe connection in the exhaust manifold. These valves aid initial warmup in cold weather by restricting exhaust gas flow slightly. The heat generated by this restriction is transferred to the intake manifold where it results in improved fuel vaporization.

The operation of the exhaust control valve should be checked every 6 months or 6,000 miles. Make sure that the thermostatic spring is hooked on the stop pin and that the tension holds the valve shut. Rotate the counterweight by hand and make sure that it moves freely through about 90° of rotation. A valve which is operating properly will open when light finger pressure is applied (cold engine). Lubricate the shaft bushings with a mixture of penetrating oil and graphite. Operate the valve manually a few times to work in the lubricant.

Battery

FLUID LEVEL (EXCEPT "MAINTENANCE FREE" BATTERIES)

Check the battery electrolyte level at least once a month, or more often in hot weather or during periods of extended car operation. The level can be checked through the case on translucent polypropylene batteries; the cell caps must be removed on other models. The

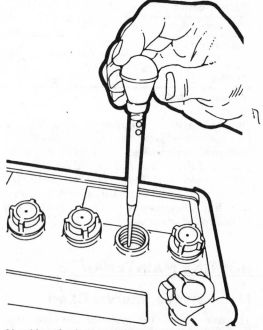

Checking the battery with a battery hydometer

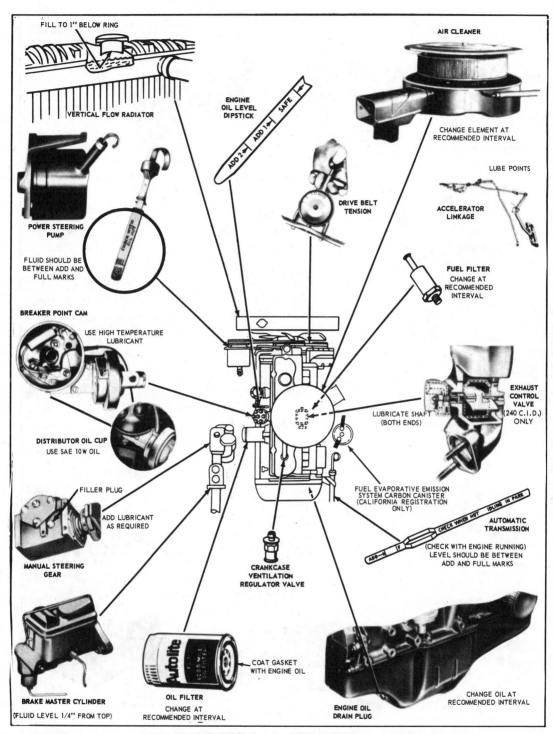

FILL TO 1" BELOW RING

VERTICAL FLOW RADIATOR

ENGINE OIL LEVEL DIPSTICK

ADD 2 — ADD 1 — SAFE

AIR CLEANER

CHANGE ELEMENT AT RECOMMENDED INTERVAL

LUBE POINTS

ACCELERATOR LINKAGE

POWER STEERING PUMP

FLUID SHOULD BE BETWEEN ADD AND FULL MARKS

DRIVE BELT TENSION

FUEL FILTER CHANGE AT RECOMMENDED INTERVAL

BREAKER POINT CAM

USE HIGH TEMPERATURE LUBRICANT

DISTRIBUTOR OIL CUP USE SAE 10W OIL

LUBRICATE SHAFT (BOTH ENDS)

EXHAUST CONTROL VALVE (240 C.I.D.) ONLY

FILLER PLUG

ADD LUBRICANT AS REQUIRED

FUEL EVAPORATIVE EMISSION SYSTEM CARBON CANISTER (CALIFORNIA REGISTRATION ONLY)

CHECK WHEN HOT — IDLING IN PARK

AUTOMATIC TRANSMISSION

(CHECK WITH ENGINE RUNNING) LEVEL SHOULD BE BETWEEN ADD AND FULL MARKS

MANUAL STEERING GEAR

CRANKCASE VENTILATION REGULATOR VALVE

COAT GASKET WITH ENGINE OIL

BRAKE MASTER CYLINDER (FLUID LEVEL 1/4" FROM TOP)

OIL FILTER CHANGE AT RECOMMENDED INTERVAL

ENGINE OIL DRAIN PLUG

CHANGE OIL AT RECOMMENDED INTERVAL

Six-cylinder engine lubrication points

electrolyte level in each cell should be kept filled to the split ring inside, or the line marked on the outside of the case.

If the level is low, add only distilled water, or colorless, odorless drinking water, through the opening until the level is correct. Each cell is completely separate from the others, so each must be checked and filled individually.

If water is added in freezing weather, the car should be driven several miles to allow the water to mix with the electrolyte. Otherwise, the battery could freeze.

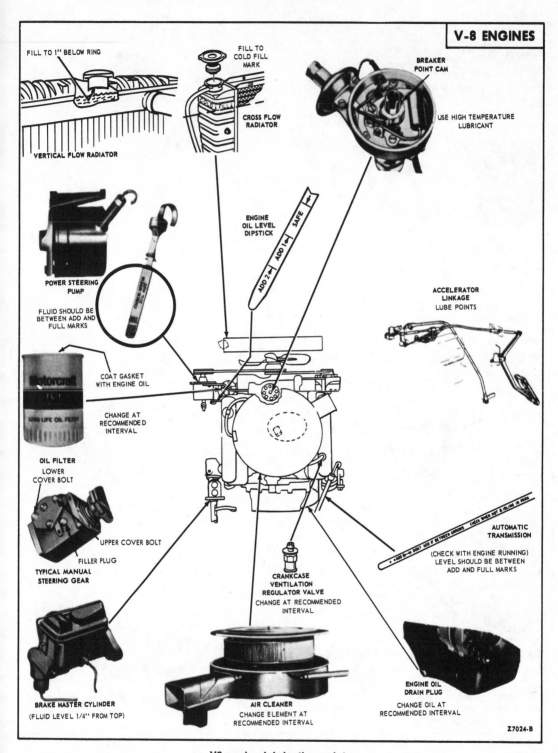

FILL TO 1" BELOW RING

VERTICAL FLOW RADIATOR

FILL TO COLD FILL MARK

CROSS FLOW RADIATOR

BREAKER POINT CAM

USE HIGH TEMPERATURE LUBRICANT

POWER STEERING PUMP

FLUID SHOULD BE BETWEEN ADD AND FULL MARKS

ENGINE OIL LEVEL DIPSTICK

ADD 2   ADD 1   SAFE

ACCELERATOR LINKAGE LUBE POINTS

Motorcraft FL.1 LONG LIFE OIL FILTER

COAT GASKET WITH ENGINE OIL

CHANGE AT RECOMMENDED INTERVAL

OIL FILTER

LOWER COVER BOLT

ADD IF DON'T ADD IF BETWEEN ARROWS   CHECK WHEN HOT & IDLING IN PARK

AUTOMATIC TRANSMISSION

(CHECK WITH ENGINE RUNNING) LEVEL SHOULD BE BETWEEN ADD AND FULL MARKS

UPPER COVER BOLT

FILLER PLUG

TYPICAL MANUAL STEERING GEAR

CRANKCASE VENTILATION REGULATOR VALVE

CHANGE AT RECOMMENDED INTERVAL

BRAKE MASTER CYLINDER

(FLUID LEVEL 1/4" FROM TOP)

AIR CLEANER

CHANGE ELEMENT AT RECOMMENDED INTERVAL

ENGINE OIL DRAIN PLUG

CHANGE OIL AT RECOMMENDED INTERVAL

Z7024-B

V8 engine lubrication points

SPECIFIC GRAVITY (EXCEPT "MAINTENANCE FREE" BATTERIES)

At least once a year, check the specific gravity of the battery, It should be between 1.20 and 1.26 at room temperature.

The specific gravity can be checked with the use of an hydrometer, an inexpensive instrument available from many sources, including auto parts stores. The hydrometer has a squeeze bulb at one end and a nozzle at the other. Battery electrolyte is sucked into the hydrometer until the float is lifted from its seat. The specific gravity is then read by noting the position of the float. Generally, if after charging, the specific gravity between any two cells varies more than 50 points (.050), the battery is bad and should be replaced.

It is not possible to check the specific gravity in this manner on sealed ("maintenance free") batteries, Instead, the indicator built into the top of the case must be relied on to display any signs of battery deterioration. If the indicator is dark, the battery can be assumed to be OK. If the indicator is light, the specific gravity is low, and the battery should be charged or replaced.

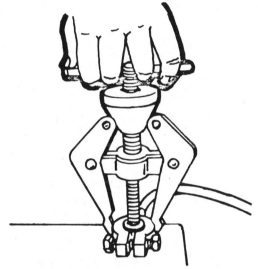

Use a puller to remove the battery cable

CABLES AND CLAMPS

Once a year, the battery terminals and the cable clamps should be cleaned. Loosen the clamps and remove the cables, negative cable first. On batteries with posts on top, the use of a puller specially made for the purpose is recommended. These are inexpensive, and available in auto parts stores. Side terminal battery cables are secured with a bolt.

Clean the cable clamps and the battery terminal with a wire brush, until all corrosion, grease, etc. is removed and the metal is shiny. It is especially important to clean the inside of the clamp thoroughly, since a small deposit of foreign material or oxidation there will prevent a sound electrical connection and inhibit either starting or charging. Special tools are available for cleaning these parts, one type for conventional batteries and another type for side terminal batteries.

Before installing the cables, loosen the battery hold-down clamp or strap, remove the

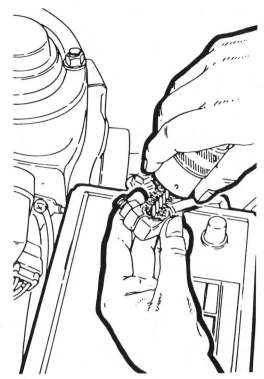

Clean battery cable clamps with a wire brush

battery and check the battery tray. Clear it of any debris, and check it for soundness. Rust should be wire brushed away, and the metal given a coat of anti-rust paint. Replace the battery and tighten the hold-down clamp or strap securely, but be careful not to overtighten, which will crack the battery case.

After the clamps and terminals are clean, reinstall the cables, negative cable last; do not hammer on the clamps to install. Tighten the clamps securely, but do not distort them. Give the clamps and terminals a thin external coat of grease after installation, to retard corrosion.

Check the cables at the same time that the terminals are cleaned. If the cable insulation is cracked or broken, or if the ends are frayed, the cable should be replaced with a new cable of the same length and gauge.

NOTE: *Keep flame or sparks away from the battery; it gives off explosive hydrogen gas. Battery electrolyte contains sulphuric acid. If you should splash any on your skin or in your eyes, flush the affected area with plenty of clear water; if it lands in your eyes, get medical help immediately.*

REPLACEMENT

When it becomes necessary to replace the battery, select a battery with a rating equal to or greater than the battery originally installed. Deterioration, embrittlement and just plain aging of the battery cables, starter motor, and associated wires makes the battery's job harder in successive years. The slow increase in electrical resistance over time makes it prudent to install a new battery with a greater capacity than the old. Details on battery removal and installation are covered in Chapter 3.

Drive Belt Adjustment

Once a year or at 12,000 mile intervals, the tension (and condition) of the alternator, power steering (if so equipped), air conditioning (if so equipped), and Thermactor air pump drive belts should be checked, and, if necessary, adjusted. Loose accessory drive belts can lead to poor engine cooling and diminish alternator, power steering pump, air conditioning compressor or Thermactor air pump output. A belt that is too tight places a severe strain on the water pump, alternator, power steering pump, compressor or air pump bearings.

Replace any belt that is so glazed, worn or stretched that it cannot be tightened sufficiently. On vehicles with matched belts, replace both belts. New belts are to be adjusted to a tension of 140 lbs (½ in., ⅜ in., and $^{15}/_{32}$ in. wide belts) or 80 lbs (¼ in. wide belts) measured on a belt tension gauge. Any belt that has been operating for a minimum of 10 minutes is considered a used belt. In the first 10 minutes, the belt should stretch to its maximum extent. After 10 minutes, stop the engine and recheck the belt tension. Belt tension for a used belt should be maintained at 110 lbs (all except ¼ in. wide belts) or 60 lbs (¼ in. wide belts). If a belt tension gauge is not available, the following procedures may be used.

ALTERNATOR (FAN DRIVE) BELT

All except "Serpentine" (single) belt

1. Position a ruler perpendicular to the drive belt at its longest run. Test the tightness of the belt by pressing it firmly with your thumb. The deflection should not exceed ¼ in.

2. If the deflection exceeds ¼ in., loosen the alternator mounting and adjusting arm bolts.

3a. On 1968–72 V8 and 6 cylinder models, use a pry bar or broom handle to move the alternator toward or away from the engine until the proper tension is reached.

CAUTION: *Apply tension to the front of the alternator only. Positioning the pry bar against the rear end housing will damage the alternator.*

3b. On 1973–and later V8 models, place a

Arrows point out attaching bolts. Turning adjusting nut clockwise increases tension—counterclockwise decreases tension

1 in. open-end or adjustable wrench on the adjusting arm bolt and pull on the wrench until the proper tension is achieved.

4. Holding the alternator in place to maintain tension, tighten the adjusting arm bolt. Recheck the belt tension. When the belt is properly tensioned, tighten the alternator mounting bolt.

POWER STEERING DRIVE BELT

All Six-Cylinder and 1971–72 V8 Models

1. Holding a ruler perpendicular to the drive belt at its longest run, test the tightness of the belt by pressing it firmly with your thumb. The deflection should not exceed ¼ in.

2. To adjust the belt tension, loosen the adjusting and mounting bolts on the front face of the steering pump cover plate (hub side).

3. Using a pry bar or broom handle on the pump hub as shown, move the power steering pump toward or away from the engine until the proper tension is reached. Do not pry against the reservoir as it is relatively soft and easily deformed.

4. Holding the pump in place, tighten the adjusting arm bolt and then recheck the belt tension. When the belt is properly tensioned tighten the mounting bolts.

1973–and later V8 Models (except single drive belt)

1. Position a ruler perpendicular to the drive belt at its longest run. Test the tightness of the belt by pressing it firmly with your thumb. The deflection should be about ¼ in.

2. To adjust the belt tension, loosen the three bolts in the three elongated adjusting slots at the power steering pump attaching bracket.

HOW TO SPOT WORN V-BELTS

V-Belts are vital to efficient engine operation—they drive the fan, water pump and other accessories. They require little maintenance (occasional tightening) but they will not last forever. Slipping or failure of the V-belt will lead to overheating. If your V-belt looks like any of these, it should be replaced.

Cracking or weathering

This belt has deep cracks, which cause it to flex. Too much flexing leads to heat build-up and premature failure. These cracks can be caused by using the belt on a pulley that is too small. Notched belts are available for small diameter pulleys.

Softening (grease and oil)

Oil and grease on a belt can cause the belt's rubber compounds to soften and separate from the reinforcing cords that hold the belt together. The belt will first slip, then finally fail altogether.

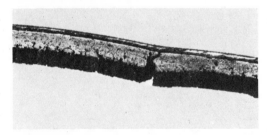

Glazing

Glazing is caused by a belt that is slipping. A slipping belt can cause a run-down battery, erratic power steering, overheating or poor accessory performance. The more the belt slips, the more glazing will be built up on the surface of the belt. The more the belt is glazed, the more it will slip. If the glazing is light, tighten the belt.

Worn cover

The cover of this belt is worn off and is peeling away. The reinforcing cords will begin to wear and the belt will shortly break. When the belt cover wears in spots or has a rough jagged appearance, check the pulley grooves for roughness.

Separation

This belt is on the verge of breaking and leaving you stranded. The layers of the belt are separating and the reinforcing cords are exposed. It's just a matter of time before it breaks completely.

3. Turn the steering pump drive belt adjusting nut as required until the proper deflection is obtained. Turning the adjusting nut clockwise will increase tension and decrease deflection; counterclockwise will decrease tension and increase deflection.

4. Without disturbing the pump, tighten the three attaching bolts.

AIR CONDITIONING COMPRESSOR DRIVE BELT

1. Position a ruler perpendicular to the drive belt at its longest run. Test the tightness of the belt by pressing it firmly with your thumb. The deflection should not exceed ¼ in.

2. If the engine is equipped with an idler pulley, loosen the idler pulley adjusting bolt, insert a pry bar between the pulley and the engine (or in the idler pulley adjusting slot), and adjust the tension accordingly. If the engine is not equipped with an idler pulley, the alternator must be moved to accomplish this adjustment, as outlined under "Alternator (Fan Drive) Belt."

3. When the proper tension is reached, tighten the idler pulley adjusting bolt (if so equipped) or the alternator adjusting and mounting bolts.

THERMACTOR AIR PUMP DRIVE BELT

1. Position a ruler perpendicular to the drive belt at its longest run. Test the tightness of the belt by pressing it firmly with your thumb. The deflection should be about ¼ in.

2. To adjust the belt tension, loosen the adjusting arm bolt slightly. If necessary, also loosen the mounting belt slightly.

3. Using a pry bar or broom handle, pry against the pump rear cover to move the pump toward or away from the engine as necessary.

CAUTION: *Do not pry against the pump housing itself, as damage to the housing may result.*

4. Holding the pump in place, tighten the adjusting arm bolt and recheck the tension. When the belt is properly tensioned, tighten the mounting bolt.

SINGLE DRIVE BELT—V8 MODELS

(Serpentine Drive Belt)

Some late models (starting in 1979) feature a single, wide, ribbed V-belt that drives the water pump, alternator and power steering. To install a new belt, simply retract the belt tensioner with a pry bar and slide the old belt off of the pulleys. Slip on a new belt and re-

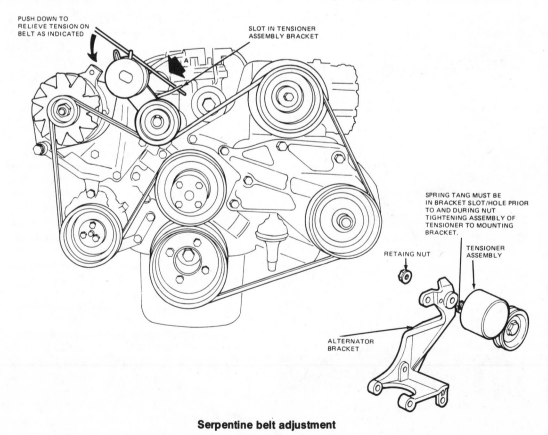

Serpentine belt adjustment

lease the tensioner. The spring powered tensioner eliminates the need for periodic adjustments.

Cooling System

At least once every 2 years, the engine cooling system should be inspected, flushed, and refilled with fresh coolant. If the coolant is left in the system too long, it loses its ability to prevent rust and corrosion. If the coolant has too much water, it won't protect against freezing.

The pressure cap should be looked at for signs of age or deterioration. Fan belt and other drive belts should be inspected and adjusted to the proper tension.

Hose clamps should be tightened, and soft or cracked hoses replaced. Damp spots, or accumulations of rust or dye near hoses, water pump or other areas, indicate possible leakage, which must be corrected before filling the system with fresh coolant.

CHECK THE RADIATOR CAP

While you are checking the coolant level, check the radiator cap for a worn or cracked gasket. If the cap doesn't seal properly, fluid will be lost and the engine will overheat.

Worn caps should be replaced with a new one.

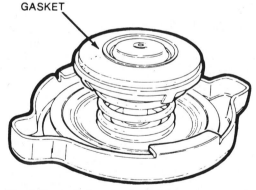

GASKET

Check the radiator cap gasket for cuts or cracks

CLEAN RADIATOR OF DEBRIS

Periodically clean any debris—leaves, paper, insects, etc.—from the radiator fins. Pick the large pieces off by hand. The smaller pieces can be washed away with water pressure from a hose.

Carefully straighten any bent radiator fins with a pair of needle nose pliers. Be careful— the fins are very soft. Don't wiggle the fins back and forth too much. Straighten them once and try not to move them again.

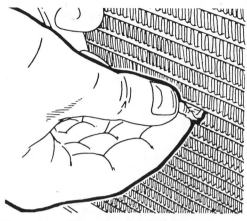

Clean the radiator fins of debris

DRAIN AND REFILL THE COOLING SYSTEM

Completely draining and refilling the cooling system every two years at least will remove accumulated rust, scale and other deposits. Coolant is a 50-50 mixture of ethylene glycol and water for year round use. Use a good quality antifreeze with water pump lubricants, rust inhibitors and other corrosion inhibitors along with acid neutralizers.

1. Drain the existing antifreeze and coolant. Open the radiator and engine drain petcocks, or disconnect the bottom radiator hose, at the radiator outlet.

NOTE: *Before opening the radiator petcock, spray it with some penetrating lubricant.*

2. Close the petcock or re-connect the lower hose and fill the system with water.

3. Add a can of quality radiator flush.

4. Idle the engine until the upper radiator hose gets hot.

5. Drain the system again.

6. Repeat this process until the drained water is clear and free of scale.

7. Close all petcocks and connect all the hoses.

8. If equipped with a coolant recovery system, flush the reservoir with water and leave empty.

9. Determine the capacity of your cooling system (see capacities specifications). Add a 50/50 mix of quaility antifreeze (ethylene glycol) and water to provide the desired protection.

10. Run the engine to operating temperature.

11. Stop the engine and check the coolant level.

12. Check the level of protection with an anti-freeze tester, replace the cap and check for leaks.

HOW TO SPOT BAD HOSES

Both the upper and lower radiator hoses are called upon to perform difficult jobs in an inhospitable environment. They are subject to nearly 18 psi at under hood temperatures often over 280°F., and must circulate nearly 7500 gallons of coolant an hour—3 good reasons to have good hoses.

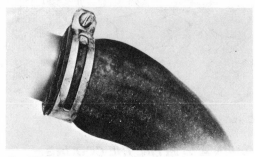

A good test for any hose is to feel it for soft or spongy spots. Frequently these will appear as swollen areas of the hose. The most likely cause is oil soaking. This hose could burst at any time, when hot or under pressure.

Swollen hose

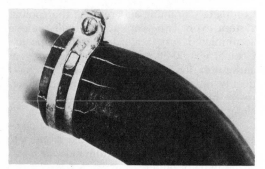

Cracked hoses can usually be seen but feel the hoses to be sure they have not hardened; a prime cause of cracking. This hose has cracked down to the reinforcing cords and could split at any of the cracks.

Cracked hose

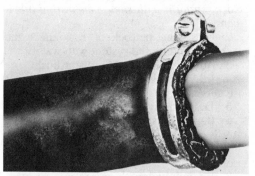

Weakened clamps frequently are the cause of hose and cooling system failure. The connection between the pipe and hose has deteriorated enough to allow coolant to escape when the engine is hot.

Frayed hose end (due to weak clamp)

Debris, rust and scale in the cooling system can cause the inside of a hose to weaken. This can usually be felt on the outside of the hose as soft or thinner areas.

Debris in cooling system

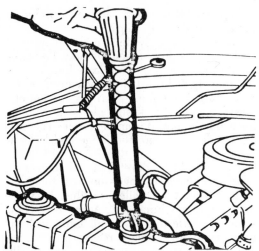

Testing coolant protection with an antifreeze tester

Air Conditioning

SAFETY PRECAUTIONS

There are two particular hazards associated with air conditioning systems and they both relate to the refrigerant gas.

First, the refrigerant gas is an extremely cold substance. When exposed to air, it will instantly freeze any surface it comes in contact with, including your eyes. The other hazard relates to fire. Although normally non-toxic, refrigerant gas becomes highly poisonous in the presence of an open flame. One good whiff of the vapor formed by burning refrigerant can be fatal. Keep all forms of fire (including cigarettes) well clear of the air conditioning system.

Any repair work to an air conditioning system should be left to a professional. Do not, under any circumstances, attempt to loosen or tighten any fittings or perform any work other than that outlined here.

CHECKING FOR OIL LEAKS

Refrigerant leaks show up as oily areas on the various components because the compressor oil is transported around the entire system along with the refrigerant. Look for only spots on all the hoses and lines, and especially on the hose and tubing connections. If there are oily deposits, the system may have a leak, and you should have it checked by a qualified repairman.

NOTE: *A small area of oil on the front of the compressor is normal and no cause for alarm.*

KEEP THE CONDENSER CLEAR

Periodically inspect the front of the condenser for bent fins or foreign material (dirt, bugs, leaves, etc.) If any cooling fins are bent, straighten them carefully with needlenosed pliers. You can remove any debris with a stiff bristle brush or hose.

OPERATE THE A/C SYSTEM PERIODICALLY

A lot of A/C problems can be avoided by simply running the air conditioner at least once a week, regardless of the season. Let the system run for at least 5 minutes a week (even in the winter), and you'll keep the internal parts lubricated as well as preventing the hoses from hardening.

REFRIGERANT LEVEL CHECK

There are two ways to check refrigerant level, depending on how your model is equipped.

With Sight Glass

The first order of business when checking the sight glass is to find the sight glass. It will either be in the head of the receiver/drier, or in one of the metal lines leading from the top of the receiver/drier. Once you've found it, wipe it clean and proceed as follows:

1. With the engine and the air conditioning system running, look for the flow of refrigerant through the sight glass. If the air conditioner is working properly, you'll be able to see a continuous flow of clear refrigerant through the sight glass, with perhaps an occasional bubble at very high temperatures.

2. Cycle the air conditioner on and off to make sure what you are seeing is clear refrigerant. Since the refrigerant is clear, it is possible to mistake a completely discharged system for one that is fully charged. Turn the system off and watch the sight glass. If there is refrigerant in the system, you'll see bubbles during the off cycle. If you observe no bubbles when the system is running, and the air flow from the unit in the car is delivering cold air, everything is OK.

3. If you observe bubbles in the sight glass while the system is operating, the system is

Typical air conditioning sight glass

low on refrigerant. Have it checked by a professional.

4. Oil streaks in the sight glass are an indication of trouble. Most of the time, if you see oil in the sight glass, it will appear as a series of streaks, although occasionally it may be a solid stream of oil. In either case, it means that part of the charge has been lost.

Without Sight Glass

On vehicles that are not equipped with sight glasses, it is necessary to feel the temperature difference in the inlet and outlet lines at the receiver/drier to gauge the refrigerant level. Use the following procedure:

1. Locate the receiver/drier. It will generally be up front near the condenser. It is shaped like a small fire extinguisher and will always have two lines connected to it. One line goes to the expansion valve and the other goes to the condenser.

2. With the engine and the air conditioner running, hold a line in each hand and gauge their relative temperatures. If they are both the same approximate temperature, the system is correctly charged.

3. If the line from the expansion valve to the receiver/drier is a lot colder than the line from the receiver/drier to the condenser, then the system is overcharged. It should be noted that this is an extremely rare condition.

4. If the line that leads from the receiver/drier to the condenser is a lot colder than the other line, the system is undercharged.

5. If the system is undercharged or overcharged, have it checked by a professional air conditioning mechanic.

Windshield Wipers

For maximum effectiveness and longest element life, the windshield and wiper blades should be kept clean. Dirt, tree sap, road tar and so on will cause streaking, smearing and blade deterioration if left on the glass. It is advisable to wash the windshield carefully with a commercial glass cleaner at least once a month. Wipe off the rubber blades with the wet rag afterwards. Do not attempt to move the wipers by hand; damage to the motor and drive mechanism will result.

If the blades are found to be cracked, broken or torn, they should be replaced immediately. Replacement intervals will vary with usage, although ozone deterioration usually limits blade life to about one year. If the wiper pattern is smeared or streaked, or if the blade chatters across the glass, the elements should

be replaced. It is easiest and most sensible to replace the elements in pairs.

There are basically three different types of refills, which differ in their method of replacement. One type has two release buttons, approximately one-third of the way up from the ends of the blade frame. Pushing the buttons down releases a lock and allows the rubber filler to be removed from the frame. The new filler slides back into the frame and locks in place.

The second type of refill has two metal tabs which are unlocked by squeezing them together. The rubber filler can then be withdrawn from the frame jaws. A new refill is installed by inserting the refill into the front frame jaws and sliding it rearward to engage the remaining frame jaws. There are usually four jaws; be certain when installing that the refill is engaged in all of them. At the end of its travel, the tabs will lock into place on the front jaws of the wiper blade frame.

The third type is a refill made from polycarbonate. The refill has a simple locking device at one end which flexes downward out of the groove into which the jaws of the holder fit, allowing easy release. By sliding the new refill through all the jaws and pushing through the slight resistance when it reaches the end of its travel, the refill will lock into position.

Regardless of the type of refill used, make sure that all of the frame jaws are engaged as the refill is pushed into place and locked. The metal blade holder and frame will scratch the glass if allowed to touch it.

ARM AND BLADE REPLACEMENT

A detailed description and procedures for replacing the wiper arm and blade is found in Chapter five.

Fluid Level Checks
ENGINE OIL

The oil level in the engine should be checked at fuel stops. The check should be made with the engine warm and switched off for a period of about one minute so that the oil has time to drain down into the crankcase. Pull out the dipstick, wipe it clean and reinsert it. The level of the oil must be kept within the "SAFE" area (on older models between the "ADD" and "F" marks), above the "ADD 1" mark on the dipstick. If the oil level is kept about the "SAFE" area, heavy oil consumption will result. If the level remains below the "ADD 1" mark, severe engine damage may result. The "ADD 1" and "ADD 2" refer to US measure quarts. Remember that in Canada, the Imperial measure quart is used and it is equal to 1.2 US quarts.

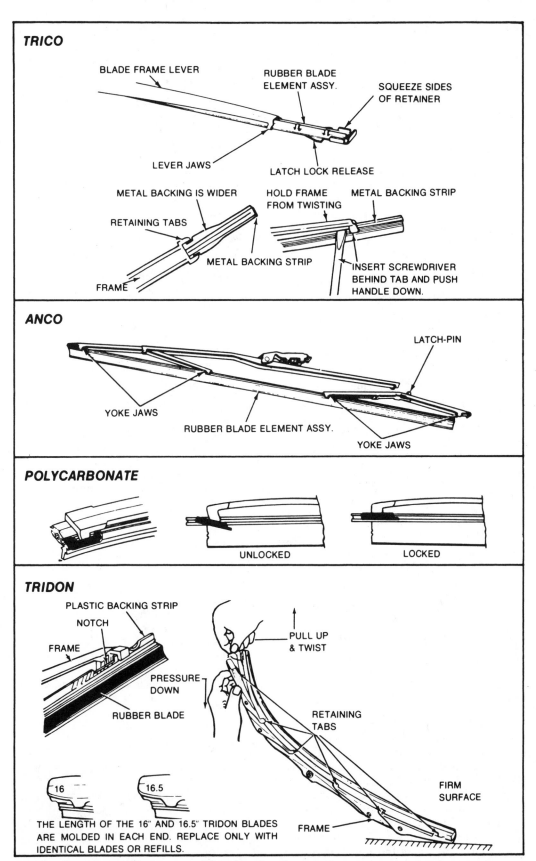

TRICO

BLADE FRAME LEVER

RUBBER BLADE ELEMENT ASSY.

SQUEEZE SIDES OF RETAINER

LEVER JAWS

LATCH LOCK RELEASE

METAL BACKING IS WIDER

HOLD FRAME FROM TWISTING

METAL BACKING STRIP

RETAINING TABS

METAL BACKING STRIP

FRAME

INSERT SCREWDRIVER BEHIND TAB AND PUSH HANDLE DOWN.

ANCO

LATCH-PIN

YOKE JAWS

RUBBER BLADE ELEMENT ASSY.

YOKE JAWS

POLYCARBONATE

UNLOCKED

LOCKED

TRIDON

PLASTIC BACKING STRIP

NOTCH

FRAME

PULL UP & TWIST

PRESSURE DOWN

RUBBER BLADE

RETAINING TABS

FIRM SURFACE

16   16.5

THE LENGTH OF THE 16" AND 16.5" TRIDON BLADES ARE MOLDED IN EACH END. REPLACE ONLY WITH IDENTICAL BLADES OR REFILLS.

FRAME

Wiper insert replacement

When adding oil, make sure that it is the same type and viscosity rating as the oil already in the crankcase.

MANUAL TRANSMISSION FLUID

At the recommended intervals in the maintenance schedule, the fluid level in the manual transmission should be checked. With the car standing perfectly level, apply the parking brake, set the transmission in Neutral, stop the engine and block all four wheels. Wipe all dirt and grease from the filler plug on the side of the transmission. Using a sliding T-bar handle or an adjustable wrench, remove the filler plug. The lubricant should be level with the bottom of the filler hole. If required, add SAE 90 manual transmission fluid to the proper level using a syringe. Install the filler plug.

AUTOMATIC TRANSMISSION FLUID

At the recommended intervals in the maintenance schedule, the automatic transmission fluid level should be checked. The level should also be checked if abnormal shifting behavior is noticed. With the car standing on a level surface, firmly apply the parking brake. Run the engine at idle until normal operating temperature is reached. Then, with the right foot firmly planted on the brake pedal, shift the transmission selector through all the positions, allowing sufficient time in each range to engage the transmission. Shift the selector into Park (P). With the engine still running, pull out the transmission dipstick, located at the right rear of the engine compartment. Wipe it clean and reinsert it, pushing it down until it seats in the tube. Pull it out and check the level. The level should be between the "ADD" and "FULL" marks. Add AFT Type F, CJ or Dexron II (depending on the year of your car) as required through the dipstick tube.

> CAUTION: *Do not overfill the transmission, as foaming and loss of fluid through the vent may cause the transmission to malfunction.*

> CAUTION: *While leaning over a running engine; be sure all loose clothing is secure, watch out for rotating parts (fan, belts, etc.).*

BRAKE MASTER CYLINDER FLUID

At the recommended intervals in the maintenance schedule, the fluid in the master cylinder should be checked. Before checking the level, carefully wipe off the master cylinder cover to remove any dirt or water that would fall into the fluid reservoir. Then push the retaining clip to one side and remove the cover and seal. The fluid level should be maintained at ¼ in. from the top of the reservoir. Fill as

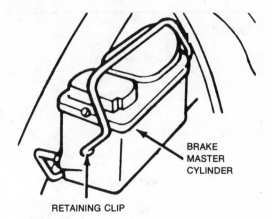

BRAKE MASTER CYLINDER

RETAINING CLIP

Master cylinder cover retaining clip

necessary with heavy-duty brake fluid meeting DOT 3 or 4 specifications.

COOLANT

The coolant level in the radiator should be checked on a monthly basis, preferably when the engine is cold. On a cold engine, the coolant level should be maintained at one inch below the filler neck on vertical flow radiators, and 2½ in. below the filler neck at the "COLD Fill" mark on crossflow radiators. On cars equipped with the Coolant Recovery System, the level is maintained at the "COLD LEVEL" mark in the translucent plastic expansion bottle. Fill as necessary with a mixture of 50% water and 50% ethylene glycol antifreeze, to ensure proper rust, freezing and boiling protection. If you have to add coolant more often than once a month or if you have to add more than one quart at a time, check the cooling system for leaks. Also check for water in the crankcase oil, indicating a blown cylinder head gasket.

> CAUTION: *Exercise extreme care when removing the cap from a hot radiator. Wait a few minutes until the engine has time to cool somewhat, then wrap a thick towel around the radiator cap and slowly turn it counterclockwise to the first stop. Step back and allow the pressure to release from the cooling system. Then, when the steam has stopped venting, press down on the cap, turn it one more stop counterclockwise and remove the cap.*

REAR AXLE FLUID

At the recommended intervals in the maintenance schedule, the rear axle fluid level should be checked. With the car standing perfectly level, apply the parking brake, set the transmission in Park or 1st gear, stop the engine and block all four wheels. Wipe all dirt and grease from the filler plug area. Using a sliding T-bar handle (⅜ in.) or an adjustable wrench, remove the filler plug. The fluid level must be maintained at ½ in. from the bottom of the filler plug hole.

To check the fluid level in the axle, bend a clean, straight piece of wire to a 90° angle and insert the bent end of the wire into the axle while resting it on the lower edge of the filler hole. Fill as necessary with SAE 90 hypoid gear lube, using a suction gun. If your car is equipped with Traction-Lok add Friction Modifier if required. Install the filler plug.

MANUAL STEERING GEAR LUBRICANT

If there is binding in the steering gear or if the wheels do not return to a straight-ahead position after a turn, the lubricant level of the steering gear should be checked. Remove the filler plug using a ¹¹/₁₆ in. open-end wrench and remove the lower cover bolt using a ⁹/₁₆ in. wrench, to expose both holes. Slowly turn the steering wheel to the left until it stops. At this point, lubricant should be rising in the lower cover bolt hole. Then slowly turn the steering wheel to the right until it stops. At this point, lubricant should be rising in the filler plug hole. If the lubricant does not rise when the wheel is turned, add a small amount of SAE 90 steering gear lubricant until it does. Replace the cover bolt and the filler plug when finished.

POWER STEERING RESERVOIR FLUID

At the recommended intervals in the maintenance schedule, the fluid level in the power steering reservoir (if so equipped) should be checked. Run the engine until the fluid reaches operating temperature. Turn the steering wheel from lock-to-lock several times to relieve the system of any trapped air. Turn off the engine. Unscrew the cap and dipstick assembly from the reservoir. The level must be maintained between the "FULL" mark and the end of the dipstick. Fill as necessary with ATF Type F.

BATTERY ELECTROLYTE

The fluid level in the battery cells should be checked on a monthly basis and more frequently in hot, dry weather. To fill the battery, ordinary tap water may be used except in areas known to have a high mineral or alkali content in the water. In these areas, distilled water must be used. The fluid level should be maintained at the "FULL TO RING" mark. If water is added during freezing weather, drive the car for several miles afterward to mix the water and the battery electrolyte. If water is needed frequently, check for a cracked battery case or a faulty voltage regulator or alternator.

CAUTION: *Keep lighted cigarettes or any other flame or spark, away from the open battery cells. Highly combustible hydrogen gas is always present in the cells.*

WINDSHIELD WASHER

Check the level of the windshield washer solution in the translucent reservoir tank at the same time the oil is being checked.

Add a mixture of one part commercial solvent to two parts water to the reservoir, as necessary. If you live in a cold area where the water might freeze, mix one part antifreeze windshield washer solution to one part water.

CAUTION: *Do not operate the windshield washer when the fluid reservoir is empty; this can cause the pump motor to burn out.*

Tires

INFLATION PRESSURE

Tire inflation is the most ignored item of auto maintenance. Gasoline mileage can drop as much as .8% for every 1 pound per square inch (psi) of under inflation.

Two items should be a permanent fixture in every glove compartment; a tire pressure gauge and a tread depth gauge. Check the tire air pressure (including the spare) regularly with a pocket type gauge. Kicking the tires won't tell you a thing, and the gauge on the service station air hose is notoriously inaccurate.

The tire pressures recommended for your car are usually found on the left door or in the owner's manual. Ideally, inflation pressure should be checked when the tires are cool. When the air becomes heated it expands and the pressure increases. Every 10° rise (or drop) in temperature means a difference of 1 psi, which also explains why the tire appears to lose air on a very cold night. When it is impossible to check the tires "cold," allow for pressure build-up due to heat. If the "hot" pressure exceeds the "cold" pressure by more than 15 psi, reduce your speed, load or both. Otherwise internal heat is created in the tire. When the heat approaches the temperature at which the tire was cured, during manufacture, the tread can separate from the body.

CAUTION: *Never counteract excessive pressure build-up by bleeding off air pressure (letting some air out). This will only further raise the tire operating temperature.*

Before starting a long trip with lots of luggage, you can add about 2–4 psi to the tires to make them run cooler, but never exceed the maximum inflation pressure on the side of the tire.

Capacities

Year	Engine No. Cyl Displacement (Cu In.)	Engine Crankcase Add 1 Qt For New Filter	Transmission Pts To Refill After Draining			Drive Axle (pts)	Gasoline Tank (gals) ■	Cooling System (qts)	
			Manual						
			3-Speed	4-Speed	Automatic			With Heater	With A/C
1968	6-240	4	3.5	—	See	5	25	13	13
	8-302	4	3.5	—	chart	5	25	13.7	13.7
	8-390	4	3.5	4.0	below	5	25	20.2	20.2
	8-427	5	—	4.0		5	25	20.6	20.6
	8-428	4	—	4.0		5	25	19.4	19.4
1969	6-240	4	3.5	—		5	24.5	14.3	14.3
	8-302	4	3.5	—		4.5	24.5	15.4	15.6
	8-390	4	3.5	—		4.5	24.5	20.1	20.5
	8-428P	4	—	—		4.5	24.5	19.7	19.7
	8-429	4	—	4.0		4.5	24.5	20.5	21.5
1970	6-240	4	3.5	—		5	24.5	14.4	14.4
	8-302	4	3.5	—		4.5	24.5	15.4	15.6
	8-351	4	3.5	—		4.5	24.5	16.5	16.9
	8-390	4	3.5	—		4.5	24.5	20.1	20.5
	8-428P	4	—	—		4.5	24.5	19.7	19.7
	8-429	4	—	—	See	4.5	24.5	18.6	19.0
1971	6-240	4	3.5	—	chart	5	22.5	14.1	14.1
	8-302	4	3.5	—	below	4.5	22.5	15.2	15.6
	8-351	4	3.5	—		4.5	22.5	16.3	16.7
	8-390	4	—	—		4.5	22.5	20.3	26.3
	8-400	4	—	—		4.5	22.5	17.6	17.6
	8-429	4	—	—		4.5	22.5	18.8	18.8
1972	6-240	4	—	—		4	22	14.2	14.2
	8-302	4	—	—		4.5	22	15.2	15.2
	8-351	4	—	—		4.5	22	16.3	16.3
	8-400	4	—	—		5	22	17.7	18.3
	8-429	4	—	—		5	22	18.8	19.5
1973	8-351	4	—	—		4.5	22	16.3	16.3
	8-400	4	—	—		5	22	17.7	18.3
	8-429	4	—	—		5	22	18.8	19.5
1974–77	8-351	4	—	—		4.5	22 ③ ④	16.3	①
	8-400	4	—	—	See	5	22 ③ ④	18.0	18.0
	8-460	4 ②	—	—	chart	5	22 ③ ④	19.4	19.4
1978	8-302	4	—	—	below	5	24.2	16.9	16.9
	8-351	4	—	—		5	24.2	16.9	16.9
	8-400	4	—	—		5	24.2	16.9	16.9
	8-460	4	—	—		5	24.2	18.6	19.0
1979	8-302	4	—	—		3.5	19.0	13.3	13.4
	8-351	4	—	—		4.0	19.0	13.3	13.4

Capacities (cont.)

Year	Engine No. Cyl Displacement (Cu In.)	Engine Crankcase Add 1 Qt For New Filter	Transmission Pts To Refill After Draining			Drive Axle (pts)	Gasoline Tank (gals) ▪	Cooling System (qts)	
			Manual		Automatic			With Heater	With A/C
			3-Speed	4-Speed					
1980	8-302	4 ⑤	—	—		3.5 ⑥	19	13.0	13.3
	8-351	4 ⑤	—	—	See	3.5 ⑥	19	13.9	14.0
1981	8-255	4 ⑤	—	—	chart	3.5 ⑥	20	14.8	15.2
	8-302	4 ⑤	—	—	below	3.5 ⑥	20 ⑦	13.0	13.4
	8-351	4 ⑤	—	—		3.5 ⑥	20	13.8 ⑧	13.8 ⑧
1982	8-255	4 ⑤	—	—		4.0	20	14.8	15.2
	8-302	4 ⑤	—	—		4.0	20 ⑦	13.0	13.4
	8-351	4 ⑤	—	—		4.0	20	13.8	13.8
1983	8-302	4 ⑤	—	—		4.0	20 ⑦	13.0	13.4
	8-351	4 ⑤	—	—		4.0	20	13.8	13.8

① 351W—17.1 qts; 351C—16.3 qts; 351M—16.3 qts
② 460 Police Interceptor—7½ qts with filter and oil cooler
③ 1975–77 Sedans—24.2 gals
④ Sedan with auxiliary tank—32.3 gals
  Wagon with auxiliary tank—29.0 gals
⑤ Two drain plugs are used on the oil pan
⑥ 4 pts with 8.5 in ring gear
⑦ 18.0 gal with EFI—18.5 gal wagons with EFI

⑧ Trailer towing H.D. system—15.0 qts
▪ Station Wagons:
  '68–'70—20 gals
  '71—22 gals
  '72–'78—21 gals
  '79–'81—20 gals
P Police
— Not applicable

Automatic Transmission Refill Capacities (Pts)

Year	Code	Capacities
1968–69	U, Z	26
1968–79	W	20.5
1968–76	X, Y	22
1970–79	U, Z	25.5
1980	W	20
	X	22
	T	24
	U	23.6
1981 and later	T	24

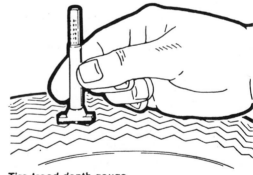

Tire tread depth gauge

TREAD DEPTH

All tires made since 1968, have 8 built-in tread wear indicator bars that show up as ½″ wide smooth bands across the tire when ¹/₁₆″ of tread remains. The appearance of tread wear indicators means that the tires should be replaced. In fact, many states have laws prohibiting the use of tires with less than ⁶/₁₆″ tread.

You can check your own tread depth with

A penny used to determine tread depth

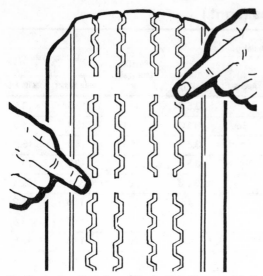

Replace a tire that shows the built-in "bump strip"

an inexpensive gauge or by using a Lincoln head penny. Slip the Lincoln penny into several tread grooves. If you can see the top of Lincoln's head in 2 adjacent grooves, the tires have less than 1/16" tread left and should be replaced. You can measure snow tires in the same manner by using the "tails" side of the Lincoln penny. If you can see the top of the Lincoln memorial, it's time to replace the snow tires.

TIRE ROTATION

Tire rotation is recommended every 6000 miles or so, to obtain maximum tire wear. The pattern you use depends on whether or not your car has a usable spare. Radial tires should not be cross-switched (from one side of the car to the other); they last longer if their direction of rotation is not changed. Snow tires sometimes have directional arrows molded into the side of the carcass; the arrow shows the direction of rotation. They will wear very rapidly if the rotation is reversed. Studded tires will lose their studs if their rotational direction is reversed.

NOTE: *Mark the wheel position or direction of rotation on radial tires or studded snow tires before removing them.*

CAUTION: *Spare tires, other than the conventional type, are only for temporary, emergency use. Never use this non-conventional type spare for tire rotation or as a regular tire.*

STORAGE

Store the tires at the proper inflation pressure if they are mounted on wheels. Keep them in a cool dry place, laid on their sides. If the tires are stored in the garage or basement, do not let them stand on a concrete floor; set them on strips of wood.

BUYING NEW TIRES

When buying new tires, give some thought to the following points, especially if you are considering a switch to larger tires or a different profile series:

1. All four tires must be of the same construction type. This rule cannot be violated. Radial, bias, and bias-belted tires must not be mixed.

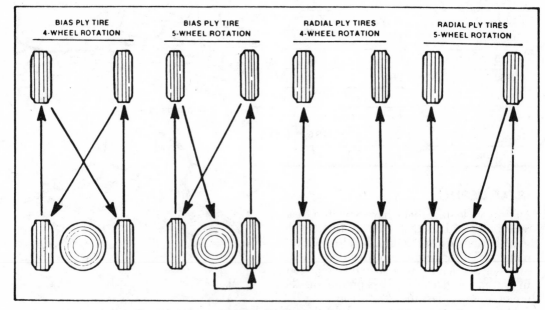

Tire rotation patterns

Maintenance Interval Chart

Operation	'68–'70	'71	'72	'73	'74	'75	'76	'77–'79	'80	'81–'83
ENGINE										
Air cleaner replacement—6 cyl	12	12	12	—	—	—	—	—	—	—
Air cleaner replacement—V8	24	24	12	12	24	20	20	30	30	30
Air intake temperature control system check	12	12	12	12	12	15	15	20	22.5	22.5
Carburetor idle speed and mixture, fast idle, throttle solenoid adj	12	12	12	12	24	15	15	22.5	30	30
Cooling system check	12	12	12	12	12	15	15	12	12	12
Coolant replacement; system draining and flushing	24	24	24	24	24	40	40	45	52.5	52.5
Crankcase breather cap cleaning	6	6	6	12	12	20	20	30	52.5	52.5
Crankcase breather filter replacement (in air cleaner)	24	6	6	8	24	20	20	30	52.5	52.5
Distributor breaker points inspection	12	12	12	12	6	—	—	—	—	—
Distributor breaker points replacement	12	12	12	24	24	—	—	—	—	—
Distributor cap and rotor inspection	12	12	12	24	①	15	15	22.5	22.5	22.5
Drive belts adjustment	12	12	12	12	12	15	15	22.5	30	30
Evaporative control system check; inspect carbon canister	—	12	12	12	24	20	20	30	52.5	52.5
Exhaust control valve (heat riser) lubrication and inspection	6	6	6	8	6	15	15	15	15	15
Exhaust gas recirculation system (EGR) check	—	—	—	12	12	15	15	15	15	15
Fuel filter replacement	12	12	12	12	6	15	10	10	12	12
Ignition timing adjustment	12	12	12	12	②	⑥	⑥	⑥	⑥	⑥
Intake manifold bolt torque check (V8 only)	12	12	12	24	12	15	15	15	15	15
Oil change	6	6	6	4	6	5	5	7.5	7.5	7.5
Oil filter replacement	6	6	6	8	12	10	10	15	15	15
PCV system valve replacement, system cleaning	12	12	12	12	24	20	20	22.5	52.5	52.5
Spark plug replacement; plug wire check	12	12	12	12	③	15	15	22.5	30	30
Thermactor air injection system check	12	—	—	—	24	15	15	22.5	22.5	22.5
CHASSIS										
Automatic transmission band adjustment	④⑤	⑤	⑤	⑤	⑤	⑤	⑤	⑤	⑤	⑤
Automatic transmission fluid level check	6	6	6	8	12	15	15	15	15	15
Brake system inspection, lining replacement	30	30	30	24	24	25	30	30	30	30
Brake master cylinder reservoir fluid level check	6	6	6	8	12	15	30	30	30	30
Clutch pedal free-play adjustment	6	6	—	—	—	—	—	—	—	—

Maintenance Interval Chart (cont.)

Operation	'68–'70	'71	'72	'73	'74	'75	'76	'77–'79	'80	'81–'83
CHASSIS										
Front suspension ball joints and steering linkage lubrication	36	36	36	36	36	30	30	30	30	30
Front wheel bearings cleaning, adjusting and repacking	30	30	30	24	24	25	30	30	30	30
Manual transmission fluid level check	6	6	—	—	—	—	—	—	—	—
Power steering pump reservoir fluid level check	6	6	6	4	6	15	15	15	15	15
Rear axle fluid level check	6	6	6	8	12	15	15	15	15	15
Steering arm stop lubrication; steering linkage inspection	6	12	12	12	12	15	15	15	15	15

① Conventional ignition—24; electronic ignition—18
② Conventional ignition—12; electronic ignition—18
③ Conventional ignition—12; electronic ignition—18
④ Normal service—36,000 mi. only; severe (fleet) service—6,000/18,000/36,000 mi. intervals—1968 only
⑤ Normal service—12,000 mi. only; severe (fleet) service—6,000/18,000/30,000 mi. intervals
⑥ Periodic adjustment unnecessary

2. The wheels should be the correct width for the tire. Tire dealers have charts of tire and rim compatibility. A mismatch will cause sloppy handling and rapid tire wear. The tread width should match the rim width (inside bead to inside bead) within an inch. For radial tires, the rim width should be 80% or less of the tire (not tread) width.

3. The height (mounted diameter) of the new tires can change speedometer accuracy, engine speed at a given road speed, fuel mileage, acceleration, and ground clearance. Tire manufacturers furnish full measurement specifications.

4. The spare tire should be useable, at least for short distance and low speed operation, with the new tires.

5. There shouldn't be any body interference when loaded, on bumps, or in turns.

Fuel Filter Replacement

Every 12,000 miles or 12 months, the fuel filter must be replaced. The filter is located in-line at the carburetor inlet. The procedure for replacing the fuel filter is as follows:

1. Remove the air filter.

2. Loosen the retaining clamp(s), securing the fuel inlet hose to the fuel filter. If the hose has crimped retaining clamps, these must be cut off and replaced.

3. Pull the hose off the fuel filter.

4. Unscrew the fuel filter from the carburetor and discard the gasket, if so equipped.

5. Install a new gasket, if so equipped, and screw the filter into the carburetor.

6. Install a new retaining clamp onto the fuel hose. Push the hose onto the fuel filter and tighten the clamp.

7. Start the engine and check for leaks.

8. Install the air filter.

LUBRICATION

Oil Recommendations

When adding the oil to the crankcase or changing the oil or filter, it is important that oil of an equal quality to original equipment be used in your car. The use of inferior oils may void your warranty. Generally speaking, oil that has been rated SE or SF (1980 and later) heavy duty detergent, by the American Petroleum Institute will prove satisfactory.

Oil of the SE/SF variety performs a multitude of functions in addition to its basic job of reducing friction of the engine's moving parts. Through a balanced formula of polymeric dispersants and metallic detergents, the oil prevents high temperature and low temperature deposits and also keeps sludge and dirt particles in suspension. Acids, particularly sulphuric acid, as well as other byproducts of combustion of sulphur fuels, are neutralized by the oil. These acids, if permitted to concentrate, may cause corrosion and rapid wear of the internal parts of the engine.

It is important to choose an oil of the proper viscosity for climatic and operational conditions. Viscosity is an index of the oil's thickness at different temperatures. A thicker oil

Oil Viscosity— Temperature Chart

When Outside Temperature Is Consistently	Use SAE Viscosity Number
SINGLE GRADE OILS	
−10°F to 32°F	10W
10°F to 60°F	20W-20
32°F to 90°F	30
Above 60°F	40
MULTIGRADE OILS	
Below 32°F	5W-30*
−10°F to 90°F	10W-30
Above −10°F	10W-40
Above 10°F	20W-40

*When sustained high-speed operation is anticipated, use the next higher grade.

(higher numerical rating) is needed for high temperature operation, whereas thinner oil (lower numerical rating) is required for cold weather operation. Due to the need for an oil that embodies both these characteristics in parts of the country where there is wide temperature variation within a small period of time, multigrade oils have been developed. Basically, a multigrade oil is thinner at low temperatures and thicker at high temperatures. For example, a 20W-40 oil exhibits the characteristics of a 20 weight oil when the car is first started and the oil is cold. Its lighter weight allows it to travel to the lubricating surfaces quicker and offer less resistance to starter motor cranking than, let's say, a straight 30 weight oil. But after the engine reaches operating temperature, the 20W-40 oil begins acting like a straight 40 weight oil, its heavier weight providing greater lubricating protection and less susceptibility to foaming than a straight 30 weight oil. Whatever your driving needs, the oil viscosity-temperature chart should prove useful in selecting the proper grade. The SAE viscosity rating is printed or stamped on the top of every oil container.

Fuel Recommendations

It is important that you use fuel of the proper octane rating in your car. Octane rating is based on the quantity of anti-knock compounds added to the fuel and it determines the speed at which the gas will burn. The lower the octane rating, the faster the fuel will burn and a greater percentage of compounds in the fuel prevent spark ping (knock), detonation and preignition (dieseling).

NOTE: *Catalytic converters were installed on most models since 1974.*

CAUTION: *Un-leaded gasoline must be used on cars equipped with a catalytic converter.*

Changing Engine Oil and Filter

At the recommended intervals in the maintenance schedule, the oil and filter are changed. After the engine has reached operating temperature, shut it off, firmly apply the parking brake, block the wheels, place a drip pan beneath the oil pan and remove the drain plug. Allow the engine to drain thoroughly before replacing the drain plug.

NOTE: *Most V8 engines (since 1979) have two oil pan drain plugs. Both plugs must be removed when draining the oil.*

Place the drip pan beneath the oil filter. To remove the filter, turn it counterclockwise using a strap wrench. Wipe the contact surface of the new filter clean of all dirt and coat the rubber gasket with clean engine oil. Clean the mating surface of the adapter on the block. To install, hand turn the new filter clockwise until the gasket just contacts the cylinder block.

NOTE: *Do not use a strap wrench to install.* Then hand-turn the filter ½ additional turn. Unscrew the filler cap on the valve cover and fill the crankcase to the proper level on the dipstick with the recommended grade of oil. Install the cap, start the engine and operate at fast idle. Check the oil filter contact area and the drain plug for leaks.

Certain operating conditions may warrant more frequent oil changes. If the vehicle is used for short trips, where the engine does not have a chance to fully warm-up before it is shut off, water condensation and low temperature deposits may make it necessary to change the oil sooner. If the vehicle is used mostly in stop-and-go traffic, corrosive acids and high temperature deposits may necessitate shorter oil changing intervals. The shorter intervals also apply to industrial or rural areas where

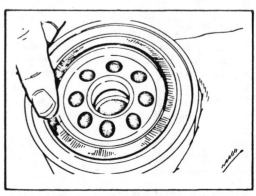

Lubricate the gasket on the new filter with clean engine oil. A dry gasket may not make a good seal and will allow the filter to leak

high concentrations of dust and other airborne particulate matter contaminate the oil. Finally, if the car is used for towing trailers, a severe load is placed on the engine causing the oil to "thin-out" sooner, making necessary the shorter oil changing intervals.

Chassis Greasing

FRONT SUSPENSION BALL JOINTS

Every 3 years or 36,000 miles, the upper and lower ball joints must be lubricated. Fords are not equipped with grease fittings at the ball joints. Instead, they use plugs, one at the top of the upper ball joint and another at the underside of the lower ball joint, which must be removed prior to greasing.

If you are using a jack to raise the front of the car, be sure to install jack stands, block the rear wheels and fully apply the parking brake. If the car has been parked in a temperature below 20°F for any length of time, park it in a heated garage for a half an hour or so until the ball joints loosen up enough to accept the grease. Wipe all accummulated dirt from around the ball joint lubrication plugs. Remove the plugs with a ³/₁₆ in. socket wrench. Using a hand-operated, low pressure grease gun fitted with a rubber tip and loaded with a suitable chassis grease, force lubricant into the joint only until the joint boot begins to swell.

NOTE: *Do not force lubricant out of the rubber boat as this destroys the weathertight seal.*

Install the grease plugs.

STEERING LINKAGE

At the recommended intervals in the maintenance schedule, the steering linkage must be lubricated. Grease fittings are not installed from the factory. Instead, plugs are used, which must be removed prior to lubrication. The linkage may be lubricated without raising the car.

If the car has been parked in a temperature below 20°F for any length of time, park it in a heated garage for a half an hour or so until the linkage joints loosen up enough to accept the grease. Wipe all accumulated dirt from around the steering joint plugs at each tie-rod end. Remove the plugs with a ³/₁₆ in. socket wrench. Using a hand-operated, low pressure grease gun fitted with a rubber tip and loaded with suitable chassis grease, force lubricant into the holes. When grease begins to escape from the hole, insert the plugs.

STEERING ARM STOPS

At the recommended intervals in the maintenance schedule, the steering arm stops must be cleaned and lubricated. The stops are located on the inside of the steering arm and at the upturned end of the suspension strut where the strut attaches to the lower control arm. Clean all friction points and apply a suitable chassis grease as per the chassis lubrication diagram.

MANUAL TRANSMISSION AND CLUTCH LINKAGE

On models so equipped, apply a small amount of chassis grease to the pivot and friction points of the transmission and clutch linkage as per the chassis lubrication diagram.

AUTOMATIC TRANSMISSION LINKAGE

On models so equipped, apply a small amount of 10W engine oil to the kickdown and shaft linkage pivot points.

PARKING BRAKE LINKAGE

At yearly intervals or whenever binding is noticeable in the parking brake linkage, lubricate the cable guides, levers and linkage with a suitable chassis grease.

BODY LUBRICATION

At 12 month intervals, the door, hood and trunk hinges, checks, and latches should be greased with a white grease such as Lubriplate®. Also the lock cylinders should be lubricated with a few drops of graphite lubricant.

DRAIN HOLE CLEANING

The doors and rocker panels of your car are equipped with drain holes to allow water to drain out of the inside of the body panels. If the drain holes become clogged with dirt, leaves, pine needles, etc., the water will remain inside the panels, causing rust. To prevent this, open the drain holes with a screwdriver. If your car is equipped with rubber dust valves instead, simply open the dust valve with your finger.

WHEEL BEARINGS

The procedures for servicing wheel bearings may be found in chapter nine.

PUSHING AND TOWING

When using jumper cables to jump start a car, a few precautions must be taken to avoid both charging system damage and damage to yourself should the battery explode. The old "positive to positive and negative to negative" jumper cable rule of thumb has been scrapped for a new revised procedure (see the special

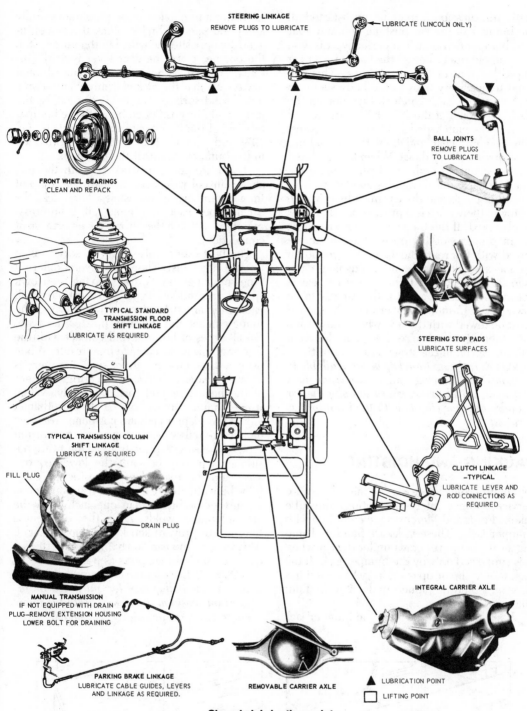

STEERING LINKAGE
REMOVE PLUGS TO LUBRICATE

LUBRICATE (LINCOLN ONLY)

BALL JOINTS
REMOVE PLUGS
TO LUBRICATE

FRONT WHEEL BEARINGS
CLEAN AND REPACK

TYPICAL STANDARD
TRANSMISSION FLOOR
SHIFT LINKAGE
LUBRICATE AS REQUIRED

STEERING STOP PADS
LUBRICATE SURFACES

TYPICAL TRANSMISSION COLUMN
SHIFT LINKAGE
LUBRICATE AS REQUIRED

FILL PLUG

DRAIN PLUG

CLUTCH LINKAGE
–TYPICAL
LUBRICATE LEVER AND
ROD CONNECTIONS AS
REQUIRED

INTEGRAL CARRIER AXLE

MANUAL TRANSMISSION
IF NOT EQUIPPED WITH DRAIN
PLUG–REMOVE EXTENSION HOUSING
LOWER BOLT FOR DRAINING

PARKING BRAKE LINKAGE
LUBRICATE CABLE GUIDES, LEVERS
AND LINKAGE AS REQUIRED.

REMOVABLE CARRIER AXLE

▲ LUBRICATION POINT

☐ LIFTING POINT

Chassis lubrication points

"jump starting" page at the end of this chapter). Here it is. First, remove all the battery cell covers and cover the cell openings with a clean, dry cloth. Then, connect the positive cable of the assist battery to the positive pole of your battery to the engine block of your car. This will prevent the possibility of a spark from the negative assist cable igniting the highly ex-

plosive hydrogen and oxygen battery fumes. Once your car is started, allow the engine to return to idle speed before disconnecting the jumper cables, and don't cross the cables. Replace the cell covers and discard the cloth. Now if your car fails to start by jump starting and it is equipped with manual transmission, it may be push started. Cars equipped with automatic transmission cannot be pushstarted. If the bumper of the car pushing you and your car's bumper do not match perfectly, it is wise to tie an old tire either on the back of your car or on the front of the pushing car. This will avoid unnecessary trips to the body shop. To push start the car, switch the ignition to the "ON" position (not the "START" position) and depress the clutch pedal. Place the transmission in Third gear and hold the accelerator pedal about halfway down. When the car speed reaches about 10 mph, gradually release the clutch pedal and the engine should start.

If all else fails and the car must be towed to a garage, there are a few precautions that must be observed. If the transmission and rear axle are in proper working order, the car can be towed with the rear wheels on the ground for distances under 15 miles at speeds no greater than 30 mph. If the transmission or rear is known to be damagad or if the car has to be towed over 15 miles or over 30 mph, the car must be towed with the rear wheels raised and the steering wheel locked so that the front wheels remain in the straight-ahead position.

NOTE: *If the ignition key is not available to unlock the steering and transmission lock system, it will be necessary to dolly the car under the rear wheels with the front wheels raised.*

JACKING AND HOISTING

When it becomes necessary to raise the car for service, proper safety precautions must be taken. Fords and Mercurys are equipped with bumper jacks. These jacks are fine for changing a tire, but never crawl under the car when it is supported only by the bumper jack. If the jack should slip or tip over, as jacks sometimes do, you would be pinned under 2 tons of automobile.

When raising the car with the bumper jack to change a tire, follow these precautions: Fully apply the parking brake, block the wheel diagonally opposite the wheel to the raised, stop the engine, place the gear lever in Park (automatic) or 1st or Reverse gear (manual), and make sure that the jack is firmly planted on a level, solid surface. On 1968–70 models, the jack should be positioned beneath the bumper inboard of the bumper-to-frame brackets. On 1971 and later models, notches are provided in the bumpers to insert the jack hook.

If you are going to work beneath the car, always install jackstands beneath an adjacent frame member. When using a floor jack, the car may be raised at a frame rail, front crossmember, or at either front lower arm strut connection.

The best way to raise a car for service is to use a garage hoist. There are several different types of garage hoists, each having their own special precautions. Types you most often will encounter are the drive-on (ramp type), the frame contact and the twin post or rail type. On all types of hoists, avoid contact with the steering linkage as damage may result. When using a drive-on type, make sure that there is enough clearance between the upright flanges of the hoist rails and the underbody. When using a frame contact hoist, make sure that all four of the adapter pads are positioned squarely on a frame rail. When using a twin post or rail type, make sure that the front adapters are positioned squarely beneath the lower control arms and the rear adapters positioned carefully beneath the rear axle housing at points no further outboard than one inch from the circumference welds near the differential housing (to prevent shock absorber damage). Always raise the car slowly, observing the security of the hoist adapters as it is raised.

NOTE: *If it is desired to unload the front suspension ball joints for purposes of inspection, position the jack beneath the lower control arm of the subject ball joints.*

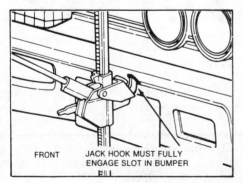

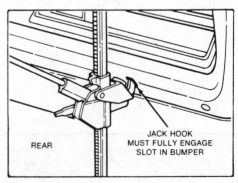

FRONT   JACK HOOK MUST FULLY ENGAGE SLOT IN BUMPER

REAR   JACK HOOK MUST FULLY ENGAGE SLOT IN BUMPER

Bumper jack installation—1971–77 models

JUMP STARTING A DEAD BATTERY

The chemical reaction in a battery produces explosive hydrogen gas. This is the safe way to jump start a dead battery, reducing the chances of an accidental spark that could cause an explosion.

Jump Starting Precautions

1. Be sure both batteries are of the same voltage.
2. Be sure both batteries are of the same polarity (have the same grounded terminal).
3. Be sure the vehicles are not touching.
4. Be sure the vent cap holes are not obstructed.
5. Do not smoke or allow sparks around the battery.
6. In cold weather, check for frozen electrolyte in the battery.
7. Do not allow electrolyte on your skin or clothing.
8. Be sure the electrolyte is not frozen.

Jump Starting Procedure

1. Determine voltages of the two batteries; they must be the same.
2. Bring the starting vehicle close (they must not touch) so that the batteries can be reached easily.
3. Turn off all accessories and both engines. Put both cars in Neutral or Park and set the handbrake.
4. Cover the cell caps with a rag—do not cover terminals.
5. If the terminals on the run-down battery are heavily corroded, clean them.
6. Identify the positive and negative posts on both batteries and connect the cables in the order shown.
7. Start the engine of the starting vehicle and run it at fast idle. Try to start the car with the dead battery. Crank it for no more than 10 seconds at a time and let it cool off for 20 seconds in between tries.
8. If it doesn't start in 3 tries, there is something else wrong.
9. Disconnect the cables in the reverse order.
10. Replace the cell covers and dispose of the rags.

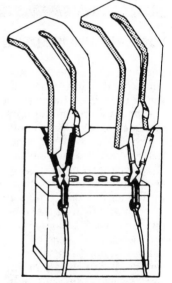

Side terminal batteries occasionally pose a problem when connecting jumper cables. There frequently isn't enough room to clamp the cables without touching sheet metal. Side terminal adaptors are available to alleviate this problem and should be removed after use.

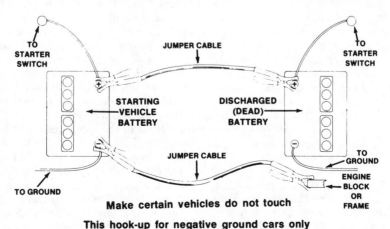

Make certain vehicles do not touch

This hook-up for negative ground cars only

Tune-Up and Performance Maintenance

T2

TUNE-UP PROCEDURES

The tune-up may be the most important maintenance procedure that you can perform on your car. A good tune-up is essential for the efficient and economical operation, as well as the long life of your car's engine.

The interval between tune-ups is a variable factor which depends on the year and engine of your car and upon the way you drive. It is generally correct to say that no car equipped with breaker point type ignition should be driven more than 12,000 miles between tune-ups, especially in this age of emission controls and increased fuel costs.

Ford Motor Company, and auto makers in general, have been attempting to produce the "maintenance-free" automobile for some time now. One of the most significant advancements along the "maintenance-free" line has been the introduction of the solid state, or breakerless, ignition system. The breakerless ignition system completely eliminates the points and condenser used in conventional (point type) distributors. Since you no longer have to install these parts, and since dwell is preset and cannot be adjusted, a number of tune-up steps are eliminated. In addition, spark plug life is considerably longer, and overall reliability is greatly increased.

This section gives specific procedures on how to tune-up your car and is intended to be as complete and basic as possible. Chapter three contains a description and troubleshooting guide for the "solid state" electronic ignition. Chapter eleven contains a more generalized section for tune-ups which includes troubleshooting diagnosis for the more experienced weekend mechanic.

CAUTION: *When working with a running engine, make sure that there is proper ventilation. Also make sure that the transmission is in Neutral or firmly in Park (unless otherwise specified) and the parking brake is fully applied. Always keep hands, long hair, clothing, neckties and tools well clear of the hot exhaust manifold(s) and radiator. When the ignition is running, do not grasp the ignition wires, distributor cap, or coil wire, as a shock in excess of 20,000 volts may result. Whenever working around the distributor, even if the engine is not running, make sure that the ignition is switched off.*

Spark Plugs

The job of the spark plug is to ignite the air/fuel mixture in the cylinder as the piston approaches the top of the compression stroke. The ignited mixture then expands and forces the piston down on the power stroke.

The average life of a spark plug is approximately 12,000 miles; 22,500 miles for models equipped with electronic ignition. This is, however, dependent on the mechanical condition of the engine, the type of fuel that is used, and the type of driving conditions. For some people, spark plugs will last 5,000 miles and for others, 15,000 to 30,000 miles.

Your car came from the factory with resistor spark plugs. Resistor spark plugs help to limit the amount of radio frequency energy that is given off by the automotive ignition system. Radio frequency energy results in the annoying buzzing or clicking you sometimes hear on your radio or the jumping picture you see on your TV when a car pulls into the driveway.

The electrode end of the spark plug (the end that goes into the cylinder) is also a very good indicator of the mechanical condition of your engine. If a spark plug should foul and begin to misfire, you will have to find the condition that caused the plug to foul and correct it. It is also a good idea to occasionally give all the plugs the once-over to get an idea how the inside of your engine is doing. A small amount of deposit on a spark plug, after it has been in

Tune-Up Specifications

When analyzing compression test results, look for uniformity among cylinders rather than specific pressures.

Year	Engine No. Cyl Displacement (cu in.)	Spark Plugs		Distributor		Ignition Timing (deg) ▲		Valves Intake Opens ■(deg)●	Fuel Pump Pressure (psi)	Idle Speed (rpm) ▲	
		Type	Gap (in.)	Point Dwell (deg)	Point Gap (in.)	Man Trans	Auto Trans			Man Trans*	Auto Trans
1968	6-240	BF-42	.034	35-40	.027	6B	6B	12	4-6	600	500
	8-302	BF-32	.034	24-29	.021	6B	6B	16	4-6	625	550②
	8-390	BF-32	.034	24-29③	.021③	6B	6B	13	4½-6½	625	550
	8-390	BF-32	.034	24-29③	.021③	6B	6B	16	4½-6½	625	550
	8-428	BF-32	.034	24-29③	.021③	6B	6B	16	4½-6½	625	550
	8-428PI	BF-32	.034	26-31	.017	—	6B	18	4½-6½	—	600
1969	6-240	BF-42	.034	35-40	.027	6B	6B	12	4-6	775/550	550
	8-302	BF-42	.034	24-29③	.021③	6B	6B	16	4½-6½	650	550②
	8-390	BF-42	.034	24-29③	.021③	6B	6B	13	4½-6½	650	550
	8-428PI	BF-32	.034	24-29③	.021③	—	6B	18	4½-6½	—	600
	8-429	BF-42	.034	26-31	.017	—	6B	16	4½-6½	—	550
	8-429	BF-42	.034	24-29③	.021③	6B	6B	16	4½-6½	650	550
1970	6-240	BF-42	.034	35-40	.027	6B	6B	12	4-6	800/500	500
	8-302	BF-42	.034	24-29	.021	6B	6B	16	4-6	575 [800/500]	575 [600/500]
	8-351W	BF-42	.034	24-29	.021	10B	10B	11	5-7	575 [700/500]	575 [600/500]
	8-390	BF-42	.034	24-29③	.021③	6B	6B	13	5-7	570/500	600/500
	8-428PI	BF-32	.034	24-29	.021	—	6B	18	4½-6½	—	600/500
	8-429	BRF-42	.034	24-29③	.021③	—	6B	16	5-7	—	600/500
	8-429	BRF-42	.034	24-29③	.021③	6B	6B	16	5-7	700/500	600/500
1971	6-240	BRF-42	.034	33-38	.027	6B	6B	18	4-6	800/500	600/500
	8-302	BRF-42	.034	24-29	.021	6B	6B	16	4-6	575 [800/500]	575 [650/500]

Tune-Up Specifications (cont.)

When analyzing compression test results, look for uniformity among cylinders rather than specific pressures.

Year	Engine No. Cyl Displacement (cu in.)	Spark Plugs Type	Spark Plugs Gap (in.)	Distributor Point Dwell (deg)	Distributor Point Gap (in.)	Ignition Timing (deg)▲ Man Trans	Ignition Timing (deg)▲ Auto Trans	Valves Intake Opens ▪(deg)●	Fuel Pump Pressure (psi)	Idle Speed (rpm)▲ Man Trans*	Idle Speed (rpm)▲ Auto Trans
1971	8-351W	BRF-42	.034	24–29	.021	6B	6B	11	5–7	575 [775/500]	575 [600/500]
	8-351C	ARF-42	.034	24–29	.021	—	6B	12	5–7	—	625/550
	8-390	BRF-42	.034	24–29	.021	—	6B	13	5–7	—	600/475
	8-400	ARF-42	.034	26–31	.017	—	10B(6B)	17	5–7	—	625/500
	8-429PI	ARF-42	.034	27½–29½	.020	—	10B	32	5–7	—	650/500
	8-429	BRF-42	.034	24–29 ③	.021 ③	—	4B	16	5–7	—	600
	8-429	BRF-42	.034	24–29 ③	.021 ③	4B	4B	16	5–7	700	600
1972	6-240	BRF-42	.034	35–39	.027	—	6B	18	4–6	—	500
	8-302	BRF-42	.034	26–30	.017	—	6B	16	5–7	—	575 [600/500]
	8-351W	BRF-42	.034	26–30	.017	—	6B	11	5–7	—	575 [600/500]
	8-351C	ARF-42	.034	26–30	.017	—	6B	12	5–7	—	600/500
	8-400	ARF-42	.034	26–30	.017	—	6B	17	5–7	—	625/500
	8-429	BRF-42	.034	26–30	.017	—	10B	8	5–7	—	600/500
	8-429PI	ARF-42	.034	26–30	.017	—	10B	32	Electric	—	650/500
1973	8-351W	BRF-42	.034	26–30	.017	—	6B	11	5–7	—	575 [600/500]
	8-351C	ARF-42	.034	26–30	.017	—	6B	12	5–7	—	600/500
	8-400	ARF-42	.034	26–30	.017	—	6B	17	5–7	—	625/500
	8-429	BRF-42	.034	26–30	.017	—	10B	8	5–7	—	600/500
	8-429PI	ARF-42	.034	26–30	.017	—	10B	32	Electric	—	650/500

1974	8-351W	BRF-42	.034[4]	26-30	.014-.020	—	6B	15	4-6	—	600/500
	8-351C	ARF-42	.044	26-30	.014-.020	—	14B	19½	5½-6½	—	700/500
	8-400	ARF-42	.044[8]	[6]	[6]	—	12B	17	5½-6½	—	625/500
	8-460	ARF-52	.054[7]	[6]	[6]	—	14B	8	5½-6½	—	650/500[5]
	8-460PI	ARF-52	.054	[6]	[6]	—	10B	18	Electric	—	700/500
1975	8-351M	ARF-42	.044	[6]	[6]	—	8B	19½	5½-6½	—	700/500
	8-400	ARF-42	.044	[6]	[6]	—	6B	17	5½-6½	—	625/500
	8-460	ARF-52	.044	[6]	[6]	—	14B	8	6.2-7.2	—	650/500
	8-460PI	ARF-52	.044	[6]	[6]	—	14B	18	Electric	—	650/500
1976	8-351M	ARF-52	.044	Electronic	—	—	12B[9]	19½	6½-7½	—	650/500
	8-400	ARF-52	.044	Electronic	—	—	10B	17	6½-7½	—	650/500
	8-460	ARF-52	.044	Electronic	—	—	8B[10]	8	7.2-8.2	—	650/500
	8-460PI	ARF-52	.044	Electronic	—	—	8B[10]	8	Electric	—	650/500
1977	8-351M	ARF-52	.050	Electronic	—	—	8B	19½	6½-7½	—	650/500
	8-400	ARF-52	.050	Electronic	—	—	8B	17	6½-7½	—	650/500
	8-460	ARF-52-6	.060	Electronic	—	—	16B	8	7-8	—	650/500
1978	8-302	ARF-52 (ARF-52-6)	.050 (.060)	Electronic	—	—	14B	16	5½-6½	—	650
	8-351W	ARF-52 (ARF-52-6)	.050 (.060)	Electronic	—	—	4B	23	4-6	—	650
	8-351M	ARF-52 (ARF-52-6)	.050 (.060)	Electronic	—	—	12B(16B)	19½	6½-7½	—	650
	8-400	ARF-52 (ARF-52-6)	.050 (.060)	Electronic	—	—	13B(16B)	17	6½-7½	—	650
	8-460	ARF-52 (ARF-52-6)	.050 (.060)	Electronic	—	—	10B	8	7¼-8¼	—	580
	8-460	ARF-52-6	.060	Electronic	—	—	16B	18	7¼-7¼	—	580
1979	8-302	ASF-52[12]	.050[12]	Electronic	—	—	14B	16	5½-6½	—	550
	8-351W	ASF-52	.050	Electronic	—	—	4B (EECII)[11]	23	6½-8	—	550

Tune-Up Specifications (cont.)

When analyzing compression test results, look for uniformity among cylinders rather than specific pressures.

Year	Engine No. Cyl Displacement (cu In.)	Spark Plugs Type	Spark Plugs Gap (In.)	Distributor Point Dwell (deg)	Distributor Point Gap (In.)	Ignition Timing (deg) ▲ Man Trans	Ignition Timing (deg) ▲ Auto Trans	Valves Intake Opens ■ (deg) ●	Fuel Pump Pressure (psi)	Idle Speed (rpm) ▲ Man Trans*	Idle Speed (rpm) ▲ Auto Trans
1980	8-302	ASF-52⑫	.050⑫	Electronic		—	6B⑫	16	5½–6½	—	550⑭
	8-351W	ASF-52	.050	Electronic		—	10B	23	6½–8	—	550⑭
1981	8-255	ASF-52	.050	Electronic		—	⑮	16	6–8	—	500⑭
	8-302	ASF-52	.050	Electronic		—	⑮	17	39½⑬	—	550⑭
	8-351	ASF-52	.050	Electronic		—	⑮	23	6½–8	—	550⑭
1982	8-255	ASF-52	.050	Electronic		—	⑮	16	6–8	—	500
	8-302	ASF-52	.050	Electronic		—	⑮	16	6½–8⑬	—	500
	8-351			Electronic		—	⑮	18	6½–8	—	600
1983	8-302	ASF-52	.050	Electronic		—	⑮	N/A	6½–8	—	600
	8-302	ASF-52	.050	Electronic		—	⑮	N/A	39½	—	550
	8-351	ASF-52	.050	Electronic		—	⑮	N/A	6½–8	—	600

▲ See text for procedure
● Figures in parentheses indicate California engine
■ All figures Before Top Dead Center
* Figures in brackets are for solenoid equipped vehicles only. In all cases where two figures are separated by a slash, the first is for idle speed with solenoid energized and the automatic transmission in Drive, while the second is for idle speed with solenoid disconnected and automatic transmission in Neutral.
① Adjust mechanical lifters, intake and exhaust, to .025 inch with engine hot
② A/C off
③ For engines equipped with single diaphragm distributors, adjust point dwell to 26–31 degrees and point gap to .017 inch
④ .044 on California models
⑤ 675/500 for California engines
⑥ Solid State (breakerless) ignition
⑦ .044 on California models
⑧ .054 on California models
⑨ 8BTDC @ 650 rpm in California
⑩ 14BTDC @ 650 rpm in California
⑪ California engines have variable EEC II timing; see the text for a description.
⑫ ASF-52-6 Calif; .060 gap; 10B;
⑬ EFI—Electronic Fuel Injection
⑭ In Drive
⑮ See underhood sticker
B Before Top Dead Center
C Cleveland
NA Not available
PI Police Interceptor
TDC Top Dead Center
W Windsor
— Not applicable
M Modified Cleveland design

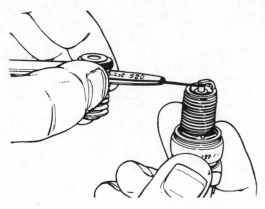

Checking the spark plug gap with a gap gauge

use for any period of time, should be considered normal.

SPARK PLUG HEAT RANGE

Spark plug heat range is the ability of the plug to dissipate heat. The longer the insulator (or the farther it extends into the engine), the hotter the plug will operate; the shorter the insulator the cooler it will operate. A plug that absorbs little heat and remains too cool will quickly accumulate deposits of oil and carbon since it is not hot enough to burn them off. This leads to plug fouling and consequently to misfiring. A plug that absorbs too much heat will have no deposits, but, due to the excessive heat, the electrodes will burn away quickly and in some instances, pre-ignition may result. Pre-ignition takes place when plug tips get so hot that they glow sufficiently to ignite the fuel/air mixture before the actual spark occurs. This early ignition will usually cause a pinging during low speeds and heavy loads.

The general rule of thumb for choosing the correct heat range when picking a spark plug is: if most of your driving is long distance, high speed travel, use a colder plug; if most of your driving is stop and go, use a hotter plug. Original equipment plugs are compromise plugs, but most people never have occasion to change

their plugs from the factory-recommended heat range.

REPLACING SPARK PLUGS

A set of spark plugs usually requires replacement before about 12,000 miles with conventional ignition systems and after about 20,000 to 30,000 miles with electronic ignition, depending on your style of driving. In normal operation, plug gap increases about 0.001 in. for every 1,000–2,500 miles. As the gap increases, the plug's voltage requirement also increases. It requires a greater voltage to jump the wider gap and about two to three times as much voltage to fire a plug at high speeds than at idle.

When you're removing spark plugs, you should work on one at a time. Don't start by removing the plug wires all at once, because unless you number them, they may become mixed up. Take a minute before you begin and number the wires with tape. The best location for numbering is near where the wires come out of the cap.

1. Twist the spark plug boot and remove the boot and wire from the plug. Do not pull on the wire itself as this will ruin the wire.

2. If possible, use a brush or rag to clean the area around the spark plug. Make sure that all the dirt is removed so that none will enter the cylinder after the plug is removed.

3. Remove the spark plug using the proper size socket. Turn the socket counterclockwise to remove the plug. Be sure to hold the socket straight on the plug to avoid breaking the plug, or rounding off the hex on the plug.

4. Once the plug is out, check it against the plugs shown in the "color" section to determine engine condition. This is crucial since plug readings are vital signs of engine condition.

5. Use a round wire feeler gauge to check the plug gap. The correct size gauge should pass through the electrode gap with a slight drag. If you're in doubt, try one size smaller and one larger. The smaller gauge should go through easily while the larger one shouldn't go through at all. If the gap is incorrect, use the electrode bending tool on the end of the gauge to adjust the gap. When adjusting the gap, always bend the side electrode. The center electrode is non-adjustable.

6. Squirt a drop of penetrating oil on the threads of the new plug and install it. Don't oil the threads too heavily. Turn the plug in clockwise by hand until it is snug.

7. When the plug is finger tight, tighten it with a wrench.

8. Install the plug boot firmly over the plug. Proceed to the next plug.

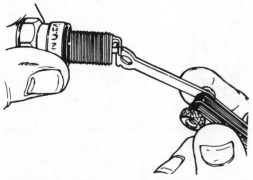

Adjusting the spark plug gap with a gapping tool

CHECKING AND REPLACING SPARK PLUG CABLES

Visually inspect the spark plug cables for burns, cuts, or breaks in the insulation. Check the spark plug boots and the nipples on the distributor cap and coil. Replace any damaged wiring. If no physical damage is obvious, the wires can be checked with an ohmmeter for excessive resistance. (See the tune-up and troubleshooting section.)

When installing a new set of spark plug cables, replace the cables one at a time so there will be no mixup. Start by replacing the longest cable first. Install the boot firmly over the spark plug. Route the wire exactly the same as the original. Insert the nipple firmly into the tower on the distributor cap. Repeat the process for each cable.

DURA-SPARK PLUG WIRES

The spark plug wires used with the DURA SPARK system are 8 mm to contain the higher output voltage. There are two types of wires used in the system and some engines will have both types. It is important to properly identify the type of wire used for each cylinder before replacements are made.

Both types are blue in color and have silicone jacketing. The insulation material underneath the jacketing may be EPDM or another silicone layer separated by glass braid. The cable incorporating EPDM is used where engine temperatures are cooler and are identified with the letters "SE" with black printing. The silicone jacket silicone insulation type is used where high engine temperatures are present and is identified with the letters "SS" with white printing.

The cables are also marked with the cylinder number, model year and date of cable manufacture (quarter and year). Service replacement wires will not have cylinder numbers, or manufacture date.

NOTE: *On any vehicle equipped with a catalytic converter, never allow the engine to run for more than 30 seconds with a spark plug wire disconnected. Use an oscilloscope for testing and diagnosis. Do not puncture wires or use adapters that can cause misfiring. Unburned fuel in the cylinders will ignite in the converter as it is exhausted and damage the converter.*

Removal

When removing spark plug wires, use great care. Grasp and twist the insulator back and forth on the spark plug to free the insulator. Do not pull on the wire directly as it may be-

come separated from the connector inside the insulator.

Installation

1. Install each wire in or on the proper terminal of the distributor cap. Be sure the terminal connector inside the insulator is fully seated. The No. 1 terminal is identified on the cap.

2. On 8-cylinder engines, remove the brackets from the old spark plug wire set and install them on the new set in the same relative position. Install the wires in the brackets on the valve rocker arm covers. Connect the wires to the proper spark plugs. Install the coil high tension lead.

The wires in the left bank bracket must be positioned in the bracket in a special order to avoid cylinder cross-fire. Be sure to position the wires in the bracket in the order from front to rear.

Whenever a DURA SPARK high tension wire is removed for any reason from a spark plug, coil or distributor terminal housing, silicone grease must be applied to the boot before it is reconnected. Using a small clean tool, coat the entire interior surface of the boot with Ford silicone grease (D7AZ 19A331-A or equivalent).

NOTE: *Should you become mixed up as to wire location, refer to the firing order illustrations.*

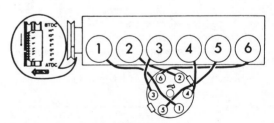

6 cylinder engine - 1,5,3,6,2,4

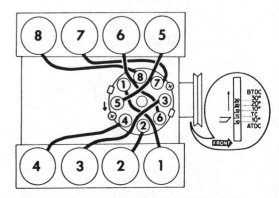

V8 engine except 351 and 400 - 1,5,4,2,6,3,7,8

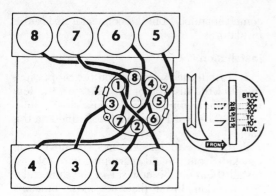

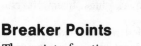

351 and 400 V8 engines - 1,3,7,2,6,5,4,8

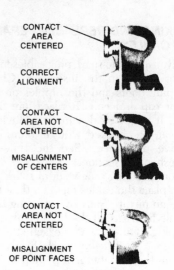

Breaker point contact alignment

Breaker Points

The points function as a circuit breaker for the primary circuit of the ignition system. The ignition coil must boost the 12 volts of electrical pressure supplied by the battery to as much as 25,000 volts in order to fire the plugs. To do this, the coil depends on the points and the condenser to make a clean break in the primary circuit.

NOTE: *Some 1974 and all 1975 and later models have electronic ignition. Breaker points are not used.*

The coil has both primary and secondary circuits. When the ignition is turned on, the battery supplies voltage through the coil to the points. The points are connected to ground, completing the primary circuit. As the current passes through the coil, a magnetic field is created in the iron center core of the coil. As the cam in the distributor turns, the points open and the primary circuit collapses. The magnetic field in the primary circuit of the coil cuts through the secondary circuit windings around the iron core. Because of the scientific phenomenon called "electromagnetic induction," the battery voltage is increased to a level sufficient to fire the spark plugs.

When the points open, the electrical charge in the primary circuit jumps the gap created between the two open contacts of the points. If this electrical charge were not transferred elsewhere, the metal contacts of the points would melt and the gap between the points would start to change rapidly. If this gap is not maintained, the points will not break the primary circuit. If the primary circuit is not broken, the secondary circuit will not have enough voltage to fire the spark plugs.

Condenser

NOTE: *Some 1974 and all 1975 and later models have electronic ignition. A condenser is not used.*

CONDITION	CAUSED BY
BURNED	INCORRECT VOLTAGE REGULATOR SETTING. RADIO CONDENSER INSTALLED TO THE DISTRIBUTOR SIDE OF THE COIL.
EXCESSIVE METAL TRANSFER OR PITTING	INCORRECT ALIGNMENT. INCORRECT VOLTAGE REGULATOR SETTING. RADIO CONDENSER INSTALLED TO THE DISTRIBUTOR SIDE OF THE COIL. IGNITION CONDENSER OF IMPROPER CAPACITY. EXTENDED OPERATION OF THE ENGINE AT SPEEDS OTHER THAN NORMAL.

Breaker point troubleshooting

The function of the condenser is to absorb excessive voltage from the points when they open and thus prevent the points from becoming pitted or burned.

It is interesting to note that the above cycle must be completed by the ignition system every time a spark fires. In a V8 engine, all of the spark plugs fire once for every two revolutions of the crankshaft. That means that in one revolution, four spark plugs fire. So when the engine is at an idle speed of 800 rpm, the points are opening and closing 3,200 times a minute.

There are two ways to check the breaker point gap: It can be done with a feeler gauge or a dwell meter. Either way you set the points, you are basically adjusting the amount of time that the points remain open. The time is measured in degrees of distributor rotation. When you measure the gap between the breaker points with a feeler gauge, you are setting the maximum amount the points will open when the rubbing block on the points is on a high point of the distributor cam. When you adjust the points with a dwell meter, you are adjusting the number of degrees that the points will remain closed before they start to open as a high point of the distributor cam approaches the rubbing block of the points.

When you replace a set of points, always replace the condenser at the same time.

When you change the point gap or dwell, you will also have changed the ignition timing. So, if the point gap or dwell is changed, the ignition timing must be adjusted also.

INSPECTION OF THE POINTS

1. Disconnect the high-tension wire from the top of the distributor and the coil.

2. Remove the distributor cap by prying off the spring clips on the sides of the cap.

3. Remove the rotor from the distributor shaft by pulling it straight up. Examine the condition of the rotor. If it is cracked or the metal tip is excessively worn or burned, it should be replaced.

4. Pry open the contacts of the points with a screwdriver and check the condition of the contacts. If they are excessively worn, burned or pitted, they should be replaced.

5. If the points are in good condition, adjust them, and replace the rotor and the distributor cap. If the points need to be replaced, follow the replacement procedure given below.

REPLACEMENT OF THE BREAKER POINTS AND CONDENSER

1. Remove the coil high-tension wire from the top of the distributor cap. Remove the distributor cap from the distributor and place it out of the way. Remove the rotor from the distributor shaft.

2. Loosen the screw that holds the condenser lead to the body of the breaker points and remove the condenser lead from the points.

3. Remove the screw that holds and grounds the condenser to the distributor body. Remove the condenser from the distributor and discard it.

4. Remove the point assembly attaching screws and adjustment lockscrews. A screwdriver with a holding mechanism will come in handy here so you don't drop a screw into the distributor and have to remove the entire distributor to retrieve it.

5. Remove the points. Wipe off the cam and apply new cam lubricant. Discard the old set of points.

6. Position the new set of points with the locating peg in the hole on the breaker plate, and install the screws that hold the assembly onto the plate. Do not tighten them all the way.

7. Attach the new condenser to the plate with the ground screw.

Rotating engine manually

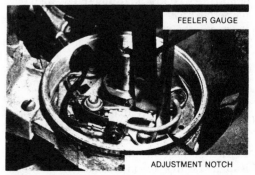

FEELER GAUGE

ADJUSTMENT NOTCH

Adjusting point gap

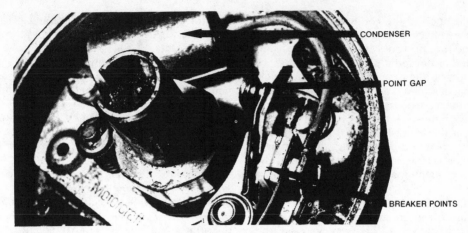

CONDENSER

POINT GAP

BREAKER POINTS

Checking the point gap

8. Attach the condenser lead to the points at the proper place.

9. Apply a small amount of cam lubricant to the shaft where the rubbing block of the points touches.

ADJUSTMENT OF THE BREAKER POINTS WITH A FEELER GAUGE

1. If the contact points of the assembly are not parallel, bend the stationary contact so they make contact across the entire surface of the contacts. Bend only the stationary bracket part of the point assembly, not the movable contact.

2. Turn the engine until the rubbing block of the points is on one of the high points of the distributor cam. You can do this by either turning the ignition switch to the start position and releasing it quickly ("bumping" the engine) or by using a wrench on the bolt that holds the crankshaft pulley to the crankshaft. Be sure to remove the wrench before starting the engine!

3. Place the correct size feeler gauge between the contacts. Make sure it is parallel with the contact surfaces.

4. With your free hand, insert a screwdriver into the notch provided for adjustment or into the eccentric adjusting screw, then twist the screwdriver to either increase or decrease the gap to the proper setting.

5. Tighten the adjustment lockscrew and recheck the contact gap to make sure that it didn't change when the lockscrew was tightened.

6. Replace the rotor and distributor cap, and the high-tension wire that connects the top of the distributor and the coil. Make sure that the rotor is firmly seated all the way onto the distributor shaft and that the tab of the rotor is aligned with notch in the shaft. Align the tab in the base of the distributor cap with the notch in the distributor body. Make sure that the cap is firmly seated on the distributor and that the retainer springs are in place. Make sure that the end of the high-tension wire is firmly placed in the top of the distributor and the coil.

Dwell Angle Setting

The dwell angle is the number of degrees of distributor cam rotation through which the breaker points remain fully closed (conducting electricity). Increasing the point gap decreases dwell, while decreasing the point gap increases dwell.

NOTE: *On cars equipped with breakerless (solid state) ignition, dwell is electronically controlled and cannot be adjusted.*

Using a dwell meter of known accuracy, connect the red lead (positive) wire of the meter to the distributor primary wire connection on the positive (+) side of the coil, and the black ground (negative) wire of the meter to a good ground on the engine (e.g. thermostat housing nut).

The dwell angle may be checked either with the distributor cap and rotor installed and the engine running, or with the cap and rotor removed and the engine cranking at starter speed. The meter gives constant reading with the engine running. With the engine cranking, the reading will fluctuate between zero degrees dwell and the maximum figure for that angle. While cranking, the maximum figure is the correct one for that setting. Never attempt to change dwell angle while the ignition is on. Touching the point contacts or primary wire connection with a metal screwdriver may result in a 12 volt shock.

To change the dwell angle, loosen the point retaining screw slightly and make the approximate correction. Tighten the retaining screw and test the dwell with the engine cranking. If the dwell appears to be correct, install the breaker point protective cover, if so equipped, the rotor and distributor cap, and test the dwell with the engine running. Take the engine through its entire rpm range and observe the dwell meter. The dwell should remain within specifications at all times. Great fluctuation of dwell at different engine speeds indicates worn distributor parts.

Following the dwell angle adjustment, the ignition timing must be checked. A 1° increase in dwell results in the ignition timing being retarded 2° and vice versa.

ADJUSTMENT OF THE BREAKER POINTS WITH A DWELL METER

1. Adjust the points with a feeler gauge as described above.

2. Connect the dwell meter to the ignition circuit according to the manufacturer's instructions. One lead of the meter is connected to a ground and the other lead is to be connected to the distributor post on the coil. An adapter is usually provided for this purpose.

3. If the dwell meter has a set line on it, adjust the meter to zero the indicator.

4. Start the engine.

NOTE: *Be careful when working on any vehicle while the engine is running. Make sure*

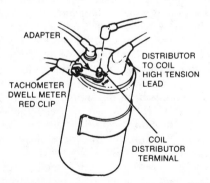

Installing dwell/tachometer adapter on coil (1974 and earlier models)

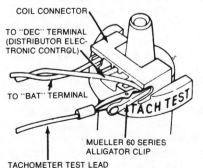

Attaching dwell/tachometer lead to coil connector (1975 and later models)

that the transmission is in Neutral or firmly in Park and that the parking brake is applied. Keep hands, clothing, tools, and the wires of the test instruments clear of the rotating fan blades.

5. Observe the reading on the dwell meter. If the reading is within the specified range, turn off the engine and remove the dwell meter.

6. If the reading is above the specified range, the breaker point gap is too small. If the reading is below the specified range, the gap is too large. In either case, the engine must be stopped and the gap adjusted in the manner previously covered. After making the adjustment, start the engine and check the reading on the dwell meter. When the correct reading is obtained, disconnect the dwell meter.

7. Check the adjustment of the ignition timing.

Distributor Cap and Ignition Rotor

During the tune-up, visually inspect the distributor cap and ignition rotor for burned or corroded contacts, cracks, carbon tracks, or moisture. Also check the fit of the rotor on the distributor shaft. If the contacts are burned or excessively corroded, if cracks or carbon tracks are detected or there is excessive play in the rotor, replace the defective part. If the cap and rotor look all right, clean the contacts and the inside of the cap and reinstall.

Ignition Timing

Ignition timing is the measurement in degrees of crankshaft rotation of the instant the spark plugs in the cylinders fire, in relation to the location of the piston, while the piston is on its compression stroke.

NOTE: *On models equipped with EEC; ignition timing procedures are neither necessary nor possible.*

Ignition timing is adjusted by loosening the distributor locking device and turning the distributor in the engine.

Ideally, the air/fuel mixture in the cylinder will be ignited (by the spark plug) and just beginning its rapid expansion as the piston passes top dead center (TDC) of the compression stroke. If this happens, the piston will be beginning the power stroke just as the compressed (by the movement of the piston) and ignited (by the spark plug) air/fuel mixture starts to expand. The expansion of the air/fuel mixture will then force the piston down on the power stroke and turn the crankshaft.

Distributor locknut

Timing light aimed at timing marks

It takes a fraction of a second for the spark from the plug to completely ignite the mixture in the cylinder. Because of this, the spark plug must fire before the piston reaches TDC, if the mixture is to be completely ignited as the piston passes TDC. This measurement is given in degrees (of crankshaft rotation) *before* the piston reaches *top dead center* (BTDC). If the ignition timing setting for your engine is six degrees (°) BTDC, this means that the spark plug must fire at a time when the piston for that cylinder is 6° before top dead center of its compression stroke. However, this only holds true while your engine is at idle speed.

As you accelerate from idle, the speed of your engine (rpm) increases. The increase in rpm means that the pistons are now traveling up and down much faster. Because of this, the spark plugs will have to fire even sooner if the mixture is to be completely ignited as the piston passes TDC. To accomplish this, the distributor incorporates means to advance the timing of the spark as engine speed increases.

The distributor in your Ford has two means of advancing the ignition timing. One is called centrifugal advance and is actuated by weights in the distributor. The other is called vacuum advance and is controlled by that large circular housing on the side of the distributor.

In addition, some distributors have a vacuum-retard mechanism which is contained in the same housing on the side of the distributor as the vacuum advance. The function of this mechanism is to retard the timing of the ignition spark under certain engine conditions. This causes more complete burning of the air/fuel mixture in the cylinder and consequently lowers exhaust emissions.

Because these mechanisms change ignition timing, it is necessary to disconnect and plug the one or two vacuum lines from the distributor when setting the basic ignition timing.

If ignition timing is set too far advanced (BTDC), the ignition and expansion of the air/fuel mixture in the cylinder will try to force the piston down the cylinder while it is still traveling upward. This causes engine "ping," a sound which resembles marbles being dropped into an empty tin can. If the ignition timing is too far retarded (after, or ATDC), the piston will have already started down on the power stroke when the air/fuel mixture ignites and expands. This will cause the piston to be forced down only a portion of its travel. This will result in poor engine performance and lack of power.

Ignition timing adjustment is checked with a timing light. This instrument is connected to the number one (No. 1) spark plug of the engine. The timing light flashes every time an electrical current is sent from the distributor, through the No. 1 spark plug wire, to the spark plug. The crankshaft pulley and the front cover of the engine are marked with a timing pointer and a timing scale. When the timing pointer is aligned with the "0" mark on the timing scale, the piston in No. 1 cylinder is at TDC of its compression stroke. With the engine running, and the timing light aimed at the timing pointer and timing scale, the stroboscopic flashes from the timing light will allow you to check the ignition timing setting of the engine. The timing light flashes every time the spark plug in the No. 1 cylinder of the engine fires. Since the flash from the timing light makes the crankshaft pulley seem stationary for a moment, you will be able to read the exact position in the No. 1 cylinder on the timing scale on the front of the engine.

NOTE: *All 1974 and later engines are equipped with conventional and "monolithic" timing features. The monolithic system employs a timing receptacle located at the front of all engines. The receptacle is designed to accept an electronic probe which connects to digital read-out equipment. On cars equipped with electronic ignition, Ford recommends that only timing lights of the inductive pickup type be used as conventional timing lights may give a false reading due to the higher coil charging currents.*

Ford recommends that the ignition timing be checked every 12 months or 2,000 miles.

The timing adjustment should always follow a breaker point gap and/or dwell angle adjustment, and be performed with the engine at normal operating temperature.

Locate the crankshaft damper/pulley and timing pointer at the front of the engine, and clean them with a solvent-soaked rag or wire brush so that the marks can be seen. Scribe a mark on the crankshaft damper/pulley and pointer with chalk or luminescent (day glo) paint to highlight the correct timing setting. Disconnect the vacuum hose(s) at the distributor vacuum capsule and plug it (them) with a pencil, golf tee, or some other small tapered object. Connect a stroboscopic timing light to the No. 1 cylinder spark plug (see "Firing Order" illustrations in Chapter 3) and to the battery terminals, according to the manufacturer's instructions. Also connect a tachometer to the engine, with one lead connected to the distributor primary wire connection at the coil and the other lead connected to a good ground.

Make sure that all of the timing light wires and tachometer wires are well clear of the engine. Start the engine and set the idle speed (if necessary) to the speed specified in the "Tune-Up Specifications" chart, using the idle speed adjusting screw(s). Then, with the engine running, aim the timing light at the pointer and at the marks on the damper/pulley. If the marks made with the chalk or paint coincide when the timing light flashes (at the specified rpm), the engine is timed correctly. If the marks do not coincide, stop the engine. Loosen the distributor locknut and start the engine again. While observing the timing light flashes on the markers, grasp the distributor vacuum capsule—not the distributor cap—and rotate the distributor until the marks do coincide. Then, stop the engine and tighten the distributor locknut, taking care not to disturb the setting. As a final check, start the engine once more to make sure that the timing marks still align.

NOTE: *If necessary, readjust the idle speed to that listed in the tune-up specs. Timing is correct only at the specified rpm.*

Once the engine is timed, reconnect the vacuum hose(s) to the distributor. Readjust, if necessary, the curb idle to specifications as outlined under "Idle Speed and Mixture Adjustment." Finally, remove the timing light and tachometer from the engine.

Valve Lash

All engines used in full-size Ford products, from 1968 to the present, are equipped with hydraulic valve lifters. Valve systems with hydraulic valve lifters operate with zero clearance in the valve train, and because of this the rocker arms are nonadjustable. The only means by which valve system clearances can be altered is by installing 0.060 in. over-or undersize pushrods; but, because of the hydraulic lifter's natural ability to compensate for slack in the valve train, all components of the valve system should be checked for wear if there is excessive play in the system.

When a valve in the engine is in the closed position, the valve lifter is resting on the base circle of the camshaft lobe and the pushrod is in its lowest position. To remove this additional clearance from the valve train, the valve lifter expands to maintain zero clearance in the valve system. When a rocker arm is loosened or removed from the engine, the lifter expands to its fullest travel. When the rocker arm is reinstalled on the engine, the proper valve setting is obtained by tightening the rocker arm to a specified limit. But with the lifter fully expanded, if the camshaft lobe is on a high point it will require excessive torque to compress the lifter and obtain the proper setting. Because of this, when any component of the valve system has been removed, a preliminary valve adjustment procedure must be followed to ensure that when the rocker arm is reinstalled on the engine and tightened, the camshaft lobe for that cylinder is in the low position. For preliminary valve adjustment procedure refer to chapter three.

Carburetor

This section contains only carburetor adjustments as they normally apply to engine tune-up. Descriptions of the carburetor and complete adjustment procedures and complete adjustment procedures can be found in Chapter 4, under "Fuel System."

When the engine in your car is running, air/fuel mixture from the carburetor is being drawn into the engine by a partial vacuum which is created by the downward movement of the pistons on the intake stroke of the four-stroke cycle of the engine. The amount of air/fuel mixture which enters the engine is controlled by throttle plate(s) in the bottom of the carburetor. When the engine is not running the throttle plate(s) is (are) closed completely blocking off the bottom of the carburetor from the inside of the engine. The throttle plates are connected, through the throttle linkage, to the accelerator in the passenger compartment of the car. After you start the engine and put the transmission in gear, you depress the accelerator to start the car moving. What you actually are doing when you depress the accelerator is opening the throttle

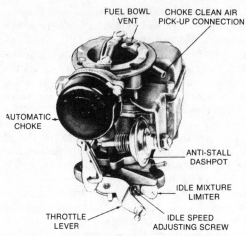

FUEL BOWL VENT
CHOKE CLEAN AIR PICK-UP CONNECTION
AUTOMATIC CHOKE
ANTI-STALL DASHPOT
IDLE MIXTURE LIMITER
THROTTLE LEVER
IDLE SPEED ADJUSTING SCREW

Carburetor adjustment—1969–71 Carter YF

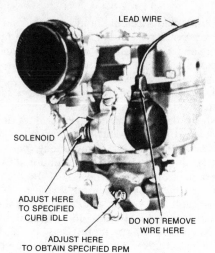

LEAD WIRE
SOLENOID
ADJUST HERE TO SPECIFIED CURB IDLE
DO NOT REMOVE WIRE HERE
ADJUST HERE TO OBTAIN SPECIFIED RPM

Carter YF with throttle solenoid positioner

plate(s) in the carburetor to admit more of the air/fuel mixture to the engine. The farther you open the throttle plates in the carburetor, the higher the engine speed becomes.

As previously stated, when the engine is not running, the throttle plates in the carburetor are closed. When the engine is idling, it is necessary to open the throttle plate slightly. To prevent having to keep your foot on the accelerator when the engine is idling, an idle speed adjusting screw was added to the carburetor. This screw has the same effect as keeping your foot slightly depressed on the accelerator. The idle speed adjusting screw contacts a lever (the throttle lever) on the outside of the carburetor. When the screw is turning in, it opens the throttle plate on the carburetor, raising the idle speed of the engine. This screw is called the curb idle adjusting screw, and the procedures in this section will tell you how to adjust it.

In addition to the curb idle adjusting screw, most engines have a throttle solenoid positioner. Ford has found it necessary to raise the idle speed on these engines to obtain a smooth engine idle. When the key is turned "off," the current to the spark plugs is cut off and the engine normally stops running. However, if an engine has a high operating temperature and a high idle speed, it is possible for the temperature of the cylinder, instead of the spark plug, to ignite the air/fuel mixture. When this happens, the engine continues to run after the key is turned off. To solve this problem, a throttle solenoid was added to the carburetor. The solenoid is a cylinder with an adjustable plunger and an electrical lead. When the ignition key is turned to "on," the solenoid plunger extends to contact the carburetor throttle lever and raise the idle speed of the engine. When the ignition key is turned "off," the solenoid is de-energized and the solenoid

plunger falls back from the throttle lever. This allows the throttle lever to fall back and rest on the curb idle adjusting screw. This closes the throttle plates far enough so that the engine will not run on.

Since it is difficult for the engine to draw the air/fuel mixture from the carburetor with the small amount of throttle plate opening that is present when the engine is idling, an idle mixture passage is provided in the carburetor. This passage delivers air/fuel mixture to the engine from a hole which is located in the bottom of the carburetor below the throttle plates. This idle mixture passage contains an adjusting screw which restricts the amount of air/fuel mixture which enters the engine at idle. The procedures given in this section will tell how to set the idle mixture adjusting screw(s).

NOTE: *With the electric solenoid disengaged, the carburetor idle speed adjusting screw must make contact with the throttle lever to prevent the throttle plates from jamming in the throttle bore when the engine is turned off.*

IDLE SPEED AND MIXTURE ADJUSTMENTS

NOTE: *In order to limit exhaust emissions, plastic caps have been installed on the idle fuel mixture screw(s) which prevent the carburetor from being adjusted to an overly rich idle fuel mixture. Under no circumstances should these limiters be modified or removed. A satisfactory idle should be obtained within the range of the limiter(s).*

Autolite 1101, Carter YF, Motorcraft 2100, Motorcraft 2150, Autolite 4100, Motorcraft 4300, Carter Thermo-Quad, Motorcraft 4350

NOTE: *The 2700/7200 VV Carburetors and Electronic fuel injection adjustments are found in Chapter 4.*

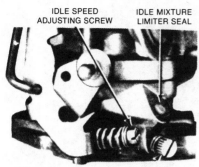

IDLE SPEED
ADJUSTING SCREW

IDLE MIXTURE
LIMITER SEAL

IDLE MIXTURE ADJUSTING SCREW

Carburetor adjustments—1968 Carter YF

1. Start the engine and run it at idle until it reaches operating temperature (about 10–20 minutes, depending on outside temperatures). Stop the engine.

2. Check the ignition timing as outlined under "Ignition Timing Adjustment."

3. Remove the air cleaner, taking note of the hose locations, and check that the choke plate is in the open position (plate in vertical position). Check the accompanying illustrations to see where the carburetor adjustment locations are. If you cannot reach them with the air cleaner installed, leave it off temporarily.

4. Attach a tachometer to the engine, with the positive wire connected to the distributor side of the ignition coil, and the negative wire connected to a good ground, such as an engine bolt.

NOTE: *In order to attach an alligator clip to the distributor side (terminal) of the coil (primary connection), it will be necessary to lift off the connector and slide a female loop type connector (commercially available) down over the terminal threads. Then push down the rubber connector over the loop connector and you have made yourself a little adaptor, to which you can connect the alligator clip of your tachometer.*

5. All idle speed adjustments are made with the headlights off (unless otherwise specified on the engine decal), with the airconditioning off (if so equipped), with all vacuum hoses connected (unless otherwise specified), with the throttle solenoid positioner activated (connected, if so equipped), and with the air cleaner on. The only problem here is that on many cars, the adjustments cannot be reached with the air cleaner installed. On these problem cars, you will have to adjust the idle speed approximately 50–100 rpm higher with the air cleaner removed so that the setting is correct when the air cleaner is installed. Also, if the air cleaner is removed, disconnect and plug the vacuum hoses for the vacuum operated heated air intake system to prevent a vacuum leak and subsequent drop in idle speed and quality. Finally, all idle speed adjustments are made in Neutral on cars with manual transmission, and in Drive on cars equipped with automatic transmission.

CAUTION: *Make sure that the parking brake is applied and all four wheels blocked.*

6a. On cars not equipped with a throttle solenoid positioner, the idle speed is adjusted with the curb idle speed adjusting screw. Start

MODEL 1101 1-V

MODELS
2100 2-V AND 4100 4-V

MODEL 4300 4-V

Idle speed screw locations

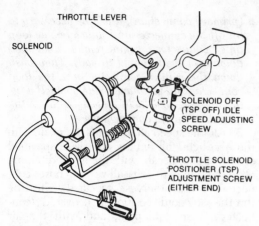

Throttle solenoid positioner adjustment—Motorcraft 2100, 2150, 4300, 4350

Idle mixture limiters installed—Motorcraft 4300 shown

the engine. Turn the curb idle speed adjusting screw inward or outward until the correct idle speed (see "Tune-Up Specifications" chart) is reached, remembering to make the 50–100 rpm allowance if the air cleaner is removed.

6b. On cars equipped with a throttle solenoid positioner, the idle speed is adjusted with solenoid adjusting crew (nut), in two stages. Start the engine. The higher speed is adjusted with the solenoid connected. Turn the solenoid adjusting screw (nut) on 1 or 4 barrel carburetors, or the entire bracket on 2 barrel carburetors, inward or outward until the correct higher idle speed (see "Tune-Up Specifications" chart) is reached, remembering to make the 50–100 rpm allownace if the air cleaner is removed. After making this adjustment on cars equipped with 2 barrel carburetors, tighten the solenoid adjusting locknut. The lower idle speed is adjusted with the solenoid lead wire disconnected near the harness (not at the carburetor). Place automatic transmission equipped cars in Neutral for this adjustment. Using the curb idle speed adjusting screw on the carburetor, turn the idle speed adjusting screw inward or outward until the correct lower idle speed (see "Tune-Up Specifications" chart) is reached, remembering again to make the 50–100 rpm allowance if the air cleaner is removed. Finally, reconnect the solenoid, slightly depress the throttle lever and allow the solenoid plunger to fully extend.

7. If removed, install the air cleaner and connect the hoses for the heated intake air system. Recheck the idle speed. If it is not correct, Step 6 will have to be repeated and the approximate corrections made.

8. To adjust the idle mixture, turn the idle mixture screw(s) inward to obtain the smoothest idle possible within the range of the limiter(s). After adjusting the mixture, it may be

necessary to readjust the idle speed as outlined in Step 6.

9. Turn off the engine and disconnect the tachometer.

NOTE: *If any doubt exists as to the proper idle mixture setting for your car, have the exhaust emission level checked at a diagnostic center or garage with an exhaust (HC/CO) analyzer.*

Motorcraft 2700 and 7200 Variable Venturi Carburetor

This carburetor was introduced in 1977 for use on California cars equipped with the 302 V8. In 1978, its usage was expanded, and in 1979 it was installed on LTD's equipped with the 302 V8. The variable Venturi carburetor is now used on all "big" Fords and Mercurys with the exception of the fuel injected version and some Canadian models. This carburetor differs substantially in both theory and operation from the rest of the carburetors discussed here. For a complete description of this carburetor, along with adjustment and overhaul procedures, see Chapter 4.

Catalytic Converter Precautions

Since 1974, most Fords and Mercurys have been equipped with catalytic converters to clean up exhaust emissions after they leave the engine. Naturally, lead-free fuel must be used in order to avoid contaminating the converter and rendering it useless. However, there are other precautions which should be taken to prevent a large amount of unburned hydrocarbon from reaching the converter. Should a sufficient amount of HC reach the converter, the unit could overheat, possibly damaging the converter or nearby mechanical components. There is even the possibility that a fire could be started. Therefore, when working on your car, the following conditions should be avoided:

1. The use of fuel system cleaning agents and additives.

2. Operating the car with a closed choke or a submerged carburetor float.

3. Extended periods of engine run-on (dieseling).

4. Turning off the ignition with the car in motion.

5. Ignition or charging system failure.

6. Misfiring of one or more spark plugs.

7. Disconnecting a spark plug wire while testing for a bad wire or plug, or poor compression in one cylinder.

8. Push or tow-starting the car, especially when hot.

9. Pumping the gas pedal when attempting to start a hot engine.

Engine and Engine Rebuilding

3

ENGINE ELECTRICAL

Solid-State Ignition

The breaker point ignition system was used through 1973 and on some 1974 models.

A breakerless (solid state) ignition system, using an armature and magnetic pickup coil assembly in the distributor and a solid state amplifer module, located between the coil and distributor, was installed in some 1974 and all 1975 and later models.

Both systems use a distributor which is driven by the camshaft at one half crankshaft rpm, a high voltage rotor, distributor cap, spark plug wiring, and an oil-filled coil.

The systems differ in the manner in which they convert electrical primary voltage (12 volt) from the battery into secondary voltage (20,000 volts or greater) to fire the spark plugs. In the conventional ignition system, the breaker points open and close as the movable breaker arm rides the rotating distributor cam, thereby opening and closing the current to the ignition coil. When the points open, they interrupt the flow of primary current to the coil, causing a collapse of the magnetic field in the coil and creating a high tension spark which is used to fire the spark plugs. In the breakerless system, a distributor shaft-mounted armature rotates past a magnetic pickup coil assembly causing fluctuations in the magnetic field generated by the pickup coil. These fluctuations in turn, cause the amplifier module to turn the ignition coil current off and mn, creating the high tension spark to fire the spark plugs. The amplifier module electronically controls the dwell, which is controlled mechanically in a conventional system by the duration which the points remain closed.

Both the conventional and breakerless ignition systems are equipped with dual advance distributors. The vacuum advance unit governs ignition timing according to engine load, while the centrifugal advance unit governs ignition timing according to engine rpm. Centrifugal advance is controlled by spring-mounted weights contained in the distributor,

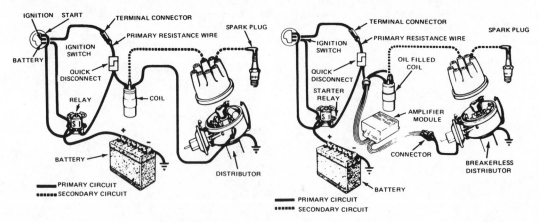

CONVENTIONAL

BREAKERLESS

Typical ignition systems

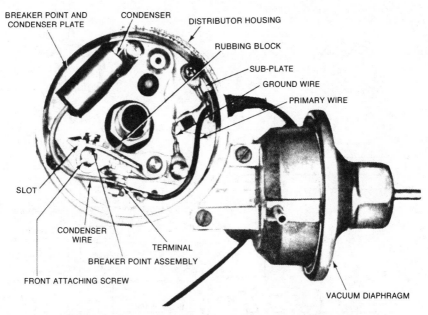

BREAKER POINT AND
CONDENSER PLATE

CONDENSER

DISTRIBUTOR HOUSING

RUBBING BLOCK

SUB-PLATE

GROUND WIRE

PRIMARY WIRE

SLOT

CONDENSER
WIRE

TERMINAL

BREAKER POINT ASSEMBLY

FRONT ATTACHING SCREW

VACUUM DIAPHRAGM

Typical breaker point distributor—cap and rotor removed

located under the breaker point mounting plate on conventional systems and under the fixed base plate on breakerless systems. As engine speed increases, centrifugal force moves the weights outward from the distributor shaft advancing the position of the distributor cam (conventional) or armature (breakerless), thereby advancing the ignition timing. Vacuum advance is controlled by a vacuum diaphragm which is mounted on the side of the distributor and attached to the breaker point mounting plate (conventional) or the magnetic

pickup coil assembly (breakerless) via the vacuum advance link. Under light acceleration, the engine is operating under a low-load condition, causing the carburetor vacuum to act on the distributor vacuum diaphragm, moving the breaker point mounting plate (conventional) or pickup coil assembly (breakerless) opposite the direction of distributor shaft rotation, thereby advancing the ignition timing.

The distributors on many models incorporate a vacuum retard mechanism. The retard mechanism is contained in the rear part of the

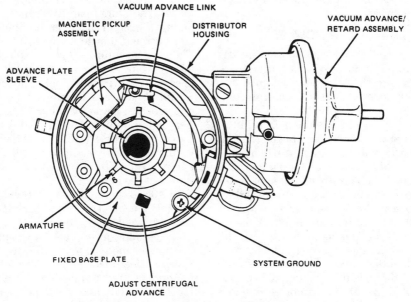

VACUUM ADVANCE LINK

MAGNETIC PICKUP
ASSEMBLY

DISTRIBUTOR
HOUSING

VACUUM ADVANCE/
RETARD ASSEMBLY

ADVANCE PLATE
SLEEVE

ARMATURE

FIXED BASE PLATE

ADJUST CENTRIFUGAL
ADVANCE

SYSTEM GROUND

Typical breakerless ignition—cap and rotor removed

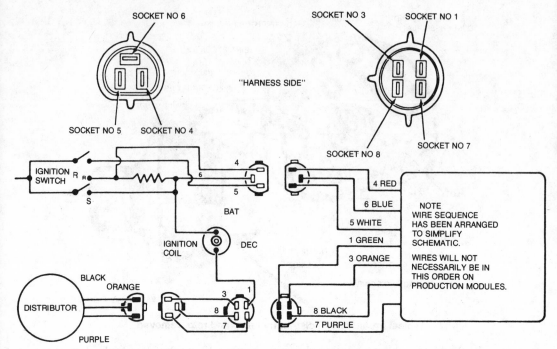

Solid state ignition testing—through 1975

vacuum diaphragm chamber. When the engine is operating under high-vacuum conditions (deceleration or idle), intake manifold vacuum is applied to the retard mechanism. The retard mechanism moves the breaker point mounting plate (conventional) or pickup coil assembly (breakerless) in the direction of distributor rotation, thereby retarding the ignition timing. Ignition retard, under these conditions, reduces exhaust emissions of hydrocarbons, although it does reduce engine efficiency somewhat.

BASIC OPERATING PRINCIPLES

The solid state (electronic) ignition system was designed primarily to provide a hotter spark necessary to fire the leaner fuel/air mixtures required by today's emission control standards.

The Ford Solid-State Ignition is a pulse-triggered, transistor controlled breakerless ignition system. With the ignition switch "on," the primary circuit is on and the ignition coil is energized. When the armature spokes approach the magnetic pick-up coil assembly, they induce a voltage which tells the amplifier to turn the coil primary current off. A timing circuit in the amplifier module will turn the current on again after the coil field has collapsed. When the current is on, it flows from the battery through the ignition switch, the primary windings of the ignition coil, and through the amplifier module circuits to

ground. When the current is off, the magnetic field built up in the ignition coil is allowed to collapse, inducing a high voltage into the secondary windings of the coil. High voltage is produced each time the field is thus built up and collapsed.

Although the systems are basically the same, Ford refers to their solid-state ignition in several different ways. 1974–76 systems are referred to simply as Breakerless systems. In 1977, Ford named their ignition systems Dura-Spark. The Dura-Spark system can be identified by the larger diameter distributor cap and larger (from 7mm to 8mm) spark plug wires. The system utilizes higher voltages up to 42,000 volts to allow wider spark plug gaps necessary to fire leaner fuel/air mixtures.

Dura-Spark was introduced in 1977, with two versions; Dura-Spark I and Dura-Spark II. The higher output Dura-Spark I is used on all California models (1977); and then only on California models equipped with the 302 V8 engine (1978–79). Dura-Spark I was discontinued at the end of 1979.

In 1980 a new version—Dura Spark III—was introduced. The Dura-Spark III system is used on models equipped with EEC (electronic engine control; refer to Chapter four).

All other models, from 1977, use the Dura-Spark II electronic ignition system.

Ford has used several different types of wiring harness on their solid-state ignition systems, due to internal circuitry changes in the

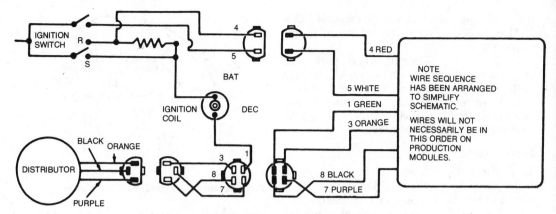

1976 and Dura Spark II ignition testing

electronic module. Wire continuity and color have not been changed, but the arrangement of the terminals in the connectors is different for each year. Schematics of the different years are included here, but keep in mind that the wiring in all diagrams has been simplified and as a result, the routing of your wiring may not match the wiring in the diagram. However, the wire colors and terminal connections are the same.

Wire color-coding is critical to servicing the Ford Solid-State Ignition. Battery current reaches the electronic module through either the *white* or *red* wire, depending on whether the engine is cranking or running. When the engine is cranking, battery current is flowing through the *white* wire. When the engine is running, battery current flows through the *red* wire. All distributor signals flow through the *orange* and *purple* wires. The *green* wire carries primary current from the coil to the module. The *black* wire is a ground between the distributor and the module. Up until 1975, a *blue* wire provides transient voltage protection. In 1976, the *blue* wire was dropped when a zener diode was added to the module. The *orange* and *purple* wires which run from the stator to the module must *always* be connected to the same color wire at the module.

If these connections are crossed, polarity will be reversed and the system will be thrown out of phase. Some replacement wiring harnesses were sold with the wiring crossed, which complicates the problem considerably. As previously noted, the *black* wire is the ground wire. The screw which grounds the black wire also, of course, grounds the entire primary circuit. If this screw is loose, dirty, or corroded, a seemingly incomprehensible ignition problem will develop. Several other cautions should be noted here. Keep in mind that on vehicles equipped with catalytic converters, any test that requires removal of a spark plug wire while the engine is running should be kept to a thirty second maximum. Any longer than this may damage the converter. In the event you are testing spark plug wires, do not pierce them. Test the wires at their terminals only.

Ignition system troubles are caused by a failure in the primary and/or the secondary circuit; incorrect ignition timing; or incorrect distributor advance. Circuit failures may be caused by shorts, corroded or dirty terminals, loose connections, defective wire insulation, cracked distributor cap or rotor, defective pickup coil assembly or amplifier module, defective distributor points or fouled spark plugs.

BASIC TROUBLESHOOTING

Except Electronic Engine Control (EEC) Systems

NOTE: *Troubleshooting procedures are not given for the EEC systems because of their great complexity.*

Before troubleshooting the Dura Spark I system, a ballast resistor must be hooked in series with the ignition coil, or the coil and module could be damaged. See the special procedures for Dura Spark I at the end of this troubleshooting section for instructions.

The following precedures can be used to determine whether the ignition system is working or not. If these procedures fail to correct the problem, a full troubleshooting procedure should be performed by a qualified service department.

Preliminary Checks

1. Check the battery's state of charge and connections.

2. Inspect all wires and connections for breaks, cuts, abrasions, or burn spots. Repair as necessary.

3. Unplug all connectors one at a time and inspect for corroded or burned contacts. Re-

pair and plug connectors back together. DO NOT remove the Di-electric compound in the connectors.

4. Check for loose or damaged spark plug or coil wires. A wire resistance check is given at the end of this section. If the boots or nipples are removed on 8mm ignition wires, reline the inside of each with silicone di-electric compound (Motorcraft WA 10).

Special Tools

To perform the following tests, two special tools are needed; the ignition test jumper shown in the illustration and a modified spark plug. Use the illustration to assemble the ignition test jumper. The test jumper must be used when performing the following tests. The modified spark plug (1977 and later) is basically a spark plug with the side electrode removed. Ford makes a special tool called a Spark Tester for this purpose, which besides not having a side electrode is equipped with a spring clip so that it can be grounded to engine metal. It is recommended that the Spark Tester be used as there is less chance of being shocked.

Run Mode Spark Test

NOTE: *The wire colors given here are the main color of the wires, not the dots or stripe marks.*

STEP 1

1. Remove the distributor cap and rotor from the distributor.

2. With the ignition off, turn the engine over by hand until one of the teeth on the distributor armature aligns with the magnet in the pick-up coil.

3. Remove the coil wire from the distributor cap. On 1977 and later models, install the modified spark plug (see Special Tools) in the coil wire terminal and using insulated pliers, hold the spark plug base against the engine block. On earlier models, use insulated pliers

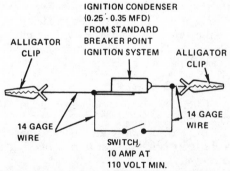

Make a special jumper wire to test the Dura Spark ignition

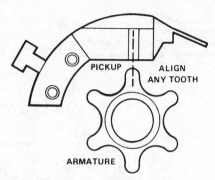

Align the armature tooth with the pickup

and hold the coil wire terminal ¼ inch from the engine block or head.

4. Turn the ignition to RUN (not START) and tap the distributor body with a screwdriver handle. There should be a spark at the modified spark plug or at the coil wire terminal.

5. If a good spark is evident, the primary circuit is OK: perform Start Mode Spark Test. If there is no spark, proceed to Step 2.

STEP 2

1. Unplug the module connector(s) which contain(s) the green and black module leads.

2. In the harness side of the connector(s), connect the special test jumper (see special tools) between the leads which connect to the green and black leads of the module pig tails. Use paper clips on connector socket holes to make contact. Do not allow clips to ground.

3. Turn the ignition switch to RUN (not START) and close the test jumper switch. Leave closed for about one second, then open. Repeat several times. There should be a spark each time the switch is opened. On Dura Spark I systems, close the test switch for 10 seconds on the first cycle. After that, one second is adequate.

4. If there is NO spark, the problem is probably in the primary circuit through the ignition switch, the coil, the green lead or the black lead, or the ground connection in the distributor. Perform Step 3. If there IS a spark, the primary circuit wiring and coil are probably OK. The problem is probably in the distributor pick-up, the module red wire, or the module. Perform Step 6.

STEP 3

1. Disconnect the test jumper lead from the black lead and connect it to a good ground. Turn the test jumper switch on and off several times as in Step 2.

2. If there is NO spark, the problem is probably in the green lead, the coil, or the coil feed circuit. Perform Step 5.

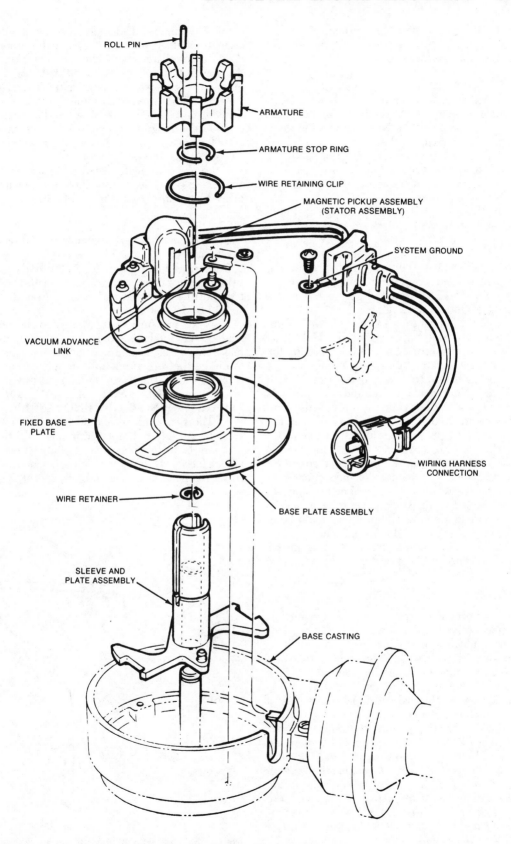

ROLL PIN

ARMATURE

ARMATURE STOP RING

WIRE RETAINING CLIP

MAGNETIC PICKUP ASSEMBLY
(STATOR ASSEMBLY)

SYSTEM GROUND

VACUUM ADVANCE
LINK

FIXED BASE
PLATE

WIRING HARNESS
CONNECTION

WIRE RETAINER

BASE PLATE ASSEMBLY

SLEEVE AND
PLATE ASSEMBLY

BASE CASTING

Breakerless V8 distributor disassembled

3. If there IS spark, the problem is probably in the black lead or the distributor ground connection. Perform Step 4.

STEP 4

1. Connect an ohmmeter between the black lead and ground. With the meter on its lowest scale, there should be NO measureable resistance in the circuit. If there is resistance, check the distributor ground connection and the black lead from the module. Repair as necessary, remove the ohmmeter, plug in all connections and repeat Step 1.

If there is NO resistance, the primary ground wiring is OK. Perform Step 6.

STEP 5

1. Disconnect the test jumper from the green lead and ground and connect it between the TACH-TEST terminal of the coil and a good ground on the engine.

2. With the ignition switch in the RUN position, turn the jumper switch on. Hold it on for about one second then turn it off as in Step 2. Repeat several times. There should be a spark each time the switch is turned off. If there is NO spark, the problem is probably in the primary circuit running through the ignition switch to the coil BAT terminal, or in the coil itself. Check coil resistance (test given later in this section), and check the coil for internal shorts or opens. Check the coil feed circuit for opens, shorts or high resistance. Repair as necessary, reconnect all connectors and repeat Step 1. If there IS spark, the coil and its feed circuit are OK. The problem could be in the green lead between the coil and the module. Check for open or short, repair as necessary, reconnect all connectors and repeat Step 1.

STEP 6

To perform this step, a voltmeter which is not combined with a dwellmeter is needed. The slight needle oscillations (½ V) you'll be looking for may not be detectable on the combined voltmeter/dwellmeter unit.

1. Connect a voltmeter between the orange and purple leads on the harness side of the module connectors.

CAUTION: *On catalytic converter equipped cars, disconnect the air supply line between the Thermactor by-pass valve and the manifold before cranking the engine with the ignition off. This will prevent damage to the catalytic converter. After testing, run the engine for at least 3 minutes before reconnecting the by-pass valve, to clear excess fuel from the exhaust system.*

2. Set the voltmeter on its lowest scale and

crank the engine. The meter needle should oscillate slightly (about ½ volt). If the meter does not oscillate, check the circuit through the magnetic pick-up in the distributor for open, shorts, shorts to ground and resistance. Resistance between the orange and purple leads should be 400–1000 ohms, and between each lead and ground should be more than 70,000 ohms. Repair as necessary, reconnect all connectors and repeat Step 1.

If the meter oscillates, the problem is probably in the power feed to the module (red wire) or in the module itself. Proceed to Step 7.

STEP 7

1. Remove all meters and jumpers and plug in all connectors.

2. Turn the ignition switch to the RUN position and measure voltage between the battery positive terminal and engine ground. It should be 12 volts.

3. Next, measure voltage between the red lead of the module and engine ground. To make this measurement, it will be necessary to pierce the red wire with a straight pin and connect the voltmeter to the straight pin and to ground. **DO NOT ALLOW THE STRAIGHT PIN TO GROUND ITSELF.**

4. The two readings should be within one volt of each other. If not within one volt, the problem is in the power feed to the red lead. Check for shorts, open, or high resistance and correct as necessary. After repairs, repeat Step 1.

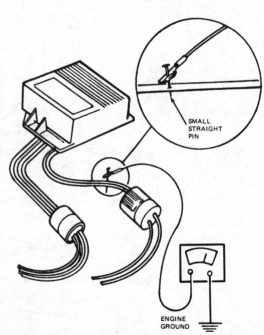

Pierce the wire with a straight pin to connect tester

If the readings are within one volt, the problem is probably in the module. Replace with a good module and repeat Step 1. If this corrects the problem, reconnect the old module and repeat Step 1. If problem returns, replace the module.

Start Mode Spark Test

NOTE: *The wire colors given here are the main colors of the wires, not the dots or stripe marks.*

1. Remove the coil wire from the distributor cap. On 1977 and later models, install the modified spark plug mentioned under "Special Tools", above, in the coil wire and ground it to engine metal either by its spring clip (Spark Tester) or by holding the spark plug shell against the engine block with insulated pliers. On 1976 and earlier models, hold the coil wire terminal ¼ in. from the engine block or head with insulated pliers.

CAUTION: *See "CAUTION" under Step 6 of "Run Mode Spark Test", above.*

2. Have an assistant crank the engine using the ignition switch and check for spark. If there IS good spark, the problem is most probably in the distributor cap, rotor, ignition cables or spark plugs. If there is NO spark, proceed to Step 3.

3. Measure the battery voltage. Next, measure the voltage at the white wire of the module while cranking the engine. To make this measurement, it will be necessary to pierce the white wire with a straight pin and connect the voltmeter to the straight pin and to ground. **DO NOT ALLOW THE STRAIGHT PIN TO GROUND ITSELF.** The battery voltage and the voltage at the white wire should be within one volt of each other. If the readings are not within one volt of each other, check and repair the feed through the ignition switch to the white wire. Recheck for spark (Step 1). If the readings are within one volt of each other, or if there is still NO spark after power feed to white wire is repaired, proceed to Step 4.

4. Measure the coil BATT terminal voltage while cranking the engine. The reading should be within one volt of battery voltage. If the readings are not within one volt of each other, check and repair the feed through the ignition switch to the coil. If the readings are within one volt of each other, the problem is probably in the ignition module. Substitute another module and repeat test for spark (Step 1).

TROUBLESHOOTING DURA SPARK I

The above troubleshooting procedures may be used on Dura Spark I systems with a few variations. The Dura Spark I module has internal connections which shut off the primary circuit in the run mode when the engine stalls. To perform the above troubleshooting procedures, it is necessary to by-pass these connections. However, with these connections by-passed, the current flow in the primary becomes so great that it will damage both the ignition coil and module unless a ballast resistor is installed in series with the primary circuit at the BAT terminal of the ignition coil. Such a resistor is available from Ford (Motorcraft part number DY-36). A 1.3 ohm, 100 watt wire-wound power resistor can also be used.

To install the resistor, proceed as follows.

1975 Test Sequence

	Test Voltage Between	Should Be	If Not, Conduct
Key On	Socket #4 and Engine Ground	Battery Voltage ± 0.1 Volt	Module Bias Test
	Socket #1 and Engine Ground	Battery Voltage ± 0.1 Volt	Battery Source Test
Cranking	Socket #5 and Engine Ground	8 to 12 volts	Cranking Test
	Jumper #1 to #8 Read #6	more than 6 volts	Starting Circuit Test
	Pin #7 and Pin #8	½ volt minimum AC or any DC volt wiggle	Distributor Hardware Test
Key Off	Socket #7 and #3 Socket #8 and Engine Ground Socket #7 and Engine Ground Socket #3 and Engine Ground	400 to 800 ohms 0 ohms more than 70,000 ohms	Magnetic Pick-up (Stator) Test
	Socket #4 and Coil Tower Socket #1 and Pin #6	7,000 to 13,000 ohms 1.0 to 2.0 ohms	Coil Test
	Socket #1 and Engine Ground	more than 4.0 ohms	Short Test
	Socket #4 and Pin #6	1.0 to 2.0 ohms	Resistance Wire Test

1976 Test Sequence

	Test Voltage Between	Should Be	If Not, Conduct
Key On	Socket #4 and Engine Ground	Battery Voltage ± 0.1 Volt	Battery Source Test
	Socket #1 and Engine Ground	Battery Voltage ± 0.1 Volt	Battery Source Test
Cranking	Socket #5 and Engine Ground	8 to 12 volts	Check Supply Circuit (starting) through Ignition Switch
	Jumper #1 to #8 Read #6	more than 6 volts	Starting Circuit Test
	Pin #3 and Pin #8	½ volt minimum AC or any DC volt wiggle	Distributor Hardware Test
Key Off	Socket #8 and #3 Socket #7 and Engine Ground Socket #8 and Engine Ground Socket #3 and Engine Ground	400 to 800 ohms 0 ohms more than 70,000 ohms more than 70,000 ohms	Magnetic Pick-up (Stator) Test
	Socket #4 and Coil Tower	7,000 to 13,000 ohms	Coil Test
	Socket #1 and Engine Ground	more than 4.0 ohms	Short Test

NOTE: *The resistor will become very hot during testing.*

1. Release the BAT terminal lead from the coil by inserting a paper clip through the hole in the rear of the horseshoe coil connector and manipulating it against the locking tab in the connector until the lead comes free.

2. Insert a paper clip in the BAT terminal of the connector on the coil. Using jumper leads, connect the ballast resistor.

3. Using a straight pin, pierce both the red and white leads of the module to short these two together. This will by-pass the internal connections of the module which turns off the ignition circuit when the engine is not running.

CAUTION: *Pierce the wires only AFTER the ballast resistor is in place or you could damage the ignition coil and module.*

4. With the ballast resistor and by-pass in place, proceed with the troubleshooting procedures above.

Module Identification

The identity of the ignition module and of the ignition system itself (Dura Spark I, II, etc.) can be discovered by examining the color of the sealing block on the module.

Ignition Coil

CHECKING IGNITION COIL RESISTANCE

NOTE: *Refer to Chapter eleven for checking the coil on a breaker point fired ignition system.*

Electronic Ignition

1. Run the engine until it reaches operating temperature (coil must be hot). However, if

COLOR	SYSTEM
• Red	Dura Spark I
• Blue	Dura Spark II
• Yellow	Dura Spark II with Dual Mode (except 1981)
• White	Dura Spark II with Cranking Retard
• Brown	Dura Spark III and other EEC controlled systems
• Yellow	Universal Ignition Module (1981)
• Green	Early Solid State Ignition

the engine will not start and the coil cannot be tested hot, the procedures and resistance values are close enough on a cold coil to determine if the no start problem comes from the coil.

2. Disconnect the high tension lead from the center of the coil.

3. Measure primary resistance with an ohmmeter connecting the coil minus and positive terminals. Primary resistance must be 0.5–1.5 ohms for Dura-Spark I through 1977, and 0.71–2.0 ohms 1978 and later. It must measure 1.0–2.0 ohms for Dura-Spark II through 1977 and the 1974–76 Solid State system. For 1978 and later Dura-Spark II, it must be 1.3–1.23 ohms.

4. Measure secondary resistance, connecting the ohmmeter between the coil tower contact (center contact) and the plus terminal of the coil. Secondary resistance must be 7,000–13,000 ohms for Dura-Spark I through 1977. 1978 and later Dura-Spark I systems must read 7350–8250 ohms, the Dura-Spark II figure is 7700–9300 ohms and the Solid State, 7,000–13,000 ohms.

Dura-Spark

	Test Voltage Between	Should Be	If Not, Conduct
Key On	Socket #4 and Engine Ground	Battery Voltage ± 0.1 Volt	Module Bias Test
	Socket #1 and Engine Ground	Battery Voltage ± 0.1 Volt	Battery Source Test
Cranking	Socket #5 and Engine Ground	8 to 12 volts	Cranking Test
	Jumper #1 to #8—Read Coil "Bat" Term & Engine Ground	more than 6 volts	Starting Circuit Test
	Sockets #7 and #3	½ volt minimum wiggle	Distributor Hardware Test
Key Off	Sockets #7 and #3 Socket #8 and Engine Ground Socket #7 and Engine Ground Socket #3 and Engine Ground	400 to 800 ohms 0 ohms more than 70,000 ohms more than 70,000 ohms	Magnetic Pick-up (Stator) Test
	Socket #4 and Coil Tower	7,000 to 13,000 ohms	Coil Test
	Socket #1 and Coil "Bat" Term	1.0 to 2.0 ohms Breakerless & Dura-Spark II	
		0.5 to 1.5 ohms Dura-Spark I	
	Socket #1 and Engine Ground	more than 4.0 ohms	Short Test
	Socket #4 and Coil "Bat" Term (Except Dura-Spark I)	1.0 to 2.0 ohms Breakerless	Resistance Wire Test
		0.7 to 1.7 ohms Dura-Spark II	

5. If the resistances test alright, but the coil is still suspected, have the coil tested on a coil tester. If the reading differs from your original test, check for a defective harness. If no defect is found in the wiring, replace the coil.

Distributor

REMOVAL AND INSTALLATION

NOTE: *All models with EEC (See Chapter 4) have the distributor locked into place during assembly. Only qualified repair centers should service these units.*

1. On all V8 engines, remove the air cleaner assembly, taking note of the hose locations, to gain access to the distributor.

2. On models equipped with a conventional ignition system, disconnect the primary wire at the coil. On models equipped with breakerless ignition, disconnect the distributor wiring connector from the vehicle wiring harness.

3. Noting the position of the vacuum line(s) on the distributor diaphragm, disconnect the lines at the diaphragm. Unsnap the two distributor cap retaining clamps and remove the cap. Position the cap and ignition wires to one side.

4. Using chalk or paint, carefully mark the position of the distributor rotor in relation to the distributor housing and mark the position of the distributor housing in relation to the en-

gine block. When this is done, you should have a line on the distributor housing directly in line with the tip of the rotor and another line on the engine block directly in line with the mark on the distributor housing. This is very important because the distributor must be reinstalled in the exact same location from which it was removed, if correct ignition timing is to be maintained.

5. Remove the distributor hold-down bolt and clamp. Remove the distributor from the engine.

NOTE: *Do not crank the engine while the distributor is removed. If the engine was disturbed with the distributor removed, you will have to retime the engine.*

6a. If the engine was cranked (disturbed) with the distributor removed, it will now be necessary to retime the engine. If the distributor has been installed incorrectly and the engine will not start, remove the distributor from the engine and start over again. Hold the distributor close to the engine and install the cap on the distributor in its normal position. Locate the No. 1 spark plug tower on the distributor cap. Scribe a mark on the body of the distributor directly below the No. 1 spark plug wire tower on the distributor cap. Remove the distributor cap from the distributor and move the distributor and cap to one side. Remove the No. 1 spark plug and crank the engine over until the No. 1 cylinder is on its compression stroke. To accomplish this, place a wrench on the lower engine pulley and turn the engine slowly in a clockwise (6 cylinder) or counterclockwise (V8) direction until the TDC mark on the crankshaft damper aligns with the timing pointer. If you place your finger in the No. 1 spark plug hole, you will feel air escaping as the piston rises in the combustion chamber. On conventional ignition systems, the rotor must be at No. 1 firing position to install the distributor. On breakerless ignition systems, one of the armature segments must be aligned with the stator as shown in the accompanying illustration to install the distributor. Make sure that the oil pump intermediate shaft properly engages the distributor shaft. It may be necessary to crank the engine with the starter, after the distributor drive gear is partially engaged, in order to engage the oil pump intermediate shaft. Install, but do not tighten the retaining clamp and bolt. Rotate the distributor to advance the timing to a point where the armature tooth is aligned properly (breakerless ignition) or to a point where the points are just starting to open (conventional ignition). Tighten the clamp.

b. If the engine was not cranked (disturbed) when the distributor was removed, position the distributor in the block with the rotor aligned with the mark previously scribed on the distributor body and the marks on the distributor body and cylinder block in alignment. Install the distributor hold-down bolt and clamp fingertight.

7. Install the distributor cap and wires.

8. On models equipped with conventional ignition connect the primary wire at the coil. On models equipped with breakerless ignition, connect the distributor wiring connector to the wiring harness.

9. Check the ignition timing as outlined in Chapter 2.

10. Install the air cleaner, if removed.

Charging System

The charging system is composed of the alternator, alternator regulator, charging system warning light, battery, and fuse link wire.

A failure of any component of the charging system can cause the entire system to stop functioning. Because of this, the charging system can be very difficult to troubleshoot when problems occur.

When the ignition key is turned on, current flows from the battery, through the charging system indicator light on the instrument panel, to the voltage regulator, and to the alternator. Since the alternator is not producing any current, the alternator warning light comes on. When the engine is started, the alternator begins to produce current and turns the alternator light off. As the alternator turns and produces current, that current is divided in two ways: part to the battery to charge the battery and power the electrcial components of the vehicle, and part is returned to the alternator to enable it to increase its output. In this sit-

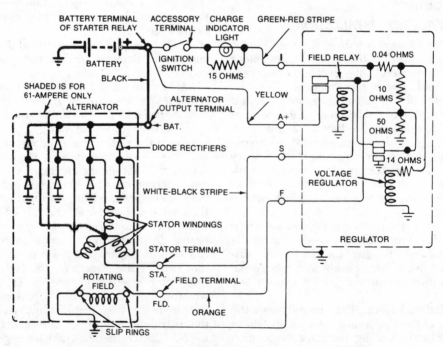

Alternator charging circuit w/indicator light—rear terminal type

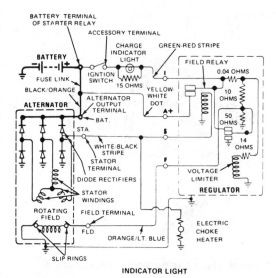

Alternator charging circuit w/indicator light—side terminal type

uation, the alternator is receiving current from the battery and from itself. A voltage regulator is wired into the current supply to the alternator to prevent it from receiving too much current which would cause it to put out too much current. Conversely, if the voltage regulator does not allow the alternator to receive enough current, the battery will not be fully charged and will eventually go dead.

The battery is connected to the alternator at all times, whether the ignition key is turned on or not. If the battery were shorted to ground, the alternator would also be shorted. This would damage the alternator. To prevent this, a fuse link is installed in the wiring between the battery and the alternator on all 1970 and later models. If the battery is shorted, the fuse link is melted, protecting the alternator.

Since the alternator, the alternator regulator, the charging system warning light, the battery and the fuse link are all interconnected, the failure of one component can cause the others to become inoperative.

ALTERNATOR PRECAUTIONS

Several precautions must be observed with alternator equipped vehicles to avoid damaging the unit. They are as follows:

1. If the battery is removed for any reason, make sure that it is reconnected with the correct polarity. Reversing the battery connections may result in damage to the oneway rectifiers.

2. When utilizing a booster battery as a starting aid, always connect it as described at the end of Chapter One.

3. Never use a fast charger as a booster to start cars with alternating-current (AC) circuits.

4. When servicing the battery with a fast charger, always disconnected the car battery cables.

5. Never attempt to polarize an alternator.

6. Avoid long soldering times when replacing diodes or transistors. Prolonged heat is damaging to alternators.

7. Do not use test lamps of more than 12 volts (V) for checking diode continuity.

8. Do not short across or ground any of the terminals on the alternator.

9. The polarity of the battery, alternator, and regulator must be matched and considered before making any electrical connections within the system.

10. Never separate the alternator on an open circuit. Make sure that all connections within the circuit are clean and tight.

11. Disconnect the battery terminals when performing any service on the electrical system. This will eliminate the possibility of accidental reversal of polarity.

12. Disconnect the battery ground cable if arc welding is to be done on any part of the car.

CHARGING SYSTEM TROUBLESHOOTING

There are many different types of charging system problems and most require expensive tools to diagnose. When one component of the system fails completely and the charging system warning light comes on, it is a little easier to locate the source of the problem. We will deal with only a complete failure of the system which causes the battery to go dead.

You will need two testing instruments for use in this section. They are both relatively cheap and readily available. The first is a current indicator. This device, when placed on a wire which has current passing through it, measures the current in amps. The other is a test light. This is simply a pointed screwdriver which contains a light bulb and has a ground wire attached to it. When the pointed end is touched to an electrical component that should have current running to it, and the ground wire is attached to a good ground, the light in the handle will come on to verify that current is indeed coming to the component.

This test works under three assumptions:

A. The battery is known to be good and fully charged;

B. The alternator belt is in good condition and adjusted to the proper tension;

C. All connections in the system are clean and tight.

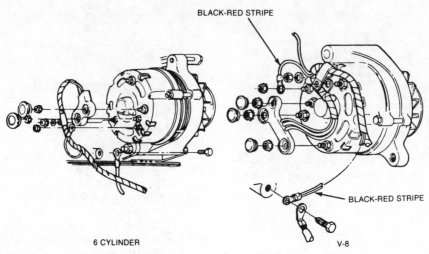

BLACK-RED STRIPE

BLACK-RED STRIPE

6 CYLINDER

V-8

1968–72 alternator wiring harness connections—typical Autolite except 65 ampere unit

NOTE: *In order for the current indicator to give a valid reading, the car must be equipped with battery cables which are of the same gauge size and quality as original equipment battery cables.*

1. Turn off all electrical components on the car. Make sure the doors of the car are closed. If the car is equipped with a clock, disconnect the clock by removing the lead wire from the rear of the clock. Disconnect the positive battery cable from the battery and connect the ground wire on a test light to the disconnected positive battery cable. Touch the probe end of the test light to the positive battery post. The test light should not light. If the test light does light, there is a short or open circuit on the car. See Chapter 5 for troubleshooting procedures for this problem.

2. Disonnnect the voltage regulator wiring harness connector at the voltage regulator. Turn on the ignition key. Connect the wire on a test light to a good ground (engine bolt). Touch the probe end of a test light to the ig-nition wire connector into the voltage regulator wiring connector. This wire corresponds to the "I" terminal on the regulator. If the test light goes on, the charging system warning light circuit is complete. If the test light does not come on and the warning light on the instrument panel is on, either the resistor wire, which is parallel with the warning light, or the wiring to the voltage regulator, is defective. If the test light does not come on and the warning light is not on, either the bulb is defective or the power supply wire from the battery through the ignition switch to the bulb has an open circuit. Connect the wiring harness to the regulator.

3. Examine the fuse link wire in the wiring harness from the starter relay to the alternator. If the insulation on the wire is cracked or split, the fuse link may be melted. Connect a test light to the fuse link by attaching the ground wire on the test light to an engine bolt and touching the probe end of the light to the bottom of the fuse link wire where it splices

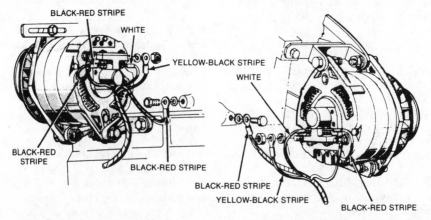

BLACK-RED STRIPE

WHITE

YELLOW-BLACK STRIPE

WHITE

BLACK-RED STRIPE

BLACK-RED STRIPE

BLACK-RED STRIPE

YELLOW-BLACK STRIPE

BLACK-RED STRIPE

1968–72 alternator wiring harness connections—Leece-Neville 65 ampere unit

into the alternator output wire. If the bulb in the test light does not light, the fuse link is melted.

4. Start the engine and place a current indicator on the positive battery cable. Turn off all electrical accessories and make sure the doors are closed. If the charging system is working properly, the gauge will show a charge of about 5 amps. If the system is not working properly, the gauge will show a draw of about 5 amps. A charge moves the needle toward the battery, a draw moves the needle away from the battery. Turn the engine off.

5. Disconnect the wiring harness from the voltage regulator at the regulator connector. Connect a male spade terminal (solderless connector) to each end of a jumper wire. Insert one end of the wire into the wiring harness connector which corresponds to the "A" terminal on the regulator. Insert the other end of the wire into the wiring harness connector which corresponds to the "F" terminal on the regulator. Position the connector with the jumper wire installed so that it cannot contact any metal surface under the hood. Position a current indicator gauge on the positive battery cable. Have an assistant start the engine. Observe the reading on the current indicator. Have your assistant slowly raise the speed of the engine to about 2,000 rpm or until the current indicator needle stops moving, whichever comes first. Do not run the engine for more than a short period of time in this condition. If the wiring harness connector or jumper wire becomes excessively hot during this test, turn off the engine and check for a grounded wire in the regulator wiring harness. If the current indicator shows a charge of about three amps less than the output of the alternator, the alternator is working properly. If the previous tests showed a draw, the voltage regulator is defective. If the gauge does not show the proper charging rate, the alternator is defective.

Alternator

REMOVAL AND INSTALLATION

While internal alternator repairs are possible, they require special tools and training. Therefore, it is advisable to replace a defective alternator, or have it repaired by a qualified shop.

1. Disconnect the negative battery cable from the battery.

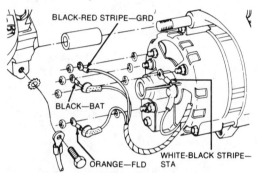

1968-72 alternator wiring harness connections —Autolite 65 ampere unit

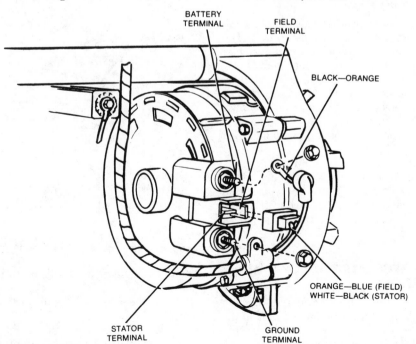

1972 and later alternator wiring harness connections—Autolite (Motorcraft) side terminal unit

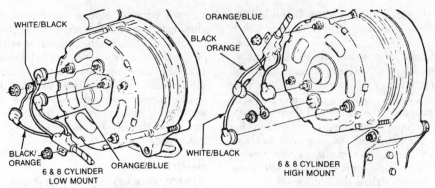

WHITE/BLACK

ORANGE/BLUE

BLACK
ORANGE

BLACK/
ORANGE

ORANGE/BLUE

WHITE/BLACK

6 & 8 CYLINDER
LOW MOUNT

6 & 8 CYLINDER
HIGH MOUNT

1973 and later Motorcraft alternator wiring harness connections—rear terminal units

2. Disconnect the wires from the rear (rear terminal) or side (side terminal) of the alternator.

3. Loosen the alternator mounting bolts and remove the drive belt.

4. Remove the alternator mounting bolts and spacer (if equipped), and remove the alternator.

5. To install, position the alternator on its brackets and install the attaching bolts and spacer (if so equipped).

6. Connect the wires to the alternator.

7. Position the drive belt on the alternator pulley. Adjust the belt tension as outlined in Chapter 1 under "Alternator Drive Belt Tension Adjustment."

8. Connect the negative battery cable.

Voltage Regulator

Voltage regulators used through 1978 were either electromechanical or transistorized. The electromechanical regulator is not adjustable, and has to be replaced as a unit when faulty. The transistorized regulator is adjustable by means of a screw located in the transistor circuit board. The cover of the electromechanical regulator is held in place by non-removable rivets, while the transistorized regulator cover is held on by Phillips screws.

Beginning in 1979, only solid state regulators were used. One type is used only on vehicles with an ammeter. The other type is used on warning light equipped vehicles. The solid state regulators are preset at the factory and it is not possible to adjust them.

VOLTAGE REGULATOR REMOVAL AND INSTALLATION

1. Remove the battery ground cable. On models with the regulator mounted behind the battery, it is necessary to remove the battery hold-down, and to move the battery.

2. Remove the regulator mounting screws.

FIELD COIL TERMINAL

FIELD RELAY TERMINAL

CHARGE INDICATOR
LIGHT TERMINAL

BATTERY TERMINAL FOR
FIELD SUPPLY VOLTAGE

Motorcraft electro-mechanical regulator connections

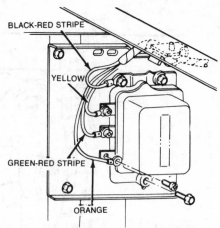

BLACK-RED STRIPE

YELLOW

GREEN-RED STRIPE

ORANGE

Leece-Neville regulator connections

3. Disconnect the regulator to the wiring harness.

4. Connect the new regulator to the wiring harness.

5. Mount the regulator to the regulator mounting plate. The radio suppression condenser mounts under one mounting screw; the

ground lead under the other mounting screw. Tighten the mounting screws.

6. If the battery was moved to gain access to the regulator, position the battery and install the hold-down. Connect the battery ground cable, and test the system for proper voltage regulation.

TESTING

Motorcraft

Any electro-mechanical regulator which does not perform to specifications must be replaced. A transistorized regulator may be adjusted if not up to specifications as per the test. The accompanying illustration shows the voltage limiter adjustment screw location beneath the regulator cover.

Before proceeding with the test, make sure that the alternator drive belt tension is properly adjusted, the battery has a good charge (specific gravity of 1.250 or better), and that all charging system electrical connections are clean and tight. A voltmeter is needed for this test. The test is as follows:

1. Connect a voltmeter to the battery, with the positive lead to the battery positive terminal and the negative lead to the battery negative terminal. Turn off all electrical equipment. Check and record the voltmeter reading with the engine stopped.

2. Connect a tachometer to the engine, with the red (positive) lead to the distributor terminal on the ignition coil and the black (negative) lead to a good ground, such as an engine bolt.

3. Place the transmission in Neutral or Park and start the engine. Increase the engine speed to 1,800–2,200 rpm for 2–3 minutes to bring the engine and regulator to operating temperature. Check and record the voltmeter reading. It should now be 1 to 2 volts higher than the first reading. This is the regulated voltage reading. If the reading is less than 1 volt or greater than 2½ volts, the regulator must be replaced or adjusted.

4. If the reading is between 1 and 2 volts, turn on the headlights and heater blower to load the alternator. The voltage should not decrease more than ½ volt from the regulated voltage reading in Step 3. If the voltage drop is greater than ½ volt, the regulator should be replaced.

Leece-Neville Electro-Mechanical Unit

1. Connect a voltmeter to the battery post terminals.

2. Start the engine. Disconnect the regulator field (F) lead and connect it to the battery terminal of the regulator.

CAUTION: *Do not run the engine with the regulator wiring in this position any longer than necessary as excessive voltage could damage the alternator.*

3. Stop the engine. Disconnect the field (F) lead from the battery terminal and reconnect it to the field terminal on the regulator. If the

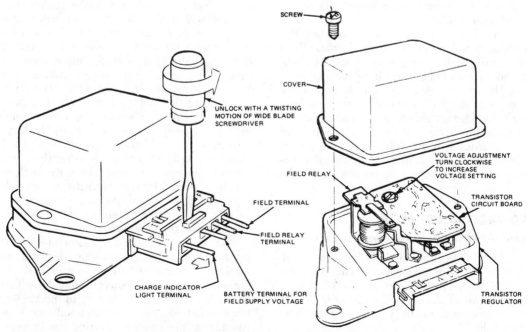

Motorcraft transistorized regulator adjustment

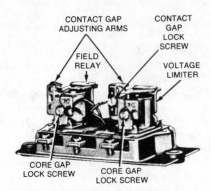

Leece-Neville regulator gap adjustments

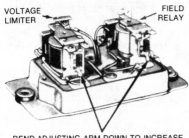

BEND ADJUSTING ARM DOWN TO INCREASE
VOLTAGE SETTING BEND ADJUSTING ARM
UP TO DECREASE VOLTAGE SETTING.

Leece-Neville regulator voltage adjustments

voltmeter reads 15–20 volts or greater, the regulator is defective and must be replaced.

Field Relay Test

NOTE: *Make sure that the battery has a good charge (specific gravity of 1.250) for this test. Connect the voltmeter as in the "Regulator Test."*

1. Without turning on the engine, turn the ignition switch on and off several times. Each time the switch is turned on, a definite clicking sound should be heard in the regulator.

2. If no click is heard, check for battery voltage at the IGN terminal of the regulator with the ignition switch in the IGN position. With battery voltage at the IGN terminal and if no clicking is heard while operating the ignition switch, the field relay is defective necessitating replacement of the voltage regulator unit.

VOLTAGE ADJUSTMENT
Leece-Neville Electro-Mechanical Unit

1. Run the engine for 10–15 minutes to allow the regulator to reach operating temperature. Connect a voltmeter across the battery posts. Turn off all electrical equipment. Check the voltage at the battery. It should be 13.9–14.1 volts.

2. The voltage control adjustment (voltage

limiter) is adjusted at the component closest to the F terminal. Remove the regulator cover. Voltage may be increased by raising the spring tension and decreased by lowering the spring tension. To adjust the spring tension, move the lower spring mounting tab.

NOTE: *Voltage will drop about ½ volt when the regulator cover is installed and should be compensated for in the adjustment.*

3. After making the adjustment, cycle the regulator by stopping and starting the engine. This will indicate if the adjustment is stable. If the voltage reading has changed, follow Steps 1 and 2 until the correct voltage is obtained.

Starting System

The battery is the first link in the chain of mechanisms which work together to provide cranking of the automobile engine. In most modern cars, the battery is a lead-acid electrochemical device consisting of six two-volt (2 V) subsections connected in series so the unit is capable of producing approximately 12 V of electrical pressure. Each subsection, or cell, consists of a series of positive and negative plates held a short distance apart in a solution of sulfuric acid and water. The two types of plates are of dissimilar metals. This causes a chemical reaction to be set up, and it is this reaction which produces current flow from the battery when its positive and negative terminals are connected to an electrical appliance such as a lamp or motor. The continued transfer of electrons would eventually convert the sulfuric acid in the electrolyte to water, and make the two plates identical in chemical composition. As electrical energy is removed from the battery, its voltage output tends to drop. Thus, measuring battery voltage and battery electrolyte composition are two ways of checking the ability of the unit to supply power. During the starting of the engine, electrical energy is removed from the battery. However, if the charging circuit is in good condition and the operating conditions are normal, the power removed from the battery will be replaced by the alternator which will force electrons back through the battery, reversing the normal flow, and restoring the battery to its original chemical state.

The battery and starting motor are linked by very heavy electrical cables designed to minimize resistance to the flow of current. Generally, the major power supply cable that leaves the battery goes directly to the starter, while other electrical system needs are supplied by a smaller cable. During starter operation, power flows from the battery to the

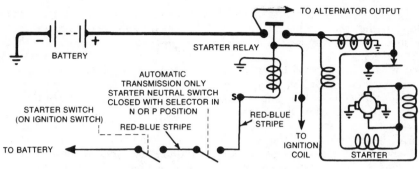

Positive engagement starter circuit

starter and is grounded through the car's frame and the battery's negative ground strap.

The starting motor is a specially designed, direct current electric motor capable of producing a very great amount of power for its size. One thing that allows the motor to produce a great deal of power is its tremendous rotating speed. It drives the engine through a tiny pinion gear (attached to the starter's armature), which drives the very large flywheel ring gear at a greatly reduced speed. Another factor allowing it to produce so much power is that only intermittent operation is required of it. Thus, little allowance for air circulation is required, and the windings can be built into a very small space.

The starter solenoid is a magnetic device which employs the small current supplied by the starting switch circuit of the ignition switch. This magnetic action moves a plunger which mechanically engages the starter.

Positive engagement Ford starters, except those used with 429 and 460 V8 engines, employ a separate relay, mounted away from the starter, to switch the motor and solenoid cur-

rent on and off, from the battery. The relay thus replaces the solenoid electrical switch, but does not eliminate the need for a solenoid mounted on the starter used to mechanically engage the starter drive gears. The relay is used to reduce the amount of current the starting switch must carry. On solenoid actuated starters installed in 429 and 460 V8 engines, the contacts in the solenoid take the place of the relay.

The starting switch circuit consists of the starting switch contained within the ignition switch, a transmission neutral safety switch or clutch pedal switch which prevents the car from being started in any gear but Neutral or Park (automatic only), and the wiring necessary to connect these in series with the starter solenoid or relay.

A pinion, which is a small gear, is mounted to a one-way drive clutch. This clutch is splined to the starter armature shaft. When the ignition switch is moved to the "start" position, the solenoid plunger slides the pinion toward the flywheel ring gear via a collar and spring. If the teeth on the pinion and flywheel match

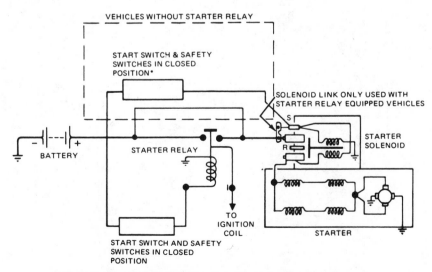

Solenoid actuated starter circuit—with and without starter relay

properly, the pinion will engage the flywheel immediately. If the gear teeth butt one another, the spring will be compressed and will force the gears to mash as soon as the starter turns far enough to allow them to do so. As the solenoid plunger reaches the end of its travel, it closes the contacts that connect the battery and starter and then the engine is cranked.

As soon as the engine starts, the flywheel ring gear begins turning fast enough to drive the pinion at an extremely high rate of speed. At this point, the one-way clutch begins allowing the pinion to spin faster than the starter shaft so that the starter will not operate at excessive speed. When the ignition switch is released from the starter position, the solenoid is de-energized, and a spring contained within the solenoid assembly pulls the gear out of mesh and interrupts the current flow to the starter.

Starter

All 6 cylinder models, and V8 models except the 429 and 460 V8 engines, use the positive engagement starter. This medium-duty unit uses a remote starter relay to open and close the circuit to the battery.

The starter installed in 429 and 460 V8 models is the solenoid actuated starter. This heavy-duty unit uses an outboard solenoid mounted atop the starter which has an internal electrical switch to open and close the circuit to the battery.

If, for some reason (such as an engine swap),

a solenoid actuated starter is installed in a car originally equipped with a starter relay (any car not originally equipped with a 429 or 460 V8), a special connector link must be installed on the starter solenoid. This link connects the battery terminal with the solenoid operating windings. Therefore, when the key is turned to the Start position, the starter solenoid is actuated, sending battery current to the solenoid. The solenoid than operates the starter through the solenoid internal contacts. See the accompanying illustration for the proper installation of the connector link.

REMOVAL AND INSTALLATION

1. Disconnect the negative battery cable.
2. Raise the front of the car and install jackstands beneath the frame. Firmly apply the parking brake and place blocks in back of the rear wheels.
3. Disconnect the heavy starter cable at the starter. On solenoid actuated starters (429 and 460 V8 only), label and disconnect the wires from the solenoid.
4. Turn the front wheels fully to the right. On many models, it will be necessary to remove the two bolts retaining the steering idler arm to the frame to gain access to the starter.
5. Remove the starter mounting bolts and remove the starter.
6. Reverse the above procedure to install. Torque the mounting bolts to 15–20 ft. lbs. and the idler arm retaining bolts to 28–35 ft. lbs. (if removed). Make sure that the nut securing the heavy cable to the starter is snugged down tightly.

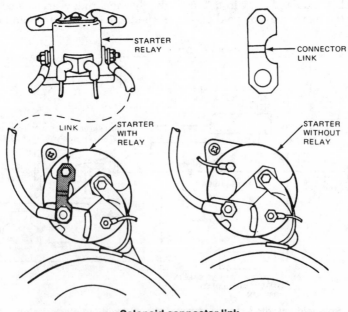

Solenoid connector link

STARTER OVERHAUL

Solenoid Actuated Starter

DISASSEMBLY

1. Disconnect the copper strap from the starter terminal on the solenoid, remove the retaining screws and remove the solenoid from the drive housing.

2. Loosen the retaining screw and slide the brush cover band back on the starter frame for access to the brushes.

3. Remove the commutator brushes from their holders. Hold each spring away from the brush with a hook, while sliding the brush out of the holder.

4. Remove the through-bolts and separate the drive-end housing, starter frame and brush end plate assemblies.

5. Remove the solenoid plunger and shift fork assembly. If either the plunger or fork is to be replaced, they can be separated by removing the roll pin.

6. Remove the armature and drive assembly from the frame. Remove the drive stop ring and slide the drive assembly off the armature shaft.

7. Remove the drive stop ring retainer from the drive housing.

CLEANING AND INSPECTION

1. Do not wash the drive because the solvent will wash out the lubricant, causing the

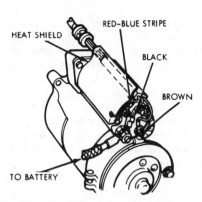

Solenoid actuated starter connections

drive to slip. Use a brush or compressed air to clean the drive, field coils, armature, commutator, armature shaft front end plate, and rear end housing. Wash all other parts in solvent and dry the parts.

2. Inspect the armature windings for broken or burned insulation and unsoldered connections.

3. Check the armature for open circuits and grounds.

4. Check the commutator for run-out. Inspect the armature shaft and the two bearings for scoring and excessive wear. On a starter with needle bearings, apply a small amount of grease to the needles. If the commutator is rough, or more than 0.005 in. out-of-round, turn it down.

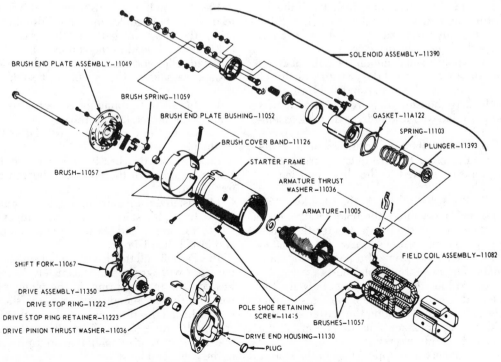

Solenoid actuated starter disassembled

5. Check the brush holders for broken springs and the insulated brush holders for shorts to ground. Tighten any rivets that may be loose. Replace the brushes if worn to ¼ in. in length.

6. Check the brush spring tension. Replace the springs if the tension is not within specified limits (80 ounces minimum).

7. Inspect the field coils for burned or broken insulation and continuity. Check the field brush connections and lead insulation. A brush kit is available. All other assemblies are to be replaced rather than repaired.

8. Examine the wear pattern on the starter drive teeth. The pinion teeth must penetrate to a depth greater than ½ the ring gear tooth depth, to eliminate premature ring gear and starter drive failure.

9. Replace starter drives and ring gears with milled, pitted or broken teeth or evidence of inadequate engagement.

ASSEMBLY

1. Install a small amount of Lubriplate® on the armature shaft splines. Install the drive assembly on the armature shaft and install a new stop ring.

2. Apply a small amount of Lubriplate on the shift lever pivot pin. Position the solenoid plunger and shift lever assembly in the drive housing.

3. Place a new retainer in the drive housing. Apply a small amount of Lubriplate to the drive end of the armature shaft. Place the armature and drive assembly into the drive housing. Be sure that the shift lever tangs properly engage the drive assembly.

4. Apply a small amount of Lubriplate on the commutator end of the armature shaft.

5. Position the frame and field assembly to the drive housing. Be sure that the frame is properly indexed to the drive housing assembly.

6. Position the brush plate assembly to the frame assembly. Be sure that the brush plate is properly indexed to the drive housing assembly.

7. Place the brushes in their holders. Pull each spring away from the holder with a hook to allow entry of the brush. Center the brush springs on the brushes. Press the insulated brush leads away from all other interior components to prevent possible shorts.

8. Position the rubber gasket between the solenoid mounting and the upper outside surface of the frame. Position the starter solenoid with the metal gasket (if used), and install the solenoid mounting screws.

9. Connect the copper strap to the starter terminal on the solenoid.

10. Position the cover band and tighten the retaining screw.

11. Connect the starter to a battery to check its operation.

BRUSH REPLACEMENT
Positive Engagement Starter

Replace the starter brushes when they are worn to ¼ in. Always install a complete set of new brushes.

1. Loosen and remove the brush cover band, gasket, and starter drive plunger lever cover. Remove the brushes from their holders.

2. Remove the two through-bolts from the starter frame.

3. Remove the drive end housing and the plunger lever return spring.

4. Remove the starter drive plunger lever pivot pin and lever, and remove the armature.

5. Remove the brush end plate.

6. Remove the ground brush retaining screws from the frame and remove the brushes.

7. Cut the insulated brush leads from the field coils, as close to the field connection point as possible.

8. Clean and inspect the starter motor.

9. Replace the brush end plate if the insulator between the field brush holder and the end plate is cracked or broken.

10. Position the new insulated field brushes lead on the field coil connection. Position and crimp the clip provided with the brushes to hold the brush lead to the connection. Solder the lead, clip, and connection together using rosin core solder. Use a 300-watt soldering iron.

11. Install the ground brush leads to the frame with the retaining screws.

12. Clean the commutator with 00 or 000 sandpaper.

13. Position the brush end plate to the starter frame, with the end plate boss in the frame slot.

14. Install the armature in the starter frame.

15. Install the starter drive gear plunger lever to the frame and starter drive assembly, and install the pivot pin.

16. Partially fill the drive end housing bearing bore with grease (approximately ¼ full). Position the return spring on the plunger lever, and the drive end housing to the starter frame. Install the through-bolts and tighten to specified torque (55 to 75 in. lbs.). Be sure that the stop ring retainer is seated properly in the drive end housing.

17. Install the commutator brushes in the

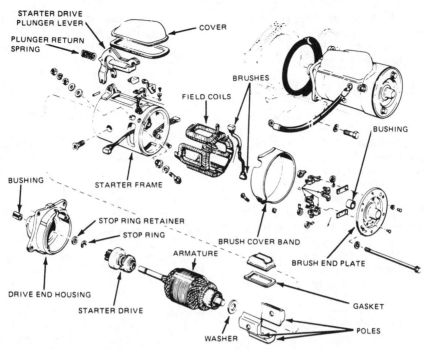

STARTER DRIVE
PLUNGER LEVER

PLUNGER RETURN
SPRING

COVER

BRUSHES

FIELD COILS

BUSHING

BUSHING

STARTER FRAME

STOP RING RETAINER

STOP RING

BRUSH COVER BAND

ARMATURE

BRUSH END PLATE

DRIVE END HOUSING

STARTER DRIVE

GASKET

WASHER

POLES

Positive engagement starter disassembled

brush holders. Center the brush springs on the brushes.

18. Position the plunger lever cover and brush cover band, with its gasket, on the starter. Tighten the bank retaining screw.

19. Connect the starter to a battery to check its operation.

Solenoid Actuated Starter

Replace the starter brushes when they are worn to ¼ in. Always install a complete set of new brushes.

1. Disconnect the copper strap from the starter terminal on the solenoid.

2. Loosen the retaining screw and slide the brush cover band back on the starter frame for access to the brushes.

3. Remove the commutator brushes from their holders. Hold each spring away from the brush with a hook, while sliding the brush out of the holder.

4. Remove the through-bolts and separate the drive end housing, starter frame and brush end plate assemblies.

5. Remove the ground brush retaining screws from the frame and remove the brushes.

6. Cut the insulated brush leads from the field coils, as close to the field connection point as possible.

7. Clean and inspect the starter motor.

8. Replace the brush end plate, if the insulator between the field brush holder and the end plate is cracked or broken.

9. Position the new insulated field brushes' lead on the field coil connection. Position and crimp the clip provided with the brushes to hold the brush lead to the connection. Solder the lead, clip, and connection together, using rosin core solder. Use a 300-watt soldering iron.

10. Install the ground brush leads to the frame with the retaining screws.

11. Clean the commutator with 00 or 000 sandpaper.

12. Apply a small amount of Lubriplate on the commutator end of the armature shaft.

13. Position the rubber gasket over the solenoid plunger lever, then position the frame to the end housing so that the wide slot in the frame clears the plunger lever and the end housing dowel is indexed with its frame slot.

14. Position the brush plate assembly to the frame assembly. Be sure that the brush plate is properly indexed to the frame. Install the through-bolts, making certain that the insulated brush lead is not between the through-bolt and the frame, and tighten to 45 to 85 in. lbs.

15. Place the brushes in their holders. Pull each spring away from the holder with a hook to allow entry of the brush. Press the insulated brush leads away from all the other interior components to prevent possible shorts.

16. Slide the cover band into position and tighten the retaining screw.

17. Connect the copper strap to the starter terminal on the solenoid.

18. Connect the starter to a battery to check its operation.

STARTER DRIVE REPLACEMENT

All Except 429 and 460 V8 (Positive Engagement Type)

1. Remove the starter from the engine.
2. Remove the brush cover band.
3. Remove the starter drive plunger lever cover.
4. Loosen the through-bolts just enough to allow removal of the drive end housing and the starter drive plunger lever return spring.
5. Remove the pivot pin which attaches the starter drive plunger lever to the starter frame and remove the lever.
6. Remove the stop-ring retainer and stop-ring from the armature shaft.
7. Remove the starter drive from the armature shaft.
8. Inspect the teeth on the starter drive. If they are excessively worn, inspect the teeth on the ring gear of the flywheel. If the teeth on the flywheel are excessively worn, the flywheel ring gear should be replaced.
9. Apply a thin coat of white grease to the armature shaft, in the area in which the starter drive operates.
10. Install the starter drive on the armature shaft and install a new stop-ring.
11. Position the starter drive plunger lever on the starter frame and install the pivot pin. *Make sure the plunger lever is properly engaged with the starter drive.*

12. Install a new stop-ring retainer on the armature shaft.
13. Fill the drive end housing bearing fore ¼ full with grease.
14. Position the starter drive plunger lever return spring and the drive end housing to the starter frame.
15. Tighten the starter through-bolts to 55–75 in. lbs.
16. Install the starter drive plunger lever cover and the brush cover band on the starter.
17. Install the starter.

Battery

REMOVAL AND INSTALLATION

1. Loosen the battery cable bolts and spread the ends of the battery cable terminals.
2. Disconnect the negative battery cable first.
3. Disconnect the positive battery cable.
4. Remove the battery hold-down.
5. Wearing heavy gloves, remove the battery from under the hood. *Be careful not to tip the battery and spill acid on yourself or the car during removal.*
6. To install, wearing heavy gloves, place the battery in its holder under the hood. *Use care not to spill the acid.*
7. Install the battery hold-down.
8. Install the positive battery cable first.
9. Install the negative battery cable.
10. Apply a *light* coating of grease to the cable ends.

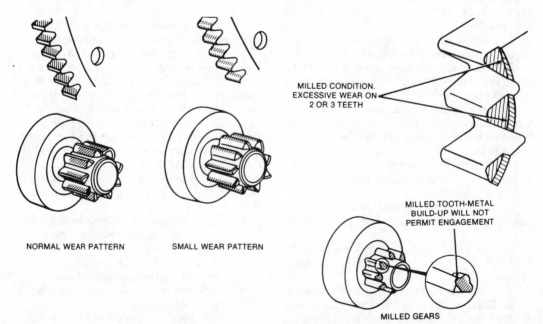

NORMAL WEAR PATTERN

SMALL WEAR PATTERN

MILLED CONDITION.
EXCESSIVE WEAR ON
2 OR 3 TEETH

MILLED TOOTH-METAL
BUILD-UP WILL NOT
PERMIT ENGAGEMENT

MILLED GEARS

Starter drive ring and pinion wear patterns

ENGINE MECHANICAL

A number of different engines have been used in Fords and Mercurys from 1968 through 1981. All of the engines use conventional cast-iron, water-cooled blocks. The cylinder heads are of the overhead valve design and the valves are actuated by pushrods and hydraulic valve lifters. The engines fall into five basic families.

A 240 cubic inch, inline six-cylinder engine is used in some models between 1968 and 1972. Unlike some of the smaller six-cylinder engines used in other Ford products, this six has a detachable intake manifold.

The second family is a remarkable series of small and medium sized V8 engines. They are; the 255, 302 and 351 Windsor engines. The 302 was the standard engine from 1968 through 1972 and then again from 1978 through 1980. The 351W medium sized V8 was installed in various models from 1969. In 1981 the 255 cubic inch V8 became the standard engine, installed in the Ford and Mercury, replacing the 302. The "new" engine is derived from the 302.

The 255 features weight reduction by about sixty pounds (from the 302) and has been designed to be adaptable to a variety of fuel metering systems. In 1981, the 302 and 351 (and a high output version of the 351, for police and towing) were offered as options. The 255 cu. in. engine has been dropped for the 1983 model year. 302 and 351 cu. in. engines are the only ones available. The 351 cu. in. is available in a standard or high output version.

The third engine family includes the 351 Cleveland, 351 Modified, and the 400 V8s. The 351C is used on 1972–74 models. The 351M, which is a modified Cleveland design, is used starting in 1975. The 400 V8 is installed in 1971–78 models. This family of engines is based on the smaller 302–351W series, but enjoys a higher volumetric efficiency quotient due to its larger valves and better breathing semi-hemispherical combustion chambers.

The fourth engine family includes the 390 and 428 cubic inch V8s. The 390 V8 may be found in 1968–71 models. The 428 V8 is used in 1968–71 models. These engines are the last

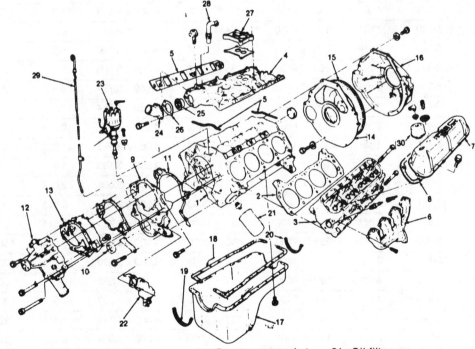

1. Cylinder block	11. Front cover gasket	21. Oil filter
2. Cylinder head gasket	12. Water pump	22. Fuel pump
3. Cylinder head	13. Water pump gasket	23. Distributor
4. Intake manifold	14. Rear cover plate	24. Thermostat housing
5. Intake manifold gasket	15. Flywheel	25. Thermostat
6. Exhaust manifold	16. Flywheel housing	26. Thermostat gasket
7. Valve cover	17. Oil pan	27. Carburetor spacer
8. Valve cover gasket	18. Oil pan gasket	28. Heater hose fitting
9. Front cover	19. Front main seal	29. Dipstick
10. Front cover seal	20. Rear main seal	30. Filler cap

Exploded view of stationary engine components—255, 302 and 351V

General Engine Specifications

Year	Engine No. Cyl Displacement (cu in.)	Carburetor Type	Advertised Horsepower @ rpm ■	Advertised Torque @ rpm (ft. lbs.) ■	Bore and Stroke (in.)	Advertised Compression Ratio	Oil Pressure @ 2050 rpm
1968	6-240	1 bbl	150 @ 4000	234 @ 2200	4.000 x 3.180	9.2:1	35–60
	8-302	2 bbl	210 @ 4400	295 @ 2400	4.000 x 3.000	9.5:1	35–60
	8-390	2 bbl	270 @ 4400	390 @ 2600	4.050 x 3.784	9.5:1	35–60
	8-390	2 bbl	280 @ 4400	403 @ 2600	4.050 x 3.784	10.5:1	35–60
	8-390	4 bbl	315 @ 4600	427 @ 2800	4.050 x 3.784	10.5:1	35–60
	8-428	4 bbl	345 @ 4600	462 @ 2800	4.130 x 3.984	10.5:1	35–60
	8-428PI	4 bbl	360 @ 5400	459 @ 3200	4.130 x 3.984	10.5:1	35–60
	8-429	4 bbl	360 @ 4600	480 @ 2800	4.360 x 3.590	10.5:1	35–60
1969	6-240	1 bbl	150 @ 4000	234 @ 2200	4.000 x 3.180	9.2:1	35–60
	8-302	2 bbl	210 @ 4400	295 @ 2400	4.000 x 3.000	9.5:1	35–60
	8-390	2 bbl	270 @ 4400	390 @ 2600	4.050 x 3.784	9.5:1	35–60
	8-390	2 bbl	280 @ 4400	430 @ 2600	4.050 x 3.784	10.5:1	35–60
	8-428PI	4 bbl	360 @ 5400	459 @ 3200	4.130 x 3.984	10.5:1	35–60
	8-429	2 bbl	320 @ 4400	460 @ 2200	4.360 x 3.590	10.5:1	35–60
	8-429	4 bbl	360 @ 4600	476 @ 2800	4.360 x 3.590	11.0:1	35–60
1970	6-240	1 bbl	150 @ 4000	234 @ 2200	4.000 x 3.180	9.2:1	35–60
	8-302	2 bbl	210 @ 4400	295 @ 2400	4.000 x 3.000	9.5:1	35–60
	8-351 W	2 bbl	250 @ 4600	355 @ 2600	4.000 x 3.500	9.5:1	35–60
	8-390	2 bbl	270 @ 4400	390 @ 2600	4.050 x 3.784	9.5:1	35–60
	8-428 PI	4 bbl	360 @ 5400	459 @ 3200	4.130 x 3.984	10.5:1	35–60
	8-429	2 bbl	320 @ 4400	460 @ 2200	4.360 x 3.590	10.5:1	35–60
	8-429	4 bbl	360 @ 4600	476 @ 2800	4.360 x 3.590	11.0:1	35–60
1971	6-240	1 bbl	140 @ 4000	230 @ 2200	4.000 x 3.180	8.9:1	35–60
	8-302	2 bbl	210 @ 4600	296 @ 2600	4.000 x 3.000	9.0:1	35–60
	8-351 W	2 bbl	240 @ 4600	350 @ 2600	4.000 x 3.500	8.9:1	35–60
	8-390	2 bbl	255 @ 4400	376 @ 2600	4.050 x 3.784	9.5:1	35–60
	8-400	2 bbl	260 @ 4400	400 @ 2200	4.000 x 4.000	9.0:1	50–70
	8-429	2 bbl	320 @ 4400	460 @ 2200	4.360 x 3.590	10.5:1	35–75
	8-429	4 bbl	360 @ 4600	480 @ 2800	4.360 x 3.590	10.5:1	35–75
	8-429 PI	4 bbl	370 @ 5400	450 @ 3400	4.360 x 3.590	11.0:1	35–75
1972	6-240	1 bbl	103 @ 3800	170 @ 2200	4.000 x 3.180	8.5:1	35–60
	8-302	2 bbl	140 @ 4000	239 @ 2000	4.000 x 3.000	8.5:1	35–60
	8-351 W	2 bbl	153 @ 3800	266 @ 2000	4.000 x 3.500	8.3:1	35–60
	8-351 C	2 bbl	163 @ 3800	277 @ 2000	4.000 x 3.500	8.6:1	35–60
	8-400	2 bbl	172 @ 4000	298 @ 2200	4.000 x 4.000	8.4:1	50–70
	8-429	4 bbl	208 @ 4400	322 @ 2800	4.362 x 3.590	8.5:1	35–75
	8-429	4 bbl	212 @ 4400	327 @ 2600	4.362 x 3.590	8.5:1	35–75
	8-460	4 bbl	200 @ 4400	326 @ 2800	4.362 x 3.850	8.5:1	35–75
	8-460	4 bbl	212 @ 4400	342 @ 2800	4.362 x 3.850	8.5:1	35–75

General Engine Specifications (cont.)

Year	Engine No. Cyl Displacement (cu in.)	Carburetor Type	Advertised Horsepower @ rpm ■	Advertised Torque @ rpm (ft. lbs.) ■	Bore and Stroke (in.)	Advertised Compression Ratio	Oil Pressure @ 2050 rpm
1973	8-351 W	2 bbl	153 @ 3800	266 @ 2000	4.000 x 3.500	8.3:1	35–60
	8-351 C	2 bbl	163 @ 3800	277 @ 2000	4.000 x 3.500	8.6:1	35–60
	8-400	2 bbl	172 @ 4000	298 @ 2200	4.000 x 4.000	8.4:1	50–70
	8-429	4 bbl	208 @ 4400	322 @ 2800	4.362 x 3.590	8.5:1	35–75
	8-429	4 bbl	212 @ 4400	327 @ 2600	4.362 x 3.590	8.5:1	35–75
	8-460	4 bbl	200 @ 4400	326 @ 2800	4.362 x 3.850	8.5:1	35–75
	8-460	4 bbl	212 @ 4400	342 @ 2800	4.362 x 3.850	8.5:1	35–75
1974	8-351 W	2 bbl	162 @ 4000	275 @ 2200	4.000 x 3.500	8.2:1	45–65
	8-351 C	2 bbl	163 @ 4200	278 @ 2000	4.000 x 3.500	8.0:1	45–75
	8-400	2 bbl	170 @ 3400	330 @ 2000	4.000 x 4.000	8.0:1	45–75
	8-460	4 bbl	195 @ 3800	335 @ 2600	4.362 x 3.850	8.0:1	35–65
	8-460 PI	4 bbl	275 @ 4400	395 @ 2800	4.362 x 3.850	8.8:1	25–65
1975	8-351 M	2 bbl	148 @ 3800 ①	243 @ 2400 ②	4.000 x 3.500	8.0:1	45–75
	8-400	2 bbl	158 @ 3800 ③	276 @ 2000 ④	4.000 x 4.000	8.0:1	45–75
	8-460	4 bbl	218 @ 4000	369 @ 2600 ⑤	4.362 x 3.850	8.0:1	35–65
	8-460 PI	4 bbl	226 @ 4000	374 @ 2600	4.362 x 3.850	8.0:1	35–65
1976–77	8-351 M	2 bbl	152 @ 3800	274 @ 1600	4.000 x 3.500	8.0:1	45–75
	8-400 ⑥	2 bbl	180 @ 3800	336 @ 1800	4.000 x 4.000	8.0:1	45–75
	8-460	4 bbl	202 @ 3800	352 @ 1600	4.362 x 3.850	8.0:1	35–65
	8-460 PI	4 bbl	202 @ 3800	352 @ 1600	4.362 x 3.850	8.0:1	35–65
1978	8-302	2 bbl	134 @ 3400	248 @ 1600	4.000 x 3.000	8.4:1	40–60
	8-351 W	2 bbl	144 @ 3200	277 @ 1600	4.000 x 3.500	8.3:1	40–60
	8-351 M	2 bbl	145 @ 3400	273 @ 1800	4.000 x 3.500	8.0:1	50–75
	8-400	2 bbl	160 @ 3800	314 @ 1800	4.000 x 4.000	8.0:1	50–75
	8-460	4 bbl	202 @ 4000	348 @ 2000	4.362 x 3.850	8.0:1	35–65
	8-460 PI	4 bbl	202 @ 3800	352 @ 1600	4.362 x 3.850	8.0:1	35–65
1979	8-302	VV	134 @ 3400	248 @ 1600	4.000 x 3.000	8.4:1	40–60
	8-351 W	2 bbl	144 @ 3200	277 @ 1600	4.000 x 3.500	8.3:1	40–60
	8-351 W Calif.	VV	139 @ 3200	270 @ 1600	4.000 x 3.500	8.3:1	40–60
1980–81	8-255	VV	119 @ 3800	194 @ 2200	3.680 x 3.000	8.8:1	40–60
	8-302	VV	130 @ 3600	230 @ 1600	4.000 x 3.000	8.4:1	40–60
	8-351 W	VV	140 @ 3400	265 @ 2000	4.000 x 3.500	8.3:1	40–60
1982	8-255	VV	119 @ 3800	194 @ 2200	3.680 x 3.000	8.8:1	40–60
	8-302	VV	130 @ 3600	230 @ 1600	4.000 x 3.000	8.4:1	40–60
	8-302	EFI	130 @ 3400	230 @ 2200	4.000 x 3.000	8.4:1	40–60
	8-351	VV	140 @ 3400	265 @ 2000	4.000 x 3.500	8.3:1	40–60

General Engine Specifications (cont.)

Year	Engine No. Cyl Displacement (cu in.)	Carburetor Type	Advertised Horsepower @ rpm ▪	Advertised Torque @ rpm (ft. lbs.) ▪	Bore and Stroke (in.)	Advertised Compression Ratio	Oil Pressure @ 2050 rpm
1983	8-302	VV	130 @ 3600	230 @ 1600	4.000 x 3.000	8.4 : 1	40–60
	8-302	EFI	130 @ 3400	230 @ 2200	4.000 x 3.000	8.4 : 1	40–60
	8-351	VV	140 @ 3400	265 @ 2000	4.000 x 3.500	8.4 : 1	40–60

▪ Beginning 1972, horsepower and torque are SAE net figures. They are measured at the rear of the transmission with all accessories installed and operating. Since the figures vary when a given engine is installed in different models, some are representative rather than exact.

W Windsor Design
C Cleveland Design
M Modified Cleveland Design
PI Police Intercepter
VV Variable Venturi
① California cars—150 @ 3800 rpm

② California cars—244 @ 2800 rpm
③ California cars—144 @ 3600 rpm
④ California cars—255 @ 2200 rpm
⑤ California cars—367 @ 2600 rpm
⑥ California only—400 cu in. engine equipped with 4 bbl carburetor

Valve Specifications

Year	Engine No. Cyl Displacement (cu in.)	Seat Angle (deg)	Face Angle (deg)	Spring Test Pressure (lbs @ in.)	Spring Installed (lbs @ in.)	Stem to Guide Clearance (in.)		Stem Diameter (in.)	
						Intake	Exhaust	Intake	Exhaust
1968	6-240	45	44	197 @ 1.30	1¹¹/₁₆	.0010–.0027	.0010–.0027	.3420	.3420
	8-302	45	44	180 @ 1.23	1²¹/₃₂	.0010–.0027	.0015–.0032	.3420	.3415
	8-390	45	44	220 @ 1.38	1¹³/₁₆	.0010–.0024	.0015–.0032	.3715	.3710
	8-427	①	②	268 @ 1.31	1¹³/₁₆	.0010–.0024	.0020–.0034	.3715	.3705
	8-428	45	44	220 @ 1.38	1¹³/₁₆	.0010–.0024	.0015–.0032	.3715	.3710
	8-429	45	44	253 @ 1.33	1¹³/₁₆	.0010–.0027	.0010–.0027	.3420	.3420
1969	6-240	45	44	197 @ 1.30	1¹¹/₁₆	.0010–.0027	.0010–.0027	.3420	.3420
	8-302	45	44	180 @ 1.23	1²¹/₃₂	.0010–.0027	.0015–.0032	.3420	.3415
	8-390	45	44	220 @ 1.38	1¹³/₁₆	.0010–.0027	.0015–.0032	.3715	.3710
	8-429	45	44	251 @ 1.33	1¹³/₁₆	.0010–.0027	.0010–.0027·	.3420	.3420
1970	6-240	45	44	197 @ 1.30	1¹¹/₁₆	.0010–.0027	.0010–.0027	.3420	.3420
	8-302	45	44	180 @ 1.23	1²¹/₃₂	.0010–.0027	.0015–.0032	.3420	.3415
	8-351	45	44	215 @ 1.34	1²⁵/₃₂	.0010–.0027	.0010–.0027	.3420	.3415
	8-390	①	44	220 @ 1.38	1¹³/₁₆	.0010–.0027	.0015–.0032	.3715	.3710
	8-429	45	44	253 @ 1.33	1¹³/₁₆	.0010–.0027	.0010–.0027	.3420	.3420
1971	6-240	45	44	197 @ 1.30	1¹¹/₁₆	.0010–.0027	.0010–.0027	.3420	.3420
	8-302	45	44	180 @ 1.23	1²¹/₃₂	.0010–.0027	.0015–.0032	.3420	.3415
	8-351 ③	45	44	215 @ 1.34	1²⁵/₃₂	.0010–.0027	.0015–.0032	.3420	.3415
	8-351 ④	45	44	210 @ 1.42	1¹³/₁₆	.0010–.0027	.0015–.0032	.3420	.3415
	8-390	①	44	220 @ 1.38	1¹³/₁₆	.0010–.0027	.0015–.0032	.3715	.3710
	8-400	45	44	226 @ 1.39	1¹³/₁₆	.0010–.0027	.0015–.0032	.3420	.3415
	8-429	45	45	253 @ 1.33	1¹³/₁₆	.0010–.0027	.0015–.0032	.3420	.3415
1972	6-240	45	44	197 @ 1.30	1¹¹/₁₆	.0010–.0027	.0010–.0027	.3420	.3420
	8-302	45	44	200 @ 1.31	1¹¹/₁₆	.0010–.0027	.0015–.0032	.3420	.3415

Valve Specifications (cont.)

Year	Engine No. Cyl Displacement (cu in.)	Seat Angle (deg)	Face Angle (deg)	Spring Test Pressure (lbs @ in.)	Spring Installed (lbs @ in.)	Stem to Guide Clearance (in.)		Stem Diameter (in.)	
						Intake	Exhaust	Intake	Exhaust
1972	8-351 ③	45	44	215 @ 1.34	$1^{25}/_{32}$	.0010–.0027	.0015–.0032	.3420	.3415
	8-351 ④	45	44	210 @ 1.42	$1^{13}/_{16}$	.0010–.0027	.0015–.0032	.3420	.3415
	8-400	45	44	226 @ 1.39	$1^{13}/_{16}$	.0010–.0027	.0015–.0032	.3420	.3415
	8-429	45	45	229 @ 1.33	$1^{13}/_{16}$	.0010–.0027	.0010–.0027	.3420	.3420
	8-460	45	45	229 @ 1.33	$1^{13}/_{16}$	.0010–.0027	.0010–.0027	.3420	.3420
1973–74	8-351 ③	45	44	200 @ 1.34	$1^{25}/_{32}$	.0010–.0027	.0015–.0032	.3420	.3415
	8-351 ④	45	44	210 @ 1.42 ⑤	$1^{13}/_{16}$	.0010–.0027	.0015–.0032	.3420	.3415
	8-400	45	44	226 @ 1.39	$1^{13}/_{16}$	.0010–.0027	.0015–.0032	.3420	.3415
	8-429	45	45	229 @ 1.33	$1^{13}/_{16}$	.0010–.0027	.0010–.0027	.3420	.3420
	8-460	45	45	229 @ 1.33	$1^{13}/_{16}$	.0010–.0027	.0010–.0027	.3420	.3420
1975–77	8-351 ⑥	45	44	226 @ 1.39	$1^{13}/_{16}$	.0010–.0027	.0015–.0032	.3420	.3415
	8-400	45	44	226 @ 1.39	$1^{13}/_{16}$	.0010–.0027	.0015–.0032	.3420	.3415
	8-460	45	45	253 @ 1.33	$1^{13}/_{16}$	.0010–.0027	.0010–.0027	.3420	.3420
1978–81	8-255 8-302	45	44	⑦	$1^{11}/_{16}$ ⑪	.0010–.0027	.0015–.0032	.3420	.3415
	8-351 W	45	44	⑩	$1^{13}/_{16}$ ⑪	.0010–.0027	.0015–.0032	.3420	.3415
	8-351 M	44½–45	45½–45¾	226 @ 1.39	$1^{13}/_{16}$	.0010–.0027	.0015–.0032	.3420	.3415
	8-400	44½–45	45½–45¾	226 @ 1.39	$1^{13}/_{16}$	.0010–.0027	.0015–.0032	.3420	.3415
	8-460	44½–45	45½–45¾	⑧	$1^{13}/_{16}$	.0010–.0027	.0010–.0027	.3420	.3420
	8-460 PI	44½–45	45½–45¾	⑨	$1^{13}/_{16}$	.0010–.0027	.0010–.0027	.3420	.3420
1982–83	8-255 ⑯	44½–45	45½–45¾	192 @ 1.40 ⑫	$1^{43}/_{64}$ ⑮	.0010–.0027	.0015–.0032	.3416–.3423	.3411–.3418
	8-302	45	45	204 @ 1.36 ⑬	$1^{43}/_{64}$ ⑮	.0010–.0027	.0015–.0032	.3416–.3423	.3411–.3418
	8-351	45	45	204 @ 1.33 ⑭	$1^{49}/_{64}$ ⑮	.0010–.0027	.0015–.0032	.3416–.3423	.3411–.3418

① Intake valve seat angle 30°
  Exhaust valve seat angle 45°
② Intake valve face angle 29°
  Exhaust valve face angle 44°
③ Windsor heads
④ Cleveland heads
⑤ 1974 models—226 @ 1.39
⑥ Modified Cleveland heads
⑦ 1977–78: Intake 200 @ 1.31; Exhaust: 200 @ 1.20
  1979–81: Intake 190–212 @ 1.36; Exhaust: 190–210 @ 1.20

⑧ Intake: 240 @ 1.33, Exhaust: 253 @ 1.33
⑨ Intake: 315 @ 1.32, Exhaust: 315 @ 1.33
⑩ Intake: 200 @ 1.34, Exhaust: 200 @ 1.20
⑪ Exhaust: 1⅝
⑫ Exhaust: 191 @ 1.23
⑬ Exhaust: 200 @ 1.20
⑭ Exhaust: 205 @ 1.15
⑮ Exhaust: $1^{37}/_{64}$
⑯ Discontinued in 1983

examples of the "Y"-block design, first introduced in the mid-fifties. Identifying features of these engines are the shaft-mounted rocker arms, and an intake manifold that extends beneath the valve covers.

The last group of engines includes the 429 and 460 V8s. The 429 V8 is installed in 1969–73 models. The 460 V8 may be found in full size Fords starting in 1974. It was last used in 1978. This family of engines was introduced to replace the old "Y"-block series, and is also based on the smaller 302–351W design. Identifying features of these powerplants are their great bulk and the tunnelport shaped configuration of the intake manifold.

For a definitive identification of all engines

Torque Specifications
All readings in ft. lbs.

Year	Engine No. Cyl Displacement (cu in.)	Cylinder Head Bolts	Rod Bearing Bolts	Main Bearing Bolts	Crankshaft Pulley Bolt	Flywheel to Crankshaft Bolts	Manifold	
							Intake	Exhaust
1968	6-240	70–75	40–45	60–70	130–145	75–85	25	25
	8-302	65–70	19–24	60–70	70–90	75–85	21	15½
	8-390, 428, 429	80–90	40–45	95–105	70–90	75–85	33½	15½
1969	6-240	70–75	40–45	60–70	130–150	75–85	25	25
	8-302	65–72	19–24	60–70	70–90	75–85	24	14
	8-390, 428	80–90	40–45	95–105	70–90	75–85	33½	21
	8-429	130–140	40–45	95–105	70–90	75–85	27½	30½
1970	6-240	70–75	40–45	60–70	130–150	75–85	25	25
	8-302	65–72	19–24	60–70	70–90	75–85	24	14
	8-351	95–100	40–45	95–105	70–90	75–85	23–25	18–24
	8-390	80–90	①	95–105	70–90	75–85	32–35	18–24
	8-429	130–140	40–45	95–105	70–90	75–85	27½	30½
1971	6-240	70–75	40–45	60–70	130–150	75–85	25	25
	8-302	65–72	19–24	60–70	70–90	75–85	24	14
	8-351	95–100	40–45	95–105	70–90	75–85	23–25	18–24②
	8-390	80–90	40–45	95–105	70–90	75–85	32–35	18–24
	8-400	95–105	40–45	95–105	70–90	75–85	27–33	12–16
	8-429	130–140	40–45	95–105	70–90	75–85	27½	30½
1972	6-240	70–75	40–45	60–70	130–150	75–85	23–28	23–28
	8-302	65–72	19–24	60–70	70–90	75–85	23–25	12–16
	8-351 W	105–112	40–45	95–105	100–130	75–85	23–25	18–24
	8-351C, 400	95–105③	40–45④	⑤	70–90	75–85	⑥	12–16
	8-429, 460	130–140	40–45	95–105	70–90	75–85	25–30	28–33
1973–83	8-351 W	105–112	40–45	95–105	100–130	75–85	23–25	18–24
	8-351C, 351M, 400	95–105	40–45	⑤	70–90	75–85	⑥	12–16
	8-429, 460	130–140	40–45	95–105	70–90	75–85	25–30	28–33
	8-255, 302	65–72	19–24	60–70	70–90	75–85	23–25	18–24

① 390—40–45; 428—53–58
  Tighten cylinder head bolts in 3 steps; the first 20 ft. lbs. less than maximum torque, the second 10 ft. lbs. less than maximum torque, and the third maximum torque
② 351C engine—12–16
③ 351 HO—120
④ 351 HO—40–45
⑤ ½ x 13 in. bolt—95–105
  ⅜ x 16 in. bolt—35–45
⑥ ⁵⁄₁₆ in. bolt—21–25
  ⅜ in. bolt—27–23
  ¼ in. bolt—6–9

mentioned above, see the "Engine Code" chart in Chapter 1.

Engine Removal and Installation

Before starting to tear out your engine, and tying up both yourself and your car for a length of time, there are a few preliminary steps that should be taken. Jot down those engine and transmission numbers (see Chapter 1) and make a trip to your parts dealer to order all those gaskets, hoses, belts, filters, etc. which are in need of replacement. This will help avoid last minute or weekend parts dashes that can

Piston and Ring Specification—All Engines
1968–83

	Top Compression	Bottom Compression	Oil Control	Piston to Bore Clearance
Ring gap	.010–.020	.010–.020	.015–.055 ①	—
Side clearance	.002–.004	.002–.004	Snug	—
Piston clearance	—	—	—	.0014–.0022②

① 1972–74; 351 and 400 is .015–.069   ② 255, 302 and 351W is .0018–.0026

tie up a car even longer. Also, have enough oil, antifreeze, transmission fluid, etc. on hand for the job.

If the car is still running, have the engine, engine compartment, and underbody steam cleaned, or at least hosed off at one of those coin-operated, do-it-yourself car washes. The less dirt, the better. Have all of the necessary tools together. These should include a sturdy hydraulic jack and a pair of jackstands of sufficient capacity, a chain/pulley engine hoist of sufficient test strength, a wooden block and a small jack to support the oil pan or transmission, a can of penetrating fluid to help loosen rusty nuts and bolts, a few jars or plastic containers to store and identify used engine hardware, and a punch or bottle of brush paint to matchmark adjacent parts to aid reassembly. Once you have all of your parts, tools, and fluids together, proceed with the task.

ENGINE REMOVAL

1. Scribe the hood hinge outline on the underside of the hood, disconnect the hood and remove.

2. Drain the entire cooling system and the engine oil.

3. Remove the air cleaner, disconnect the battery at the cylinder head. On automatic transmission-equipped cars, disconnect oil cooler lines at the radiator. Label and disconnect all emission control hoses and electrical leads.

4. Remove the upper and lower radiator hoses from the engine and, if the engine is equipped with a fan shroud, disconnect the shroud from the radiator and position it rearward. Remove the radiator from the car.

5. Remove the fan attaching screws and remove the fan, fan spacer and shroud from the engine as an assembly. Loosen and remove all drive belts.

6. Disconnect the heater hoses from the engine. If the vehicle is equipped with power steering, remove the pump from the engine and position it out of the way.

7. Remove the alternator mounting bolts and ground wire from the block and remove the alternator. Disconnect the carburetor and kick-down linkage from the engine.

8. On models with power brakes, remove the vacuum line from the engine. On cars with air conditioning, remove the compressor mounting bracket from the engine and position the compressor out of the way without disconnecting the refrigerant lines.

NOTE: *If the compressor lines do not have*

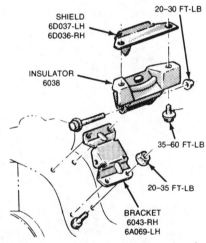

302, 351V front engine supports (255 similar)

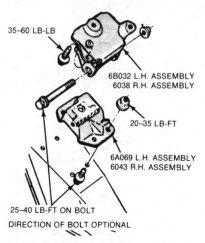

351C, 351M, 400 V8 front engine supports

Crankshaft and Connecting Rod Specifications
All measurements are given in inches

Year	Engine No. Cyl Displacement (cu in.)	Crankshaft				Connecting Rod		
		Main Brg Journal Dia	Main Brg Oil Clearance	Shaft End-Play	Thrust on No.	Journal Diameter	Oil Clearance	Side Clearance
1968	6-240	2.3986-2.3990	.0008-.0024	.004-.008	5	2.1232-2.1246	.0007-.0028	.014-.020
	8-302	2.2486-2.2490	.0005-.0024	.004-.008	3	2.1232-2.1246	.0007-.0028	.014-.020
	8-390, 427, 428, 429	2.7488-2.7492	.0008-.0012	.004-.008	3	2.4384-2.4388	.0007-.0028	.014-.020
1969	6-240	2.3982-2.3990	.0005-.0015	.004-.008	5	2.1228-2.1236	.0008-.0015	.006-.013
	8-302	2.2482-2.2490	.0005-.0015	.004-.008	3	2.1228-2.1236	.0008-.0015	.010-.020
	8-390	2.7484-2.7492	.0013-.0025	.004-.010	3	2.4380-2.4388	.0008-.0015	.010-.020
	8-428	2.7484-2.7492	.0010-.0020	.004-.010	3	2.4380-2.4388	.0020-.0030	.010-.020
	8-429	2.9994-3.0002	.0005-.0015	.004-.008	3	2.4992-2.5000	.0008-.0015	.010-.020
1970	6-240	2.3982-2.3990	.0005-.0015	.004-.008	5	2.1228-2.1236	.0008-.0026	.006-.013
	8-302	2.2482-2.2490	.0005-.0015	.004-.008	3	2.1228-2.1236	.0008-.0026	.010-.020
	8-351	2.9994-2.3002	.0013-.0025	.004-.008	3	2.3103-2.3111	.0008-.0026	.010-.020
	8-390	2.7484-2.7492	.0005-.0025	.004-.008	3	2.4380-2.4388	.0008-.0026	.010-.020
	8-428	2.7484-2.7492	.0008-.0020	.004-.008	3	2.4380-2.4388	.0008-.0026	.010-.020
	8-429	2.9994-3.0002	.0005-.0025	.004-.008	3	2.4992-2.5000	.0008-.0026	.010-.020
1971	6-240	2.3982-2.3990	.0005-.0022	.004-.008	5	2.1228-2.1236	.0008-.0026	.006-.013
	8-302	2.2482-2.2490	.0005-.0024①	.004-.008	3	2.1228-2.1236	.0008-.0026	.010-.020
	8-351W	2.9994-3.0002	.0013-.0030	.004-.008	3	2.3103-2.3111	.0008-.0026	.010-.020
	8-351C	2.7484-2.7492	.0009-.0026	.004-.010	3	2.3103-2.3111	.0008-.0026	.010-.020
	8-390	2.7484-2.7492	.0008-.0020	.004-.008	3	2.4380-2.4388	.0010-.0030	.010-.020

Year	Engine						
1972	8-400	2.9994–3.0002	.0009–.0026	.004–.010	3	2.3103–2.3111	.0008–.0026	.010–.020
	8-429	2.9994–3.0002	.0005–.0025	.004–.008	3	2.4992–2.5000	.0008–.0028	.010–.020
	6-240	2.3982–2.3990	.0005–.0022	.004–.008	5	2.1228–2.1236	.0008–.0026	.006–.013
	8-302	2.2482–2.2490	.0005–.0024 ①	.004–.008	3	2.1228–2.1236	.0008–.0026	.010–.020
	8-351W	2.9994–3.0002	.0008–.0026	.004–.008	3	2.3103–2.3111	.0008–.0026	.010–.020
	8-351C	2.7484–2.7492	.0011–.0028	.004–.010	3	2.3103–2.3111	.0011–.0026	.010–.020
	8-400	2.9994–3.0002	.0011–.0028	.004–.010	3	2.3103–2.3111	.0011–.0026	.010–.020
	8-429	2.9994–3.0002	.0010–.0020 ②	.004–.008	3	2.4992–2.5000	.0008–.0028	.010–.020
	8-460	2.9994–3.0002	.0010–.0020 ②	.004–.008	3	2.4992–2.5000	.0008–.0026	.010–.020
1973–74	8-351W	2.9994–3.0002	.0008–.0026	.004–.008	3	2.3103–2.3111	.0008–.0026	.010–.020
	8-351C	2.7484–2.7492	.0011–.0028	.004–.010	3	2.3103–2.3111	.0011–.0026	.010–.020
	8-400	2.9994–3.0002	.0011–.0028	.004–.010	3	2.3103–2.3111	.0011–.0026	.010–.020
	8-429	2.9994–3.0002	.0010–.0020 ②	.004–.008	3	2.4992–2.5000	.0008–.0028	.010–.020
	8-460	2.9994–3.0002	.0010–.0020 ②	.004–.008	3	2.4992–2.5000	.0008–.0026	.010–.020
1975–77	8-351M	2.9994–3.0002	.0009–.0026	.004–.008	3	2.3103–2.3111	.0008–.0026	.010–.020
	8-400	2.9994–3.0002	.0009–.0026	.004–.008	3	2.3103–2.3111	.0008–.0026	.010–.020
	8-460	2.9994–3.0002	.0009–.0027 ③	.004–.008	3	2.4992–2.5000	.0008–.0028	.010–.020
1978–83	8-255, 302	2.2482–2.2490	.0005–.0015 ④	.004–.008	3	2.1228–2.1236	.0008–.0015	.010–.020
	8-351W	2.9994–3.0002	.0008–.0015	.004–.008	3	2.3103–2.3111	.0008–.0015	.010–.020
	8-351M, 400	2.9994–3.0002	.0008–.0015	.004–.008	3	2.3103–2.3111	.0008–.0015	.010–.020
	8-460	2.9994–3.0002	.0008–.0015	.004–.008	3	2.4992–2.5000	.0008–.0015	.010–.020

① #1—.0001–.0018
② #1—.010–.015
③ #1 bearing—.0004–.0022 in.
④ #1 bearing—.0001–.0015

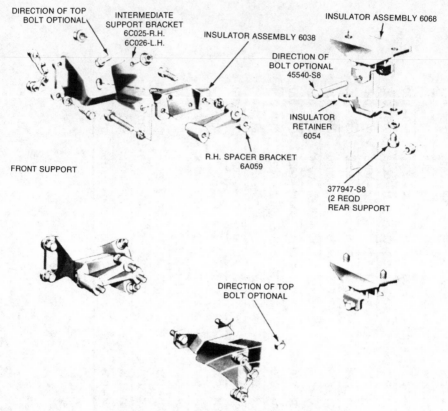

Six-cylinder engine front and rear supports

enough slack to move the compressor out of the way without disconnecting the refrigerant lines, the air conditioning system must be evacuated, using the required tools, before the refrigerant lines can be disconnected.

CAUTION: *Evacuating the air conditioning system should be left to an expert.*

9. Disconnect fuel tank line at the fuel pump and plug the line.

10. Disconnect the coil and distributor primary wire harness. Disconnect wires at the oil pressure and water temperature-sending units.

11. Remove the starter and dust seal.

12. On a car equipped with a manual transmission, remove the clutch retracting spring. Disconnect the clutch equalizer shaft and arm bracket at the underbody rail and remove the arm bracket and equalizer.

13. Raise the car. Install jackstands be-

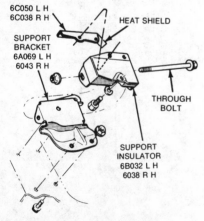

1969–71 429 V8 front engine supports

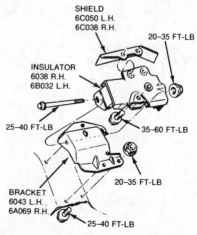

1973–78 429, 460 V8 front engine supports

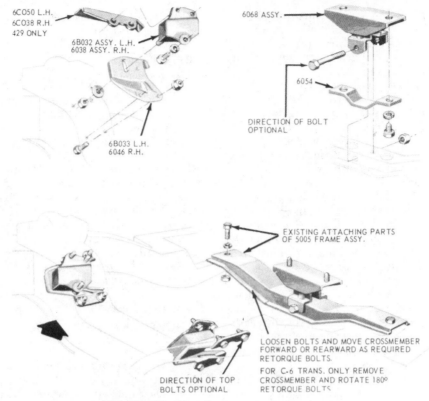

6C050 L.H.
6C038 R.H.
429 ONLY

6B032 ASSY. L.H.
6038 ASSY. R.H.

6B033 L.H.
6046 R.H.

6068 ASSY.

6054

DIRECTION OF BOLT
OPTIONAL

EXISTING ATTACHING PARTS
OF 5005 FRAME ASSY.

LOOSEN BOLTS AND MOVE CROSSMEMBER
FORWARD OR REARWARD AS REQUIRED
RETORQUE BOLTS.

FOR C-6 TRANS. ONLY REMOVE
CROSSMEMBER AND ROTATE 180°
RETORQUE BOLTS

DIRECTION OF TOP
BOLTS OPTIONAL

390, 428 V8 engine front and rear supports

neath the frame. Remove the flywheel or converter housing upper retaining bolts.

14. Disconnect the exhaust pipe or pipes at the exhaust manifold. Disconnect the right and left motor mount at the underbody bracket. Remove the flywheel or converter housing cover.

15. On a car with manual transmission remove the flywheel housing lower retaining bolts.

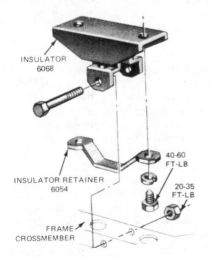

INSULATOR
6068

INSULATOR RETAINER
6054

40-60
FT-LB

20-35
FT-LB

FRAME
CROSSMEMBER

Rear engine support—All V8

16. On a car with automatic transmission, disconnect throttle valve vacuum line at the intake manifold, disconnect the converter from the flywheel. Remove the converter housing lower retaining bolts. On a car with power steering, disconnect power steering pump from cylinder head. Remove the drive belt and wire steering pump out of the way.

17. Lower the car. Support the transmission and flywheel or converter housing with a jack.

CAUTION: *On models with automatic transmission, be sure the converter "breaks" loose from the flywheel and stays firmly mounted on the transmission.*

18. Attach an engine lifting hook. Lift the engine up and out of the compartment and onto an adequate work stand.

ENGINE INSTALLATION

1. Attach engine sling and lifting device. Then lift engine from work stand.

2. Lower the engine into the engine compartment. Be sure the dowels in the block engage the holes in the flywheel housing. On a car with automatic transmission, start the converter pilot into the crankshaft. Make sure the converter mounting bolts line up with the flywheel holes. On a car with manual transmis-

sion, start the transmission main drive gear into the clutch disc. If the engine hangs up after the shaft enters, rotate the crankshaft slowly (with transmission in gear) until the shaft and clutch disc splines mesh.

3. Install the flywheel or converter housing upper bolts.

4. Install engine support insulator to bracket retaining nuts. Disconnect engine lifting sling and remove lifting brackets.

5. Raise front of car. Install exhaust packing gaskets and connect exhaust line/s and tighten attachments.

6. Position dust seal and install starter.

7. On cars with manual transmissions, install remaining flywheel housing-to-engine bolts. Connect clutch release rod. Position the clutch equalizer bar and bracket and install retaining bolts. Install clutch pedal retracting spring.

8. On cars with automatic transmissions, attach the converter to the flywheel. Install the converter housing inspection cover. Install the remaining converter housing retaining bolts.

9. Remove the support from the transmission and lower the car.

10. Connect engine ground strap and coil primary wire.

11. Connect water temperature gauge wire and the heater hose at coolant outlet housing. Connect accelerator rod at the bellcrank.

12. On cars with automatic transmission, connect the transmission filler tube bracket. Connect the throttle valve vacuum line.

13. On cars with power steering, install the drive belt and power steering pump bracket. Install the bracket retaining bolts. Adjust drive belt to proper tension.

14. Remove plug from the fuel tank line. Connect the flexible fuel line and the oil pressure sending unit wire.

15. Install the pulley, belt spacer, and fan. Adjust belt tension.

16. Install the alternator and the negative battery cable. Connect all emission control hoses and electrical leads disconnected to remove the engine.

17. In vehicles with power brakes, connect vacuum line at intake manifold. On cars with air conditioning, install compressor on mounting bracket.

18. Install radiator. Connect radiator hoses. Fill the cooling system.

19. On cars with automatic transmissions, connect oil cooler lines.

20. Install oil filter. Connect heater hose at water pump, after bleeding the system.

21. Bring crankcase to level with correct grade of oil. Run engine at fast idle and check for leaks. Install air cleaner and make final engine adjustments.

22. Install and adjust hood.

23. Road-test car.

Valve Cover
REMOVAL AND INSTALLATION

1. Remove the air cleaner and heat chamber air inlet hose, if so equipped.

2. Remove the automatic choke tube, if so equipped, and the fresh air tube from the valve cover.

3. Remove the thermactor bypass valve and air supply hoses, as needed.

4. Disconnect the spark plug wires. Remove the wire bracket if necessary.

5. Remove any other necessary parts, then remove the valve cover.

6. Installation is the reverse of removal.

NOTE: *Always use new gaskets when installing the valve covers.*

Cylinder Head
REMOVAL AND INSTALLATION
Six-Cylinder

1. Drain coolant and remove air cleaner. Disconnect battery cable at cylinder head.

2. Disconnect exhaust pipe at manifold.

3. Disconnect accelerator retracting spring, choke control cable and accelerator rod at carburetor.

4. Disconnect fuel line and distributor control vacuum line at the carburetor.

5. Disconnect coolant tubes from carburetor spacer. Disconnect coolant and heater hoses.

6. Disconnect distributor control vacuum line at distributor and fuel inlet line at the filter. Remove lines as an assembly.

7. On an engine equipped with positive crankcase ventilation, disconnect the emission exhaust tube.

8. Disconnect spark plug wires at the plugs and the small wire from the termperature-sending unit. On an engine equipped with a Thermactor exhaust emission control system, disconnect the air pump hose at the air manifold assembly. Unscrew the tube nuts and remove the air manifold. Disconnect the anti-backfire valve air and vacuum lines at the intake manifold. On a car equipped with power brakes, disconnect the brake vacuum line at the intake manifold.

9. Remove the rocker arm cover.

10. Loosen the rocker arm stud nut so that the rocker arm can be rotated to one side. Remove valve pushrods and keep them in sequence.

11. Remove one cylinder head bolt from each end and install two 7/16 in. x 14 guide studs.

12. Remove remaining cylinder head bolts, then remove cylinder head.

13. Prior to installation, clean head and block surfaces.

14. Apply sealer to both sides of head gasket. Position gasket over guide studs or dowel pins.

NOTE: *Apply gasket sealer only to steel shim head gaskets. Steel-asbestos composite head gaskets are to be installed without any sealer.*

15. Install new gasket on the exhaust pipe flange.

16. Lift the cylinder head over the guide studs and slide it carefully into place while guiding the exhaust manifold studs into the exhaust pipe flange.

17. Coat cylinder head attaching bolts with water-resistant sealer and install (but do not tighten), the head bolts.

18. Torque the head, in proper sequence, and in three progressive steps to 75 ft. lbs.

19. Lubricate both ends of the pushrods and insert them in their original bores and sockets.

20. Lubricate valve stem tips and rocker arm pads.

21. Position the rocker arms and tighten the stud nuts enough to hold the pushrods in position.

22. Do a preliminary, cold valve lash adjustment.

23. Install exhaust pipe-to-manifold nuts and lockwashers. Torque to 17–22 ft. lbs.

24. Connect radiator and heater hoses. Connect coolant tubes at the carburetor spacer.

25. Connect distributor vacuum line and the carburetor fuel line. Connect battery cable to cylinder head.

26. On engines equipped with positive crankcase ventilation, clean components throughly and install.

NOTE: *On engines equipped with a Thermactor exhaust emission control system, install the air manifold assembly on the cylinder head. Connect the air pump outlet hose to the air manifold. Connect the anti-backfire valve, air and vacuum lines to the intake manifold.*

27. Connect accelerator rod pull-back spring. Connect choke control cable and the accelerator rod at the carburetor.

28. Connect distributor control vacuum line at distributor. Connect carburetor fuel line at fuel filter.

29. Connect temperature sending unit wire at sending unit. Connect spark plug wires.

30. Completely fill and bleed the cooling system.

31. Run engine for a minimum of 30 minutes at 1,200 rpm to stabilize engine temperature. Then, check for coolant and oil leaks.

32. Adjust engine idle mixture speed. Check valve lash and adjust, if necessary.

33. Install valve rocker arm cover, then the air cleaner.

All V8

1. Drain the cooling system.

2. Remove the intake manifold and the carburetor as an assembly, following the procedures under "Intake Manifold Removal."

3. Disconnect the spark plug wires, marking them as to placement. Position them out of the way of the cylinder head. Remove spark plugs.

4. Disconnect the resonator or muffler inlet pipe(s) at the exhaust manifold(s).

NOTE: *On some 351 and 400 engines, it may be necessary to remove the exhaust manifolds from the cylinder heads to gain access to the lower head bolts.*

5. Disconnect the battery ground cable at the cylinder head (if applicable).

6. Remove the rocker arm covers.

7. On cars with air conditioning, remove the mounting bolts and the drive belt, and position the compressor out of the way of the cylinder head. Remove the compressor upper mounting bracket from the cylinder head.

CAUTION: *If the compressor refrigerant lines do not have enough slack to permit repositioning of the compressor without first disconnecting the refrigerant lines, the air conditioning system will have to be evacuated by a trained air conditioning servicemen. Under no circumstances should an untrained person attempt to disconnect the air conditioning refrigerant lines.*

8. In order to remove the left cylinder head, on cars equipped with power steering, it may be necessary to remove the steering pump and bracket, remove the drive belt, and wire or tie the pump out of the way, but in such a way as to prevent the loss of its fluid.

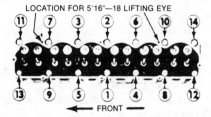

Six-cylinder head bolt torque sequence

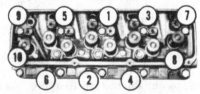

V8 cylinder head bolt torque sequence

9. In order to remove the right head it may be necessary to remove the alternator mounting bracket bolt and spacer, the ignition coil, and the air cleaner inlet duct from the right cylinder head.

10. In order to remove the left cylinder head on a car equipped with a Thermactor exhaust emission control system, disconnect the hose from the air manifold on the left cylinder head.

11. If the right cylinder head is to be removed on a car equipped with a Thermactor exhaust emission control system, remove the Thermactor air pump and its mounting bracket. Disconnect the hose from the air manifold on the right cylinder head.

12. On 390 and 428 engines, unbolt the rocker arm shafts from front to back, two turns at a time, and remove the rocker shaft and arm assembly. On all other V8 engines, loosen the rocker arm stud nuts or mounting bolts enough to rotate the rocker arms to one side in order to facilitate the removal of the pushrods. On all V8 engines, remove the pushrods in sequence, so that they may be installed in their original positions. On all V8 engines except the 390 and 428 V8, remove the exhaust valve stem caps.

NOTE: *After rotating the rocker arms from the valve stems, remove the exhaust valve caps from the stems of the exhaust valves. They are small and easy to lose. Remember to reinstall them.*

13. Remove the cylinder head attaching bolts, noting their positions. Lift the cylinder head off the block. Remove and discard the old cylinder head gasket.

14. Prior to installation, clean all surfaces where gaskets are to be installed. These include the cylinder head, intake manifold, rocker arm (valve) cover, and the cylinder block contact surfaces.

15. Position the new cylinder head gasket over the cylinder dowels on the block. Coat the head bolts with water-resistant sealer. Position new gaskets on the muffler inlet pipes at the exhaust manifold flange.

16. Position the cylinder head to the block, and install the head bolts, each in its original position. On all engines on which the exhaust manifold has been removed from the head to facilitate removal, it is necessary to properly guide the exhaust manifold studs into the muffler inlet pipe flange when installing the head.

17. Following the cylinder head torque sequence diagrams, step-torque the cylinder head bolts in three stages. First, torque the bolts to 20 ft. lbs. less than the maximum figure listed in the "Torque Specifications" chart. Second, torque the bolts to 10 ft. lbs. less than

the maximum figure. Finally, torque the bolts to the maximum figure in the chart. At this point, tighten the exhaust manifold-to-cylinder head attaching bolts to specifications.

18. Tighten the nuts on the exhaust manifold studs at the muffler inlet flanges to 18 ft. lbs.

19. Clean and inspect the pushrods one at a time. Clean the oil passage within each pushrod with a suitable solvent and blow the passage out with compressed air. Check the ends of the pushrods for nicks, grooves, roughness, or excessive wear. Visually inspect the pushrods for straightness, and replace any bent ones. Do not attempt to straighten pushrods.

20. Install the pushrods in their original positions. Apply Lubriplate or a similar product to the valve stem tips and to the pushrod guides in the cylinder head. Install the exhaust valve stem caps.

21. On 390 and 428 V8 engines, the intake manifold and rocker arm and shaft assemblies must now be installed. When tightening down the rocker arm shaft assembly, make sure that the oil holes face downward, the identification notch faces downward and toward the front (right bank) or toward the rear (left bank), and that the crankshaft damper has the "XX" mark aligned with the pointer. The rocker arms bolts are tightened front to rear, two turns at a time, to avoid bending pushrods.

22. On all V8 engines except the 390 and 428, apply white grease to the fulcrum seats and sockets. Turn the rocker arms to their proper positions and tighten the stud nuts or mounting bolts enough to hold the rocker arms in position. Make sure that the lower ends of the pushrods have remained properly seated in the valve lifters.

23. On all V8 engines except the 390 and 428, perform a preliminary valve adjustment.

24. Apply a coat of oil-resistant sealer to the upper side of the new valve cover gasket. Position the gasket on the valve cover with the cemented side of the gasket facing the valve cover. Install the valve covers and tighten the bolts to 3–5 ft. lbs.

25. Install the intake manifold and carburetor.

26. Refer to Steps 7–11 (inclusive) of the "Removal" procedure and reverse the procedures if applicable to your car.

27. Adjust all drive belts which were removed.

28. Refill the cooling system.

29. Connect the battery ground cable at the cylinder head (if applicable).

30. Install the spark plugs and connect the spark plug wires.

31. Start the engine and check for leaks.

32. With the engine running, check and adjust the carburetor idle speed and mixture.

33. With the engine running, listen for abnormal valve noises or irregular idle and correct them.

CLEANING AND INSPECTING

Chip carbon away from the valve heads, combustion chambers, and ports, using a chisel made of hardwood. Remove the remaining deposits with a stiff wire brush.

NOTE: *Be sure that the deposits are actually removed, rather than burnished.*
Clean the remaining cylinder head parts with cleaning solvent. Do not remove the protective coating from the springs. Check for cracks and/or damage. Repair as needed.

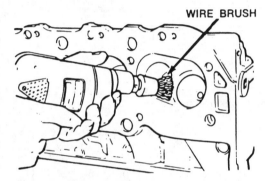

Removing the carbon from the cylinder head with a wire brush and electric drill

RESURFACING

NOTE: *Resurfacing should only be performed by a reputable machine shop. The following you can do to determine if resurfacing is necessary.*
Place a straight-edge across the gasket surface of the cylinder head. Using feeler gauges, determine the clearance at the center of the straight-edge. If warpage exceeds .003" in a 6" span, or .006" over the total length, the cylinder head must be resurfaced.

NOTE: *If warpage exceeds the manufactur-*

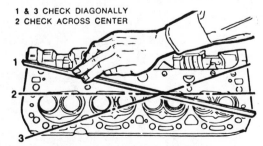

Checking the cylinder head for warpage

er's maximum tolerance for material removal, the cylinder head must be replaced.

When milling the cylinder heads of V-type engines, the intake manifold mounting position is altered, and must be corrected by milling the manifold flange a proportionate amount.

CAUTION: *Do not plane or grind more than .010 in. from the original cylinder head gasket surface.*

PRELIMINARY VALVE ADJUSTMENT

All engines used in full-size Ford products, from 1968 to the present, are equipped with hydraulic valve lifters. Valve systems with hydraulic valve lifters operate with zero clearance in the valve train, and because of this the rocker arms are nonadjustable. The only means by which valve system clearances can be altered is by installing 0.060 in. over or undersize pushrods; but, because of the hydraulic lifter's natural ability to compensate for slack in the valve train, all components of the valve system should be checked for wear if there is excessive play in the system.

When a valve in the engine is in the closed position, the valve lifter is resting on the base circle of the camshaft lobe and the pushrod is in its lowest position. To remove this additional clearance from the valve train, the valve lifter expands to maintain zero clearance in the valve system. When a rocker arm is loosened or removed from the engine, the lifter expands to its fullest travel. When the rocker arm is reinstalled on the engine, the proper valve setting is obtained by tightening the rocker arm to a specified limit. But with the lifter fully expanded, if the camshaft lobe is on a high point it will require excessive torque to compress the lifter and obtain the proper setting. Because of this, when any component of the valve system has been removed, a preliminary valve adjustment procedure must be followed to ensure that when the rocker arm is reinstalled on the engine and tightened, the camshaft lobe for that cylinder is in the low position.

Six-Cylinder

1. Crank the engine until the TDC mark on the crankshaft damper is aligned with timing pointer on the cylinder front cover.

2. Scribe a mark on the damper at this point.

3. Scribe two more marks on the damper, each equally spaced from the first mark (see illustration).

4. With the engine on TDC of the compression stroke, (mark A aligned with the pointer) back off the rocker arm adjusting nut

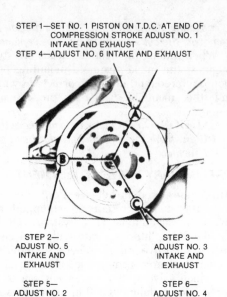

STEP 1—SET NO. 1 PISTON ON T.D.C. AT END OF
COMPRESSION STROKE ADJUST NO. 1
INTAKE AND EXHAUST
STEP 4—ADJUST NO. 6 INTAKE AND EXHAUST

STEP 2—	STEP 3—
ADJUST NO. 5	ADJUST NO. 3
INTAKE AND	INTAKE AND
EXHAUST	EXHAUST

STEP 5—	STEP 6—
ADJUST NO. 2	ADJUST NO. 4
INTAKE AND	INTAKE AND
EXHAUST	EXHAUST

Position of crankshaft for preliminary valve adjustment—six-cylinder

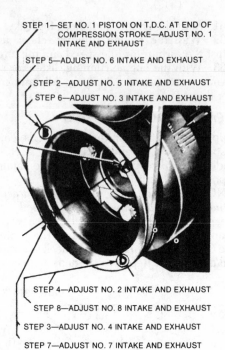

STEP 1—SET NO. 1 PISTON ON T.D.C. AT END OF
COMPRESSION STROKE—ADJUST NO. 1
INTAKE AND EXHAUST

STEP 5—ADJUST NO. 6 INTAKE AND EXHAUST

STEP 2—ADJUST NO. 5 INTAKE AND EXHAUST

STEP 6—ADJUST NO. 3 INTAKE AND EXHAUST

STEP 4—ADJUST NO. 2 INTAKE AND EXHAUST

STEP 8—ADJUST NO. 8 INTAKE AND EXHAUST

STEP 3—ADJUST NO. 4 INTAKE AND EXHAUST

STEP 7—ADJUST NO. 7 INTAKE AND EXHAUST

Position of crankshaft for preliminary valve adjustment—1968–69 302 V8 without positive stop rocker arm stud

until there is end-play in the pushrod. Tighten the adjusting nut until all clearance is removed, then tighten the adjusting nut one additional turn on 1969 and later models and ¾ of a turn on all 1968 models. To determine when all clearance is removed from the rocker arm, turn the pushrod with the fingers. When the pushrod can no longer be turned, all clearance has been removed.

5. Repeat this procedure for each valve, turning the crankshaft ⅓ turn to the next mark each time and following the engine firing order of 1-5-3-6-2-4.

1968–69 302 V8

NOTE: *This procedure for the early 302 V8 engine is designed for engines in which the rocker arm mounting studs do not incorporate a positive stop shoulder on the mounting stud. These engines were originally equipped with this kind of stud. However, due to production differences, it is possible some early 302 engines may be encountered that are equipped with positive stop rocker arm mounting studs. Before following this procedure, verify that the rocker arm mounting studs do not incorporate a positive stop shoulder. On studs without a positive stop, the shank portion of the stud that is exposed just above the cylinder head is the same diameter as the threaded portion, at the top of the stud, to which the rocker arm retaining nut attaches. If the shank portion of the stud is of greater diameter than the threaded portion, this identifies it as a*

positive stop rocker arm stud and the procedure for the 351 engine should be followed.

1. Crank the engine until the No. 1 cylinder is at TDC of the compression stroke and

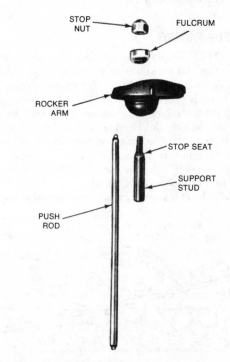

Positive stop rocker arm stud and nut

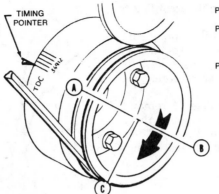

With No. 1 at TDC at end of compression stroke make a chalk mark at points B and C approximately 90 degrees apart.

TIMING POINTER

POSITION A – No. 1 at TDC at end of compression stroke.

POSITION B – Rotate the crankshaft 180 degrees (one half revolution) clockwise from POSITION A.

POSITION C – Rotate the crankshaft 270 degrees (three quarter revolution) clockwise from POSITION B.

Position of crankshaft for preliminary valve adjustment—1969–75 302, 351, 400, 429 and 460 V8

the timing pointer is aligned with the mark on the crankshaft damper.

2. Scribe a mark on the damper at this point.

3. Scribe three more marks on the damper, dividing the damper into quarters (see illustration).

4. With mark A aligned with the timing pointer, adjust the valves on the No. 1 cylinder by backing off the adjusting nut until the pushrod has free play in it. Then, tighten the nut until there is no free play in the rocker arm. This can be determined by turning the pushrod while tightening the nut; when the pushrod can no longer be turned, all clearance has been removed. After the clearance has been removed, tighten the nut an additional ¾ of a turn.

5. Repeat this procedure for each valve, turning the crankshaft ¼ turn to the next mark each time and following the engine firing order of 1-5-4-2-6-3-7-8.

All Other V8 Engines

1. Crank the engine until the No. 1 cylinder is at TDC of the compression stroke and the timing pointer is aligned with the mark on the crankshaft damper.

2. Scribe a mark on the damper at this point.

3. Scribe two additional marks on the damper (see illustration).

4. With the timing pointer aligned with mark A on the damper, tighten the following valves to the specified torque:
- *255, 302, 429, and 460* No. 1, 7 and 8 Intake; No. 1, 5, and 4 Exhaust
- *351 and 400* No. 1, 4, and 8 Intake; No. 1, 3, and 7 Exhaust

5. Rotate the crankshaft 180° to point B and tighten the following valves:
- *255, 302, 429, and 460* No. 5 and 4 Intake; No. 2 and 6 Exhaust

- *351 and 400* No. 3 and 7 Intake; No. 2 and 6 Exhaust

6. Rotate the crankshaft 270° to point C and tighten the following valves:
- *255, 302, 429, and 460* No. 2, 3, and 6 Intake; No. 7, 3, and 8 Exhaust
- *351 and 400* No. 2, 5, and 6 Intake; No. 4, 5, and 8 Exhaust

7. Rocker arm tightening specifications are: 255, 302 and 351W—tighten nut until it contacts the rocker shoulder, then torque to 18–20 ft. lbs.; 351C and 400—tighten bolt to 18–25 ft. lbs.; 428 and 460—tighten nut until it contacts rocker shoulder, then torque to 18–22 ft. lbs.

Valves and Springs
REMOVAL AND INSTALLATION

1. Remove the cylinder head as previously outlined.

2. Invert the cylinder head, and number the valve faces front to rear, using a permanent felt-tip marker.

3. Remove the rocker arms with shaft(s) or balls and nuts. Wire the sets of rockers, balls

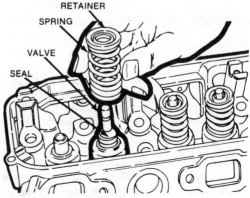

Installing valve stem seals

and nuts together, and identify according to the corresponding valve.

4. Using an appropriate valve spring compressor, compress the valve springs. Lift out the keepers with needlenose pliers, release the compressor, and remove the valve, spring, and spring retainer.

5. Installation is the reverse of removal, with the following recommendations. Always install a new valve stem seal. Use a ⅝" deep wall socket and a light hammer to seat the new seal.

INSPECTION

Check for burned and/or damaged valves. Repair or replace as necessary. Place the spring on a flat surface next to a square. Measure the height of the spring, and rotate it against the edge of the square to measure distortion. If spring height varies (by comparison) by more than ¹⁄₁₆" or if distortion exceeds ¹⁄₁₆", replace the spring. In addition to evaluating the spring as above, test the spring pressure at the installed height using a valve spring tester. A tolerance of ∓ 5 lbs. is permissible.

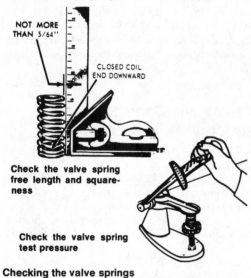

Check the valve springs:

NOT MORE THAN 5/64"

CLOSED COIL END DOWNWARD

Check the valve spring free length and square-ness

Check the valve spring test pressure

Checking the valve springs

REFACING

NOTE: *This procedure should only be performed by a qualified machine shop.*

Using a valve grinder, resurface the valves according to specifications given earlier in this chapter.

CAUTION: *Valve face angle is not always identical to valve seat angle.*

A minimum margin of ¹⁄₃₂" should remain after grinding the valve. The valve stem top should also be squared and resurfaced, by placing the

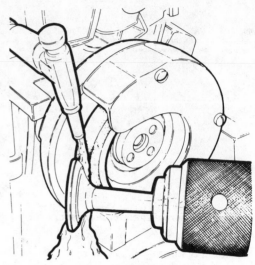

Valve grinding by machine

stem in the V-block of the grinder, and turning it while pressing lightly against the grinding wheel.

NOTE: *Do not grind sodium filled exhaust valves on a machine. These should be hand lapped.*

VALVE GUIDES

Ford Motor Company engines use integral valve guides. Mercury and Ford dealers offer valves with oversize stems for worn guides.

Valve Guides

NOTE: *This procedure should only be attempted by a qualified machine shop.*

If it becomes necessary to ream a valve guide, to install a valve with a larger stem, reaming kits are available. The Ford kit contains the following reamer and pilot combinations.

.003 in. oversize reamer with a standard pilot.

.015 in. oversize reamer with a .003 in oversize pilot.

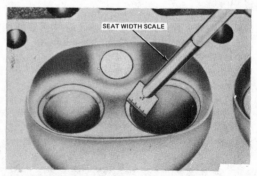

Checking the valve seat width

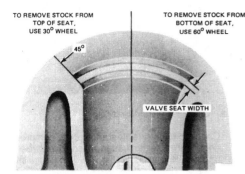

TO REMOVE STOCK FROM
TOP OF SEAT,
USE 30° WHEEL

TO REMOVE STOCK FROM
BOTTOM OF SEAT,
USE 60° WHEEL

45°

VALVE SEAT WIDTH

Facing the valve seat

.030 in. oversize reamer with a .015 in. oversize pilot.

When replacing a standard size valve, with an oversize one, always start with the (smallest oversize first and then the next smallest) so not to overload the reamers.

CAUTION: *Always reface the valve seats after the guide has been reamed. Use a suitable scraper to break the sharp corner at the top of the guide.*

Valve Seats

Resurfacing the valve seats is necessary when refacing the valves. This is necessary to provide a compression-tight fit.

NOTE: *This procedure should only be attempted by a qualified machine shop.*

Grind the seats to a 45° angle. Remove only enough stock to clean up pits, grooves, or to correct seat run-out. After the seat has been refaced, use a machinists scale to measure seat width.

If the seat width exceeds the maximum limit remove enough stock from the top and/or bottom to bring into specifications. The valve seats of all engines use a 60° angle grinding wheel to remove stock from the bottom of the seats (raise the seats) and a 30° angle wheel to remove stock from the top of the seats (lower the seats).

The finished seat should contact the approximate center of the valve face.

Rocker Arms

390 and 428 V8 engines utilize shaft-mounted rocker arm assemblies. Removal and installation procedures for these rocker arm assemblies are included under the "Cylinder Head Removal and Installation" procedure. Remember that the oil holes must always face downward and that the large rocker shaft retaining bolt is always the second from the front of the engine. In all cases, the torque sequence for the rocker shaft retaining bolts is from the front to the rear of the engine, two

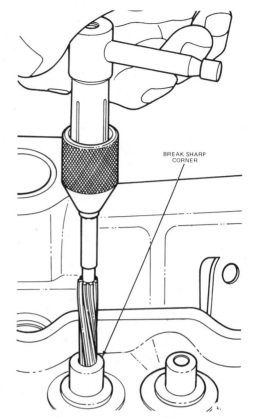

BREAK SHARP
CORNER

Reaming the valve guides—typical

turns at a time. Torque the retaining bolts to 40–45 ft. lbs.

The 240 six-cylinder and all other V8 engines are equipped with individual stud-mounted or pedestal bolt and fulcrum mounted rocker arms. Use the following procedure to remove the rocker arms:

1. Disconnect the choke heat chamber air hose, the air cleaner and inlet duct assembly,

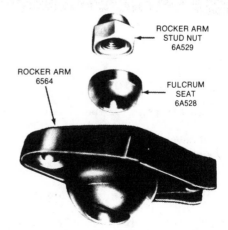

ROCKER ARM
STUD NUT
6A529

ROCKER ARM
6564

FULCRUM
SEAT
6A528

Valve rocker arm and related parts—240 six, 302 V8, 351W V8

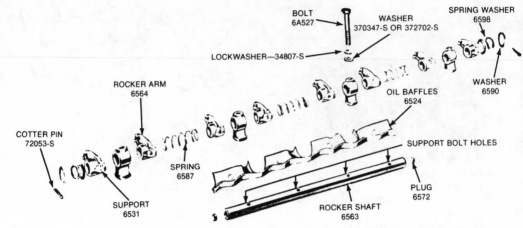

BOLT
6A527

WASHER
370347-S OR 372702-S

SPRING WASHER
6598

LOCKWASHER—34807-S

ROCKER ARM
6564

OIL BAFFLES
6524

WASHER
6590

COTTER PIN
72053-S

SUPPORT BOLT HOLES

SPRING
6587

PLUG
6572

SUPPORT
6531

ROCKER SHAFT
6563

390, 428 V8 valve rocker arm shaft assembly

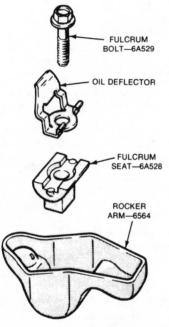

FULCRUM
BOLT—6A529

OIL DEFLECTOR

FULCRUM
SEAT—6A528

ROCKER
ARM—6564

Valve rocker arm and related parts—fulcrum mounted

the choke heat tube, PCV valve and hose and the EGR hoses (if so equipped).

2. On models so equipped, disconnect the Thermactor by-pass valve and air supply hoses.

3. Label and disconnect the spark plug wires at the plugs. Remove the plug wires from the looms.

4. Remove the valve cover attaching bolts and remove the cover(s).

5. Remove the valve rocker arm stud nut, fulcrum seat, and then the rocker arm.

6. Reverse the above procedure to install, taking care to adjust the valve lash as outlined under "Preliminary Valve Adjustment."

Intake Manifold

REMOVAL AND INSTALLATION

All V8

1. Drain the cooling system.

2. Disconnect the upper radiator hose and water pump by-pass hose from the thermostat housing. Disconnect the water temperature sending unit wire. Remove the heater hose from the automatic choke housing and disconnect the hose from the intake manifold.

3. Remove the air cleaner. Disconnect the automatic choke heat chamber air inlet hose at the inlet tube near the right valve cover. Remove the crankcase ventilation hose and intake duct assembly. On all models so equipped, disconnect the Thermactor air hose from the check valve at the rear of the intake manifold and loosen the hose clamp at the bracket. Remove the air hose and Thermactor air by-pass valve from the bracket and position it to one side.

4. Remove all carburetor linkage and automatic transmission kick-down linkage that attaches to the manifold. Disconnect the fuel line, choke heat tube, and any vacuum lines from the carburetor or intake manifold, marking them for installation.

5. Disconnect the distributor vacuum hoses from the distributor. Remove the distributor cap and mark the relative position of the rotor on the distributor housing. Disconnect the spark plug wires at the spark plugs and the primary and secondary wires from the coil. Remove the distributor hold-down bolt and remove the distributor.

6. If equipped with air conditioning, remove the brackets retaining the compressor to the intake manifold.

7. On 390 and 428 engines, remove the valve covers the rocker arm assemblies and the

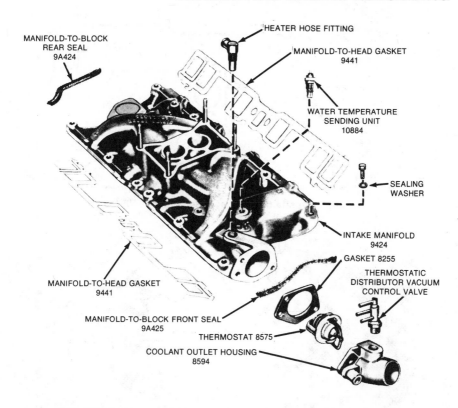

302, 351V intake manifold assembly—255, 428, 429 and 460 similar

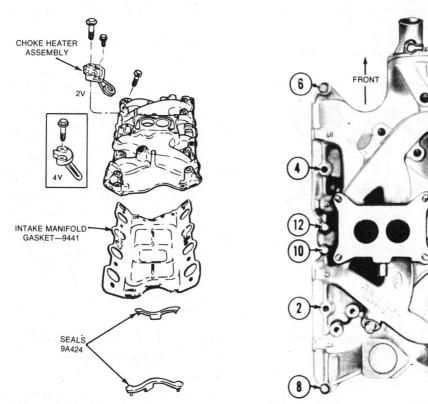

351C, 351M, 400 V8 intake manifold assembly

Intake manifold torque sequence—255 and 302 V8

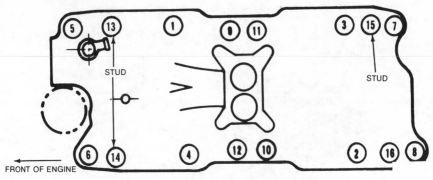

Intake manifold torque sequence—351W V8

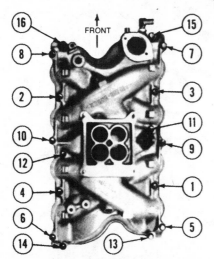

Intake manifold torque sequence—429, 460 V8

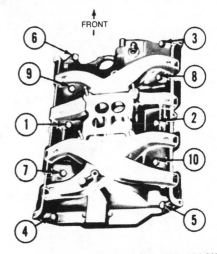

Intake manifold torque sequence—390, 428 V8

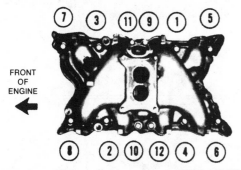

Intake manifold torque sequence—351C, 351M, 400 V8

pushrods. The rocker arms should be removed by backing off each of the four bolts two turns at a time, from front to back. Keep the pushrods in order so that they can be installed in their original positions.

8. Remove the manifold attaching bolts. Lift off the intake manifold and carburetor as an assembly.

NOTE: *If it is necessary to pry the manifold to loosen it from the engine, be careful not*

to damage any gasket sealing surfaces. Always discard all old gaskets and attaching bolt sealing washers.

9. Clean all gasket surfaces and firmly cement new gaskets in place, using non-hardening sealer. Apply $1/16$ inch bead of silicone RTV sealer at the points where the intake gasket and end seals interlock, and along the full length of the seals. Make sure that the gaskets interlock with the seal tabs, and that the gasket holes align with those in the cylinder heads.

10. Reverse the above procedure to install, taking care to run a finger around the seal area on the installed manifold to make sure that the seals did not slip out during installation. Finally, torque the intake manifold bolts in the proper sequence, and recheck the torque after the engine is warm.

Intake and Exhaust Manifold
REMOVAL AND INSTALLATION
Six-Cylinder

1. Remove the air cleaner. Remove the carburetor linkage and kick down linkage from the engine.

2. Disconnect the fuel line from the carburetor and all vacuum lines from the manifolds.

3. Remove the negative battery cable, then remove the alternator mounting bolts and remove the alternator from the engine with the wires attached.

4. Disconnect the muffler inlet pipe from the engine.

5. Remove the manifold attaching parts from the engine, and remove the two manifolds as an assembly.

6. To separate the manifolds, remove the carburetor and then remove the nuts which secure the manifolds together.

7. Clean all gasket areas and reverse above procedure to install; using all new gaskets. Torque to specifications listed in the "Torque Specifications" chart.

Exhaust Manifold
REMOVAL AND INSTALLATION
All V8

1. On the right exhaust manifold, remove the air cleaner and intake duct assembly.

2. Disconnect the automatic choke heat chamber air inlet hose from the inlet tube near the right valve cover. Remove the automatic choke heat tube.

3. Remove the nuts or bolts retaining the heat stove to the exhaust manifold and remove the stove.

4. Disconnect the exhaust manifold(s) from the muffler inlet pipe(s).

5. Remove the manifold retaining bolts and washers and the manifold(s).

6. Reverse the above procedure to install, using new inlet pipe gaskets. Torque the exhaust manifold retaining bolts to specifications, in sequence from the centermost bolt outward. Start the engine and check for exhaust leaks.

Timing Gear Cover
REMOVAL AND INSTALLATION
Six-Cylinder

1. Drain the cooling system and the crankcase.

2. Remove the radiator from the car.

3. Loosen and remove all engine drive belts.

4. On vehicles with power steering, disconnect the pump mounting bracket from the cylinder front cover and position the pump and bracket out of the way.

5. On models with air conditioning, remove the condenser mounting bolts and position the condenser out of the way. *Do not disconnect the refrigerant lines.*

6. Disconnect and remove the fan and fan spacer.

7. Remove any accessory drive pulleys from the crankshaft damper. Remove the capscrew and washer from the crankshaft end; then, using a puller, remove the crankshaft damper.

8. Remove the alternator adjusting arm bolt and position the arm out of the way. Remove the dipstick.

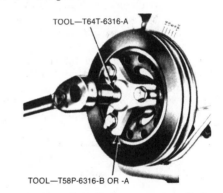

Removing crankshaft damper—six-cylinder and 390, 428 V8

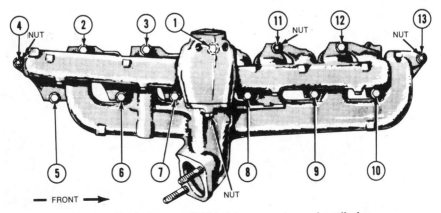

Intake and exhaust manifold torque sequence—six cylinder

9. Remove the bolts retaining the timing cover to the block. Remove the front cover and accessory drive belt idler pulley assembly (if so equipped), and discard the gasket.

10. Reverse the above procedure to install, using a new gasket. Torque the timing cover bolts to 15–20 ft. lbs.

Timing Gear Cover and Chain
REMOVAL AND INSTALLATION
All V8

1. Drain the cooling system and crankcase.

2. Disconnect the negative battery cable.

3. If equipped with a fan shroud, disconnect it from the radiator and position rearward.

4. Remove the radiator. Remove the fuel pump.

5. Remove the fan attaching bolts, the fan, fan spacer and shroud from the engine.

6. Loosen and remove all engine drive belts.

7. Remove the power steering pump mounting bracket and position the pump and bracket out of the way.

8. If equipped with air conditioning, remove the compressor and condenser and position them out of the way. *Do not disconnect the refrigerant lines.*

9. Disconnect the alternator adjusting arm from the engine and position it out of the way.

10. If equipped with Thermactor, remove the pump from the engine.

11. Disconnect the heater hose and bypass hose from the water pump.

12. Remove any accessory drive pulleys from the crankshaft damper and remove the crankshaft front bolt and washer.

TIMING MARKS

Aligning timing marks—all V8s

13. Using a puller, remove the crankshaft damper from the engine.

14. On 390 and 428 V8, use a suitable tool to pull the crankshaft sleeve away from the cylinder front cover. Remove the sleeve from the engine.

15. Remove the front cover attaching bolts and the front oil pan bolts.

16. Remove the cover from the engine.

17. Remove the crankshaft front oil-slinger.

18. To check timing chain free-play, rotate the crankshaft in a clockwise direction until all slack is removed from the left-side of the chain. Scribe a mark on the engine parallel to the

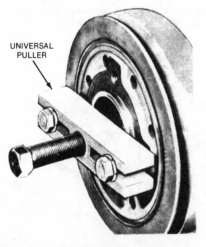

UNIVERSAL PULLER

Removing crankshaft damper—V8 except 390, 428 V8

TOOL—T52L-6306-AEE or 6306-AJ

Installing crankshaft damper—all engines

Fuel pump eccentric and front oil slinger
installed—all V8 except 390, 428 V8

present position of the chain. Next, rotate the crankshaft in a counterclockwise direction to remove all the slack from the right-side of the chain. Force the left-side of the chain outward with the fingers and measure the distance between the present position of the chain and the reference mark on the engine. If the distance exceeds ½ in., replace the chain and sprockets.

19. To replace the chain and sprockets, crank the engine until the timing marks are aligned as shown in the illustration.

20. Remove the camshaft sprocket attaching bolt and remove the chain and sprockets from the engine by sliding them forward as an assembly.

21. To install, position the chain and

sprockets on the engine, making sure that the timing marks on the sprockets are aligned.

22. Clean all gasket surfaces. Trim away the exposed portion of the oil pan gasket flush with the front of the block. (See timing cover oil seal replacement).

23. Cut and position the required portion of a new gasket to the oil pan, applying sealer to both sides of it.

24. Reinstall the front cover, applying oil-resistant sealer to the new gasket.

25. Install the components that were removed from the engine by reversing the removal procedure.

Timing Gear and Camshaft
REMOVAL AND INSTALLATION
Six-Cylinder

1. Remove the timing case cover.
2. Mark the location of the grille center support and hood lock assembly in relation to the radiator support. Remove the grille, center support, and hood lock as an assembly.
3. Remove the air cleaner and valve cover.
4. Disconnect the fuel pump outlet line and remove the fuel pump from the engine.
5. Loosen the rocker arm nuts and position the rocker arms to the side so the pushrods can be removed. Keep the pushrods in order so that they can be returned to their original location in the engine.
6. Remove the pushrod cover from the side of the engine, and, using a magnet, remove the lifters from their bores. Keep the lifters in order so that they can be returned to their original location in the engine.
7. Rotate the engine until the timing marks are aligned on the timing gears.
8. Remove the camshaft thrust plate screws.
9. Remove the camshaft by pulling it slowly out the front of the engine. Use care

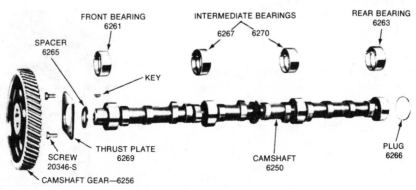

Six-cylinder camshaft and related parts

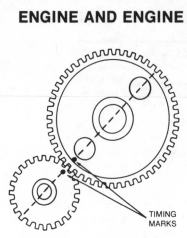

Aligning timing marks—six-cylinder

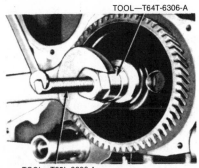

TOOL—T64T-6306-A

TOOL—T65L-6306-A

Installing camshaft timing gear

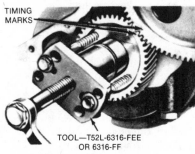

TIMING MARKS

TOOL—T52L-6316-FEE OR 6316-FF

Removing crankshaft timing gear

not to damage the camshaft lobes or journals while removing the cam from the engine.

10. Place the camshaft/gear assembly in a press and press the cam from the gear.

11. Position new gear on camshaft and press into position.

12. Using a puller, remove the crankshaft timing gear.

13. Using a suitable tool, press the new gear onto the crankshaft.

14. Before installing the camshaft in the engine, coat the lobes with lubriplate and the journals and all valve train components with heavy oil.

15. Reverse above procedure to install, following recommended torque settings and performing preliminary valve adjustment before starting engine.

Camshaft

REMOVAL AND INSTALLATION
All V8

1. Remove the intake manifold.

2. Remove the cylinder front cover, timing chain and sprockets as outlined previously.

3. Remove the rocker arm covers.

4. On 390 and 428 engines it is necessary to remove the rocker arm shafts to remove the intake manifold. On all other engines with individual rocker arms, loosen the rocker arm fulcrum bolts and rotate the rocker arms to the side.

5. Remove the pushrods and lifters and keep them in order so that they can be installed in their original location.

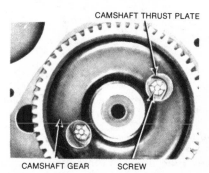

CAMSHAFT THRUST PLATE

CAMSHAFT GEAR   SCREW

Camshaft thrust plate screw locations—six-cylinder

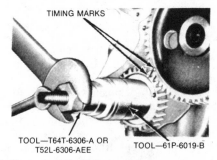

TIMING MARKS

TOOL—T64T-6306-A OR T52L-6306-AEE   TOOL—61P-6019-B

Installing crankshaft timing gear

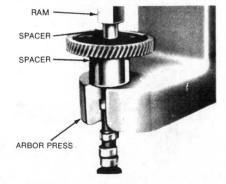

RAM

SPACER

SPACER

ARBOR PRESS

Removing the camshaft gear using a press

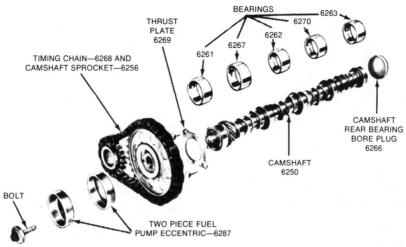

V8 camshaft and related parts—typical

6. Remove the camshaft thrust plate and washer if so equipped. Remove the camshaft from the front of the engine. On certain engine/chassis combinations it may be necessary to remove the grille to gain adequate clearance to remove the camshaft. Use care not to damage the camshaft lobes or journals while removing the cam from the engine.

7. Before installing the camshaft in the engine, coat the lobes with lubriplate and the journals and all valve train components with heavy oil.

8. Reverse above procedure to install.

9. On all engines with individually mounted rocker arms, a preliminary valve adjustment must be performed before starting the engine.

BEARING REMOVAL

1. Remove the camshaft, flywheel, and crankshaft.

2. Push the pistons to the top of the cylinders.

3. Remove the rear camshaft bearing plug.

4. Remove the camshaft bearings, using a camshaft bearing removal tool.

5. Installation is the reverse of removal. Thoroughly oil the camshaft before reinstalling.

CHECKING CAMSHAFT

Degrease the camshaft, using solvent, and clean out all oil holes. Visually inspect cam lobes and bearing journals for excessive wear. If a lobe is questionable, check all lobes as indicated below. If a journal or lobe is worn, the camshaft must be reground or replaced.

NOTE: *If a journal is worn, there is a good chance that the bushings are worn.*

If lobes and journals appear intact, place the front and rear journals in V-blocks, and rest a dial indicator on the center journal. Rotate the camshaft to check straightness. If deviation exceeds .001", replace the camshaft.

Check the camshaft lobes with a micrometer, by measuring the lobes from the nose to base and again at 90° (see illustration). The lift

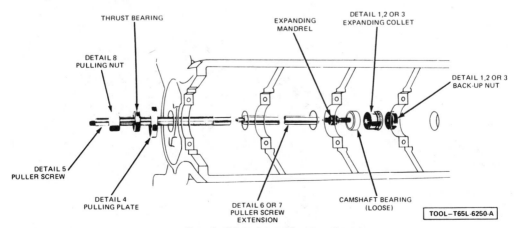

Camshaft bearing replacement

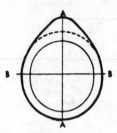

Camshaft lobe measurement

is determined by subtracting the second measurement from the first. If all exhaust lobes and all intake lobes are not identical, the camshaft must be reground or replaced.

Timing Gear Cover Oil Seal
REPLACEMENT
All Engines

It is a recommended procedure to replace the cover seal any time that the timing (front) cover is removed.

1. With the cover removed from the engine, drive the old seal from the rear of the cover with a pin punch. Clean out the recess in the cover.

2. Coat the new seal with grease (to ease installation) and drive it into the cover until it is fully seated. Check the seal after installation to be sure that the spring is properly positioned in the seal.

Pistons and Connecting Rods
REMOVAL AND INSTALLATION

1. Drain crankcase and remove oil pan. Remove oil baffle tray if so equipped.

2. Drain cooling system and remove cylinder head or heads.

3. Remove any ridge and/or deposits from the upper end of cylinder bores with a ridge reamer.

4. Check rods and pistons for identification numbers and, if necessary, number them.

5. Remove connecting rod capnuts and caps. Push the rods away from the crankshaft and install caps and nuts loosely to their respective rods.

6. Push pistons and rod assemblies up and out of the cylinders.

7. Prior to installation, lightly coat pistons, rings and cylinder walls with light engine oil.

8. With bearing caps removed, install pieces of protective rubber hose on bearing cap bolts.

9. Install each piston in its respective bore, using thread guards on each assembly. Guide the rod bearing into place on the crankcase journal.

TOOL—T68P-6700-A

Installing the front engine oil seal

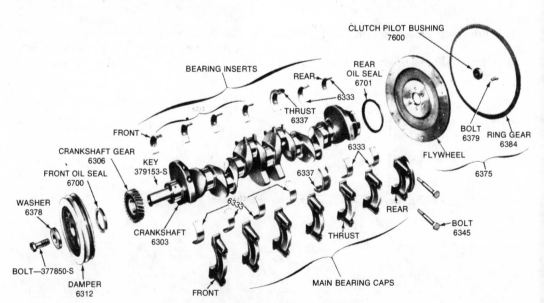

Crankshaft and related parts—six-cylinder

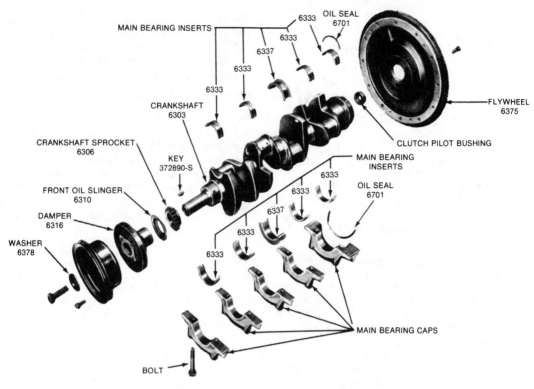

Crankshaft and related parts—typical V8

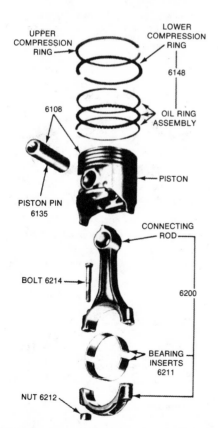

Typical piston, connecting rod and related parts

10. Remove thread guards from connecting rods and install lower half of bearing and cap. Check clearances.

11. Install oil pan.

12. Install cylinder head.

13. Refill crankcase and cooling system.

14. Start engine, bring to operating temperature and check for leaks.

ROD BEARING REPLACEMENT

1. Clean the journals. Inspect journals and thrust faces for nicks, or burrs, that will cause premature wear.

NOTE: *When replacing standard bearings with new bearings, it is recommended to fit the bearings to minimum specified clearance.*

2. Place a plastigauge on the bearing surface across the full width of the bearing cap about ¼ in. off center.

3. Install cap and tighten bolts to specifications. Do not turn the crankshaft while the plastigauge is in place.

4. Remove the cap. Using the plastigauge scale check width at widest point to get minimum clearance. Check also at the narrowest point. The difference is known as journal taper.

5. If clearance exceeds limits, try undersized bearings.

6. After bearings have been fitted, apply a

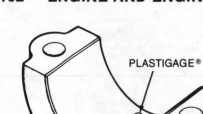

PLASTIGAGE®

Plastigauge installed on the lower bearing shell—typical

light coat of oil to the journal and bearing. Install the cap and tighten to specifications.

PISTON PIN REPLACEMENT

The piston pin clearance is designed to maintain adequate clearance under all engine operating conditions. Because of this, the piston and piston pin are a matched set and not serviced separately.

Inspect piston pin bores and piston pins for wear. Piston pin bores and piston pins must be free of varnish or scuffing when being measured. The piston pin should be measured with a micrometer and the piston pin bore should be measured with a dial bore gauge or an inside micrometer. If clearance is in excess of

the .001″ wear limit, the piston and piston pin assembly should be replaced.

NOTE: *The piston pin must be pressed in and out. This procedure should only be performed by a qualified machine shop.*

PISTON RING REPLACEMENT

Before replacing rings, inspect cylinder bores.

1. If cylinder bore is in satisfactory condition, place each ring in bore in turn and square it in bore with head of piston. Measure ring gap. If ring gap is greater than limit, get new ring. If ring gap is less than limit, file end of ring to obtain correct gap.

2. Check ring side clearance by installing

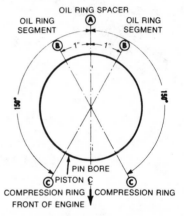

Piston ring spacing

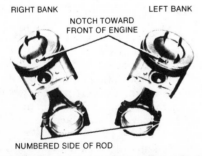

Correct piston and rod position—six-cylinder

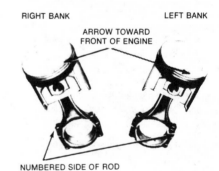

Correct piston and rod position—351C, 351M, 400 V8

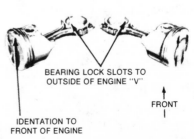

Correct piston and rod position—255, 302, 351V, 429 and 460 V8

Correct piston and rod position—390, 428 V8

rings on piston, and inserting feeler gauge to correct dimension between ring and lower land. Gauge should slide freely around ring circumference without binding. Any wear will form a step on lower land. Replace any pistons having high steps. Before checking ring side clearance be sure ring grooves are clean and free of carbon, sludge, or grit.

3. Space ring gaps at equal intervals around piston circumference. Be sure to install piston in its original bore. Install short lengths of rubber tubing over connecting rod bolts to prevent damage to rod journal. Install ring compressor over rings on piston. Lower piston rod assembly into bore until ring compressor contacts block. Using wooden handle of hammer, push piston into bore while guiding rod onto journal.

CLEANING AND INSPECTION

Remove the deposits from the piston surfaces using cleaning solvent.

NOTE: *Do not use a caustic cleaning solution or wire brush to clean pistons.*

Clean the ring grooves with a ring groove cleaner. Make sure the oil ring slots (or holes) are clean.

Carefully inspect pistons for fractures at the ring lands, skirts, pin bosses, and for scuffed, rough or scored skirts. Replace any pistons that are questionable.

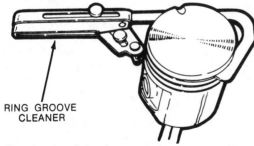

RING GROOVE CLEANER

Cleaning the piston ring grooves

ENGINE LUBRICATION

Oil Pan

REMOVAL AND INSTALLATION

Six-Cylinder

1. Drain crankcase and cooling system.
2. Disconnect upper hose at outlet elbow and lower hose at radiator. Remove the radiator.
3. Disconnect flexible fuel line at fuel pump.
4. With automatic transmission, disconnect kick-down rod at bellcrank assembly. On

car with manual transmission, disconnect clutch linkage.
5. Raise car on hoist.
6. Disconnect starter cable at starter. Remove retaining bolts and remove starter.
7. Remove nuts on both engine front support insulator-to-support brackets.
8. Remove bolt and insulator, rear support insulator-to-crossmember and insulator-to-transmission extension housing.
9. Raise transmission, remove support insulator, lower transmission, to crossmember.
10. Raise engine with transmission jack and place 3 in. thick wood blocks between both front support insulators and intermediate support brackets.
11. Remove oil pan retaining bolts and oil pump mounting bolts. With oil pump in pan, rotate crankshaft as needed to remove pan.
12. Install in reverse of above.

1968–69 302, 351 V8

1. Remove oil level dipstick. Drain oil pan.
2. Disconnect stabilizer bar from lower control arms, and pull ends down.
3. Remove oil pan attaching bolts and position pan on front crossmember.
4. Remove one oil inlet tube bolt and loosen the other to position tube out of way to remove pan.
5. Turn crankshaft as required for clearance to remove pan.
6. Install in reverse of above.

All Other V8 Engines Through 1978

1. Remove the shroud from the radiator and position it rearward over the fan. Disconnect the battery negative cable.
2. Raise and support the car on jackstands. Drain the oil. Position the transmission cooler lines out of the way, if necessary. Remove the sway bar attaching bolts and move the sway bar forward on the struts.
3. Remove nuts and lockwashers from the engine front support insulator-to-intermediate support bracket.
4. Install a block of wood on a jack and position a jack under the leading edge of the pan.
5. Raise the engine approximately 1¼ in. and insert a 1 in. block between the insulators and crossmember. Remove the floor jack. On 351C, 351M, 400, and 460 V8s, remove the starter. On 460 V8s through 1977, remove the oil filter.
6. Remove the oil pan attaching screws and lower the pan to the frame crossmember.
7. Turn the crankshaft to obtain clearance between the crankshaft counterweight and the rear of the pan.

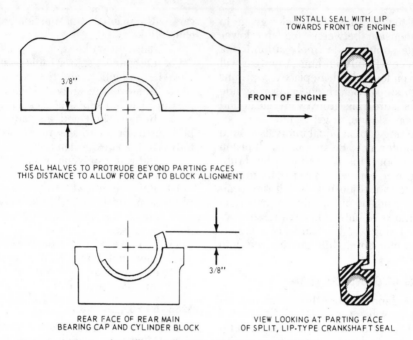

INSTALL SEAL WITH LIP
TOWARDS FRONT OF ENGINE

3/8''

FRONT OF ENGINE

SEAL HALVES TO PROTRUDE BEYOND PARTING FACES
THIS DISTANCE TO ALLOW FOR CAP TO BLOCK ALIGNMENT

3/8''

REAR FACE OF REAR MAIN
BEARING CAP AND CYLINDER BLOCK

VIEW LOOKING AT PARTING FACE
OF SPLIT, LIP-TYPE CRANKSHAFT SEAL

Installing split-type rubber rear oil seal

8. Remove the oil pump attaching bolts.

9. Position the tube and the screen out of the way and remove the pan.

10. To install, clean the gasket mounting surfaces thoroughly. Coat the surfaces on the block and pan with sealer. Position the pan side gaskets on the engine block.

11. Install the front cover oil seal on the cover, with the tabs over the pan side gaskets. Install the rear main cap seal with the tabs over the pan side gaskets.

12. Install the pan mounting bolts, tightening them on each side from the center outwards to 9–11 ft. lbs. for $5/16$ in. bolts, 7–9 ft. lbs. for ¼ in. bolts. Complete the installation by reversing Steps 1–5.

1979 and Later Without EGR Cooler

1. Remove the air cleaner and disconnect the accelerator and kickdown rods at the carburetor.

2. Remove the accelerator mounting bracket bolts and remove the bracket.

3. Remove the fan shroud attaching bolts and position the shroud up and over the fan.

4. Disconnect the windshield wiper motor wiring from the harness and remove the wiper motor.

5. Disconnect the windshield washer hose.

6. Remove the wiper motor mounting cover.

7. Remove the dipstick and remove the dipstick retaining bolt from the exhaust manifold.

8. Raise the car and support on jackstands. Drain the crankcase.

NOTE: *Engines with dual sump must be drained by removing both drain plugs.*

9. Disconnect the fuel line at the fuel pump.

10. Disconnect the inlet pipes from the exhaust manifold.

11. Remove the dipstick tube from the oil pan.

12. Loosen the rear engine mount attaching nuts. Remove the engine mount through bolts.

13. Remove the shift selector crossover bolts and remove the crossover.

14. Disconnect the transmission kickdown rod.

15. Remove the torque converter cover.

16. Remove the brake line retainer from the front crossmember.

17. Place a jack under the engine and raise it as far as it will go.

18. Place a small block of wood between each engine mount and the chassis brackets to support the engine. Remove the jack.

19. Remove the oil pan attaching bolts and lower the oil pan.

20. Remove the three oil pump attaching bolts from the cylinder block and allow the pump to fall into the pan.

21. Remove the oil pan from the car.

22. Inspect the oil pan for damage. Thoroughly clean the oil pump pick-up tube and screen assembly.

23. Reverse to install. See Steps 10–12 of

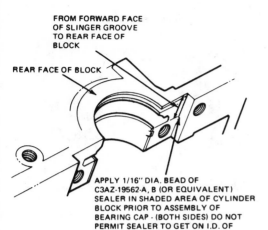

FROM FORWARD FACE OF SLINGER GROOVE TO REAR FACE OF BLOCK

REAR FACE OF BLOCK

APPLY 1/16" DIA. BEAD OF C3AZ-19562-A, B (OR EQUIVALENT) SEALER IN SHADED AREA OF CYLINDER BLOCK PRIOR TO ASSEMBLY OF BEARING CAP - (BOTH SIDES) DO NOT PERMIT SEALER TO GET ON I.D. OF SPLIT LIP SEAL

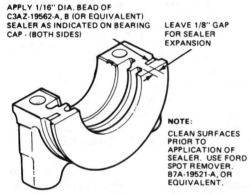

APPLY 1/16" DIA. BEAD OF C3AZ-19562-A, B (OR EQUIVALENT) SEALER AS INDICATED ON BEARING CAP - (BOTH SIDES)

LEAVE 1/8" GAP FOR SEALER EXPANSION

NOTE: CLEAN SURFACES PRIOR TO APPLICATION OF SEALER. USE FORD SPOT REMOVER. B7A-19521-A, OR EQUIVALENT.

Applying silicone sealer to rear main bearing cap and block

the procedure for cars through 1978 for gasket installation details.

1979 And Later With EGR Cooler, EEC, or MCU

1. Refer to Steps 1–7 of the above procedure.

2. Remove the Thermactor air pump tube retaining clamp. Remove the air cross-over tube from the rear of the engine.

3. Raise the car and drain the crankcase.

4. Remove the filler tube from the oil pan and drain the transmission.

5. Remove the starter motor.

6. Remove the fuel line from the fuel pump.

7. Disconnect the inlet pipes from the exhaust manifold.

8. Remove the exhaust gas oxygen sensor from the exhaust manifold.

9. Disconnect the air tube attaching clamps from the torque converter.

10. Remove the torque converter inspection cover.

11. Disconnect the exhaust pipes at the catalytic converter outlet.

12. Remove the catalytic converter secondary air tube. Remove the inlet pipes at the exhaust manifold.

13. Refer to Steps 11–23 of the 1978 procedure.

Crankshaft and Main Bearings
REMOVAL AND INSTALLATION

NOTE: *This procedure assumes that the engine is removed from the vehicle.*

1. Drain the crankcase and block.

2. Disconnect the plug wires and remove their brackets.

3. Disconnect the coil to distributor high tension lead, at the coil.

4. Remove the distributor cap, plug wires and spark plugs.

5. Remove the fuel pump, oil filter, alternator and its mounting brackets.

6. Remove the crankshaft pulley and the vibration damper.

7. Remove the front cover and water pump as an assembly.

8. Remove the timing chain and sprockets.

9. Remove the flywheel and rear cover plate.

10. Remove the oil pan and oil pump.

11. Mark all bearing caps (rods and mains) before removing them.

12. Remove the bearing caps.

13. Drive the pistons to the top of their bore. Be careful not to score the crankshaft with the rod bolts.

14. Gently remove the crankshaft from the block.

15. Installation is the reverse of removal.

NOTE: *Follow the rod bearing installation procedure when installing the main bearings.*

CLEANING AND INSPECTION

Clean bearing inserts and caps in solvent. Dry them with compressed air.

NOTE: *Do not scrape gum or varnish deposits from bearing shells.*

Inspect each bearing carefully. Bearings that have scored, chipped, or worn surfaces should be replaced. Check bearing clearances with a plasti-gauge. Replace any that are not within specifications.

REGRINDING JOURNALS

NOTE: *This procedure should be done by a qualified machine shop.*

Rear Main Bearing Oil Seal

REPLACEMENT

1968–69 302, 351 V8

NOTE: *The rear oil seal originally installed in these engines is a rope (fabric) type seal. However, all service replacements are of the rubber type. To remove the rope type seal and install the rubber type, the following procedure is used.*

1. Drain the crankcase and remove the oil pan. (See oil pan removal).
2. Remove the lower half of the rear main bearing cap and, after removing the old seal from the cap, drive out the pin in the bottom of the seal groove with a punch.
3. Loosen all main bearing caps and allow the crankshaft to lower slightly.

NOTE: *The crankshaft should not be allowed to drop more than 1/32 in.*

4. With a 6 in. length of 3/16 in. brazing rod, drive up on either exposed end of the top half of the oil seal. When the opposite end of the seal starts to protrude, have a helper grasp it with pliers and gently pull while the driver end is being tapped.
5. After removing both halves of the rope seal and the retaining pin from the lower half of the bearing cap, follow Steps 4 through 10 of the following procedure for 1970–76 engines to install the rubber seal.

All Other V8 Engines

NOTE: *The rear oil seal installed in these engines is a rubber type seal.*

1. Loosen all main bearing cap bolts, lowering crankshaft slightly but not more than 1/32 in.
2. Remove rear main cap, and remove upper and lower halves of seal. On block half of seal, use seal removing tool or insert a small metal screw into end of seal with which to draw it out.
3. Clean seal grooves with solvent and dip replacement seal in clean engine oil.
4. Install upper seal half in its groove in block with lip toward front of engine by rotating it on seal journal of crankshaft until approximately 3/8 in. protrudes below parting surface.
5. Tighten other main caps and torque to specification.
6. Install lower seal half in rear main cap with lip to front and approximately 3/8 in. of seal protrudes to mate with upper seal.
7. Install rear main cap and torque.
8. Dip side seals in engine oil and install them. Tap seals in last half inch if necessary. Do not cut protruding ends of seals.

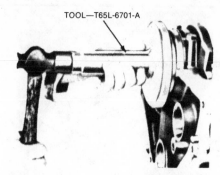

TOOL—T65L-6701-A

Installing crankshaft rear oil seal—1968–69 six-cylinder

1968–69 Six-Cylinder

If the rear main bearing oil seal is the only operation involved, it can be replaced in the car according to the following procedure.

NOTE: *If the oil seal is being replaced in conjunction with a rear main bearing replacement, the engine must be removed from the car.*

1. Remove the starter.
2. On cars equipped with automatic transmissions, remove the transmission. On cars equipped with manual transmissions, remove the transmission, clutch, flywheel and engine rear cover plate.
3. With an awl, punch holes in the main bearing oil seal, on opposite sides of the crankshaft and just above the bearing cap to cylinder block split line. Insert a sheet metal screw in each hole. With two large screwdrivers, pry the oil seal out.
4. Clean the oil recess in the cylinder block, main bearing cap and the crankshaft sealing surface.
5. Lubricate the entire oil seal. Then, install and drive the seal into its seat 0.005 in. below the face of the cylinder block with Ford tool T-65L-6701-A, or a socket of the proper diameter.
6. The remaining procedure is the reverse of removal.

Oil Pump

REMOVAL AND INSTALLATION

1. Remove the oil pan as outlined under the previous applicable "Oil Pan Removal and Installation" procedure.
2. On 255, 302 and 351W V8 applications, remove the oil pump inlet tube and screen assembly.
3. Remove the oil pump attaching bolts. Lower the oil pump, gasket, and intermediate driveshaft from the crankcase. If not already removed, remove and clean the inlet tube and screen assembly.

Typical oil pump and inlet tube installed—390, 428 V8 shown

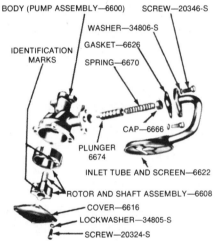

Typical oil pump disassembled—six-cylinder shown

4. To install, prime the oil pump by filling either the inlet or outlet port with engine oil. Rotate the pump shaft to distribute the oil within the pump body.

5. Position the intermediate driveshaft into the distributor socket. With the shaft firmly seated in the socket, the stop on the shaft should contact the roof of the crankcase. Remove the shaft and position the stop as necessary.

6. Insert the intermediate driveshaft into the oil pump. Using a new gasket, install the pump and shaft as an assembly. Do not attempt to force the pump into position if it will not seat readily. If necessary, rotate the intermediate driveshaft hex into a new position so that it will mesh with the distributor shaft.

7. Torque the oil pump attaching bolts to 12–15 ft. lbs. on the six-cylinder engines, 22–

32 ft. lbs. on the 255, 302 and 351W V8, 25–35 ft. lbs. on the 351C, 351M and 400 V8, and 20–25 ft. lbs. on the 390, 428, 429, and 460 V8.

8. Clean and install the inlet tube and screen assembly.

9. Install the oil pan as previously outlined under "Oil Pan Removal and Installation."

OVERHAUL

NOTE: *Internal components are not serviced separately. Pumps that have damaged parts must be replaced.*

Check the inside of the pump housing, outer race and rotor for damage or excessive wear. Also check the mating surface of the pump cover for wear. Minor scuff marks are normal, but if the surface is scored or grooved, replace the pump.

Flywheel and Ring Gear
REMOVAL AND INSTALLATION

1. Jack up the vehicle and support it with jack-stands.

2. Remove the driveshaft and transmission. NOTE: *On cars with automatic transmissions be careful not to drop the torque converter.*

3. Remove the flywheel.

4. Installation is the reverse of removal. Torque the flywheel bolts 75–85 ft. lbs.

Ring Gear—Manual Transmission Only

Heat the ring gear, with a torch, on the engine side only. Then drive it off the flywheel with a hammer. Do not hit the flywheel when removing the ring gear. The new flywheel is reinstalled by heating it also.

CAUTION: *Do not heat the new ring gear above 500°F. If this limit is exceeded, the temper will be removed from the teeth.*

Checking flywheel face runout

Inspection

Check the flywheel for cracks, heat checks or other damage that will make it unfit for service. Machine the surface if it is scored or worn (manual transmission only). If necessary to remove more than .045 in., replace the flywheel.

Use a dial indicator to check runout. Runout should not exceed .030 in. (manual transmission) .060 in. (automatic transmission). Remember to hold the crankshaft fully forward or rearward so that end play will not be mistaken for runout.

ENGINE COOLING

All Ford engines are liquid-cooled by a solution of water and ethylene glycol antifreeze. In addition to the freeze protection properties of the antifreeze solution, the solution has a higher boiling point than plain water, thereby preventing overheating in many cases, and contains anticorrosion and water pump lubrication additives.

The coolant circulates via the rotating motion of the water pump. It passes from the radiator, through the lower radiator hose, past the water pump, through the cooling passages of the engine, past the thermostat (if open), through the upper radiator hose and back into the radiator. As the hot coolant passes through the radiator, outside air is drawn through the radiator cooling fins by the engine fan. Heat is exchanged prior to the coolant's recirculation through the engine. Heat is supplied to the car's interior by by-passing a portion of the coolant through the heater core.

When the engine is cold, the thermostat, located in a housing between the top of the engine and the upper radiator hose, is closed and prevents the coolant from passing into the radiator. This causes the coolant in the engine to heat quickly, thereby shortening the time needed for the engine to reach its normal operating temperature. When the coolant reaches a predetermined temperature, the thermostat opens and the normal cooling cycle resumes.

Later models are equipped with a coolant recovery system. These systems use a plastic recovery reservoir and a non-vented radiator cap to contain coolant expansion. When adding coolant to these systems, add coolant to the reservoir only, not the radiator.

On models equipped with automatic transmission, the lower section (down-flow) or left-side (crossflow) of the radiator contains an automatic transmission fluid cooler. Oil from the transmission is transported by a pair of metal

hydraulic lines, under pressure, to the radiator's bottom (or left) section, where it is cooled.

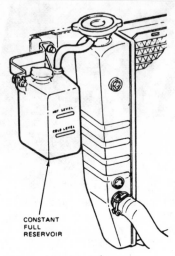

CONSTANT
FULL
RESERVOIR

Constant-full cooling system

Radiator

REMOVAL AND INSTALLATION

1. Drain the cooling system.
2. Disconnect the upper and lower hoses at the radiator.
3. On cars with automatic transmissions, disconnect the oil cooler lines at the radiator.
4. On vehicles with a fan shroud, remove the shroud retaining screws and position the shroud out of the way.
5. Remove the radiator attaching bolts and lift out the radiator.
6. If a new radiator is to be installed, transfer the petcock from the old radiator to the new one. On cars with automatic transmissions, transfer the oil cooler line fittings from the old radiator to the new one.
7. Position the radiator and install, but do not tighten, the radiator support bolts. On cars with automatic transmissions, connect the oil cooler lines. Then tighten the radiator support bolts.
8. On vehicles with a fan shroud, reinstall the shroud.
9. Connect the radiator hoses. Close the radiator petcock. Then fill and bleed the cooling system.
10. Start the engine and bring to operating temperature. Check for leaks.
11. On cars with automatic transmissions, check the cooler lines for leaks and interference. Check the transmission fluid level.

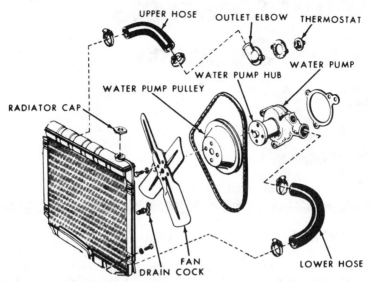

UPPER HOSE   OUTLET ELBOW   THERMOSTAT

WATER PUMP HUB   WATER PUMP

WATER PUMP PULLEY

RADIATOR CAP

FAN   DRAIN COCK   LOWER HOSE

Cooling system and related parts—typical V8 with downflow radiator

Water Pump

REMOVAL AND INSTALLATION

1. Drain the cooling system.

2. On 351C, 351M, and 400 V8 engines, disconnect the negative battery cable.

3. If equipped with a fan shroud, remove the shroud attaching bolts and position the shroud over the fan.

4. Remove the fan and spacer from the water pump shaft. Remove the shroud, if so equipped.

5. Remove the air conditioning drive belt and idler pulley, if so equipped. Remove the alternator, power steering and Thermactor drive belts, if so equipped. Remove the power steering pump attaching bolts, if so equipped, and position it to one side (leaving it connected).

6. Remove all accessory brackets which attach to the water pump. Remove the water pump pulley.

7. Disconnect the lower radiator hose, heater hose, and the water pump by-pass hose at the water pump.

8. Remove the bolts attaching the water pump and gasket surfaces. On the 429 and 460 V8, remove the water pump backing plate and replace the gasket.

NOTE: *The 240 six-cylinder engine originally had a one-piece gasket for the cylinder front cover and the water pump. Trim away the old gasket at the edge of the cylinder cover and replace with a service gasket.*

10. Coat both sides of a new gasket with water-resistant sealer and place it on the front cover. Install the water pump and tighten the attaching bolts diagonally, in rotation, to 12–15 ft. lbs. (255, 302, 351, 400 V8), 15–20 ft. lbs. (240 Six, 429, 460, V8) or 20–25 ft. lbs. (390, 428 V8).

11. Connect the lower radiator hose, heater hose, and water pump by-pass hose at the water pump.

12. Install all accessory brackets attaching to the water pump. Install the pump pulley on the pump shaft.

RECESS

BRIDGE

FLATS

Installing thermostat

Emission Controls and Fuel System

EMISSION CONTROLS

There are three types of automobile pollutants that concern automotive engineers: crankcase fumes, exhaust gases and gasoline vapors from evaporation. The devices and systems used to limit these pollutants are commonly called emission control equipment.

Emission Control Equipment

1968 through 1973

Emission controls between 1968 and 1973 are fairly simple compared to later systems. Below are listed the emission controls common to—but not necessarily on all models: Air pump, Closed positive crankcase ventilation (PCV), Calibrated carburetor and distributor, Dual vacuum advance on the distributor, Deceleration valve (6 cylinder), Heated air cleaner, Vapor control system-canister storage, Fresh air intake tube to the air cleaner, Electronic distributor modulator, various Vacuum check valves and EGR (exhaust gas recirculation).

1974

Late 1973 and 1974 models use an Exhaust Gas Recirculation System (EGR) to control oxides of nitrogen. On V8 engines, exhaust gases travel through the exhaust gas crossover passage in the intake manifold. A portion of these gases is diverted into a spacer which is mounted under the carburetor. The EGR control valve, which is attached to the rear of the spacer, consists of a vacuum diaphragm with an attached plunger which normally blocks off exhaust gases from entering the intake manifold. The EGR valve is controlled by a vacuum line from the carburetor which passes through a ported vacuum switch. The EGR ported vacuum switch provides vacuum to the EGR valve at coolant temperatures above 125°F. The vacuum diaphragm then opens the

EGR valve permitting exhaust gases to flow through the carburetor spacer and enter the intake manifold where they combine with the fuel mixture and enter the combustion chambers. The exhaust gases are relatively oxygen-free and tend to dilute the combustion charge. This lowers peak combustion temperature thereby reducing oxides of nitrogen.

All models with a 351C, 400, or 460 V8 use the new Delay Vacuum By-Pass (DVB) spark control system. This system provides two paths by which carburetor vacuum can reach the distributor vacuum advance. The system consists of a spark delay valve, a check valve, a solenoid vacuum valve, and an ambient temperature switch. When the ambient temperature is below 49°F, the temperature switch contacts are open and the vacuum solenoid is open (de-energized). Under these conditions, vacuum will flow from the carburetor, through the open solenoid, and to the distributor. Since the spark delay valve resists the flow of carburetor vacuum, the vacuum will always flow through the vacuum solenoid when it is open, since this is the path of least resistance. When the ambient temperature rises above 60°F, the contacts in the temperature switch (which is located in the door post) close. This passes ignition switch current to the solenoid, energizing the solenoid. This blocks one of the two vacuum paths. All distributor vacuum must now flow through the spark delay valve. When carburetor vacuum rises above a certain level on acceleration, a rubber valve in the spark delay valve blocks vaccum from passing through the valve for from 5 to 30 seconds.

After this time delay has elapsed, normal vacuum is supplied to the distributor. When the vacuum solenoid is closed, (temperature above 60°), the vacuum line from the solenoid to the distributor is vented to atmosphere. To prevent the vacuum that is passing through the spark delay valve from escaping through the solenoid into the atmosphere, a one-way check valve is installed in the vacuum line from the solenoid to the distributor.

In order to meet 1974 California emission control standards, all 1974 Ford cars sold in that state are equipped with a Thermactor (air injection) system to control hydrocarbons and carbon monoxide. The EGR system is retained to control oxides of nitrogen.

1975

All full size Ford Motor Co. cars are equipped with catalytic converters. California models are equipped with two converters, while models sold in the 49 states have only one unit.

Catalytic converters convert noxious emissions of hydrocarbons (HC) and carbon monoxide (CO) into harmless carbon dioxide and water. The units are installed in the exhaust system ahead of the mufflers and are designed, if the engine is properly tuned, to last 50,000 miles before replacement.

In addition to the converters, most 1975 Ford, Mercury and Thunderbird cars are equipped with the Thermactor air pump (air injection system) previously mentioned. The air injection system, which afterburns the uncombusted fuel mixture in the exhaust ports, is needed with the converters to prevent an overly rich mixture from reaching the converter, and to help supply oxygen to aid in converter reaction.

Other emission control equipment for 1975 includes a carryover of the Positive Crankcase Ventilation (PCV) System, the Fuel Evaporative Control System, and exhaust gas recirculation.

Emission control related improvements for 1975 include standard Solid State (breakerless) Ignition, induction hardened exhaust valve seats, exhaust manifold redesign, vacuum operated heat riser valves, and improved carburetors with more precise fuel metering control and a mechanical high-speed bleed system.

All cars equipped with the 460 V8 engine use a Cold Start Spark Advance (CSSA) System in 1975 to aid in cold start driveability. Basically, the system will allow full vacuum advance to the distributor until the coolant temperature reaches 125°F.

1976

For 1976, the complexity of emission control equipment has been reduced on Ford products. The average number of emission control components has been reduced from 25 to 11 on most cars. All 1976 models have catalytic converters. In addition, a new proportional exhaust gas recirculation system has been introduced. Exhaust backpressure regulates the EGR valve spark port vacuum signal to modulate the recirculation of gases, matching EGR flow to engine load.

1977-79

Most emission controls are carryover from 1976. One exception, however, is the EEC II (Electronic Engine Control) system. It is installed on all Mercurys with the optional 351W V8, and on LTDs sold in California with that engine.

The system is based on EEC I (EEC systems are described later in this chapter), but certain components have been changed to improve performance and reliability, and to reduce complexity and cost. EEC II controls spark timing, EGR, and air/fuel ratio (mixture). A solid state module incorporating a digital microprocessor and other integrated circuits interprets information sent by seven sensors, calculates spark advance, EGR flow rate and fuel-flow trim, and sends electrical signals to control the ignition module, EGR valve actuator, and an electric stepper motor in the carburetor. EEC II also controls purging of vapors in the storage canister to prevent over-rich mixtures, high-altitude fuel mixture adjustments, Thermactor (air pump) air flow, and cold engine (fast idle) functions. Because the throttle idle position, ignition timing and mixture are controlled electronically, these functions cannot be adjusted in the conventional manner.

1980

The major change in the emission control system for 1980 is in the EEC. The new system, EEC III, performs the same function as EEC II but uses a new electronic control module. The EEC system computes information and makes any necessary changes about 30 times a second, controlling the fuel-air mixture, EGR, ignition timing and the air flow to the exhaust emission system.

1981 and later

The application of EEC III is continued. A Microprocessor Control Unit (MCU) system is installed on 255 and 302 V8s sold in California, and all 351 V8s sold nationwide. MCU is installed with a feedback carburetor system. Components include an oxygen sensor, a variable-mixture carburetor, a three-way oxidation/reduction catalytic converter, an air pump, and the MCU module.

Briefly, the three-way catalyst, which oxidizes HC and CO into H_2O and CO_2, and reduces NOx into N_2 and O_2, is only able to operate efficiently within a narrow range of exhaust gas content. An ideal air/fuel ratio (14.7:1, which is called stoichiometry) is needed for the converter to work properly. The oxygen sensor, installed in the exhaust manifold, monitors the exhaust mixture and sends a signal to the MCU. The MCU then determines whether the air/fuel mixture is correct; if not, it sends a signal to the carburetor mixture control solenoid vacuum valve, altering the mixture slightly to bring it back within the narrow band required by the converter.

The Thermactor (air pump) system provides the converter with oxygen for the oxidation reaction.

Ford Electronic Engine Control System

EEC I

Ford's EECI system was introduced in 1978, on the Lincoln Versailles. Designed to precisely control ignition timing, EGR and Thermactor (air pump) flow, the system consists of an Electronic Control Assembly (ECA), seven monitoring sensors, a Dura Spark II ignition module and coil, a special distributor assembly, and an EGR system designed to operate on air pressure.

The ECA is a solid state micro computer, consisting of a processor assembly and a calibration assembly. The processor continuously receives inputs from the seven sensors, which it converts to usable information for the calculating section of the computer. It also performs ignition timing, Thermactor and EGR flow calculations, processes the information and sends out signals to the ignition module and control solenoids to adjust the timing and flow of the systems accordingly. The calibration assembly contains the memory and programming for the processor.

Processor inputs come from sensors monitoring manifold pressure, barometric pressure, engine coolant temperature, inlet air temperature, crankshaft position, throttle position, and EGR valve position.

The manifold absolute pressure sensor determines changes in intake manifold pressure (barometric pressure minus manifold vacuum) which result from changes in engine load and speed, or in atmospheric pressure. Its signal is used by the ECA to set part throttle spark advance and EGR flow rate.

Barometric pressure is monitored by a sensor mounted on the firewall. Measurements taken are converted into a useable electrical signal. The ECA uses this reference for altitude-dependent EGR flow requirements.

Engine coolant temperature is measured at the rear of the intake manifold by a sensor

consisting of a brass housing containing a thermistor (resistance decreases as temperature rises). When reference voltage (about 9 volts, supplied by the processor to all sensors) is applied to the sensor, the resistance can be measured by the resulting voltage drop. Resistance is then interpreted as coolant temperature by the ECA. This sensor replaces both the PVS and EGR PVS in conventional systems. EGR flow is cut off by the ECA when a predetermined temperature value is reached. The ECA will also advance initial ignition timing to increase idle speed if the coolant overheats due to prolonged idle. A faster idle speed increases coolant and radiator air flow.

Inlet air temperature is measured by a sensor mounted in the air cleaner. It functions in the same way as the coolant sensor. The ECA uses its signal for proper spark advance and Thermactor flow. At high inlet temperatures (above 90°F) the ECA modifies timing advance to prevent spark knock.

The crankshaft is fitted with a four-lobed powdered metal pulse ring, positioned 10° BTDC. Its position is constantly monitored by the crankshaft position sensor. Signals are sent to the ECA describing both the position of the crankshaft at any given moment, and the frequency of the pulses (engine rpm). These signals are used to determine optimum ignition timing advance. If either the sensor or wiring is broken, the ECA will not receive a signal, and thus be unable to send any signal to the ignition module. This will prevent the engine from starting.

The throttle position sensor is a rheostat connected to the throttle plate shaft. Changes in throttle plate angle change the resistance value of the reference voltage supplied by the processor. Signals are interpreted in one of three ways by the ECA:

- Closed throttle (idle or deceleration)
- Part throttle (cruise)
- Full throttle (maximum acceleration)

A position sensor is built into the EGR valve. The ECA uses its signal to determine EGR valve position. The valve and position sensor are replaced as a unit, should either fail.

CAUTION: *Because of the complicated nature of this system, special diagnostic tools are necessary for troubleshooting. Any troubleshooting without these tools must be limited to mechanical checks of connectors and wiring.*

The distributor is locked in place during engine manufacture; no rotational adjustment is possible for initial ignition timing, since all timing is controlled by the ECA. There are no mechanical advance mechanisms or adjustments under the rotor, thus there is no need to remove it except for replacement.

EEC II

The second generation EEC II system was introduced in 1979 on full size Fords and Mercurys. It is based on the EEC I system used on the Versailles, but some changes have been made to reduce complexity and cost, increase the number of controlled functions, and improve reliability and performance.

In general, the EEC II system operates in the same manner as EEC I. An Electronic Control Assembly (ECA) monitors reports from six sensors, and adjusts the EGR flow, ignition timing, Thermactor (air pump) air flow, and carburetor air/fuel mixture in response to the incoming signals. Although there are only six sensors, seven conditions are monitored. The sensors are: (1) Engine Coolant Temperature, (2) Throttle Position, (3) Crankshaft Position, (4) Exhaust Gas Oxygen, (5) Barometric and Manifold Absolute Pressure, and (6) EGR Valve Position. These sensors function in the same manner as the EEC I sensors, and are described in the EEC I section. Note that inlet air temperature is not monitored in the EEC II system, and that the barometric and manifold pressure sensors have been combined into one unit. One more change from the previous system is in the location of the crankshaft sensor: it is mounted on the front of the engine, behind the vibration damper and crankshaft pulley.

The biggest difference between EEC I and EEC II is that the newer system is capable of continually monitoring and adjusting the carburetor air/fuel ratio. Monitoring is performed by the oxygen sensor installed in the right exhaust manifold; adjustment is made via an electric stepper motor installed on the model 7200 VV carburetor.

The stepper motor has four separate armature windings, which can be sequentially energized by the ECA. As the motor varies the position of the carburetor metering valve, the amount of control vacuum exposed to the fuel bowl is correspondingly altered. Increased vacuum reduces pressure in the fuel bowl, causing a leaner air/fuel mixture, and vice versa. During engine starting and immediately after, the ECA sets the motor at a point dependent on its initial position. Thereafter, the motor position is changed in response to the ECA calculations of the six input signals.

EEC II is also capable of controlling purging of vapors from the evaporative emission control storage canister. A canister purge solenoid, a combination solenoid and valve, is located in the line between the intake manifold purge fitting and the carbon canister. It controls the flow of vapors from the canister to the intake manifold, opening and closing in response to signals from the ECA.

CAUTION: *As is the case with EEC I, diagnosis and repair of the system requires special tools and equipment.*

The distributor is locked in place during engine manufacture; no rotational adjustment is possible for initial ignition timing, since all timing is controlled by the ECA. There are no mechanical advance mechanisms or adjustments under the ignition rotor, and thus there is no need to remove it except for replacement.

Air/fuel mixture is entirely controlled by the ECA; no adjustments are possible.

EEC III

EEC III was introduced in 1980. It is a third generation system developed entirely from EEC II. The only real differences between EEC II and III are contained within the Electronic Control Assembly (ECA) and the Dura-Spark ignition module. The EEC III system uses a separate program module which plugs into the main ECA module. This change allows various programming calibrations for specific applications to be made to the program module, while allowing the main ECA module to be standardized. Additionally, EEC III uses a Dura-Spark III ignition module, which contains fewer electronic functions than the Dura-Spark II module; the functions have been incorporated into the main ECA module. There is no interchangeability between the Dura-Spark II and III modules.

NOTE: *Since late 1979 emission controls and air/fuel mixtures have been controlled by various electronic methods. An electronically controlled feedback carburetor is used to precisely calibrate fuel metering, many vacuum check valves, solenoids and regulators have been added and the electronic control boxes (ECU and MCU) can be calibrated and programmed in order to be used by different engines and under different conditions.*

NOTE: *Because of the complicated nature of the Ford system, special tools and procedures are necessary for testing and troubleshooting.*

The following emission control devices described can be tested and maintained, any not mentioned should be serviced by qualified mechanics using the required equipment.

Positive Crankcase Ventilation System

All 1968 and later models are equipped with a positive crankcase ventilation (PCV) system to control crankcase blow-by vapors. The system consists of a PCV valve and oil separator mounted on top of the valve cover, a nonventilated oil filter cap, and a pair of hoses supplying filtered intake air to the valve cover and delivering the crankcase vapors from the valve cover to the intake manifold (six-cylinder) or carburetor (V8).

The system functions as follows:

When the engine is running, a small portion of the gases which are formed in the combustion chamber leak by the piston rings and enter the crankcase. Since these gases are under pressure, they tend to escape from the crankcase and enter the atmosphere. If these cases are allowed to remain in the crankcase for any period of time, they contaminate the engine oil and cause sludge to build up in the crankcase. If the gases are allowed to escape into the atmosphere, they pollute the air, with unburned hydrocarbons.

The job of the crankcase emission control equipment is to recycle these gases back into the engine combustion chamber where they are reburned.

The crankcase (blow-by) gases are recycled in the following way: as the engine is running, clean, filtered air is drawn through the air filter and into the crankcase. As the air passes through the crankcase, it picks up the combustion gases and carries them out of the crankcase, through the oil separator, through the PCV valve, and into the induction system. As they enter the intake manifold, they are drawn into the combustion chamber where they are reburned.

The most critical component in the system is the PCV valve. This valve controls the amount of gases which are recycled into the combustion chamber. At low engine speeds, the valve is partially closed, limiting the flow of the gases into the intake manifold. As engine speed increases, the valve opens to admit greater quantities of the gases into the intake manifold. If the valve should become blocked or plugged, the gases will be prevented from escaping from the crankcase by the normal route. Since these gases are under pressure, they will find their own way out of the crankcase. This alternate route is usually a weak oil seal or gasket in the engine. As the gas escapes by the gasket, it also creates an oil leak. Besides causing oil leaks, a clogged PCV valve also allows these gases to remain in the crankcase for an extended period of time, promoting the formation of sludge in the engine.

PCV VALVE TEST—WITH TACHOMETER

1. See if any deposits are present in the carburetor passages, the oil filler cap or the hoses. Clean these as required.

2. Connect a tachometer, as instructed by its manufacturer, to the engine.

3. With engine idling, do one of the following:

   a. Remove the PCV valve hose from the crankcase or the oil filter connection.

   b. On cars with the PCV valve located in a grommet on the valve cover, remove both the valve and the grommet.

   NOTE: *If the valve and the hoses are not clogged up, a hissing sound should be present.*

4. Check the tachometer reading. Place a finger over the valve or hose opening (a suction should be felt).

5. Check the tachometer again. The engine speed should have dropped at least 50 rpm. It should return to normal when the finger is removed from the opening.

6. If the engine does not change speed or if the change is less than 50 rpm, the hose is clogged or the valve is defective. Check the hose first. If the hose is not clogged, replace, do not attempt to repair, the PCV valve.

7. Test the new valve in the above manner, to make sure that it is operating properly.

PCV VALVE TEST—WITHOUT TACHOMETER

With the engine running, pull the PCV valve and hose from the valve rocker cover rubber grommet. Block off the end of the valve with your finger. A strong vacuum should be felt.

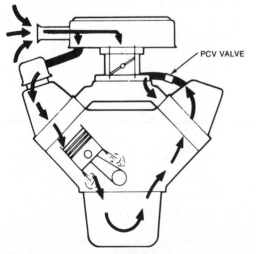

Positive crankcase ventilation system operation —V8

Shake the valve; a clicking noise indicates it is free. Replace the valve if it is suspected of being blocked.

REMOVAL AND INSTALLATION

1. Pull the PCV valve and hose from the rubber grommet in the rocker arm cover or from the oil filler cap.

2. Remove the PCV valve from the hose. Inspect the inside of the PCV valve. If the valve is gummy it can be cleaned in a suitable, safe solvent. However, replacing a clogged, gummed up PCV valve with a new one is suggested.

3. Soak the rubber ventilation hose(s) in a low volatility petroleum base solvent to loosen the deposits. Pass a suitable cleaning brush through them and blow out with compressed air or let air-dry.

4. Thoroughly wash the crankcase breather cap (if equipped) in solvent and shake dry. Do not dry with compressed air; damage to the filtering material may result.

5. Replace any hard or cracked hoses or ones that are clogged and cannot be cleaned.

6. The installation of the hoses and PCV valve is in the reverse order of removal.

Fuel Evaporative Control System

1970 models manufactured for sale in California, and all 1971 and later models nationwide are equipped with a fuel evaporative control system to prevent the evaporation of unburned gasoline. The 1970 system consists of a sealed fuel tank filler cap, an expansion area at the top of the gas tank, a combination vapor separator and expansion tank assembly, a 3-way vapor control valve, a carbon canister located in the engine compartment which stores these vapors, and the hoses which connect this equipment. The 1971 and later system consists of a special-vacuum/pressure re-

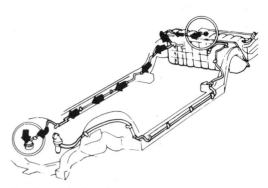

Routing of fuel tank vapors

lief filler cap, and expansion area at the top of the fuel tank, a foam-filled vapor separator mounted on top of the fuel tank, a carbon canister which stores fuel vapors and hoses which connect this equipment. On both systems, the carburetor fuel bowl vapors are retained within the fuel bowl until the engine is started, at which point they are internally vented into the engine for burning.

The system functions as follows:

Changes in atmospheric temperature cause the gasoline in fuel tanks to expand or contract. If this expansion and consequent vaporization takes place in a conventional fuel tank, the fuel vapors escape through the filler cap or vent hose and pollute the atmosphere. The fuel evaporative emission control system prevents this by routing the gasoline vapors to the engine where they are burned.

As the gasoline in the fuel tank of a parked car begins to expand due to heat, the vapor that forms moves to the top of the fuel tank. The fuel tanks on all 1970 and later cars are enlarged so that there exists an area representing 10–20% of the total fuel tank volume above the level of the fuel tank filler tube where these gases may collect. The vapors then travel upward into the vapor separator which prevents liquid gasoline from escaping from the fuel tank. The fuel vapor is then drawn through the vapor separator outlet hose, through the 3-way vapor control valve (1970 only), then to the charcoal canister in the engine compartment. The vapor enters the canister, passes through a charcoal filter, and then exits through the canister's grated bottom. As the vapor passes through the charcoal, it is cleansed by hydrocarbons, so that the air that passes out of the bottom of the canister is free of pollutants.

When the engine is started, vacuum from the carburetor draws fresh air into the canister. As the entering air passes through the charcoal in the canister, it picks up the hydrocarbons that were deposited there by the fuel vapors. This mixture of hydrocarbons and fresh air is then carried through a hose to the air

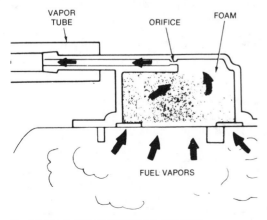

Fuel vapors entering vapor separator

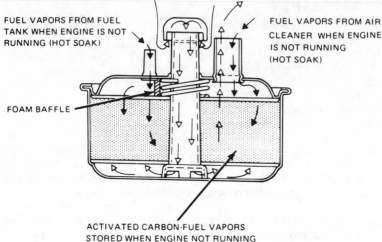

FLOW OF FRESH AIR TO
PURGE STORED FUEL
VAPORS WHEN ENGINE
IS RUNNING

FUEL VAPORS TO AIR CLEANER TO BE
BURNED WHEN ENGINE IS RUNNING

FUEL VAPORS FROM FUEL
TANK WHEN ENGINE IS NOT
RUNNING (HOT SOAK)

FUEL VAPORS FROM AIR
CLEANER WHEN ENGINE
IS NOT RUNNING
(HOT SOAK)

FOAM BAFFLE

ACTIVATED CARBON-FUEL VAPORS
STORED WHEN ENGINE NOT RUNNING

Cross-section of charcoal canister

cleaner. In the carburetor, it combines with the incoming air/fuel mixture and enters the combustion chambers of the engine where it is burned.

On both systems, there still remains the problem of allowing air into the tank to replace the gasoline displaced during normal use and the problem of relieving excess pressure from the fuel tank should it reach a dangerous level. On 1970 systems, the 3-way control valve accomplishes this. On 1971 and later systems, the special filler cap performs this task. Under normal circumstances, the filler cap functions as a check valve, allowing air to enter the tank to replace the fuel consumed. At the same time it prevents vapors from escaping from the cap. In case of severe pressure within the tank, the filler cap valve opens, venting the pollutants to the atmosphere.

VENT-VALVE REPLACEMENT

Except for 1970 models manufactured for sale in California, the only service performed on the evaporative control system is the replacement of the charcoal (carbon) canister at the intervals listed in the maintenance schedule in Chapter 1. The above mentioned California registered 1970 models require replacement of the 3-way vent valve once a year or every 12,000 miles. The procedure is as follows.

1. Working under the vehicle, disconnect two hoses from the control valve. Remove the vent valve cover.

2. Remove two attaching bolts and remove the valve from the crossmember of the rear of the gas tank.

3. To install, position the valve to the crossmember and install two attaching bolts.

4. Connect the two hoses to the valve assembly. Install the cover.

CANISTER REMOVAL AND INSTALLATION

Loosen and remove the canister mounting bolts from the mounting bracket. Disconnect the purge hose from the air cleaner and the feed hose from the fuel tank. Discard the old canister and install a new unit. Make sure that the hoses are connected properly.

Thermactor System

The Thermactor emission control system makes use of a belt-driven air pump to inject fresh air into the hot exhaust stream through the engine exhaust ports. The result is the extended burning of those fumes which were not completely ignited in the combustion chamber, and the subsequent reduction of some of the hydrocarbon and carbon monoxide content of the exhaust emissions into harmless carbon dioxide and water.

The Thermactor system is composed of the following components:

1. Air supply pump (belt-driven)
2. Air by-pass valve
3. Check valves
4. Air manifolds (internal or external)
5. Air supply tubes (on external manifolds only).

Air for the Thermactor system is cleaned by means of a centrifugal filter fan mounted on

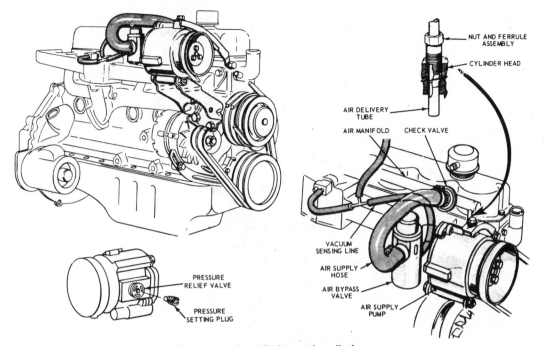

Thermactor installation—six cylinder

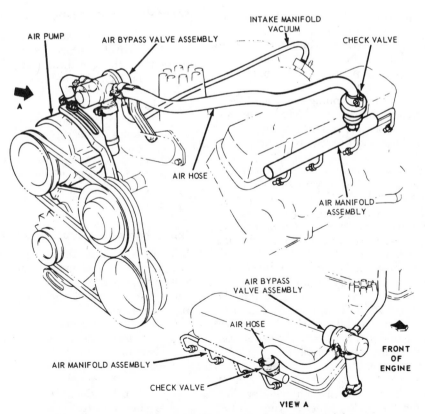

Typical thermactor installation—V8 except 390 and 428

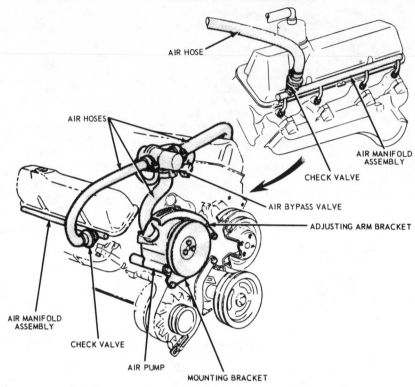

Thermactor installation—390, 428 V8

the air pump driveshaft. The air filter does not require a replaceable element.

To prevent excessive pressure, the air pump is equipped with a pressure relief valve which uses a replaceable plastic plug to control the pressure setting.

The Thermactor air pump has sealed bearings which are lubricated for the life of the unit, and pre-set rotor vane and bearing clearances, which do not require any periodic adjustments.

The air supply from the pump is controlled by the air by-pass valve, sometimes called a dump valve. During deceleration, the air by-pass valve opens, momentarily diverting the air supply through a silencer and into the atmosphere, thus preventing backfires within the exhaust system.

A check valve is incorporated in the air inlet side of the air manifolds. Its purpose is to prevent exhaust gases from backing up into the Thermactor system. This valve is especially important in the event of drive belt failure, and during deceleration, when the air by-pass valve is dumping the air supply.

The air manifolds and air supply tubes channel the air from the Thermactor air pump into the exhaust ports of each cylinder, thus completing the cycle of the Thermactor system.

THERMACTOR SYSTEM CHECKS

Before performing an extensive diagnosis of the emission control systems, verify that all specifications on the Certification Label are met, because the following systems or components may cause symptoms that appear to be emission related.

    a. Improper vacuum connections
    b. Vacuum leaks
    c. Ignition timing
    d. Plugs, wires, cap and rotor
    e. Carburetor float level
    f. Carburetor main metering jets
    g. Choke operation

Fabricating a Test Gauge Adapter

In order to test the three major components of a Thermactor system (air pump, check valve and bypass valve), a pressure gauge and adapter are required. The adapter can be fabricated as follows:

    1. Obtain these items:
        a. ½-inch pipe tee
        b. ½-inch pipe, 2 inches long and threaded at one end
        c. ½-inch pipe plug
        d. ½-inch reducer bushing or other suitable gauge adapter.
    2. Apply sealer to threaded ends of pipe,

plug and bushing. Assemble as shown in the illustration.

3. Drill $^{11}/_{32}$ inch (0.3437) diameter hole through center of pipe plug. Clean out chips after drilling.

4. Attach pressure gauge with ¼-psi increments to bushing or adapter.

Air Pump Tests

CAUTION: *Do not hammer on, pry, or bend the pump housing while tightening the drive belt or testing the pump.*

BELT TENSION AND AIR LEAKS

1. Before proceeding with the tests, check the pump drive belt tension to see if it is within specifications.

2. Turn the pump by hand. If it has seized, the belt will slip, producing noise. Disregard any chirping, squealing, or rolling sounds from inside the pump; these are normal when it is turned by hand.

3. Check the hoses and connections for leaks. Hissing or a blast of air is indicative of a leak. Soapy water, applied lightly around the area in question, is a good method for detecting leaks.

AIR OUTPUT TESTS

1. Disconnect the air supply hose at the antibackfire valve.

2. Connect a vacuum gauge, using a suitable adaptor, to the air supply hose.

NOTE: *If there are two hoses plug the second one.*

3. With the engine at normal operating temperature, increase the idle speed and watch the vacuum gauge.

4. The air flow from the pump should be steady and fall between 2–6 psi. If it is unsteady or falls below this, the pump is defective and must be replaced.

PUMP NOISE DIAGNOSIS

The air pump is normally noisy; as engine speed increases, the noise of the pump will rise in pitch. The rolling sound the pump bearings make is normal; however, if this sound becomes objectionable at certain speeds, the pump is defective and will have to be replaced.

A continual hissing sound from the air pump pressure relief valve at idle, indicates a defective valve. Replace the relief valve.

If the pump rear bearing fails, a continual knocking sound will be heard. Since the rear bearing is not separately replaceable, the pump will have to be replaced as an assembly.

Check Valve Test

1. Before starting the test, check all of the hoses and connections for leaks.

2. Detach the air supply hose(s) from the check valve(s).

3. Insert a suitable probe into the check valve and depress the plate. Release it; the plate should return to its original position against the valve seat. If binding is evident, replace the valve.

4. Repeat step 3 if two valves are used.

5. With the engine running at normal operating temperature, gradually increase its speed to 1,500 rpm. Check for exhaust gas leakage. If any is present, replace the valve assembly.

NOTE: *Vibration and flutter of the check valve at idle speed is a normal condition and does not mean that the valve should be replaced.*

Air Bypass Valve Test

1. Detach the hose, which runs from the bypass valve to the check valve, at the bypass valve hose connection.

2. Connect a tachometer to the engine. With the engine running at normal idle speed, check to see that air is flowing from the bypass valve hose connection.

3. Speed the engine up, so that it is running at 1,500–2,000 rpm. Allow the throttle to snap shut. The flow of air from the bypass valve at the check valve hose connection should stop momentarily and air should then flow from the exhaust port on the valve body or the silencer assembly.

4. Repeat step 3 several times. If the flow of air is not diverted into the atmosphere from the valve exhaust port or if it fails to stop flowing from the hose connection, check the vacuum lines and connections. If these are tight, the valve is defective and requires replacement.

5. A leaking diaphragm will cause the air to flow out both the hose connection and the exhaust port at the same time. If this happens, replace the valve.

REMOVAL AND INSTALLATION

Thermactor Air Pump

1. Disconnect the air outlet hose at the air pump.

2. Loosen the pump belt tension adjuster.

3. Disengage the drive belt.

4. Remove the mounting bolt and air pump.

5. To install, position the air pump on the mounting bracket and install the mounting bolt.

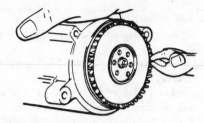

Thermactor air pump filter fan removal

6. Place drive belt in pulleys and attach the adjusting arm to the air pump.

7. Adjust the drive belt tension to specifications and tighten the adjusting arm and mounting bolts.

8. Connect the air outlet hose to the air pump.

Thermactor Air Pump Filter Fan

1. Loosen the air pump adjusting arm bolt and mounting bracket bolt to relieve drive belt tension.

2. Remove drive pulley attaching bolts and pull drive pulley off the air pump shaft.

3. Pry the outer disc loose; then, pull off the centrifugal filter fan with slip-joint pliers. CAUTION: *Do not attempt to remove the metal drive hub.*

4. Install a new filter fan by drawing it into position, using the pulley and bolts as an installer. Draw the fan evenly by alternately tightening the bolts, making certain that the outer edge of the fan slips into the housing. NOTE: *A slight interference with the housing bore is normal. After a new fan is installed, it may squeal upon initial operation, until its outer diameter sealing lip has worn in, which may require 20 to 30 miles of operation.*

Thermactor Check Valve

1. Disconnect the air supply hose at the valve. (Use a 1¼ in. crowfoot wrench, the valve has a standard, right-hand pipe thread.)

2. Clean the threads on the air manifold adaptor or air supply tube with a wire brush. Do not blow compressed air through the check valve in either direction.

3. Install the check valve and tighten.

4. Connect the air supply hose.

Thermactor Air By-pass Valve

1. Disconnect the air and vacuum hoses at the air by-pass valve body.

2. Position the air by-pass valve, and connect the respective hoses.

Improved Combustion System

All 1968 models equipped with automatic transmission, all 1969 models except the 428 Police Interceptor engine, and all 1970 and later models (regardless of other exhaust emission control equipment) are equipped with the Improved Combustion (IMCO) System. The IMCO System controls emissions arising from the incomplete combustion of the air/fuel mixture in the cylinders. The IMCO system incorporates a number of modifications to the distributor spark control system, the fuel system, and the internal design of the engine.

Internal engine modifications include the following: elimination of surface irregularities and crevices as well as a low surface area-to-volume ratio in the combustion chambers, a high-velocity intake manifold combined with short exhaust ports, selective valve timing and a higher temperature and capacity cooling system.

Modifications to the fuel system include the following: recalibrated carburetors to achieve a leaner air/fuel mixture, more precise calibration of the choke mechanism, the installation of idle mixture limiter caps and a heated air intake system.

Modifications to the distributor spark control system include the following: a modified centrifugal advance curve, the use of dual diaphragm distributors in most applications, a ported vacuum switch, a deceleration valve and a spark delay valve.

Heated Air Intake System

The heated air intake portion of the air cleaner consists of a thermostat or bimetal switch and vacuum motor and a spring-loaded temperature control door in the snorkel of the air cleaner. The temperature control door is located between the end of the air cleaner snorkel which draws in air from the engine compartment and the duct that carries heated air up from the exhaust manifold. When underhood temperature is below 90°F, the temperature control door blocks off underhood air from entering the air cleaner and allows only heated air from the exhaust manifold to be drawn into the air cleaner. When underhood temperature rises above 130°F, the temperature control door blocks off heated air from the exhaust manifold and allows only underhood air to be drawn into the air cleaner.

By controlling the temperature of the engine intake air this way, exhaust emissions are lowered and fuel economy is improved. In addition, throttle plate icing is reduced, and cold weather driveability is improved from the necessary leaner mixtures.

DUCT AND VALVE ASSEMBLY TEST

1. Either start with a cold engine or remove the air cleaner from the engine for at

least half an hour. While cooling the air cleaner, leave the engine compartment hood open.

2. Tape a thermometer, of known accuracy, to the inside of the air cleaner so that it is near the temperature sensor unit. Install the air cleaner on the engine but do not fasten its securing nut.

3. Start the engine. With the engine cold and the outside temperature less than 90°F, the door should be in the "heat on" position (closed to outside air).

4. Operate the throttle lever rapidly to one-half to three-quarters of its opening and release it. The air door should open to allow outside air to enter and then close again.

5. Allow the engine to warm up to normal temperature. Watch the door. When it opens to the outside air, remove the cover from the air cleaner. The temperature should be over 90°F and no more than 130°F; 105°F is about normal. If the door does not work within these temperature ranges, or fails to work at all, check for linkage or door binding.

If binding is not present and the air door is not working, proceed with the vacuum tests given below. If these indicate no faults in the vacuum motor and the door is not working, the temperature sensor is defective and must be replaced.

VACUUM MOTOR TEST

Be sure that the vacuum hose that runs between the temperature switch and the vacuum motor is not pinched by the retaining clip under the air cleaner. This could prevent the air door from closing.

1. Check all the vacuum lines and fittings for leaks. Correct any leaks. If none are found, proceed with the test.

2. Remove the hose which runs from the sensor to the vacuum motor. Run a hose directly from the manifold vacuum source to the vacuum motor.

3. If the motor closes the air door, it is functioning properly and the temperature sensor is defective.

4. If the motor does *not* close the door and

no binding is present in its operation, the vacuum motor is defective and must be replaced.

NOTE: *If an alternate vacuum source is applied to the motor, insert a vacuum gauge in the line by using a T-fitting. Apply at least 9 in. Hg of vacuum in order to operate the motor.*

REMOVAL AND INSTALLATION

Temperature Operated Duct and Valve Assembly

1. Remove the hex-head cap screws which secure the air intake duct and valve assembly to the air cleaner.

2. Remove the air intake duct and valve assembly from the engine.

3. If the duct and valve assembly was removed because of a suspected temperature malfunction, check the operation of the thermostat and valve plate assembly. Refer to the Air Intake Duct test for the proper procedure.

4. If inspection reveals that the valve plate is sticking or the thermostat is malfunctioning, remove the thermostat and valve plates as follows:

   a. Detach the valve plate tension spring from the valve plate using long-nose pliers. Loosen the thermostat locknut and unscrew the thermostat from the mounting bracket. Grasp the valve plate and withdraw it from the duct.

5. Install the air intake duct and valve assembly on the shroud tube.

6. Connect the air intake duct and valve assembly to the air cleaner and tighten the hex-head retaining cap screws.

7. If it was necessary to disassemble the thermostat and air duct and valve, assemble the unit as follows:

   a. Install the valve plate. Install the locknut on the thermostat, and screw the thermostat into the mounting bracket. Install the valve plate tension spring on the valve plate and duct.

   b. Check the operation of the thermostat and air duct assembly. Refer to the Air Intake Duct Test for the proper procedure. Tighten the locknut.

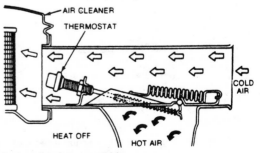

Temperature-operated duct and valve assembly

8. Install the vacuum override motor (if applicable) and check for proper operation.

Vacuum Operated Duct and Valve Assembly

1. Disconnect the vacuum hose at the vacuum motor.

2. Remove the hex head cap screws which secure the air intake duct and valve assembly to the air cleaner.

3. Remove the duct and valve assembly from the engine.

4. Position the duct and valve assembly to the air cleaner and heat stove tube. Install the attaching cap screws.

5. Connect the vacuum line at the vacuum motor.

Dual Diaphragm Distributors

Dual diaphragm distributors are installed in most 1968 and later models and appear in many different engine/transmission/equipment combinations.

The dual distributor diaphragm is a two-chambered housing which is mounted on the side of the distributor. The outer side of the housing is a distributor vacuum advance mechanism, connected to the carburetor by a vacuum hose. The purpose of the vacuum advance is to advance ignition timing according to the conditions under which the engine is operating. This device has been used on automobiles for many years now and its chief advantage is economical engine operation. The second side of the dual diaphragm is the side that has been added to help control engine exhaust emissions at idle and during deceleration.

The inner side of the dual diaphragm is connected by a vacuum hose to the intake manifold. When the engine is idling or decelerating, intake manifold vacuum is high and carburetor vacuum is low. Under these conditions, intake manifold vacuum, applied to the inner side of the dual diaphragm, retards ignition timing to promote more complete combustion of the air fuel mixture in the engine combustion chambers.

DUAL DIAPHRAGM TEST

1. Connect a timing light to the engine. Check the ignition timing.

NOTE: *Before proceeding with the tests, disconnect any spark control devices, distributor vacuum valves, etc. If these are left connected, inaccurate results may be obtained.*

2. Remove the retard hose from the distributor and plug it. Increase the engine speed. The timing should advance. If it fails to do so, then the vacuum unit is faulty and must be replaced.

3. Check the timing with the engine at normal idle speed. Unplug the retard hose and connect it to the vacuum unit. The timing should instantly be retarded. If this does not occur, the retard diaphragm has a leak and the vacuum unit must be replaced.

REMOVAL AND INSTALLATION

1. Remove the distributor cap and rotor.

2. Disconnect the vacuum lines.

3. Remove the clip that secures the diaphragm arm to the distributor advance plate.

4. Remove the screws that attach the diaphragm to the distributor (outside of the distributor).

5. Carefully remove the unit by tilting it downward to disengage the diaphragm arm from the plate.

6. Installation is the reverse of removal. Consult the instructions that come with the new diaphragm as to the calibration of the unit.

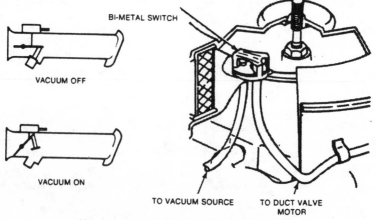

BI-METAL SWITCH

VACUUM OFF

VACUUM ON

TO VACUUM SOURCE   TO DUCT VALVE MOTOR

Vacuum-operated duct and valve assembly

Ported Vacuum Switch (Distributor Vacuum Control Valve)

The distributor vacuum control valve is a temperature-sensitive valve which screws into the water jacket of the engine. Three vacuum lines are attached to the vacuum control valve: one which runs from the carburetor to the control valve, one which runs from the control valve to the distributor vacuum advance (outer) chamber, and one which runs from the intake manifold to the distributor vacuum control valve.

During normal engine operation, vacuum from the carburetor passes through the top nipple on the distributor control valve, through the valve to the second nipple on the valve, and out the second nipple on the valve to the distributor vacuum advance chamber. When the engine is idling however, carburetor vacuum is very low, so that there is little, if any, vacuum in the passageways described above.

If the engine should begin to overheat while idling, a check ball inside the distributor vacuum control which normally blocks off the third nipple of the valve (intake manifold vacuum) moves upward to block off the first nipple (carburetor vacuum). This applies intake manifold vacuum (third nipple) to the distributor vacuum advance chamber (second nipple). Since intake manifold vacuum is very high while the engine is idling, ignition timing is advanced by the application of intake manifold vacuum to the distributor vacuum advance chamber. This raises the engine idle speed and helps to cool the engine.

PORTED VACUUM SWITCH (DISTRIBUTOR VACUUM CONTROL VALVE) TEST

1. Check the routing and connection of all vacuum hoses.
2. Attach a tachometer to the engine.
3. Bring the engine up to the normal operating temperature. The engine must not be overheated.
4. Note the engine rpm, with the transmission in neutral, and the throttle in the curb idle position.
5. Disconnect the vacuum hose from the intake manifold at the temperature-sensing valve. Plug or clamp the hose.
6. Note the idle rpm with the hose disconnected. If there is no change in rpm, the valve is good. If there is a drop of 100 or more rpm, the valve should be replaced. Replace the vacuum line.
7. Check to make sure that the all-season cooling mixture meets specifications, and that

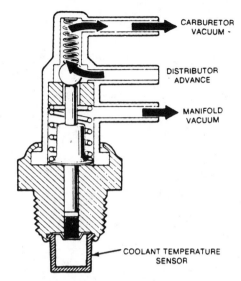

Ported vacuum switch operation

the correct radiator cap is in place and functioning.

8. Block the radiator air flow to induce a higher-than-normal temperature condition.
9. Continue to operate until the engine temperature or heat indicator shows above normal.

If engine speed by this time has increased 100 or more rpm, the temperature-sensing valve is satisfactory. If not, it should be replaced.

Deceleration Valve

Some IMCO-equipped 1968–72 engines are equipped with a distributor vacuum advance control valve (deceleration valve) which is used with dual-diaphragm distributors to further aid in controlling ignition timing. The deceleration valve is in the vacuum line which runs from the outer (advance) diaphragm to the carburetor—the normal vacuum supply for the distributor. During deceleration, the intake manifold vacuum rises causing the deceleration valve to close off the carburetor vacuum source and connect the intake manifold vacuum source to the distributor advance diaphragm. The increase in vacuum provides maximum ignition timing advance, thus providing more complete fuel combustion, and decreasing exhaust system backfiring.

DECELERATION VALVE TEST

1. Connect a tachometer to the engine and bring the engine to the normal operating temperature.

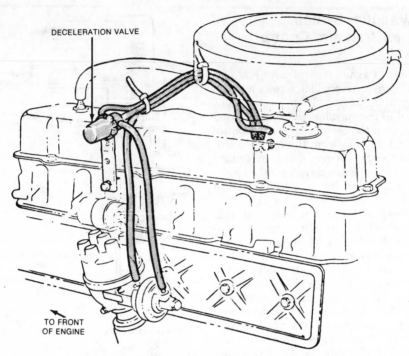

DECELERATION VALVE

TO FRONT
OF ENGINE

Deceleration valve installation—six cylinder

2. Check the idle speed and set it to specifications with the headlights on high beam, as necessary.

3. Turn off the headlights and note the idle rpm.

4. Remove the plastic cover from the valve. Slowly turn the adjusting screw counterclockwise without pressing in. After 5, and no more than 6 turns, the idle speed should suddenly increase to about 1000 rpm. If the speed does not increase after six turns, push inward on the valve spring retainer and release. Speed should now increase.

5. Slowly turn the adjusting screw clockwise until the idle speed drops to the speed noted in Step 3. Make one more turn clockwise.

6. Increase the engine speed to 2000 rpm, hold for 5 seconds, and release the throttle. The engine speed should return to idle speed within 4 seconds. If idle is not resumed in 4 seconds, back off the dashpot adjustment and repeat the check. If the idle is not resumed in 3 seconds with the dashpot back off, turn the deceleration valve adjustment screw an additional quarter turn clockwise and repeat the check. Repeat the quarter turn adjustment and idle return checks until the engine returns to idle within the required time.

7. If it takes more than one complete turn from Step 5 to meet the idle return time specification, replace the valve.

Spark Delay Valve

The spark delay valve is a plastic, spring-loaded, color-coded valve which is installed in the vacuum line to the distributor advance diaphragm on many 1971 and later models. Under heavy throttle applications, the valve will close, blocking normal carburetor vacuum to the distributor. After the designated period of closed time, the valve opens, restoring the carburetor vacuum to the distributor.

SPARK DELAY VALVE TEST

NOTE: *If the distributor vacuum line contains a cut-off solenoid, it must be open during this test.*

1. Detach the vacuum line from the dis-

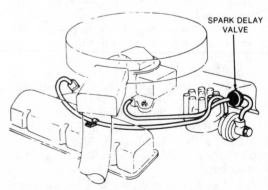

SPARK DELAY
VALVE

Spark delay valve installation—V8 shown

tributor at the spark delay valve end. Connect a vacuum gauge to the valve, in its place.

2. Connect a tachometer to the engine. Start the engine and rapidly increase its speed to 2,000 rpm with the transmission in neutral.

3. As soon as the engine speed is increased, the vacuum gauge reading should drop to zero.

4. Hold the engine speed at a steady 2,000 rpm. It should take longer than two seconds for the gauge to register 6 in. Hg. If it takes less than two seconds, the valve is defective and must be replaced.

5. If it takes longer than the number of seconds specified for the gauge to reach 6 in. Hg, disconnect the vacuum gauge from the spark delay valve. Disconnect the hose which runs from the spark delay valve to the carburetor at the valve end. Connect the vacuum gauge to this hose.

6. Start the engine and increase its speed to 2,000 rpm. The gauge should indicate 10–16 in. Hg. If it does not, there is a blockage in the carburetor vacuum port or else the hose itself is plugged or broken. If the gauge reading is within specification, the valve is defective.

7. Reconnect all vacuum lines and remove the tachometer, once testing is completed.

REMOVAL AND INSTALLATION

1. Locate the spark delay valve in the distributor vacuum line and disconnect it from the line.

2. Install a new spark delay valve in the line, making sure that the black end of the valve is connected to the line from the carburetor and the color-coded end is connected to the line from the spark delay valve to the distributor.

Distributor Modulator (Dist-O-Vac) System

1970 models equipped with automatic transmission and the 240, 302, or 390 2 bbl engines, and 1971 models equipped with automatic transmission and the 240, 390 2 bbl, or 429 4 bbl engines are equipped with a Dist-O-Vac spark control system. This system is used in conjunction with all of the IMCO system equipment except the deceleration valve.

The three components of the Dist-O-Vac system are the speed sensor, the thermal

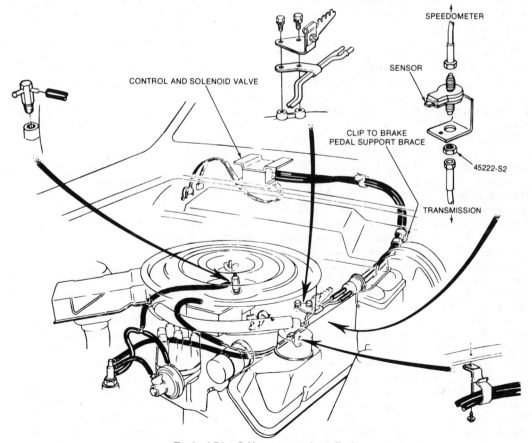

Typical Dist-O-Vac system installation

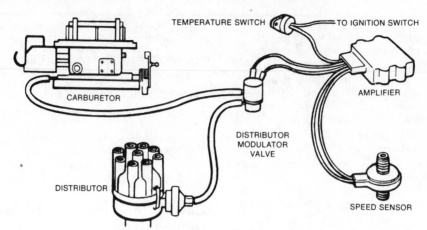

Electronic spark control system schematic

switch, and the electronic control module. The electronic control module consists of two sub-assemblies: the electronic control amplifier and the three-way solenoid valve.

The speed sensor, a small unit mounted in the speedometer cable, contains a rotating magnet and a stationary winding which is insulated from ground. The magnet, which rotates with the speedometer cable, generates a small voltage which increases directly with speed. This voltage is directed to the electronic control amplifier.

The thermal switch consists of a bimetallic-element switch which is mounted in the right door pillar and senses the temperature of the air. The switch is closed at 58°F or lower, and open at temperatures about 58°F. This switch is also connected to the electronic control amplifier.

Within the electronic control module case, there is a printed circuit board and an electronic amplifier. The speed sensor and thermal switch are connected to this assembly. The thermal switch is the dominant circuit. When the temperature of the outside air is 58°F or lower, the circuit is closed, so that regardless of speed, the electronic control amplifier will not trigger the three-way solenoid valve. At temperatures above 58°F, however, the thermal switch circuit is open, allowing the circuit from the speed sensor to take over and control the action of the solenoid valve.

The three-way solenoid valve is located within the electronic control module and below the printed circuit board of the amplifier. It is vented to the atmosphere at the top, and connected at the bottom of the carburetor spark port (small hose) and the primary (advance) side of the dual-diaphragm distributor (large hose). The large hose is also channeled through the temperature-sensing valve. The

small hose is equipped with an air bleed to provide a positive airflow in the direction of the carburetor. The air bleed purges the hose of vacuum, thus assuring that raw gasoline will not be drawn through the hose and into the distributor diaphragm.

When the thermal switch is closed (air temperature 58°F or lower), or when it is open and the speed sensor is not sending out a strong enough voltage signal (speeds below approximately 35 mph), the amplifier will not activate the solenoid valve and the valve is in the closed position, blocking the passage of air from the small tube through the large tube. With the valve in this position, the larger hose is vented to the atmosphere through the top opening in the three-way valve assembly. Consequently, no vacuum is being supplied to the primary diaphragm on the distributor, and, therefore, no vacuum advance.

When the air temperature is above 58°F and/or the speed of the car is sufficient to generate the required voltage (35 mph or faster), the valve opens, blocking the vent to the atmosphere while opening the vacuum line from the carburetor spark port to the primary diaphragm of the distributor.

Electronic Spark Control

1972 Fords manufactured for sale in California equipped with a 351C or 400 V8, and all 1972 Fords equipped with the 429 Police Interceptor engine, use the electronic spark control system.

Electronic Spark Control is a system which blocks off carburetor vacuum to the distributor vacuum advance mechanism under certain temperature and speed conditions. The Electronic Spark Control System consists of four components: a temperature sensor, a speed sensor, an amplifier, and a distributor modulator vacuum valve. The system serves to prevent ignition timing advance (by blocking off carburetor vacuum from the distributor vacuum advance mechanism) until the car reaches a speed of 35 mph when the ambient temperature is over 65°F.

The temperature sensor, which is mounted on the front face of the left door pillar, monitors the outside air temperature and relays this information to the amplifier. The amplifier, which is located under the instrument panel, controls the distributor modulator vacuum valve. The modulator valve, which is attached to the ignition coil mounting bracket, is connected into the carburetor vacuum line to the distributor, and is normally open. If the temperature of the outside air is below 48°F, the contacts in the temperature sensor are open and no signal is sent to the amplifier. Since no signal is sent to the amplifier, the amplifer does not send a signal to the distributor modulator valve, and the vacuum passage from the carburetor to the distributor vacuum advance remains open. When the outside temperature rises to 65°F or above, the contacts in the temperature sensor close, and a signal is sent to the amplifier. The amplifier relays the message to the distributor modulator, which closes to block the vacuum passage to the distributor, preventing ignition timing advance.

When the ambient temperature is 65°F or above, ignition timing advance is prevented until the amplifier receives a signal from the speed sensor that the speed of the vehicle has reached 35 mph, and the distributor modulator vacuum valve can be opened to permit ignition timing advance.

The speed sensor is a miniature generator which is connected to the speedometer cable of the car. As the speedometer cable turns, the inside of the speed sensor turns with the speedometer cable. As the speed of the car increases, a rotating magnet in the speed sensor induces an electronic current in the stationary windings in the speed sensor. This current is sent to the amplifier. As the speed of the vehicle increases, the amount of current sent to the amplifier by the speed sensor increases proportionately. When the car reaches a speed of 35 mph, the amplifier signals the distributor modulator vacuum valve to open, allowing carburetor vacuum to be sent to the distributor vacuum advance chamber. This permits the ignition timing to advance.

It should be noted that this system operates only when the ambient temperature is 65°F or above, and then only when the speed of the car is below 35 mph.

Transmission Regulated Spark System

1972 models equipped with the 240 Six or the 351W V8 and automatic transmission use a transmission regulated spark control system.

The transmission regulated spark control system (TRS) differs from the Dist-O-Vac and ESC systems in that the speed sensor and amplifier are replaced by a switch on the transmission. The switch is activated by a mechanical linkage which opens the switch when the transmission is shifted into High gear. The switch, when opened, triggers the opening of the vacuum lines to the distributor, thus providing vacuum advance. So, in short, the TRS system blocks vacuum advance to the distributor only when the outside temperature is above 65°F and the transmission is in First or Second gear.

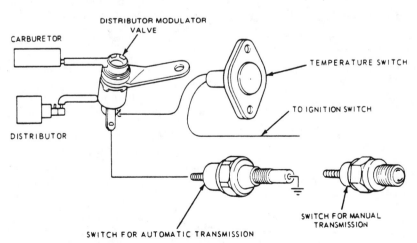

Transmission regulated spark control system schematic

ELECTRONIC SPARK CONTROL SYSTEM OPERATION TEST

1. Raise the car until the wheels are clear of the ground by at least 4 in. Support the rear of the car with jackstands.

CAUTION: *The car must be firmly supported during this test. If one of the wheels should come in contact with the ground while it is turning, it will move forward very rapidly and unexpectedly. As an extra precaution, chock the front wheels and do not stand in front of the vehicle while the wheels are turning.*

2. Disconnect the vacuum hose from the distributor vacuum advance chamber. This is the outer hose on vans with dual diaphragm vacuum advance units.

3. Connect the hose to a vacuum gauge.

4. Pour hot water on the temperature sensing switch to make sure that it is above 65°F.

5. Start the engine and apply the foot brake. Depress the clutch and shift the transmission into High gear. Release the hand brake and slowly engage the clutch.

6. Have an assistant observe the vacuum gauge while you raise the speed of the engine until the speedometer reads 35 mph, at which time the vacuum gauge should show a reading.

7. If the vacuum gauge shows a reading below 35 mph, a component in the electronic spark control system is defective. If the vacuum gauge does not show a reading, even above 35 mph, there is either a defective component in the electronic spark control system, or there is a broken or clogged vacuum passage between the carburetor and the distributor.

REMOVAL AND INSTALLATION

Dist-O-Vac and ESC Temperature Sensor

1. Open the right door and remove the two screws which attach the temperature sensor to the right door pillar.

2. Disconnect the lead wires from the temperature sensor.

3. Connect the lead wires to the new sensor.

4. Position the sensor on the door pillar and install the attaching screws.

Dist-O-Vac and ESC Speed Sensor

1. Disconnect the lead wires from the sensor.

2. Disconnect the speed sensor from the speedometer cable.

3. Position the O-rings on both ends of the new speed sensor.

4. Connect both ends of the speedometer cable to the speed sensor.

5. Connect the lead wires to the speed sensor.

ESC Amplifier

1. Locate the amplifier under the instrument panel, near the glove compartment.

2. Disconnect the wiring harness from the amplifier.

3. Remove the two amplifier attaching screws and remove the amplifier.

4. Position a new amplifier under the instrument panel and connect the wiring harness to it.

5. Install the two amplifier attaching screws.

ESC Distributor Vacuum Modulator Valve

1. Tag the hoses that attach to the modulator and disconnect them from the amplifier.

2. Disconnect the lead wires from the modulator.

3. Remove the No. 2 left front valve cover bolt (six-cylinder) or the inboard left front valve cover bolt and remove the modulator.

4. Position the new modulator on the valve cover and install the attaching bolt.

5. Connect the wires and hoses to the modulator.

Exhaust Gas Recirculation System

All 1973 and later models are equipped with an exhaust gas recirculation (EGR) system to control oxides of nitrogen.

On V8 engines, exhaust gases travel through the exhaust gas crossover passage in the intake manifold. On spacer entry equipped engines, a portion of these gases are diverted into a spacer which is mounted under the carburetor. On floor entry models, a regulated portion of exhaust gases enters the intake manifold through a pair of small holes drilled in the floor of the intake manifold riser. The EGR control valve, which is attached to the rear of the spacer or intake manifold, consists of a vacuum diaphragm with an attached plunger which normally blocks off exhaust gases from entering the intake manifold.

On all models, the EGR valve is controlled by a vacuum line from the carburetor which passes through a ported vacuum switch. The EGR ported vacuum switch provides vacuum to the EGR valve at coolant temperatures above 125°F. The vacuum diaphragm then opens the EGR valve permitting exhaust gases to flow through the carburetor spacer and enter the combustion chambers. The exhaust gases are relatively oxygen-free, and tend to

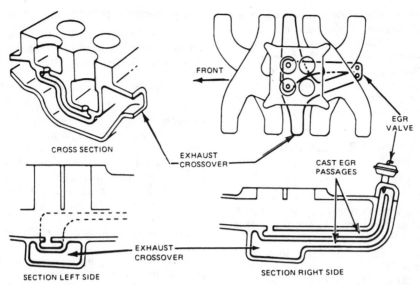

Floor entry EGR valve operation

dilute the combustion charge. This lowers peak combustion temperature thereby reducing oxides of nitrogen.

On some models equipped with a 351C, 400, 429 or 460 V8, an EGR subsystem, consisting of a speed sensor and control amplifier, prevents exhaust gases from entering the combustion mixture when the car is traveling 65 mph or faster.

System Test

1. Allow the engine to warm up, so that the coolant temperature has reached at least 125°F.

2. Disconnect the vacuum hose which runs from the temperature cut-in valve to the EGR valve at the EGR valve end. Connect a vacuum gauge to this hose with a T-fitting.

3. Increase engine speed. Do not exceed half throttle or 3,000 rpm. The gauge should indicate a vacuum. If no vacuum is present, check the following:

    a. The carburetor—look for a clogged vacuum port.

    b. The vacuum hoses—including the vacuum hoses to the transmission modulator.

    c. The temperature cut-in valve—if no vacuum is present at its outlet with the engine temperature above 125°F and vacuum available from the carburetor, the valve is defective.

4. If all the above tests are positive, check the EGR valve itself.

5. Connect an outside vacuum source and a vacuum gauge to the valve.

6. Apply vacuum to the EGR valve. The valve should open at 3–10 in. Hg, the engine

idle speed should slow down and the idle quality should become more rough.

7. If this does not happen, i.e., the EGR valve remains closed, the EGR valve is defective and must be replaced.

8. If the valve stem moves but the idle remains the same, the valve orifice is clogged and must be cleaned.

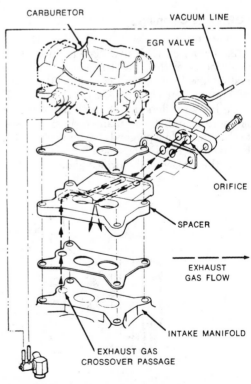

Spacer entry EGR valve operation

NOTE: *If an outside vacuum source is not available, disconnect the hose which runs between the EGR valve and the temperature cut-in valve and plug the hose connections on the cut-in valve. Connect the EGR valve hose to a source of intake manifold vacuum and watch the idle. The results should be the same as in steps 6–7, above.*

Temperature Cut-In Valve EGR Ported Vacuum Switch

VALVE BENCH TEST

1. Remove the valve from the engine.
2. Connect an outside source of vacuum to the top port on the valve. Leave the bottom port vented to the atmosphere.
3. Use ice or an aerosol spray to cool the valve below 60 °F.
4. Apply 20 in. Hg vacuum to the valve. The valve should hold a minimum of 19 in. Hg vacuum for 5 minutes without leaking down.
5. Leave the vacuum source connected to the valve and place it, along with a high temperature thermometer, into a nonmetallic, heat-resistant container full of water.
6. Heat the water. The vacuum in the valve should drop to zero once the temperature of the water reaches about 125°F.
7. Replace the valve if it fails either of the tests.

EGR Valve Cleaning

Remove the EGR valve for cleaning. Do not strike or pry on the valve diaphragm housing or supports, as this may damage the valve operating mechanism and/or change the valve calibration. Check orifice hole in the EGR valve body for deposits. A small hand drill of no more than 0.060 in. diameter may be used to clean the hole if plugged. Extreme care must be taken to avoid enlarging the hole or damaging the surface of the orifice plate.

VALVES WHICH CANNOT BE DISASSEMBLED

Valves which are riveted or otherwise permanently assembled should be replaced if highly contaminated; they cannot be cleaned.

VALVES WHICH CAN BE DISASSEMBLED

Separate the diaphragm section from the main mounting body. Clean the valve plates, stem, and the mounting plate, using a small power-driven rotary type wire brush. Take care not to damage the parts. Remove deposits between stem and valve disc by using a steel blade or shim approximately 0.028 in. thick in a sawing motion around the stem shoulder at both sides of the disc.

The poppet must wobble and move axially before reassembly.

Clean the cavity and passages in the main body of the valve with a power-driven rotary wire brush. If the orifice plate has a hole less than 0.450 in. it must be removed for cleaning. Remove all loosened debris using compressed air. Reassemble the diaphragm section on the main body using a new gasket between them. Torque the attaching screws to specification. Clean the orifice plate and the counterbore in the valve body. Reinstall the orifice plate using a small amount of contact cement to retain the plate in place during assembly of the valve to the carburetor spacer. Apply cement to only outer edges of the orifice plate to avoid restriction of the orifice.

EGR Supply Passages and Carburetor Space Cleaning

Remove the carburetor and carburetor spacer on engines so equipped. Clean the supply tube with a small power-driven rotary type wire brush or blast cleaning equipment. Clean the exhaust gas passages in the spacer using a suitable wire brush and/or scraper. The machined holes in the spacer can be cleaned by using a suitable round wire brush. Hard encrusted

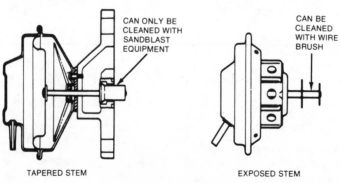

CAN ONLY BE CLEANED WITH SANDBLAST EQUIPMENT

CAN BE CLEANED WITH WIRE BRUSH

TAPERED STEM   EXPOSED STEM

EGR valve comparison

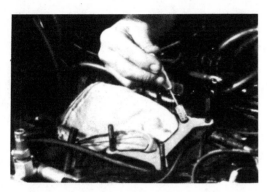

Cleaning EGR exhaust gas entry port in intake manifold

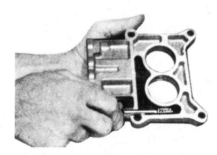

Cleaning EGR spacer exhaust passages

material should be probed loose first, then brushed out.

EGR Exhaust Gas Channel Cleaning

Clean the exhaust gas channel, where applicable, in the intake manifold, using a suitable carbon scraper. Clean the exhaust gas entry port in the intake manifold by hand passing a suitable drill bit thru the holes to auger out the deposits. Do not use a wire brush. The manifold riser bore(s) should be suitably plugged during the above action to prevent any of the residue from entering the induction system.

Delay Vacuum By-pass (DVB) System

All 1973 models equipped with the 351C, 400, 429, or 460 V8 manufactured before March 15, 1973 are equipped with the Delay Vacuum By-pass spark control system. This system provides two paths by which carburetor vacuum can reach the distributor vacuum advance. The system consists of a spark delay valve, a check valve, a solenoid vacuum valve, and an ambient temperature switch. When the ambient temperature is below 49°F, the temperature switch contacts are open and the vacuum solenoid is open (deenergized). Under these conditions, vacuum will flow from the carburetor, through the open solenoid, and to the distributor. Since the spark delay valve resists the flow of carburetor vacuum, the vacuum will always flow through the vacuum solenoid when it is open, since this is the path of least resistance. When the ambient temperature rises above 60°F, the contacts in the temperature switch (which is located in the door post) close. This passes ignition switch current to the solenoid, energizing the solenoid. This blocks one of the two vacuum paths. All distributor vacuum must now flow through the spark delay valve. When carburetor vacuum rises above a certain level on acceleration, a rubber valve in the spark delay valve blocks vacuum from passing through the valve for from 5 to 30 seconds. After this time delay has elapsed, normal vacuum is supplied to the distributor. When the vacuum solenoid is closed, (temperature above 60°), the vacuum line from the solenoid to the distributor is vented to atmosphere. To prevent the vacuum that is passing through the spark delay valve from escaping through the solenoid into the atmosphere, a one-way check valve is installed in the vacuum line from the solenoid to the distributor.

Cold Temperature Actuated Vacuum (CTAV) System

This system is installed on some 1973 models manufactured after March 15, 1973 and many 1974 models to control distributor spark advance. It is basically a refinement of the DVB or TAV spark control systems with the temperature switch relocated in the air cleaner and a latching relay added to maintain a strong vacuum signal at the distributor, whether it be EGR port or spark port carburetor vacuum, and to keep the system from intermittently switching vacuum signals when the intake air is between 49 and 60°F. When the temperature switch closes at 60°F, the latching relay (normally off) is energized and stays on until the ignition switch is turned off. The latching relay then overrides the temperature switch and forces the solenoid valve to keep the spark port vacuum system closed and open the EGR port vacuum system. This prevents full vacuum advance, once the engine is warmed-up, thereby lowering emissions.

EGR/Coolant Spark Control (CSC) System

The EGR/CSC system is used on most 1974 and later models. It regulates both distributor spark advance and the EGR valve operation according to coolant temperature by sequentially switching vacuum signals.

The major EGR/CSC system components are:

1. 95°F EGR-PVS valve;
2. Spark Delay Valve (SDV);
3. Vacuum check valve.

When the engine coolant temperature is below 82°F, the EGR-PVS valve admits carburetor EGR port vacuum (occurring at about 2,500 rpm) directly to the distributor advance diaphragm, through the one-way check valve.

At the same time, the EGR-PVS valve shuts off carburetor EGR vacuum to the EGR valve and transmission diaphragm.

When engine coolant temperature is 95°F and above, the EGR-PVS valve is actuated and directs carburetor EGR vacuum to the EGR valve and transmission instead of the distributor. At temperatures between 82–95°F, the EGR-PVS valve may be open, closed, or in mid-position.

The SDV valve delays carburetor spark vacuum to the distributor advance diaphragm by restricting the vacuum signal through the SCV valve for a predetermined time. During normal acceleration, little or no vacuum is admitted to the distributor advance diaphragm until acceleration is completed, because of (1) the time delay of the SDV valve and (2) the re-routing of EGR port vacuum if the engine coolant temperature is 95°F or higher.

The check valve blocks off vacuum signal from the SDV to the EGR-PVS so that carburetor spark vacuum will not be dissipated when the EGR-PVS is actuated above 95°F.

The 235°F PVS is not part of the EGR/CSC system, but is connected to the distributor vacuum advance to prevent engine overheating while idling (as on previous models). At idle speed, no vacuum is generated at either the carburetor spark port or EGR port and engine timing is fully retarded. When engine coolant temperature reaches 235°F, however, the valve is actuated to admit intake manifold vacuum to the distributor advance diaphragm. This advances the engine timing and speeds up the engine. The increase in coolant flow and fan speed lowers engine temperature.

EGR Venturi Vacuum Amplifier System

System Test

The amplifiers have built-in calibrations and no external adjustments are required. If the amplifier tests reveal it is malfunctioning, replace the amplifier. All connections are located on one side of the amplifier. A vacuum connector and hose assembly is used to assure that proper connections are made at the amplifier. The amplifier is retained with a sheet-metal screw.

1. Operate the engine until normal operating temperatures are reached.
2. Before the vacuum amplifier is checked, inspect all other basic components of the EGR System (EGR valve, EGR/PVS valve, hoses, routing, etc.).
3. Check vacuum amplifier connections for proper routing and installation. If necessary, refer to the typical vacuum amplifier schematic.
4. Remove hose at EGR valve.
5. Connect vacuum gauge to EGR hose. Gauge must read in increments of at least 1 in. Hg graduation.
6. Remove hose at carburetor venturi (leave off).
7. With engine at curb idle speed, vacuum gauge reading should be within ±0.3 in. Hg of specified bias valve as shown in amplifier specifications for other than zero bias. Zero bias may read from 0 to 0.5 in. Hg. If out of specification, replace amplifier.
8. Depress accelerator and release after engine has reached 1500 to 2000 rpm. After engine has returned to idle, the vacuum must return to bias noted in step 7. If bias has changed, replace amplifier. Also, if vacuum shows a marked increase (greater than 1 in. Hg) during acceleration period, the amplifier should be replaced.
9. Hook up venturi hose at carburetor with engine at curb idle rpm. If a sizeable increase in output vacuum is observed, (more than 0.5 in. Hg above step 7), check idle speed. High idle speed could increase output vacuum due to venturi vacuum increase. See engine decal for correct idle specifications.
10. Check amplifier reservoir and connections as follows: Disconnect external reservoir hose at amplifier and AP or plug. Depress accelerator rapidly to 1500 to 2000 rpm. The vacuum should increase to 4 in. Hg or more. If out of specifications, replace amplifier.

Cold Start Spark Advance (CSSA) System

All 1975–78 models using the 460 V8 are equipped with the CSSA System. It is a modification of the existing spark control system to aid in cold start driveability. The system uses a coolant temperature sensing vacuum switch located on the thermostat housing. When the engine is cold (below 125°F), it permits full manifold vacuum to the distributor advance

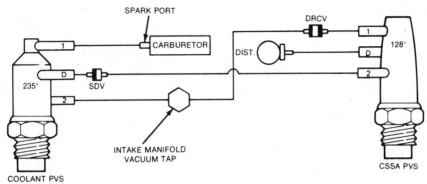

CSSA system schematic

diaphragm. After the engine warms up, normal spark control (retard) resumes.

Vacuum Operated Heat Control Valve (VOHV)

To further aid cold start driveability during engine warmup, most 1975 and later engines use a VOHV located between the exhaust manifold and the exhaust inlet (header) pipe.

When the engine is first started, the valve is closed, blocking exhaust gases from exiting from one bank of cylinders. These gases are then diverted back through the intake manifold crossover passage under the carburetor. The result is quick heat to the carburetor and choke.

The VOHV is controlled by a ported vacuum switch which uses manifold vacuum to keep the vacuum motor on the valve closed until the coolant reaches a predetermined "warm-up" valve. When the engine is warmed-up, the PVS shuts off vacuum to the VOHV, and a strong return spring opens the VOHV butterfly.

Testing the Vacuum Operated Heat Riser

Testing the vacuum operated heat riser valve is a matter of making sure it opens and closes

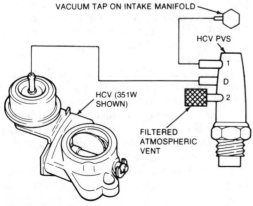

VOHV system schematic

freely. You can move it by hand to see if it works, on a warm engine. On a cold engine, the valve should be closed, and disconnecting the hose should allow it to open (engine idling). On a cold engine, there should be vacuum at the vacuum actuator. On a warm engine the vacuum should be shut off.

Catalytic Converter System

Starting in 1975 most models have a catalytic converter(s) located in the exhaust system. The converter works as a gas reactor, and its catalytic function is to speed up the heat producing chemical reaction between the exhaust gas components in order to reduce the air pollutants in the engine exhaust.

The catalyst material is contained in a sealed, honeycombed chamber. It is the surface of the catalyst material that plays a major role in the heat producing chemical reaction. There are basically three types of catalytic converters:

1. The conventional oxidation catalyst (COC); used to oxidize hydrocarbons (HC) and carbon monoxide (CO).

2. The three-way catalyst (TWC); not only works on HC and CO but also reduces nitrogen oxides (NOx).

3. The light off catalyst (LOC); arranged in series with the main catalytic converter, is designed to handle the exhaust emissions during engine warmup when the main converter has not reached the proper temperature for maximum efficiency.

In order to provide oxygen necessary to obtain the converter's maximum efficiency a secondary air source is provided by the air pump (thermactor). The system is protected by several devices that block out the secondary air when the engine is laboring under any abnormal hot or cold operating situation.

The catalytic converter is expected to function without service for at least 50,000 miles. Use of leaded fuel would quickly cause catalyst failure and an expensive repair bill.

FUEL SYSTEM

Fuel Pump

A single-action mechanical fuel pump, driven by the camshaft, is used on all models except some Police Interceptor 429 and 460 engines and the 302 fuel injected engine.

Some Police Interceptor 429 and 460 engines and the fuel injected 302 use an electric fuel pump located in the gas tank. The gas tank must be removed to service the electric fuel pump.

CAUTION: *The fuel injected 302 has the fuel system under extreme pressure. A special tool is necessary to bleed off the pressure before servicing this system. It is suggested that only qualified mechanics work on this system.*

The mechanical fuel pump is located at the lower left-side of the engine block on six-cylinder models, and at the lower left-side of the cylinder front cover on V8 models.

TESTING AND ADJUSTMENT

No adjustments may be made to the fuel pump. Before removing and replacing the old fuel pump, the following test may be made while the pump is still installed on the engine.

CAUTION: *To avoid accidental ignition of fuel during the test, first remove the coil high-tension wire from the distributor and the coil.*

1. If a fuel pressure gauge is available, connect the gauge to the engine and operate the engine until the pressure stops rising. Stop the engine and take the reading. If the reading is within the specifications given in the "Tune-Up Specifications" chart in Chapter 2, the malfunction is not in the fuel pump. Also check the pressure drop after the engine is stopped. A large pressure drop below the minimum specification indicates leaky valves. If the pump proves to be satisfactory, check the tank and inlet line.

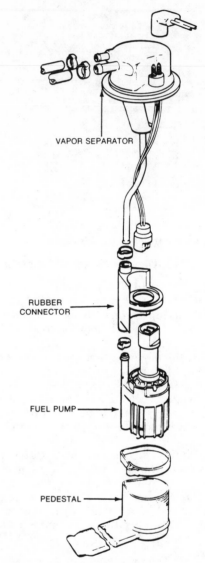

VAPOR SEPARATOR

RUBBER CONNECTOR

FUEL PUMP

PEDESTAL

Electric fuel pump and related parts

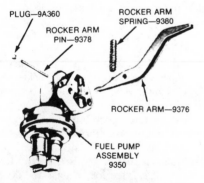

PLUG—9A360

ROCKER ARM PIN—9378

ROCKER ARM SPRING—9380

ROCKER ARM—9376

FUEL PUMP ASSEMBLY 9350

Carter permanently-sealed fuel pump—V8

2. If a fuel pressure gauge is not available, disconnect the fuel line at the pump outlet, place a vessel beneath the pump outlet, and crank the engine. A good pump will force the fuel out of the outlet in steady spurts. A worn diaphragm spring may not provide proper pumping action.

3. As a further test, disconnect and plug the fuel line from the tank at the pump, and hold your thumb over the pump inlet. If the pump is functioning properly, suction should be felt on your thumb. No suction indicates that the pump diaphragm is leaking, or that the diaphragm linkage is worn.

4. Check the crankcase for gasoline. A ruptured diaphragm may leak fuel into the engine.

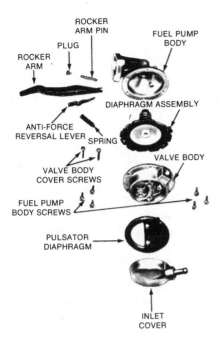

Carter Police Interceptor fuel pump disassembled

REMOVAL AND INSTALLATION

Mechanical Pump

1. Disconnect the plug and inlet and outlet lines from the fuel pump.

2. Remove the fuel pump retaining bolts and carefully pull the pump and old gasket away from the block.

3. Discard the old gasket. Clean the mating surfaces on the block and position a new gasket on the block, using oil-resistant sealer.

4. Mount the fuel pump and gasket to the engine block, being careful to insert the pump lever (rocker arm) in the engine block, aligning it correctly above the camshaft lobe.

NOTE: *If resistance is felt while positioning the fuel pump on the block, the camshaft lobe is probably on the high position. To ease installation, connect a remote engine starter switch to the engine and "tap" the switch until resistance fades.*

5. While holding the pump securely against the block, install the retaining bolts. On six-cylinder engines, torque the bolts to 12–15 ft. lbs., and on V8s, 20–24 ft. lbs.

6. Unplug and reconnect the fuel lines at the pump.

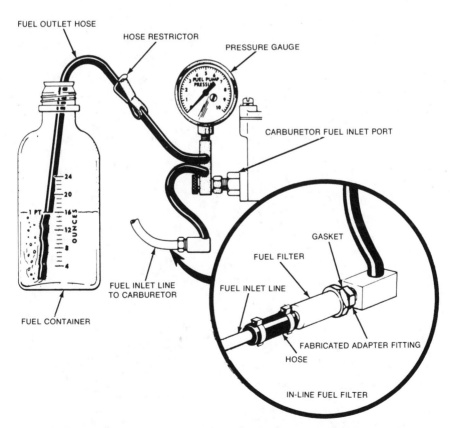

Typical fuel pump pressure and capacity test equipment

7. Start the engine and check for fuel leaks. Also check for oil leaks where the fuel pump attaches to the block.

Electric Choke

Starting in 1973, all models use an electrically-assisted choke to reduce exhaust emissions of carbon monoxide during warmup. The system consists of a choke cap, a thermostatic spring, a bimetal sensing disc (switch) and a ceramic positive temperature coefficient (PTC) heater.

The choke is powered from the center tap of the alternator, so that current is constantly applied to the temperature sensing disc. The system is grounded through the carburetor body. At temperatures below approximately 60°F, the switch is open and no current is supplied to the ceramic heater, thereby resulting in normal unassisted thermostatic spring choking action. When the temperature rises above about 60°F, the temperature sensing disc closes and current is supplied to the heater, which in turn, acts on the thermostatic spring. Once the heater starts, it causes the thermostatic spring to pull the choke plate(s) open within 1½ minutes, which is sooner than it would open if nonassisted.

ELECTRIC CHOKE OPERATIONAL TEST

1. Detach the electrical lead from the choke cap.

2. Use a jumper lead to connect the terminal on the choke cap and the wire terminal, so that the electrical circuit is still completed.

3. Start the engine.

4. Hook up a test light between the connector on the choke lead and ground.

5. The test light should glow. If it does not, current is not being supplied to the electrically-assisted choke.

6. Connect the test light between the terminal on the alternator and the terminal on the choke cap. If the light now glows, replace the lead, since it is not passing current to the choke assist.

CAUTION: *Do not ground the terminal on the alternator while performing Step 6.*

7. If the light still does not glow, the fault lies somewhere in the electrical system. Check the system out.

If the electrically-assisted choke receives power but still does not appear to be functioning properly, reconnect the choke lead and proceed with the rest of the test.

8. Tape the bulb end of the thermometer to the metallic portion of the choke housing.

9. If the electrically-assisted choke operates below 55°F, it is defective and must be replaced.

10. Allow the engine to warm up to between 80 and 100°F; at these temperatures the choke should operate for about 1½ minutes.

11. If it does not operate for this length of

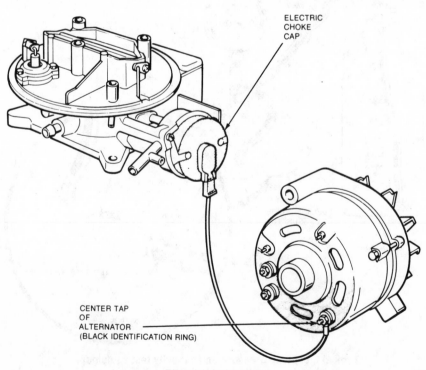

ELECTRIC
CHOKE
CAP

CENTER TAP
OF
ALTERNATOR
(BLACK IDENTIFICATION RING)

Electric choke wiring

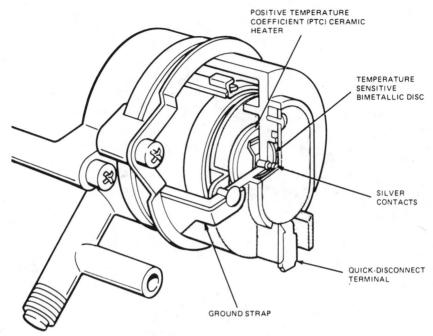

POSITIVE TEMPERATURE
COEFFICIENT (PTC) CERAMIC
HEATER

TEMPERATURE
SENSITIVE
BIMETALLIC DISC

SILVER
CONTACTS

QUICK-DISCONNECT
TERMINAL

GROUND STRAP

Electric choke components

time, check the bimetallic spring to see if it is connected to the tang on the choke lever.

12. If the spring is connected and the choke is not operating properly, replace the cap assembly.

Carburetors

Nine different carburetors have been used on full size cars from 1968 to the present. The carburetors are installed as per the following usage chart:

• Autolite 1101	1968–69 240 Six
• Carter YF	1968–72 240 Six
• Autolite (Motor-craft) 2100	1968–74 302, 351, 390, 400, 429 V8
• Motorcraft 2150	1975–79 351, 400
• Autolite 4100	1968–69 428PI V8
• Autolite (Motor-craft) 4300	1968–74, 390, 428, 429, 460 V8
• Motorcraft 4350	1975–78 400 V8 and 460 V8
• Carter Thermo-Quad®	1974 460 V8
• Motorcraft 2700 Variable Venturi (VV) and Motorcraft 7200 Variable Venturi (VV)	Used with various models and electronic engine controls

In accordance with Federal emissions regulations, all carburetors are equipped with idle mixture screw limiter caps. These caps are installed to prevent tampering with the carburetor fuel mixture screws so that the engine cannot be adjusted to a richer idle mixture.

Most models are equipped with a throttle solenoid positioner. The purpose of a throttle solenoid is to prevent the engine from running on (dieseling) after the ignition is turned off. Dieseling is a common occurrence with many cars using emission control systems that require a leaner fuel mixture, a higher operating temperature, and a higher curb idle speed. The throttle solenoid prevents running-on and dieseling by closing the throttle plate(s) after the key is turned off, thereby shutting off the air and gas to the overheated combustion chamber.

THROTTLE SOLENOID (ANTIDIESELING SOLENOID) TEST

1. Turn the ignition key on and open the throttle. The solenoid plunger should extend (solenoid energize).

2. Turn the ignition off. The plunger should retract, allowing the throttle to close.

NOTE: *With the antidieseling solenoid de-energized, the carburetor idle speed adjusting screw must make contact with the throttle shaft to prevent the throttle plates from jamming in the throttle bore when the engine is turned off.*

3. If the solenoid is functioning properly and the engine is still dieseling, check for one of the following:

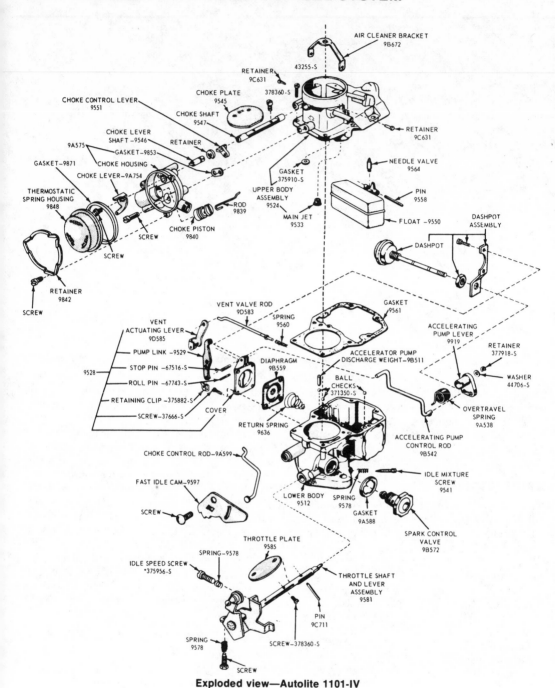

AIR CLEANER BRACKET
9B672

43255-S

RETAINER
9C631

CHOKE PLATE
9545

378360-S

CHOKE CONTROL LEVER
9551

CHOKE SHAFT
9547

RETAINER
9C631

CHOKE LEVER
SHAFT –9546

RETAINER

9A575

GASKET–9853

NEEDLE VALVE
9564

GASKET–9871

CHOKE HOUSING

PIN
9558

CHOKE LEVER–9A754

GASKET
375910-S

THERMOSTATIC
SPRING HOUSING
9848

UPPER BODY
ASSEMBLY
9524

ROD
9839

FLOAT –9550

DASHPOT
ASSEMBLY

MAIN JET
9533

SCREW

CHOKE PISTON
9840

DASHPOT

SCREW

RETAINER
9842

SCREW

VENT VALVE ROD
9D583

GASKET
9561

SPRING
9560

VENT
ACTUATING LEVER
9D585

ACCELERATING
PUMP LEVER
9919

RETAINER
377918-S

PUMP LINK –9529

DIAPHRAGM
9B559

ACCELERATOR PUMP
DISCHARGE WEIGHT–9B511

WASHER
44706-S

9528

STOP PIN –67516-S

ROLL PIN –67743-S

BALL
CHECKS
371350-S

RETAINING CLIP –375882-S

OVERTRAVEL
SPRING
9A538

SCREW–37666-S

COVER

RETURN SPRING
9636

ACCELERATING PUMP
CONTROL ROD
9B542

CHOKE CONTROL ROD–9A599

IDLE MIXTURE
SCREW
9541

FAST IDLE CAM–9597

LOWER BODY
9512

SPRING
9578

SCREW

GASKET
9A588

SPARK CONTROL
VALVE
9B572

THROTTLE PLATE
9585

SPRING–9578

IDLE SPEED SCREW
*375956-S

THROTTLE SHAFT
AND LEVER
ASSEMBLY
9581

PIN
9C711

SPRING
9578

SCREW–378360-S

SCREW

Exploded view—Autolite 1101-IV

a. High idle or engine shut off speed;
b. Engine timing not set to specification;
c. Binding throttle linkage;
d. Too low an octane fuel being used.

Correct any of these problems as necessary.

4. If the solenoid fails to function as outlined in Steps 1–2, disconnect the solenoid leads; the solenoid should de-energize. If it does not, it is jammed and must be replaced.

5. Connect the solenoid to a 12 V power source and to ground. Open the throttle so that the plunger can extend. If it does not, the solenoid is defective.

6. If the solenoid is functioning correctly and no other source of trouble can be found, the fault probably lies in the wiring between the solenoid and the ignition switch or in the ignition switch itself. Remember to reconnect the solenoid when finished testing.

NOTE: *On some 1970–71 models, dieseling*

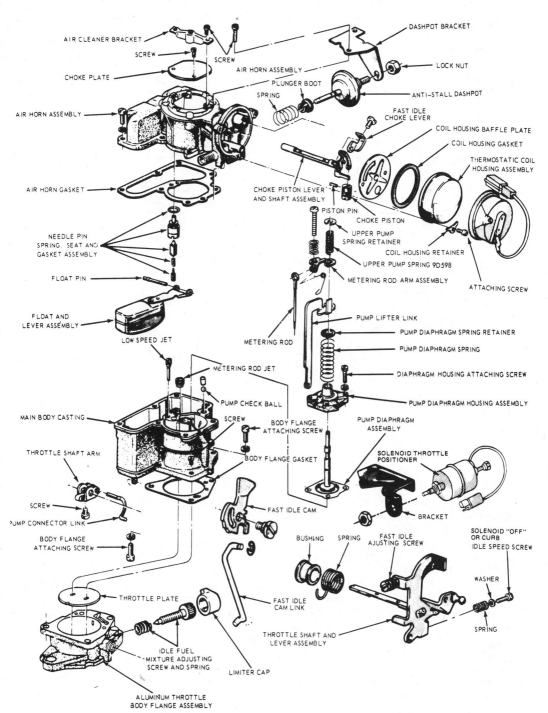

AIR CLEANER BRACKET

SCREW

CHOKE PLATE

AIR HORN ASSEMBLY

AIR HORN GASKET

NEEDLE PIN
SPRING, SEAT AND
GASKET ASSEMBLY

FLOAT PIN

FLOAT AND
LEVER ASSEMBLY

LOW SPEED JET

MAIN BODY CASTING

THROTTLE SHAFT ARM

SCREW

PUMP CONNECTOR LINK

BODY FLANGE
ATTACHING SCREW

THROTTLE PLATE

IDLE FUEL
MIXTURE ADJUSTING
SCREW AND SPRING

LIMITER CAP

ALUMINUM THROTTLE
BODY FLANGE ASSEMBLY

SCREW

AIR HORN ASSEMBLY

PLUNGER BOOT

SPRING

DASHPOT BRACKET

LOCK NUT

ANTI-STALL DASHPOT

FAST IDLE
CHOKE LEVER

COIL HOUSING BAFFLE PLATE

COIL HOUSING GASKET

THERMOSTATIC COIL
HOUSING ASSEMBLY

CHOKE PISTON LEVER
AND SHAFT ASSEMBLY

PISTON PIN

CHOKE PISTON

UPPER PUMP
SPRING RETAINER

COIL HOUSING RETAINER

UPPER PUMP SPRING 9D598

METERING ROD ARM ASSEMBLY

ATTACHING SCREW

METERING ROD

PUMP LIFTER LINK

PUMP DIAPHRAGM SPRING RETAINER

PUMP DIAPHRAGM SPRING

DIAPHRAGM HOUSING ATTACHING SCREW

PUMP DIAPHRAGM HOUSING ASSEMBLY

METERING ROD JET

PUMP CHECK BALL

SCREW

BODY FLANGE
ATTACHING SCREW

BODY FLANGE GASKET

PUMP DIAPHRAGM
ASSEMBLY

SOLENOID THROTTLE
POSITIONER

FAST IDLE CAM

BRACKET

BUSHING

SPRING

FAST IDLE
ADJUSTING SCREW

SOLENOID "OFF"
OR CURB
IDLE SPEED SCREW

WASHER

SPRING

FAST IDLE
CAM LINK

THROTTLE SHAFT AND
LEVER ASSEMBLY

Exploded view—Carter YF-IV

may occur when the engine is turned off because of feedback through the alternator warning light circuit. A diode kit is available from Ford to cure this problem. A failure of this diode may also lead to a similar problem.

REMOVAL AND INSTALLATION

1. Remove the air cleaner.
2. Disconnect the throttle cable or rod at the throttle lever. Disconnect the distributor

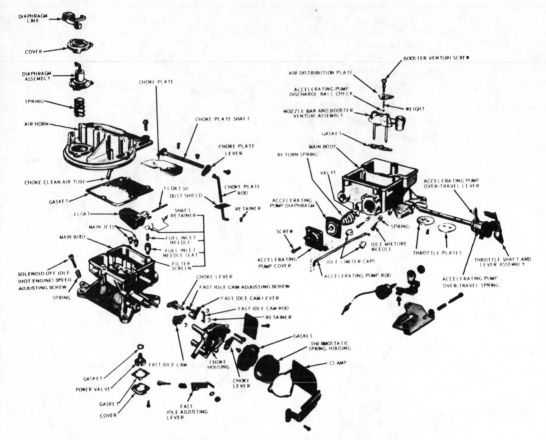

Exploded view—Motorcraft 2100-2V

vacuum line, exhaust gas recirculation line (1973 and later models), inline fuel filter, choke heat tube and the positive crankcase ventilation hose at the carburetor.

3. Disconnect the throttle solenoid (if so equipped) and electric choke assist (1973 and later models) at their connectors. Remove the wires to the carburetor on the 7200 VV.

4. Remove the carburetor retaining nuts. Lift off the carburetor carefully, taking care not to spill any fuel. Remove the carburetor mounting gasket and discard it. Remove the carburetor mounting spacer, if so equipped, from the intake manifold.

5. Prior to installation, clean the gasket mounting surfaces of the intake manifold, spacer (if so equipped), and carburetor. When using a spacer, use two new gaskets, sandwiching the spacer between the gaskets. If a spacer is not used, only one new carburetor mounting gasket is required.

6. Place the new gasket(s) and spacer (if so equipped) on the carburetor mounting studs. Position the carburetor on top of the gasket and hand tighten the retaining nuts. Then tighten the nuts in a criss-cross pattern to 10–15 ft. lbs.

7. Connect the throttle linkage, the distributor vacuum line, exhaust gas recirculation line (1973 and later models), inline fuel filter, choke heat tube, positive crankcase ventilation hose, throttle solenoid (if so equipped) and electric-choke assist (1973 and later models).

8. Adjust the curb idle speed, the idle fuel mixture and the accelerator pump stroke (Autolite-Motorcraft 2 and 4 barrel carburetors only).

OVERHAUL

All Except 2700 VV and 7200 VV

NOTE: *The 2700 VV and the 7200 VV carburetor equipped with the EEC system is electronically controlled, and an integral part of a sophisticated emission control system. Do not attempt to overhaul this carburetor.*

Efficient carburetion depends greatly on careful cleaning and inspection during overhaul, since dirt, gum, water, or varnish in or on the carburetor parts are often responsible for poor performance.

Overhaul your carburetor in a clean, dust-free area. Carefully disassemble the carburetor, referring often to the exploded views.

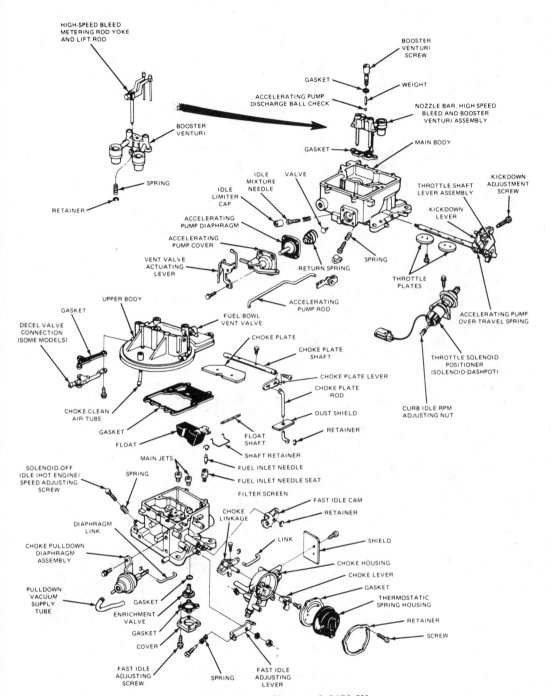

Exploded view—Motorcraft 2150-2V

Keep all similar and lookalike parts segregated during the disassembly and cleaning to avoid accidental interchange during assembly. Make a note of all jet sizes.

When the carburetor is disassembled, wash all parts (except diaphragms, electric choke units, pump plunger, and any other plastic, leather, fiber, or rubber parts) in clean carburetor solvent. Do not leave parts in the solvent any longer than is necessary to sufficiently loosen the deposits. Excessive cleaning may remove the special finish from the float bowl and choke valve bodies, leaving these parts unfit for service. Rinse all parts in clean solvent and blow them dry with compressed air or allow them to air dry. Wipe clean all cork, plastic, leather, and fiber parts with a clean, lint-free cloth.

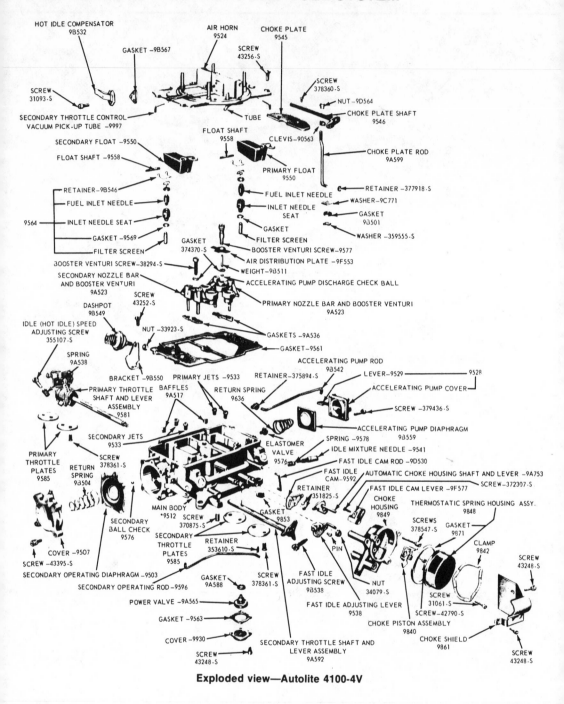

Exploded view—Autolite 4100-4V

Blow out all passages and jets with compressed air and be sure that there are no restrictions or blockages. Never use wire or similar tools to clean jets, fuel passages, or air bleeds. Clean all jets and valves separately to avoid accidental interchange.

Check all parts for wear or damage. If wear or damage is found, replace the defective parts. Especially check the following:

1. Check the float needle and seat for wear. If wear is found, replace the complete assembly.

2. Check the float hinge pin for wear and the float(s) for dents or distortion. Replace the float if fuel has leaked into it.

3. Check the throttle and choke shaft bores for wear to the throttle arm, shaft, or shaft bore will often require replacement of the throttle

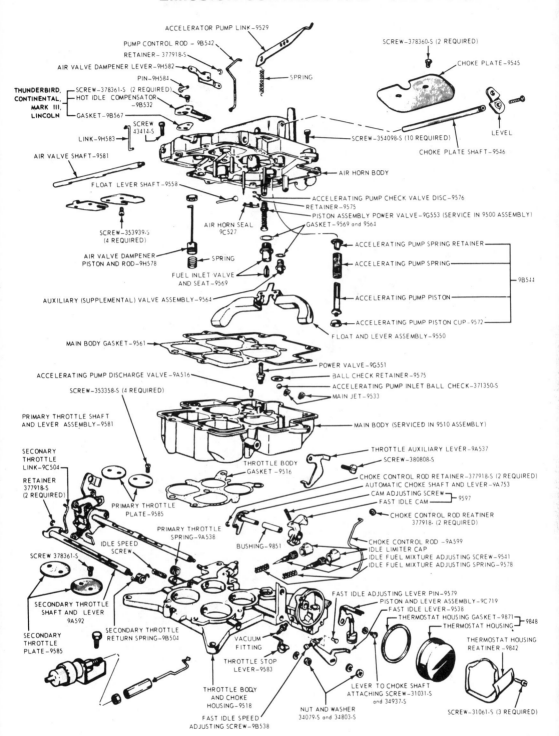

ACCELERATOR PUMP LINK-9529

PUMP CONTROL ROD - 9B542
RETAINER - 377918-S
AIR VALVE DAMPENER LEVER-9H582
PIN-9H584
THUNDERBIRD, SCREW-378361-S (2 REQUIRED)
CONTINENTAL, HOT IDLE COMPENSATOR
MARK III, -9B532
LINCOLN GASKET-9B567
SCREW
43414-S
LINK-9H583
SPRING

AIR VALVE SHAFT-9581

FLOAT LEVER SHAFT-9558

SCREW-353939-S
(4 REQUIRED)
AIR VALVE DAMPENER
PISTON AND ROD-9H578

AIR HORN SEAL
9C527
SPRING
FUEL INLET VALVE
AND SEAT-9569

AUXILIARY (SUPPLEMENTAL) VALVE ASSEMBLY-9564

MAIN BODY GASKET-9561

ACCELERATING PUMP DISCHARGE VALVE-9A516

SCREW-353358-S (4 REQUIRED)

PRIMARY THROTTLE SHAFT
AND LEVER ASSEMBLY-9581

SECONARY
THROTTLE
LINK-9C504

RETAINER
377918-S
(2 REQUIRED)

PRIMARY THROTTLE
PLATE-9585

PRIMARY THROTTLE
SPRING-9A538

IDLE SPEED
SCREW

SCREW 378361-S

SECONDARY THROTTLE
SHAFT AND LEVER
9A592

SECONDARY
THROTTLE
PLATE-9585

SECONDARY THROTTLE
RETURN SPRING-9B504

BUSHING-9851

VACUUM
FITTING

THROTTLE STOP
LEVER-9583

THROTTLE BODY
AND CHOKE
HOUSING-9518

FAST IDLE SPEED
ADJUSTING SCREW-9B538

NUT AND WASHER
34079-S and 34803-S

LEVER TO CHOKE SHAFT
ATTACHING SCREW-31031-S
and 34937-S

SCREW-378360-S (2 REQUIRED)

CHOKE PLATE-9545

LEVEL

SCREW-354098-S (10 REQUIRED)

CHOKE PLATE SHAFT-9546

AIR HORN BODY

ACCELERATING PUMP CHECK VALVE DISC-9576
RETAINER-9575
PISTON ASSEMBLY POWER VALVE-9G553 (SERVICE IN 9500 ASSEMBLY)
GASKET-9569 and 9564

ACCELERATING PUMP SPRING RETAINER
ACCELERATING PUMP SPRING
9B544
ACCELERATING PUMP PISTON
ACCELERATING PUMP PISTON CUP-9572

FLOAT AND LEVER ASSEMBLY-9550

POWER VALVE-9G551
BALL CHECK RETAINER-9575
ACCELERATING PUMP INLET BALL CHECK-371350-S
MAIN JET-9533

MAIN BODY (SERVICED IN 9510 ASSEMBLY)

THROTTLE AUXILIARY LEVER-9A537
SCREW-380808-S
THROTTLE BODY
GASKET-9516
CHOKE CONTROL ROD RETAINER-377918-S (2 REQUIRED)
AUTOMATIC CHOKE SHAFT AND LEVER-9A753
CAM ADJUSTING SCREW
FAST IDLE CAM 9597
CHOKE CONTROL ROD REATINER
377918- (2 REQUIRED)
CHOKE CONTROL ROD -9A599
IDLE LIMITER CAP
IDLE FUEL MIXTURE ADJUSTING SCREW-9541
IDLE FUEL MIXTURE ADJUSTING SPRING-9578

FAST IDLE ADJUSTING LEVER PIN-9579
PISTON AND LEVER ASSEMBLY-9C719
FAST IDLE LEVER-9538
THERMOSTAT HOUSING GASKET-9871
THERMOSTAT HOUSING
9848
THERMOSTAT HOUSING
REATINER-9842

SCREW-31061-S (3 REQUIRED)

Exploded view—Motorcraft 4300-4V

body. These parts require a close tolerance of fit; wear may allow air leakage, which could affect starting and idling.

NOTE: *Throttle shafts and bushings are not included in overhaul kits. They can be purchased separately.*

4. Inspect the idle mixture adjusting needles for burrs or grooves. Any such condition requires replacement of the needle, since you will not be able to obtain a satisfactory idle.

5. Test the accelerator pump check valves. They should pass air one way but not the other.

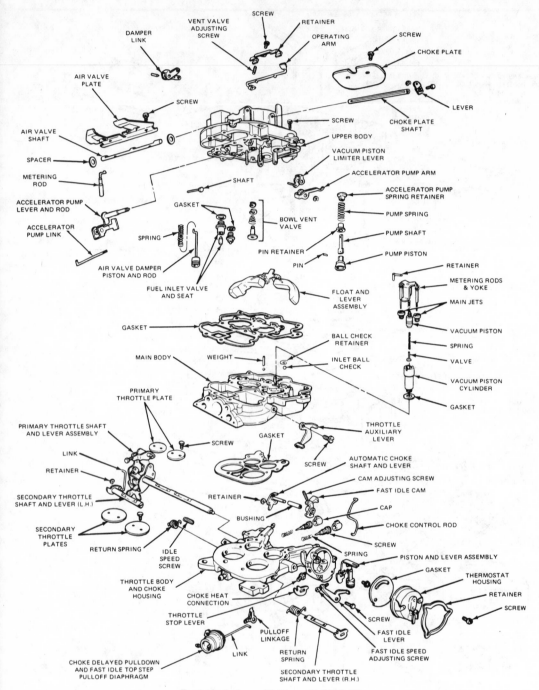

Exploded view—Motorcraft 4350-4V

Test for proper seating by blowing and sucking on the valve. Replace the valve if necessary. If the valve is satisfactory, wash the valve again to remove breath moisture.

6. Check the bowl cover for warped surfaces with a straightedge.

7. Closely inspect the valves and seats for wear and damage, replacing as necessary.

8. After the carburetor is assembled, check the choke valve for freedom of operation.

Carburetor overhaul kits are recommended for each overhaul. These kits contain all gaskets and new parts to replace those which deteriorate most rapidly. Failure to replace all parts supplied with the kit (especially gaskets) can result in poor performance later.

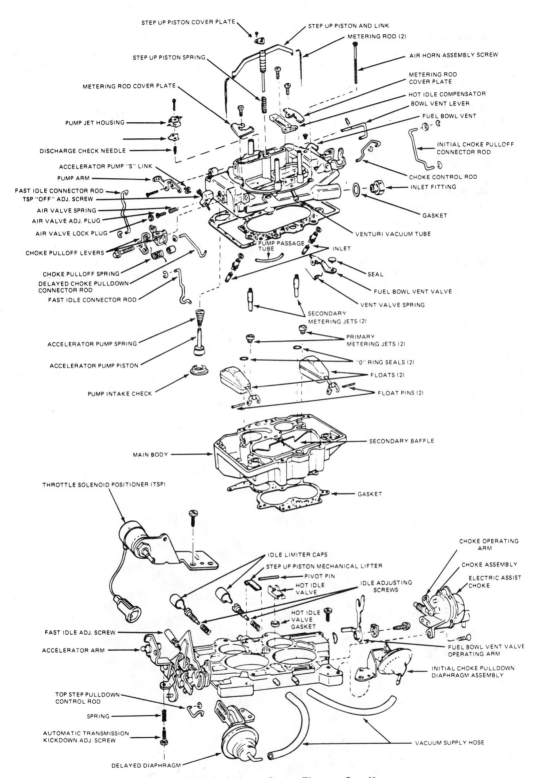

STEP UP PISTON COVER PLATE

STEP UP PISTON AND LINK

METERING ROD (2)

STEP UP PISTON SPRING

AIR HORN ASSEMBLY SCREW

METERING ROD COVER PLATE

METERING ROD
COVER PLATE

HOT IDLE COMPENSATOR
BOWL VENT LEVER

PUMP JET HOUSING

FUEL BOWL VENT

DISCHARGE CHECK NEEDLE

INITIAL CHOKE PULLOFF
CONNECTOR ROD

ACCELERATOR PUMP "S" LINK

CHOKE CONTROL ROD

PUMP ARM

INLET FITTING

FAST IDLE CONNECTOR ROD

TSP "OFF" ADJ. SCREW

AIR VALVE SPRING

GASKET

AIR VALVE ADJ. PLUG

AIR VALVE LOCK PLUG

VENTURI VACUUM TUBE

CHOKE PULLOFF LEVERS

PUMP PASSAGE
TUBE

INLET

CHOKE PULLOFF SPRING

SEAL

DELAYED CHOKE PULLDOWN
CONNECTOR ROD

FUEL BOWL VENT VALVE

FAST IDLE CONNECTOR ROD

VENT VALVE SPRING

SECONDARY
METERING JETS (2)

ACCELERATOR PUMP SPRING

PRIMARY
METERING JETS (2)

ACCELERATOR PUMP PISTON

"O" RING SEALS (2)

FLOATS (2)

PUMP INTAKE CHECK

FLOAT PINS (2)

SECONDARY BAFFLE

MAIN BODY

THROTTLE SOLENOID POSITIONER (TSP)

GASKET

CHOKE OPERATING
ARM

IDLE LIMITER CAPS

CHOKE ASSEMBLY

STEP UP PISTON MECHANICAL LIFTER

ELECTRIC ASSIST
CHOKE

PIVOT PIN

IDLE ADJUSTING
SCREWS

HOT IDLE
VALVE

FAST IDLE ADJ. SCREW

HOT IDLE
VALVE GASKET

ACCELERATOR ARM

FUEL BOWL VENT VALVE
OPERATING ARM

INITIAL CHOKE PULLDOWN
DIAPHRAGM ASSEMBLY

TOP STEP PULLDOWN
CONTROL ROD

SPRING

AUTOMATIC TRANSMISSION
KICKDOWN ADJ. SCREW

VACUUM SUPPLY HOSE

DELAYED DIAPHRAGM

Exploded view—Carter Thermo-Quad®

Some carburetor manufacturers supply overhaul kits of three basic types: minor repair; major repair; and gasket kits. Basically, they contain the following:

Minor Repair Kits:
- All gaskets
- Float needle valve
- Volume control screw
- All diaphragms
- Spring for the pump diaphragm

Major Repair Kits:
- All jets and gaskets
- All diaphragms
- Float needle valve
- Volume control screw
- Pump ball valve
- Float
- Complete intermediate rod
- Intermediate pump lever
- Some cover hold-down screws and washers

Gasket Kits:
- All gaskets

After cleaning and checking all components, reassemble the carburetor, using new parts and referring to the exploded view. When reassembling, make sure that all screws and jets are tight in their seats, but do not over-tighten as the tips will be distorted. Tighten all screws gradually, in rotation. Do not tighten needle valves into their seats; uneven jetting will result. Always use new gaskets. Be sure to adjust the float level when reassembling.

AUTOMATIC CHOKE HOUSING ADJUSTMENT

All Except VV Carburetors

By rotating the spring housing of the automatic choke, the reaction of the choke to engine temperature can be controlled. To adjust, remove the air cleaner assembly, loosen the thermostatic spring housing retaining screws and set the spring housing to the specified index mark. The marks are shown in the accompanying illustration. After adjusting the setting, tighten the retaining screws and replace the air cleaner assembly to the carburetor.

CHOKE PLATE PULL-DOWN CLEARANCE ADJUSTMENT

Autolite 1101

1. Remove the air cleaner assembly.
2. Remove the choke cover and thermo-

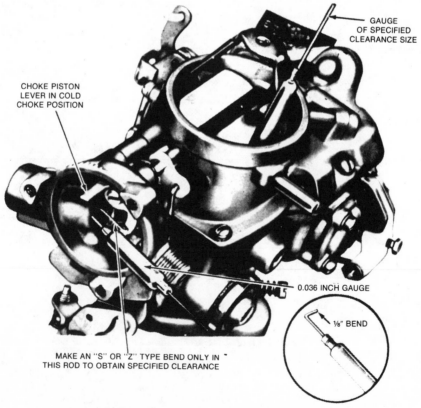

Adjusting choke plate pull-down—Autolite 1101

THERMOSTATIC SPRING HOUSING INDEX MARK

CHOKE
HOUSING
INDEX MARK

Automatic choke housing adjustment

DRILL GAUGE

CHOKE PISTON
LEVER

.026″
WIRE
GAUGE

Adjusting choke plate pull-down—Carter YF

static coil assembly. Block the throttle valve half open so that the fast idle screw does not contact the fast idle cam.

3. Bend a 0.036 in. wire gauge at a 90° angle about ⅛ in. from the end. Insert the bent end between the lower edge of the choke piston slot and the upper edge of the right-hand slot in the choke housing (see the illustration).

4. Move the piston lever counterclockwise until the gauge fits snugly in the slot. Hold the gauge in place by exerting light pressure on the lever.

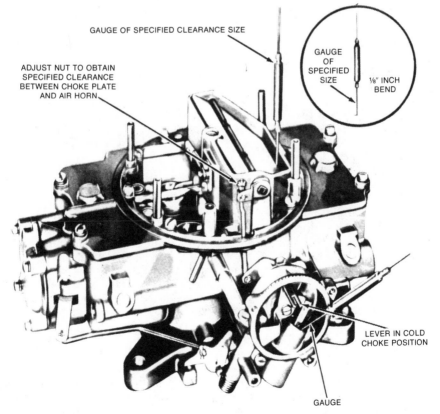

GAUGE OF SPECIFIED CLEARANCE SIZE

ADJUST NUT TO OBTAIN
SPECIFIED CLEARANCE
BETWEEN CHOKE PLATE
AND AIR HORN

GAUGE
OF
SPECIFIED
SIZE

⅛″ INCH
BEND

LEVER IN COLD
CHOKE POSITION

GAUGE

Adjusting choke plate pull-down—Autolite 2100, 4100—1968–69

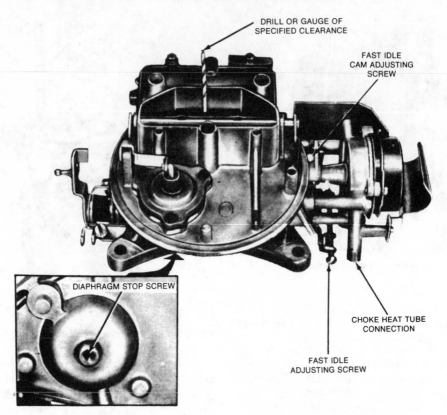

Adjusting choke plate pull-down—Motorcraft 2100 (1970–74)

5. Insert a drill or gauge of the specified thickness (see "Carburetor Specifications" chart) between the lower edge of the choke plate and the air horn wall.

6. To adjust, carefully bend the choke piston link (in an S or Z-shaped bend) until the choke plate clearance is that of the drill gauge.

7. After adjustment, install the choke cover and adjust as outlined under "Automatic Choke Housing Adjustment." Install the air cleaner.

Carter YF

1. Remove the carburetor air cleaner, and remove the choke thermostatic spring housing.

2. Bend a section of 0.026 in. diameter wire at a 90° angle approximately ⅛ in. from one end.

3. Insert the bent end of the wire gauge between the choke piston slot and the righthand slot in the choke housing. Rotate the choke piston lever counterclockwise until the gauge is snug in the piston slot.

4. Exert light pressure upon the choke piston lever to hold the gauge in position. Check the specified clearance with a drill of the correct diameter between the lower edge of the choke plate and the carburetor bore.

5. Choke plate pull-down clearance may be adjusted by bending the choke piston lever as required to obtain the desired clearance. It is recommended that the choke piston lever be removed prior to bending, in order to prevent distorting the piston link.

6. Install the choke thermostatic spring housing and gasket, and set the housing to the proper specification.

Autolite 2100, 4100

1968–69

1. Follow Steps 1–5 "Autolite 1101."

2. To adjust, turn the choke plate clevis adjusting nut (see the illustration) as required until the choke plate clearance is that of the drill gauge.

3. After adjustment, install the choke cover and adjust as outlined under "Automatic Choke Housing Adjustment." Install the air cleaner.

Autolite (Motorcraft) 2100

1970–74

1. Remove the air cleaner.

2. With the engine at its normal operating temperature, loosen the choke thermostatic spring housing retaining screws, and set the housing 90° in the rich direction.

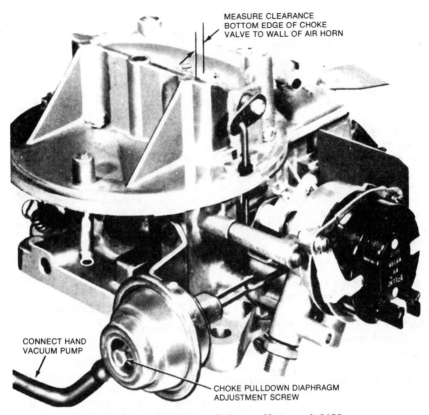

Adjusting choke plate pull-down—Motorcraft 2150

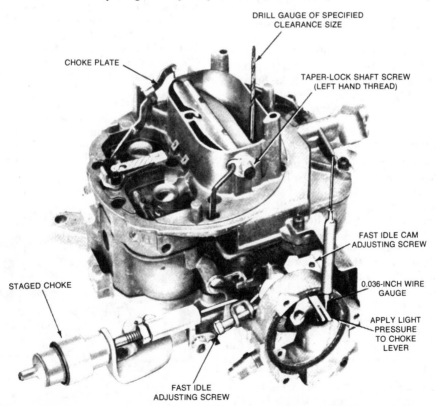

Choke plate pull-down and fast idle cam adjustment—Motorcraft 4300 (4350 similar)

3. Disconnect and remove the choke heat tube from the choke housing.

4. Turn the fast idle adjusting screw outward one full turn.

5. Start the engine. Use a drill of the specified diameter to check the clearance between the lower edge of the choke plate and the air horn wall.

6. To adjust the clearance, turn the diaphragm stopscrew (located on the underside of the choke diaphragm housing). Turning clockwise will decrease the clearance; counterclockwise will increase it.

7. Connect the choke heat tube, and set the choke thermostatic spring housing to the proper specification. Adjust the fast idle speed to specifications.

Motorcraft 2150

1. Remove the air cleaner assembly.

2. Set the throttle on the top step of the fast idle cam.

3. Noting the position of the choke housing cap, loosen the retaining screws and rotate the cap 90 degrees in the rich (closing) direction.

4. Activate the pull-down motor by manually forcing the pull-down control diaphragm link in the direction of applied vacuum or by applying vacuum to the external vacuum tube.

5. Using a drill gauge of the specified diameter, measure the clearance between the choke plate and the center of the air horn wall nearest the fuel bowl.

6. To adjust, reset the diaphragm stop on the end of the choke pull-down diaphragm.

7. After adjusting, reset the choke housing cap to the specified notch. Check and reset fast idle speed, if necessary. Install the air cleaner.

Autolite (Motorcraft) 4300, 4350

1. Follow Steps 1–5 under "Autolite 1101."

2. To adjust loosen the hex head screw (left-hand thread) on the choke plate shaft and pry the link away from the tapered shaft. Using a drill gauge 0.010 in. thinner than the specified clearance (to allow for tolerances in the linkage), insert the gauge between the lower edge of the choke plate and the air horn wall. Hold the choke plate against the gauge and maintain a light pressure in a counterclockwise direction on the choke lever. Then, with the choke piston snug against the 0.036 in. wire gauge and the choke plate against the 0.010 in. smaller drill gauge, tighten the hex head screw (left-hand thread) on the choke plate shaft. After tightening the hex head screw, make a final check using a drill gauge of the specified clearance between the choke plate and air horn.

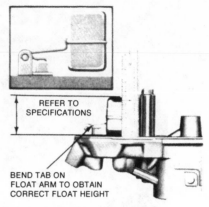

REFER TO SPECIFICATIONS

BEND TAB ON FLOAT ARM TO OBTAIN CORRECT FLOAT HEIGHT

Float level adjustment—Autolite 1101

3. After adjustment, install the choke cover and adjust as outlined under "Automatic Choke Housing Adjustment." Install the air cleaner.

FLOAT LEVEL ADJUSTMENT

Autolite 1101

1. Remove the carburetor air horn and gasket from the carburetor.

2. Measure the distance from the gasket surface of the air horn to the top of the float. If the measurement is not within the specified tolerance, bend the float arm tab as necessary to obtain the specified dimension. Be careful not to exert any pressure on the fuel inlet needle, as this will damage it and result in an improper fuel level within the float bowl.

3. Install the carburetor air horn to the main body of the carburetor, using a new gasket.

Carter YF

The float level is adjusted dry in the following manner: Remove the carburetor air horn and gasket from the carburetor. Using a gauge made to the proper dimension, invert the air

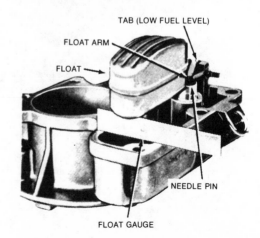

TAB (LOW FUEL LEVEL)

FLOAT ARM

FLOAT

NEEDLE PIN

FLOAT GAUGE

Float level adjustment—Carter YF

horn assembly and check the clearance between the top of the float and the bottom of the air horn. When checking the float level, the air horn should be held at eye level and the float lever arm should be resting on the pin of the needle valve. The float lever arm may be bent in order to adjust the float clearance. However, do not bend the tab at the end of the float arm, as this will prevent the float from bottoming in the fuel bowl when the bowl is empty. Using a new gasket, install the carburetor air horn.

Autolite (Motorcraft) 2100, 2150, 4100

DRY ADJUSTMENT

This preliminary setting of the float level adjustment must be done with the carburetor removed from the engine.

1. Remove the air horn and see that the float is raised and the fuel inlet needle is seated. Check the distance between the top surface of the main body (with the gasket removed) and the top surface of the float. Depress the float tab to seat the fuel inlet needle. Take a measurement near the center of the float, at a point ⅛ in. from the free end. If you are using a prefabricated float gauge, place the gauge in the corner of the enlarged end section of the fuel bowl. The gauge should touch the float near the end, but not on the end radius.

2. If necessary, bend the tab on the end of the float to bring the setting within the specified limits.

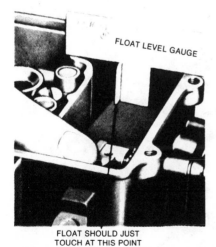

FLOAT LEVEL GAUGE

FLOAT SHOULD JUST
TOUCH AT THIS POINT

Dry float level adjustment—Motorcraft 2100, 2150, 4100

WET ADJUSTMENT

1. Bring the engine to its normal operating temperature, park the car on as nearly level a surface as possible, and stop the engine.

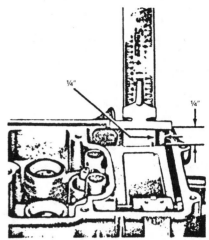

Wet float level adjustment—Motorcraft 2100, 2150, 4150

2. Remove the air cleaner assembly from the carburetor.

3. Remove the air horn retaining screws and the carburetor identification tag. Leave the air horn and gasket in position on the carburetor main body. Start the engine, let it idle for several minutes, rotate the air horn out of the way, and remove the gasket to provide access to the float assembly.

4. With the engine idling, use a standard depth scale to measure the vertical distance from the top machined surface of the carburetor main body to the level of the fuel bowl. This measurement must be made at least ¼ in. away from any vertical surface in order to assure an accurate reading.

5. Stop the engine before making any adjustment to the float level. Adjustment is accomplished by bending the float tab (which contacts the fuel inlet valve) up or down as required to raise or lower the fuel level. After making an adjustment, start the engine, and allow it to idle for several minutes before repeating the fuel level check. Repeat as necessary until the proper fuel level is attained.

6. Reinstall the air horn with a new gasket and secure it with the screws. Include the installation of the identification tag in its proper location.

7. Check the idle speed, fuel mixture, and dashpot adjustments. Install the air cleaner assembly.

Autolite (Motorcraft) 4300, 4350

1. Refer to the illustration for details of construction of a tool for checking the parallel setting of the dual pontoons.

2. Install the gauge on the carburetor and set it to the specified height.

3. Check the clearance and alignment of the

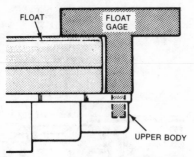

Float setting with rebuilding kit gauge—4300, 4350

pontoons to the gauge. Both pontoons should just barely touch the gauge for the proper setting. Pontoons may be aligned if necessary by slightly twisting them.

4. To adjust the float level, bend the primary needle tab down to raise the float and up to lower it.

Carter Thermo-Quad

1. Taking note of their placement, disconnect all linkages and rods which connect the bowl cover to the carburetor body.

2. Remove the 10 screws retaining the bowl cover to the body.

3. Using legs to protect the throttle valves, remove the bowl cover. Invert the bowl cover, taking care not to lose any of the small parts.

4. With the bowl cover inverted and the floats resting on the seated needle, measure

the distance between the bowl cover (new gasket installed) to the bottom side of each float.

5. If not to specifications, bend the float lever to suit.

NOTE: *Never allow the lip of the float to be pressed against the needlw when adjusting the float height.*

6. Reverse Steps 1–3 to install. Make sure that the float pin does not protrude past the edge of the bowl cover.

DECHOKE CLEARANCE ADJUSTMENT
Carter YF

1. Remove the carburetor air cleaner.

2. Hold the throttle plate to the full open position while closing the choke plate as far as possible without forcing it. Use a drill of the proper diameter (see "Carburetor Specifications" chart) to check the clearance between the choke plate and air horn.

3. Adjust as necessary by bending the pawl on the fast idle speed lever. Bend forward to increase clearance and backward to decrease clearance.

Autolite (Motorcraft) 4300, 4350

1. Remove the air cleaner assembly.

2. Remove the automatic choke spring housing from the carburetor.

3. With the throttle plate wide open and the choke plate closed as far as possible with-

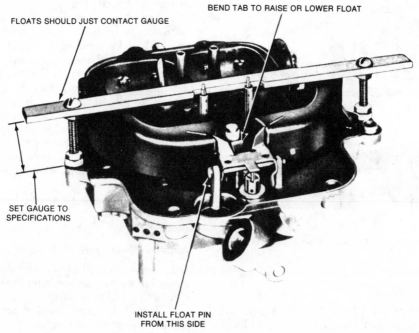

Float setting with fabricated gauge—4300, 4350

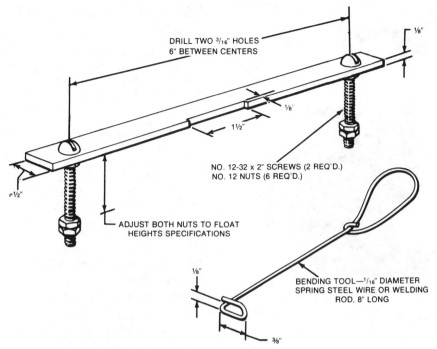

DRILL TWO ³/₁₆" HOLES
6" BETWEEN CENTERS

¹/₈"

¹/₈"

1½"

NO. 12-32 x 2" SCREWS (2 REQ'D.)
NO. 12 NUTS (6 REQ'D.)

½"

ADJUST BOTH NUTS TO FLOAT
HEIGHTS SPECIFICATIONS

¹/₈"

BENDING TOOL—¹/₁₆" DIAMETER
SPRING STEEL WIRE OR WELDING
ROD, 8" LONG

³/₈"

Float gauge and bending tool details—4300, 4350

out forcing it, insert a drill gauge of the specified diameter between the choke plate and air horn.

4. To adjust, bend the arm on the choke trip lever. Bend downward to increase clearance and upward to decrease clearance. After adjusting, recheck the clearance.

5. Install the automatic choke housing, taking care to engage the thermostatic spring with the tang on the choke lever and shaft assembly.

6. Adjust the automatic choke setting. Install the air cleaner. Adjust the idle speed and dashpot, if so equipped.

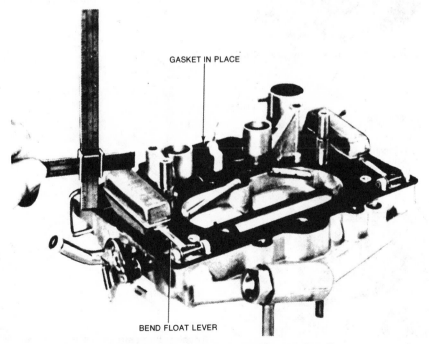

GASKET IN PLACE

BEND FLOAT LEVER

Checking float height—Carter Thermo-Quad®

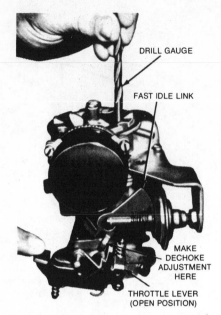

Dechoke clearance adjustment—Carter YF

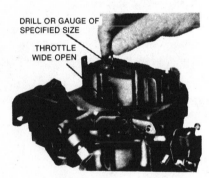

Checking dechoke clearance—Motorcraft 4300, 4350

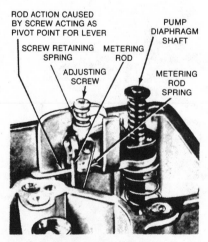

Metering rod adjustment—Carter YF

METERING ROD ADJUSTMENT

Carter YF

With the carburetor air horn and gasket removed from the carburetor, unscrew the idle speed adjusting screw until the throttle plate is tightly closed in the throttle bore. Press downward on the end of the diaphragm shaft until the metering rod arm contacts the lifter link at the diaphragm stem. With the metering rod in the preceding position, turn the rod adjustment screw (see the accompanying illustration) until the metering rod just bottoms in the body casting. Turn the metering rod adjusting screw one additional turn in the clockwise direction. Install the carburetor air horn along with a new gasket.

ACCELERATOR PUMP STROKE ADJUSTMENT

Autolite (Motorcraft) 2100, 2150, 4100

In order to keep the exhaust emission level of the engine within the specified limits, the accelerating pump stroke has been preset at the factory. The additional holes are provided for differing engine-transmission-body applications only. The primary throttle shaft lever (overtravel lever) has four holes and the accelerating pump link two holes to control the pump stroke. The accelerating pump operating rod should be in the overtravel lever hole number listed in the "Carburetor Specifications" chart, and in the inboard hole (hole closest to the pump plunger) in the accelerat-

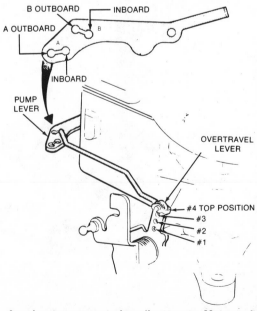

Accelerator pump stroke adjustment—Motorcraft 2100, 2150, 4100

55 WAYS TO IMPROVE FUEL ECONOMY

CHILTON'S
FUEL ECONOMY & TUNE-UP TIPS

Tune-Up • Spark Plug Diagnosis • Emission Controls

Fuel System • Cooling System • Tires and Wheels

General Maintenance

CHILTON'S FUEL ECONOMY & TUNE-UP TIPS

Fuel economy is important to everyone, no matter what kind of vehicle you drive. The maintenance-minded motorist can save both money and fuel using these tips and the periodic maintenance and tune-up procedures in this Repair and Tune-Up Guide.

There are more than 130,000,000 cars and trucks registered for private use in the United States. Each travels an average of 10-12,000 miles per year, and, in total they consume close to 70 billion gallons of fuel each year. This represents nearly ⅔ of the oil imported by the United States each year. The Federal government's goal is to reduce consumption 10% by 1985. A variety of methods are either already in use or under serious consideration, and they all affect your driving and the cars you will drive. In addition to "down-sizing", the auto industry is using or investigating the use of electronic fuel delivery, electronic engine controls and alternative engines for use in smaller and lighter vehicles, among other alternatives to meet the federally mandated Corporate Average Fuel Economy (CAFE) of 27.5 mpg by 1985. The government, for its part, is considering rationing, mandatory driving curtailments and tax increases on motor vehicle fuel in an effort to reduce consumption. The government's goal of a 10% reduction could be realized — and further government regulation avoided — if every private vehicle could use just 1 less gallon of fuel per week.

How Much Can You Save?

Tests have proven that almost anyone can make at least a 10% reduction in fuel consumption through regular maintenance and tune-ups. When a major manufacturer of spark plugs sur-

TUNE-UP

1. Check the cylinder compression to be sure the engine will really benefit from a tune-up and that it is capable of producing good fuel economy. A tune-up will be wasted on an engine in poor mechanical condition.

2. Replace spark plugs regularly. New spark plugs alone can increase fuel economy 3%.

3. Be sure the spark plugs are the correct type (heat range) for your vehicle. See the Tune-Up Specifications.

Heat range refers to the spark plug's ability to conduct heat away from the firing end. It must conduct the heat away in an even pattern to avoid becoming a source of pre-ignition, yet it must also operate hot enough to burn off conductive deposits that could cause misfiring.

The heat range is usually indicated by a number on the spark plug, part of the manufacturer's designation for each individual spark plug. The numbers in bold-face indicate the heat range in each manufacturer's identification system.

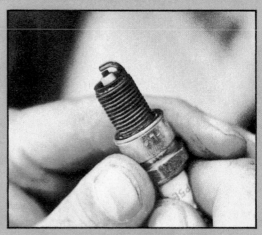

Periodically, check the spark plugs to be sure they are firing efficiently. They are excellent indicators of the internal condition of your engine.

Manufacturer	Typical Designation
AC	R **45** TS
Bosch (old)	WA **145** T30
Bosch (new)	HR **8** Y
Champion	RBL **15** Y
Fram/Autolite	**415**
Mopar	P-**62** PR
Motorcraft	BR**F**-42
NGK	BP **5** ES-15
Nippondenso	W **16** EP
Prestolite	14GR **5** 2A

On AC, Bosch (new), Champion, Fram/ Autolite, Mopar, Motorcraft and Prestolite, a higher number indicates a hotter plug. On Bosch (old), NGK and Nippondenso, a higher number indicates a colder plug.

4. Make sure the spark plugs are properly gapped. See the Tune-Up Specifications in this book.

5. Be sure the spark plugs are firing efficiently. The illustrations on the next 2 pages show you how to "read" the firing end of the spark plug.

6. Check the ignition timing and set it to specifications. Tests show that almost all cars

veyed over 6,000 cars nationwide, they found that a tune-up, on cars that needed one, increased fuel economy over 11%. Replacing worn plugs alone, accounted for a 3% increase. The same test also revealed that 8 out of every 10 vehicles will have some maintenance deficiency that will directly affect fuel economy, emissions or performance. Most of this mileage-robbing neglect could be prevented with regular maintenance.

Modern engines require that all of the functioning systems operate properly for maximum efficiency. A malfunction anywhere wastes fuel. You can keep your vehicle running as efficiently and economically as possible, by being aware of your vehicles operating and performance characteristics. If your vehicle suddenly develops performance or fuel economy problems it could be due to one or more of the following:

PROBLEM	POSSIBLE CAUSE
Engine Idles Rough	Ignition timing, idle mixture, vacuum leak or something amiss in the emission control system.
Hesitates on Acceleration	Dirty carburetor or fuel filter, improper accelerator pump setting, ignition timing or fouled spark plugs.
Starts Hard or Fails to Start	Worn spark plugs, improperly set automatic choke, ice (or water) in fuel system.
Stalls Frequently	Automatic choke improperly adjusted and possible dirty air filter or fuel filter.
Performs Sluggishly	Worn spark plugs, dirty fuel or air filter, ignition timing or automatic choke out of adjustment.

Check spark plug wires on conventional point type ignition for cracks by bending them in a loop around your finger.

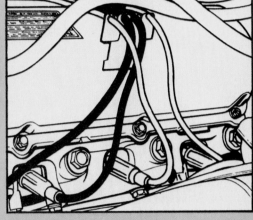

Be sure that spark plug wires leading to adjacent cylinders do not run too close together. (Photo courtesy Champion Spark Plug Co.)

have incorrect ignition timing by more than 2°.

7. If your vehicle does not have electronic ignition, check the points, rotor and cap as specified.

8. Check the spark plug wires (used with conventional point-type ignitions) for cracks and burned or broken insulation by bending them in a loop around your finger. Cracked wires decrease fuel efficiency by failing to deliver full voltage to the spark plugs. One misfiring spark plug can cost you as much as 2 mpg.

9. Check the routing of the plug wires. Misfiring can be the result of spark plug leads to adjacent cylinders running parallel to each other and too close together. One wire tends to pick up voltage from the other causing it to fire "out of time".

10. Check all electrical and ignition circuits for voltage drop and resistance.

11. Check the distributor mechanical and/or vacuum advance mechanisms for proper functioning. The vacuum advance can be checked by twisting the distributor plate in the opposite direction of rotation. It should spring back when released.

12. Check and adjust the valve clearance on engines with mechanical lifters. The clearance should be slightly loose rather than too tight.

SPARK PLUG DIAGNOSIS

Normal

APPEARANCE: This plug is typical of one operating normally. The insulator nose varies from a light tan to grayish color with slight electrode wear. The presence of slight deposits is normal on used plugs and will have no adverse effect on engine performance. The spark plug heat range is correct for the engine and the engine is running normally.

CAUSE: Properly running engine.

RECOMMENDATION: Before reinstalling this plug, the electrodes should be cleaned and filed square. Set the gap to specifications. If the plug has been in service for more than 10-12,000 miles, the entire set should probably be replaced with a fresh set of the same heat range.

Oil Deposits

APPEARANCE: The firing end of the plug is covered with a wet, oily coating.

CAUSE: The problem is poor oil control. On high mileage engines, oil is leaking past the rings or valve guides into the combustion chamber. A common cause is also a plugged PCV valve, and a ruptured fuel pump diaphragm can also cause this condition. Oil fouled plugs such as these are often found in new or recently overhauled engines, before normal oil control is achieved, and can be cleaned and reinstalled.

RECOMMENDATION: A hotter spark plug may temporarily relieve the problem, but the engine is probably in need of work.

Incorrect Heat Range

APPEARANCE: The effects of high temperature on a spark plug are indicated by clean white, often blistered insulator. This can also be accompanied by excessive wear of the electrode, and the absence of deposits.

CAUSE: Check for the correct spark plug heat range. A plug which is too hot for the engine can result in overheating. A car operated mostly at high speeds can require a colder plug. Also check ignition timing, cooling system level, fuel mixture and leaking intake manifold.

RECOMMENDATION: If all ignition and engine adjustments are known to be correct, and no other malfunction exists, install spark plugs one heat range colder.

Photos Courtesy Champion Spark Plug Co.

Carbon Deposits

APPEARANCE: Carbon fouling is easily identified by the presence of dry, soft, black, sooty deposits.

CAUSE: Changing the heat range can often lead to carbon fouling, as can prolonged slow, stop-and-start driving. If the heat range is correct, carbon fouling can be attributed to a rich fuel mixture, sticking choke, clogged air cleaner, worn breaker points, retarded timing or low compression. If only one or two plugs are carbon fouled, check for corroded or cracked wires on the affected plugs. Also look for cracks in the distributor cap between the towers of affected cylinders.

RECOMMENDATION: After the problem is corrected, these plugs can be cleaned and reinstalled if not worn severely.

MMT Fouled

APPEARANCE: Spark plugs fouled by MMT (Methycyclopentadienyl Maganese Tricarbonyl) have reddish, rusty appearance on the insulator and side electrode.

CAUSE: MMT is an anti-knock additive in gasoline used to replace lead. During the combustion process, the MMT leaves a reddish deposit on the insulator and side electrode.

RECOMMENDATION: No engine malfunction is indicated and the deposits will not affect plug performance any more than lead deposits (see Ash Deposits). MMT fouled plugs can be cleaned, regapped and reinstalled.

High Speed Glazing

APPEARANCE: Glazing appears as shiny coating on the plug, either yellow or tan in color.

CAUSE: During hard, fast acceleration, plug temperatures rise suddenly. Deposits from normal combustion have no chance to fluff-off; instead, they melt on the insulator forming an electrically conductive coating which causes misfiring.

RECOMMENDATION: Glazed plugs are not easily cleaned. They should be replaced with a fresh set of plugs of the correct heat range. If the condition recurs, using plugs with a heat range one step colder may cure the problem.

Ash (Lead) Deposits

APPEARANCE: Ash deposits are characterized by light brown or white colored deposits crusted on the side or center electrodes. In some cases it may give the plug a rusty appearance.

CAUSE: Ash deposits are normally derived from oil or fuel additives burned during normal combustion. Normally they are harmless, though excessive amounts can cause misfiring. If deposits are excessive in short mileage, the valve guides may be worn.

RECOMMENDATION: Ash-fouled plugs can be cleaned, gapped and reinstalled.

Detonation

APPEARANCE: Detonation is usually characterized by a broken plug insulator.

CAUSE: A portion of the fuel charge will begin to burn spontaneously, from the increased heat following ignition. The explosion that results applies extreme pressure to engine components, frequently damaging spark plugs and pistons.

Detonation can result by over-advanced ignition timing, inferior gasoline (low octane) lean air/fuel mixture, poor carburetion, engine lugging or an increase in compression ratio due to combustion chamber deposits or engine modification.

RECOMMENDATION: Replace the plugs after correcting the problem.

Photos Courtesy Fram Corporation

EMISSION CONTROLS

13. Be aware of the general condition of the emission control system. It contributes to reduced pollution and should be serviced regularly to maintain efficient engine operation.

14. Check all vacuum lines for dried, cracked or brittle conditions. Something as simple as a leaking vacuum hose can cause poor performance and loss of economy.

15. Avoid tampering with the emission control system. Attempting to improve fuel econ-

FUEL SYSTEM

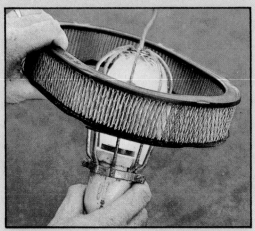

Check the air filter with a light behind it. If you can see light through the filter it can be reused.

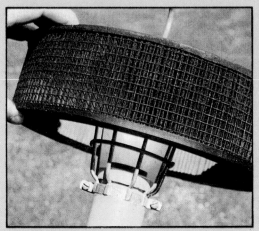

Extremely clogged filters should be discarded and replaced with a new one.

18. Replace the air filter regularly. A dirty air filter richens the air/fuel mixture and can increase fuel consumption as much as 10%. Tests show that ⅓ of all vehicles have air filters in need of replacement.

19. Replace the fuel filter at least as often as recommended.

20. Set the idle speed and carburetor mixture to specifications.

21. Check the automatic choke. A sticking or malfunctioning choke wastes gas.

22. During the summer months, adjust the automatic choke for a leaner mixture which will produce faster engine warm-ups.

COOLING SYSTEM

29. Be sure all accessory drive belts are in good condition. Check for cracks or wear.

30. Adjust all accessory drive belts to proper tension.

31. Check all hoses for swollen areas, worn spots, or loose clamps.

32. Check coolant level in the radiator or expansion tank.

33. Be sure the thermostat is operating properly. A stuck thermostat delays engine warm-up and a cold engine uses nearly twice as much fuel as a warm engine.

34. Drain and replace the engine coolant at least as often as recommended. Rust and scale

TIRES & WHEELS

38. Check the tire pressure often with a pencil type gauge. Tests by a major tire manufacturer show that 90% of all vehicles have at least 1 tire improperly inflated. Better mileage can be achieved by over-inflating tires, but never exceed the maximum inflation pressure on the side of the tire.

39. If possible, install radial tires. Radial tires deliver as much as ½ mpg more than bias belted tires.

40. Avoid installing super-wide tires. They only create extra rolling resistance and decrease fuel mileage. Stick to the manufacturer's recommendations.

41. Have the wheels properly balanced.

omy by tampering with emission controls is more likely to worsen fuel economy than improve it. Emission control changes on modern engines are not readily reversible.

16. Clean (or replace) the EGR valve and lines as recommended.

17. Be sure that all vacuum lines and hoses are reconnected properly after working under the hood. An unconnected or misrouted vacuum line can wreak havoc with engine performance.

---

23. Check for fuel leaks at the carburetor, fuel pump, fuel lines and fuel tank. Be sure all lines and connections are tight.

24. Periodically check the tightness of the carburetor and intake manifold attaching nuts and bolts. These are a common place for vacuum leaks to occur.

25. Clean the carburetor periodically and lubricate the linkage.

26. The condition of the tailpipe can be an excellent indicator of proper engine combustion. After a long drive at highway speeds, the inside of the tailpipe should be a light grey in color. Black or soot on the insides indicates an overly rich mixture.

27. Check the fuel pump pressure. The fuel pump may be supplying more fuel than the engine needs.

28. Use the proper grade of gasoline for your engine. Don't try to compensate for knocking or "pinging" by advancing the ignition timing. This practice will only increase plug temperature and the chances of detonation or pre-ignition with relatively little performance gain.

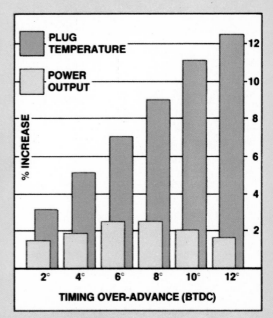

Increasing ignition timing past the specified setting results in a drastic increase in spark plug temperature with increased chance of detonation or preignition. Performance increase is considerably less. (Photo courtesy Champion Spark Plug Co.)

---

that form in the engine should be flushed out to allow the engine to operate at peak efficiency.

35. Clean the radiator of debris that can decrease cooling efficiency.

36. Install a flex-type or electric cooling fan, if you don't have a clutch type fan. Flex fans use curved plastic blades to push more air at low speeds when more cooling is needed; at high speeds the blades flatten out for less resistance. Electric fans only run when the engine temperature reaches a predetermined level.

37. Check the radiator cap for a worn or cracked gasket. If the cap does not seal properly, the cooling system will not function properly.

---

42. Be sure the front end is correctly aligned. A misaligned front end actually has wheels going in different directions. The increased drag can reduce fuel economy by .3 mpg.

43. Correctly adjust the wheel bearings. Wheel bearings that are adjusted too tight increase rolling resistance.

Check tire pressures regularly with a reliable pocket type gauge. Be sure to check the pressure on a cold tire.

GENERAL MAINTENANCE

Check the fluid levels (particularly engine oil) on a regular basis. Be sure to check the oil for grit, water or other contamination.

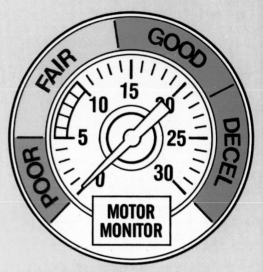

A vacuum gauge is another excellent indicator of internal engine condition and can also be installed in the dash as a mileage indicator.

44. Periodically check the fluid levels in the engine, power steering pump, master cylinder, automatic transmission and drive axle.

45. Change the oil at the recommended interval and change the filter at every oil change. Dirty oil is thick and causes extra friction between moving parts, cutting efficiency and increasing wear. A worn engine requires more frequent tune-ups and gets progressively worse fuel economy. In general, use the lightest viscosity oil for the driving conditions you will encounter.

46. Use the recommended viscosity fluids in the transmission and axle.

47. Be sure the battery is fully charged for fast starts. A slow starting engine wastes fuel.

48. Be sure battery terminals are clean and tight.

49. Check the battery electrolyte level and add distilled water if necessary.

50. Check the exhaust system for crushed pipes, blockages and leaks.

51. Adjust the brakes. Dragging brakes or brakes that are not releasing create increased drag on the engine.

52. Install a vacuum gauge or miles-per-gallon gauge. These gauges visually indicate engine vacuum in the intake manifold. High vacuum = good mileage and low vacuum = poorer mileage. The gauge can also be an excellent indicator of internal engine conditions.

53. Be sure the clutch is properly adjusted. A slipping clutch wastes fuel.

54. Check and periodically lubricate the heat control valve in the exhaust manifold. A sticking or inoperative valve prevents engine warm-up and wastes gas.

55. Keep accurate records to check fuel economy over a period of time. A sudden drop in fuel economy may signal a need for tune-up or other maintenance.

© 1980 Chilton Book Company, Radnor, PA 19089

ing pump link. If the pump stroke has been changed from the specified settings, use the following procedure to correct the stroke.

1. Release the operating rod from the retaining clip by pressing the tab end of the clip toward the rod while pressing the rod away from the clip until it disengages.

2. Position the clip over the specified hole (see "Carburetor Specification" chart) in the overtravel lever. Press the ends of the clip together and insert the operating rod through the clip and the overtravel lever. Release the clip to engage the rod.

Autolite (Motorcraft) 4300

The pump stroke is preset at the factory to limit exhaust emissions. The additional holes in the operating arm are provided for different engine applications. The stroke should not be changed from the specified hole (see "Carburetor Specifications" chart).

The only adjustments possible are the pump stroke and pump stem height. To change the pump stroke, merely remove the pivot pin and reposition it in the specified hole. To adjust the pump stem height, bend the operating rod at the angles, taking care not to cause binds in the system.

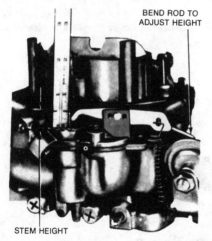

Accelerator pump stroke and piston stem height—Motorcraft 4300

Motorcraft 4350

The accelerator pump adjustment is preset at the factory for reduced exhaust emissions. Adjustment is provided only for different engine installations. The adjustment is internal, with three piston-to-shaft pin positions in the pump piston.

To check that the shaft pin is located in the specified piston hole, remove the carburetor air horn and invert it. Disconnect the accel-

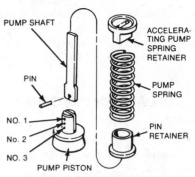

Accelerator pump stroke adjustment—Motorcraft 4350

erator pump from the operating arm by pressing downward on the spring and sliding the arm out of the pump shaft slot. Disassemble the spring and nylon keeper retaining the adjustment pin. If the pin is not in its specified hole, remove it, reposition the shaft to the correct hole in the piston assembly and reinstall the pin. Then, slide the nylon retainer over the pin and position the spring on the shaft. Finally, compress the spring on the shaft and install the pump on the pump arm.

NOTE: *Under no circumstances should you adjust the stroke of the accelerator pump by turning the vacuum limiter lever adjusting nut. This adjustment is preset at the factory and modification could result in poor cold driveability.*

ANTI-STALL DASHPOT ADJUSTMENT

All Carburetors

Having made sure that the engine idle speed and mixture are correct and that the engine is at normal operating temperature, loosen the anti-stall dashpot locking nut (see accompanying illustration). With the throttle held closed, depress the plunger with a screwdriver blade and measure the clearance between the throttle lever and the plunger tip. If the clearance is not as specified in the "Carburetor Specifi-

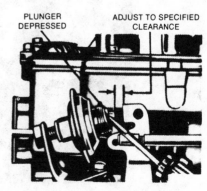

Typical anti-stall dashpot adjustment

cations" chart, turn the dashpot until the proper clearance is obtained between the throttle lever and the plunger tip. After tightening the locking nut, recheck the adjustment.

FAST IDLE CAM INDEX SETTING

Carter YF

1. Position the fast idle screw on the kick-down step of the fast idle cam against the shoulder of the high step.

2. Adjust by bending the choke plate connecting rod to obtain the specified clearance between the lower edge of the choke plate and the carburetor bore.

Autolite (Motorcraft) 2100, 4100

1968–72

1. Loosen the choke thermostatic spring housing retaining screws and position the housing 90° in the right direction.

2. Position the fast idle speed screw at the kick-down step of the fast idle cam. This kick-down step is identified by a small "V" stamped in the side of the casting.

3. Be sure that the fast idle cam is in the kick-down position while checking or adjusting the fast idle cam clearance. Check the clearance between the lower edge of the choke plate and the wall of the air horn by inserting a drill of the specified diameter between them. Adjustment may be accomplished by turning the fast idle cam adjusting screw clockwise to

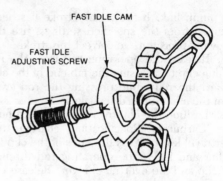

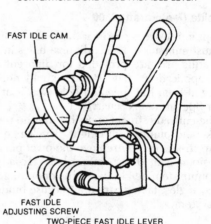

CONVENTIONAL ONE-PIECE FAST IDLE LEVER

FAST IDLE CAM

FAST IDLE
ADJUSTING SCREW
TWO-PIECE FAST IDLE LEVER
FOR 351-C AND 400 ENGINES

Fast idle cam index setting—Motorcraft 2100

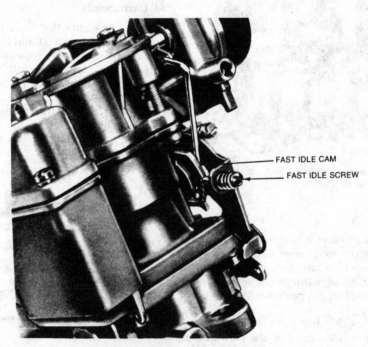

Fast idle cam index setting—Carter YF

increase or counterclockwise to decrease the clearance.

4. Set the choke thermostatic spring housing to specifications, and adjust the antistall dashpot, idle speed, and fuel mixture.

Motorcraft 2100, 2150

1973 AND LATER

1. Loosen the choke thermostatic spring housing retaining screws and rotate the housing 90° in the rich direction.

2. Position the fast idle speed screw or lever on the high step of the cam.

3. Depress the choke pull-down diaphragm against the diaphragm stop screw thereby placing the choke in the pull-down position.

4. While holding the choke pull-down diaphragm depressed, slightly open the throttle and allow the fast idle cam to fall.

5. Close the throttle and check the position of the fast idle cam or lever. When the fast idle cam is adjusted correctly, the screw should contact the "V" mark on the cam. Adjustment is accomplished by rotating the fast idle cam adjusting screw as needed.

Autolite (Motorcraft) 4300, 4350

1. Loosen the choke thermostatic spring housing retaining screws and position the housing 90° in the rich direction.

2. Position the fast idle speed screw at the kick-down step of the fast idle cam. This kick-down step is identified by a small "V" stamped in the side of the casting.

3. Be sure that the fast idle cam is in the kick-down position while checking or adjusting the fast idle cam clearance. Check the

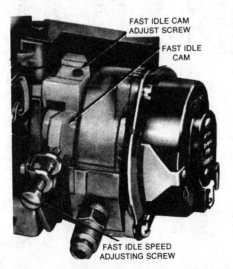

FAST IDLE CAM
ADJUST SCREW

FAST IDLE
CAM

FAST IDLE SPEED
ADJUSTING SCREW

Fast idle cam index setting—Motorcraft 4300, 4350

clearance between the lower edge of the choke plate and the wall of the air horn by inserting a drill of the specified diameter between them. Adjustment may be accomplished by turning the fast idle cam adjusting screw clockwise to increase or counterclockwise to decrease the clearance.

4. Set the choke thermostatic spring housing to specifications, and adjust the antistall dashpot, idle speed, and fuel mixture.

Model 2700 and 7200VV (Variable Venturi)

The variable venturi carburetor is similar in appearance to a conventional carburetor, and, like a conventional carburetor uses a normal float and fuel bowl system. However, the similarity ends there.

NOTE: *Any service or troubleshooting on the "VV" carburetors should be performed by qualified mechanics.*

The variable venturi (VV) carburetors are able to vary the area of venturi according to the engine load and speed requirements. In place of the normal choke plate and fixed area venturis, the VV carburetors have a pair of small oblong castings in the top of the upper carburetor body. These castings slide back and forth across the top of the carburetor in response to the air flow requirements of the engine.

Fuel is admitted into the venturi area by means of tapered metering rods that fit into the main jets. These rods are attached to the venturis, and, as the venturis open or close in response to air demand, the fuel needed to maintain the proper mixture increases or decreases as the metering rods slide into the jets. In comparison to a conventional carburetor with fixed venturis and a variable air supply, this system provides a much more precise control of the fuel-air supply during all modes of operation.

The 7200VV carburetor is the more common of the two VV carburetors. The difference between the 2700VV and the 7200VV is the feedback capability of the 7200 model.

The 7200VV feed-back carburetor varies the air-fuel ratio in response to commands from the EEC module. The air bleed feed-back system uses a stepper motor to regulate bleed air admitted into the main fuel metering system in response to a signal from the EEC. The stepper motor governs the metering rods thereby varying the air bleed; the greater the amount of air, the leaner the air-fuel mixture which aids in lower engine emissions.

Since the variable venturi, in both models, keeps air speed constant, separate idle and en-

Carburetor Specifications

Year	Fuel Level (in.) Dry	Float Adj (in.) Wet	Fast Idle Cam Index Setting (in.)	Anti-Stall Dashpot Adj (in.)	Accelerator Pump Operating Rod Position (in overtravel lever)	Dechoke Clearance Adjustment (in.)	Automatic Choke Thermostatic Spring Housing Adj	Choke Plate Pull-Down Clearance Adj (in.)
Autolite 1101								
1968–69	13/32		—	0.080	—	15/16	3 Lean	0.200
Carter YF								
1968	7/32		0.0035	0.100	—	0.250	Index	0.280
1969	7/32		0.0035	None	—	0.250	Index	0.280
1970	3/8		Man. 0.029 Auto. 0.035	Auto 7/64	—	0.250	Man.—Index Auto.—1 lean	0.225
1971	3/8		Man. 0.190 Auto. 0.200	Auto. 0.100	—	0.250	Index	Man. 0.200 Auto. 0.230
1972	3/8		0.220	0.100	—	0.250	1 Lean	0.230
Autolite (Motorcraft) 2100								
1968	302—3/8 390—31/64 351,	3/4 7/8	302 MT—0.110 302 AT—0.120 390 MT—0.170 390 AT—0.100	1/8	302—2 390—3	0.060	302 MT—Index 302 AT—1 Lean 390 All—Index	302 MT—0.120 302 AT—0.140 390 MT—0.210 390 AT—0.100
1969	302—3/8 351, 390,—31/64 429	3/4 7/8	302 All—0.110 351, 390, 429 AT— 0.100 390 MT—0.170	1/8	302 MT—3 302 AT—2 351, 390,—3 429	0.060	302 MT—2 Rich 302 AT—Index 351, 429—2 Rich 390 MT—1 Rich 390 AT—2 Rich	302 MT—0.130 302, 351 AT— 0.120 390 MT—0.210 390, 429 AT— 0.130

Year							
1970	7/16	13/16	302 All—0.130 351 MT—0.190 351 AT—0.170 390 MT—0.170 390, 429 AT—0.160	AT—1/8	302, 351 MT—3 302 AT—2 351 AT—4 390, 429—3	0.060	302 All—1 Rich 351 All—2 Lean 390 MT—1 Rich 390 AT—2 Rich 429 All—2 Rich	302 All—0.150 351 MT—0.230 390 MT—0.210 351, 390 AT—0.200 429 All—0.200
1971	7/16	13/16	302 MT—0.150 351 MT—0.190 302, 351 AT—0.130 390, 400,—0.160 429	351 AT, 400 AT—1/8 429 AT	302 MT—3 302 AT—2 351, 390,—3 400, 429,	0.060	302, 351 MT—1 Rich 302, 351 AT—Index 390 AT—Index 400, 429 AT—1 Rich	302 MT—0.170 302 AT—0.150 351 MT—0.220 351, 400 AT—0.190 390, 429 AT—0.200
1972	7/16	13/16	302, 351W—0.130 351C—0.160 400—0.150	302, 351W—1/8	302 All—2 351 All—3 400 (49 states)—4 400 (Calif.)—3	302, 400—0.060 351C, 351W—0.030	302, 351C—1 Rich 351W, 400—Index	302 All—0.150 351 W All—0.140 351C All—0.190 400 (49 states)—0.180 400 (Calif.)—0.170
1973	7/16	13/16	See procedure	None	All—3	—	351W—2 Rich 351C, 400—3 Rich	0.160①
1974	7/16	13/16	See procedure	None	351W, 351C—2 400—3	—	351W—2 Rich 351C, 400—3 Rich	0.160①

Motorcraft 2150

Year							
1975	7/16	13/16	See procedure	None	②	—	3 Rich	0.125
1976–77	7/16	13/16	See procedure	None	#2	—	③	0.160
1978–79	7/16	13/16	See procedure	None	#2	—	③	0.160

Carburetor Specifications (cont.)

Year	Fuel Level (in.) Dry	Float Adj (in.) Wet	Fast Idle Cam Index Setting (in.)	Anti-Stall Dashpot Adj (in.)	Accelerator Pump Operating Rod Position (in overtravel lever)	Dechoke Clearance Adjustment (in.)	Automatic Choke Thermostatic Spring Housing Adj	Choke Plate Pull-Down Clearance Adj (in.)
Autolite 4100								
1968–69	Primary 17/32 Secondary 11/16	20/32 11/16	0.120	3/32–1/8	#3	0.060	2 Rich	0.140
Autolite (Motorcraft) 4300								
1968	25/32		0.100	3/32	#3	0.300	MT—1 Rich AT—2 Rich	MT—0.120 AT—0.140
1969	25/32		MT—0.220 AT—0.160	MT—3/32	#2	0.300	MT—Index AT—1 Rich	MT—0.270 AT—0.230
1970	428 PI—1.0 429—25/32		428 PI—0.120 429 MT—0.220	428 PI—0.080 429—0.070	428 PI—#3 429—#2	0.300	428 PI—2 Rich 429—Index	428 PI—0.160 429 MT—0.250 429 AT—0.220
1971	49/64		0.170	1/16	#2	0.300	Index	0.220
1972	49/64		429 AT—0.200 429 PI—0.190	None	#1	0.300	429 AT—2 Rich 429 PI—Index	429 AT—0.220 429 PI—0.215
1973	429, 460 AT —.76 460 PI—.88		429 AT—0.200 460 AT—0.190 460 PI—0.200	None	#1	0.300	Index	429, 460 AT— 0.210 460 PI—0.200
1974	3/4		0.200	None	#1	0.300	Index	460 PI—0.200 460 PI—0.230

Motorcraft 4350

1975	460-4V—15/16 460 PI—31/32	0.160	None	#1	0.300	2 Rich	Initial—0.160 Delayed—0.190
1976–78	460-4V—1.0 460-PI—0.96	460 4V—0.140 460-PI—0.160	None	#2	0.300	2 Rich	Initial—0.140 Delayed—0.190 ④

Carter Thermo-Quad ®

1974	1¹¹/₁₆	0.099	None	Inner	0.130	Index	0.250

① Overrich choke setting—increase in steps of 0.020 in.
Lean choke setting—decrease clearance in steps of 0.020 in.
② D50E-BA, CA—3
D5AE-AA, EA—3
D50E-GA; D5ME-BA, FA—2
③ D6WE-AA—3 Rich
D6AE-HA, D6ME-AA—3 Rich
D6WE-BA—2 Rich
④ 460 PI—Initial—0.160
Delayed—0.210

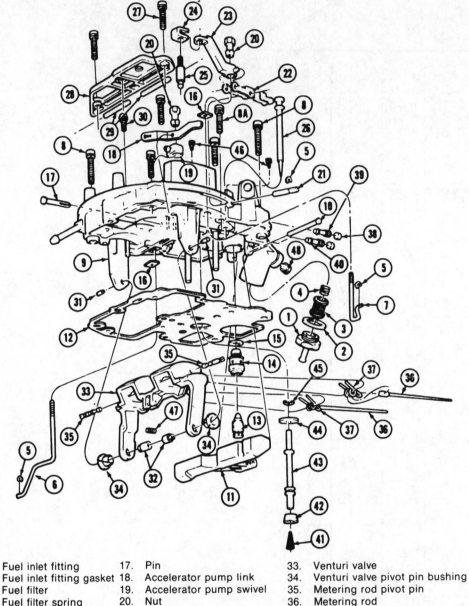

1.	Fuel inlet fitting	17.
2.	Fuel inlet fitting gasket	18.
3.	Fuel filter	19.
4.	Fuel filter spring	20.
5.	Retaining E-ring	21.
6.	Accelerator pump rod	22.
7.	Choke control rod	23.
8.	Screw	24.
8A.	Screw	
9.	Upper body	25.
10.	Float hinge pin	26.
11.	Float assembly	27.
12.	Float bowl gasket	28.
13.	Fuel inlet valve	29.
14.	Fuel inlet seat	30.
15.	Fuel inlet seat gasket	31.
16.	Dust seal	32.

1. Fuel inlet fitting
2. Fuel inlet fitting gasket
3. Fuel filter
4. Fuel filter spring
5. Retaining E-ring
6. Accelerator pump rod
7. Choke control rod
8. Screw
8A. Screw
9. Upper body
10. Float hinge pin
11. Float assembly
12. Float bowl gasket
13. Fuel inlet valve
14. Fuel inlet seat
15. Fuel inlet seat gasket
16. Dust seal

17. Pin
18. Accelerator pump link
19. Accelerator pump swivel
20. Nut
21. Choke hinge pin
22. Cold enrichment rod lever
23. Cold enrichment rod swivel
24. Control vacuum regulator adjusting nut
25. Control vacuum regulator
26. Cold enrichment rod
27. Screw
28. Venturi valve cover plate
29. Roller bearing
30. Venturi air bypass screw
31. Venturi valve pivot plug
32. Venturi valve pivot pin

33. Venturi valve
34. Venturi valve pivot pin bushing
35. Metering rod pivot pin
36. Metering rod
37. Metering rod spring
38. Cup plug
39. Main metering jet assembly
40. O-ring
41. Accelerator pump return spring
42. Accelerator pump cup
43. Accelerator pump plunger
44. Internal vent valve
45. Retaining E-ring
46. Idle trim screw
47. Venturi valve limiter adjusting screw
48. Pipe plug

Typical upper body—VV carburetor (2700VV shown)

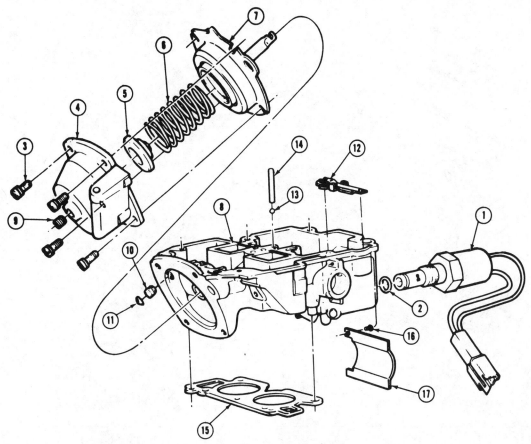

1. Cranking enrichment solenoid
2. O-ring seal
3. Screw
4. Venturi valve diaphragm cover
5. Venturi valve diaphragm spring guide
6. Venturi valve diaphragm spring
7. Venturi valve diaphragm assembly
8. Main body
9. Venturi valve adjusting screw
10. Wide open stop screw
11. Plug expansion
12. Cranking fuel control assembly
13. Accelerator pump check ball
14. Accelerator pump check ball weight
15. Throttle body gasket
16. Screw
17. Choke heat shield

Typical main body—VV carburetor (2700VV shown)

richment systems are not needed in these carburetors.

REMOVAL

1. Label and disconnect all hoses attached to the air cleaner. Remove the air cleaner.

2. Remove the throttle cable from the throttle lever. Label and disconnect all vacuum lines, emission hoses, the fuel line and electrical connections to the carburetor. On models with EEC, disconnect the TPS (throttle position sensor) at the harness connector.

3. Remove the carburetor mounting nuts and remove the carburetor.

4. Remove the mounting gasket/spacer (if equipped) and the lower gasket from the intake manifold. Always use new gaskets when reinstalling.

INSTALLATION

1. Clean the gasket mounting surfaces of the intake manifold, spacer and carburetor.

2. Install the two gaskets with the spacer in between on the intake manifold. Position the carburetor on the intake manifold and connect the spark and EGR lines before bolting the carburetor in position. Connect the TPS harness. Tighten the mounting bolts in stages to prevent damage to the mounting flange of the carburetor.

3. Connect all other lines and hoses removed.

4. Connect the throttle cable. Start the engine and allow it to warm up. Adjust the idle speed.

5. When the carburetor is removed or re-

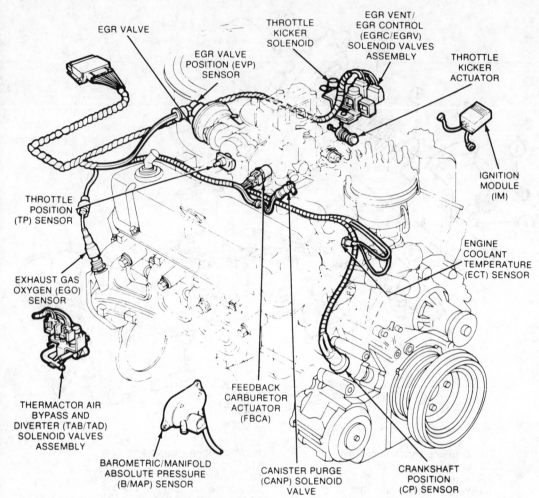

VV feedback carburetor wiring and vacuum diagram

placed it is necessary to check or adjust the transmission kickdown or throttle valve lever. Refer to the transmission chapter for procedures.

CURB IDLE SPEED

The VV carburetors may have a vacuum operated throttle modulator (VOTM) in conjunction with a solenoid, a VOTM alone, or neither of these devices. Vehicles without air conditioning should not be equipped with either a solenoid or a VOTM. Vehicles with air conditioning may have either a solenoid in conjunction with a VOTM or simply the VOTM. On all models equipped with automatic parking brake release, disconnect the vacuum line at the parking brake and plug it.

Vehicles with No Solenoid or VOTM

1. Place the transmission in drive.
2. Turn the throttle stop adjusting screw until the correct idle speed is obtained.

3. Cycle the throttle to check the idle. If the idle falls to within plus or minus 50 rpm of the specified speed, leave it alone.

Vehicles With Both a Solenoid and VOTM

1. Place the transmission in drive, turn the air conditioner on, and make sure the cold enrichment rod is fully seated.
2. Disconnect the electro-magnetic clutch.
3. Turn the screw at the rear of the solenoid/VOTM to adjust the idle speed.
4. Cycle the throttle to check the repeatability to within plus or minus 50 rpm.

NOTE: *The procedure is the same for a carburetor equipped with only a VOTM.*

1981 and Later 225, 302 and 351

NOTE: *If equipped with automatic overdrive transmission, see Idle Speed Adjustment section.*

1. Place the transmission in Park. Apply the emergency brake and block the wheels.

2. Bring the engine to normal operating temperature. Turn off all accessories and connect a tachometer.

3. On carbureted models, disconnect and plug the vacuum hose at the throttle kicker, place the transmission in the gear specified on the underhood sticker and check and adjust the curb idle rpm. Adjust at the curb idle screw at the throttle valve lever or at the saddle bracket adjusting screw.

4. On EFI engines, shut the engine off, restart it and run at 2,000 rpm for 60 seconds in neutral then let the engine idle stabilize for 15 seconds. Place the transmission in drive and check/adjust the curb idle rpm. Adjust at the saddle bracket adjusting screw. If rpm is low, turn the screw clockwise one full turn then repeat step 4 until correct rpm is reached. If the rpm is high, turn the screw counterclockwise to specific rpm and recheck.

5. On carbureted models, place transmission in Neutral or Park, rev the engine once, place the transmission in the specified gear (sticker) and recheck the curb idle rpm.

6. On EFI engines, make sure the scribe mark on the throttle position sensor is aligned with the mark on the throttle body. Adjust as necessary.

7. Reconnect the throttle kicker vacuum hose on the 7200 VV carburetor and apply pressure to the nylon nut on the accelerator pump to take up linkage clearance, then adjust the clearance between the top of the accelerator pump and the pump lever to .010 in., using the nylon nut on the pump rod. Turn the pump rod one turn counterclockwise to set the lever lash preload.

8. Reconnect all hoses.

9. To set the throttle kicker speed, set the transmission in Neutral or Park, bring the engine to normal operating temperature and turn off all accessories. Disconnect the vacuum hose

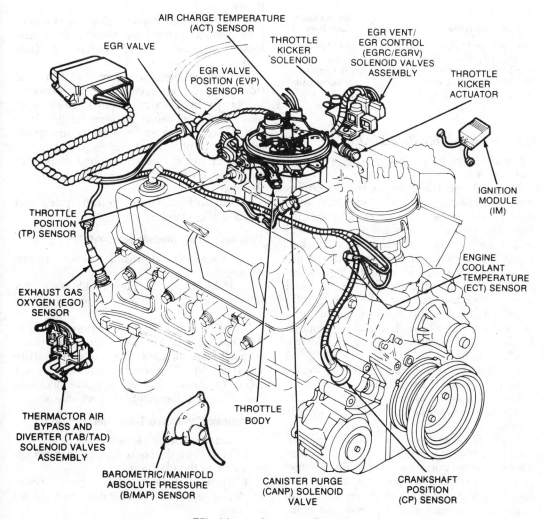

EFI wiring and vacuum diagram

at the Vacuum Operated Throttle Modulator (kicker) and connect an external vacuum source (10 in. Hg. minimum) to the kicker.

10. Place the transmission in the gear specified on the underhood sticker (apply parking brake, block wheels).

11. Disconnect the A/C compressor clutch wire, place the A/C selector to max. blower cooling and check/adjust the VOTM kicker speed. If adjustment is required, turn the saddle bracket adjusting screw.

12. Reconnect all components.

AUTOMATIC OVERDRIVE IDLE SPEED ADJUSTMENT

If the car is equipped with Ford's automatic overdrive transmission, and the idle speed is adjusted by more than 50 rpm, the adjustment screw on the linkage lever at the carburetor must also be adjusted:

Idle Speed Change	Turns on Linkage Lever Screw
• Less than 50 rpm	No change
• 500-100 rpm increase	1½ turns out
• 50-100 rpm decrease	1½ turns in
• 100-150 rpm increase	2½ turns out
• 100-150 rpm decrease	2½ turns in

ELECTRONIC FUEL INJECTION

Some 302 V8 powered cars are equipped with fuel injection.

The electronic fuel injection (EFI) includes two fuel injectors vertically mounted in a throttle body installed on the intake manifold. The throttle body resembles a conventional carburetor, but in fact retains only the fuel supply and throttle plate functions of a carburetor. Fuel is supplied by a high pressure pump mounted inside the fuel tank. A fuel pressure regulator is mounted on the throttle body just ahead of the injectors, maintaining fuel pressure at 39 psi. Excess fuel supplied by the pump is returned to the gas tank via a steel return line.

CAUTION: *Should any service be necessary on the EFI, the fuel pressure must be bled off. Use the special tool from Ford, or carefully "crack" the fuel feed line at the gas tank.*

Fuel discharge from the injectors is controlled by the EEC module, which computes engine temperature, speed, timing and fuel requirements to determine how long to electrically energize the injectors for maximum engine performance and economy and minimal emissions.

NOTE: *Any service or troubleshooting on the EFI should be performed by qualified mechanics.*

THROTTLE AND DOWNSHIFT LINKAGE ADJUSTMENT
1968 Models

1. Apply the parking brake and place selector lever in N.

2. Run engine at fast idle until it reaches normal operating temperature. Then, slow it down to normal idle.

3. Connect a tachometer to the engine.

4. Adjust engine to specified idle speed with selector in D1 or D2. Due to the vacuum parking brake release (if so equipped), the parking brake will not hold while selector is in D1 or D2. Keep service brake applied.

5. When satisfied that idle speed is correct, stop engine and adjust dashpot clearance. Check clearance between dashpot plunger and throttle lever.

6. With engine stopped, disconnect carburetor return spring from throttle lever and loosen accelerator cable conduit attaching clamp.

7. With accelerator pedal to floor and throttle lever wide open, slide cable conduit to rear (to left on six-cylinder engine) to remove slack from cable. Tighten clamp.

8. Disconnect downshift lever return spring and hold throttle lever wide open. Depress downshift rod to "through detent stop." Set downshift lever adjusting screw against throttle lever.

9. Connect carburetor return spring and downshift lever return spring.

1969 and Later Models (exc. AOT)

1. Disconnect downshift lever return spring.

2. Hold throttle shaft lever wide open, and hold downshift rod against "through detent stop."

3. Adjust downshift screw to provide 0.050–0.070 in. clearance between screw and throttle shaft lever on 1969–72 models and 0.010–0.080 in. on 1973–and later models (except AOT). On 240 cu. in. engine, tighten locknut.

4. Connect downshift lever return spring.

Automatic Overdrive Transmission (AOT)

1. Remove the air cleaner.

2. Make sure the choke linkage is off of high cam and on the idle stop.

3. Turn linkage lever adjusting screw counterclockwise until the end is flush with the lever face.

4. Turn the linkage adjusting screw clock-

wise to obtain .005 inch clearance between the end of the screw and the throttle lever.

5. Turn the linkage screw clockwise, three full turns, if possible. One turn is the minimum, if this is not possible the transmission linkage needs adjustment.

Fuel Tank

REMOVAL AND INSTALLATION

1. Block the front wheels, raise the rear of the car and support with jackstands.
2. Drain the fuel from the tank. If there is no drain plug, remove the fuel line and drain into a suitable safe container.
3. Remove all lines and hoses from the tank. Remove the filler neck attachment.
4. Support the tank and remove the nuts and bolts securing the mounting straps.
5. Lower the tank slowly, and remove from under the car.
6. Installation is the reverse of removal.

CAUTION: *No smoking. If the car is equipped with EFI, bleed the fuel pressure from the system by "cracking" the fuel feed line at the gas tank.*

Chassis Electrical

HEATER

Non-Air Conditioned Cars

BLOWER MOTOR REMOVAL AND INSTALLATION

1968–72 Models

1. Disconnect the negative battery cable.
2. Disconnect the blower motor wire leads under the hood.
3. Remove any parts mounted on the inside of the right fender apron.
4. Raise the vehicle on a hoist and remove the right front wheel.
5. Remove the fender apron-to-fender attaching bolts and lower the fender apron.
6. Insert a block of wood between the apron and the fender to gain working space.
7. Reach inside the fender apron and remove the blower motor mounting plate attaching screws.
8. Remove the blower motor, wheel and mounting plate from inside the fender as an assembly.
9. Reverse above procedure to install.

1973–78 Models

1. Disconnect the battery ground cable. Disconnect the blower motor lead wire.
2. Remove the mounting screw from the black ground wire location at the upper cowl. Remove both wires from the clip.
3. Remove the right front tire and wheel.
4. In order to get to the blower motor, an access hole must be cut out in the right front fender apron. The pattern for this hole has been outlined on the apron by the factory. It appears as a beaded line.
5. A small indentation or drill dimple is present ½ in. from the centerline of the bead. Drill a 1 in. diameter hole at this drill dimple. Be careful not to damage the heater case by overdrilling.

6. Using aircraft snips, cut along the bead to create the opening. Do not use a saber saw.
7. Remove the blower motor mounting plate screws and disconnect the cooler tube from the motor.
8. Remove the motor and wheel assembly out of the heater case and out through the access hole.
9. To install, reverse the removal procedure. Apply rope sealer to the motor mounting plate. Obtain a cover plate from your local Ford parts department, drill 8, ⅛ in. holes in the fender apron and install the cover plate.

1979 and Later Models

1. Disconnect the battery ground cable.
2. Disconnect the blower motor ground wire and engine ground wire.
3. Disconnect the wiring harness connections.
4. Remove the blower motor cooling tube.
5. Remove the four retaining screws from the mounting plate.
6. Remove the blower motor and wheel assembly. It will be necessary to turn the assembly slightly to the right and follow the contour of the wheel well.
7. Installation is the reverse of removal.

HEATER CORE REMOVAL AND INSTALLATION

Through 1978

On cars not equipped with air conditioning, the heater core is located in the left-side of the case on the engine side of the dash panel. To remove:

1. Partially drain cooling system.
2. Remove heater hoses at core.
3. Remove retaining screws, core cover and seal from plenum.
4. Remove core from plenum.
5. Install in reverse of above, applying a thin coat of silicone to the pads.

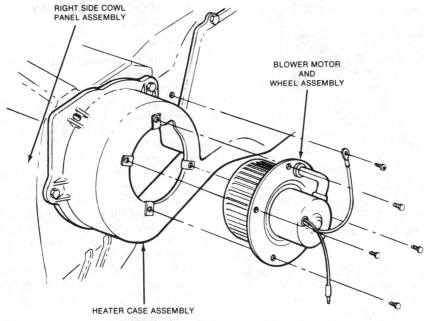

RIGHT SIDE COWL
PANEL ASSEMBLY

BLOWER MOTOR
AND
WHEEL ASSEMBLY

HEATER CASE ASSEMBLY

Typical blower motor installation

1979 and Later Models

1. It is necessary to remove the plenum assembly to reach the heater core on 1979 and later models. Drain the coolant from the system.

2. Disconnect the negative battery cable.

3. Disconnect the heater hoses from the heater core tubes. Plug the tubes to prevent leakage.

4. Remove the one bolt located beneath the wiper motor that attaches the left side of the plenum to the dash. Remove the nut that

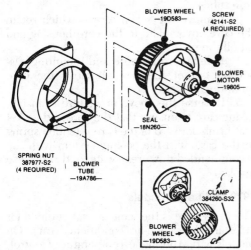

BLOWER WHEEL
—19D583—

SCREW
42141-S2
(4 REQUIRED)

BLOWER
MOTOR
—19805—

SEAL
—18N260—

SPRING NUT
387977-S2
(4 REQUIRED)

BLOWER
TUBE
—19A786—

CLAMP
384260-S32

BLOWER
WHEEL
—19D583—

Blower motor removal (1979 shown)

retains the upper left corner of the heater case.

5. Disconnect the control system vacuum supply hose from the vacuum source and push the hose and the grommet into the passenger compartment.

6. Remove the glove compartment.

7. Loosen the right still plate, and remove the right side cowl trim panel.

8. Remove the attaching bolt on the lower right side of the instrument panel.

9. Remove the instrument panel pad. There are five screws attaching the lower edge, one screw on each outboard end, and two screws near the defroster openings.

10. Disengage the temperature control cable from the top of the plenum. Disconnect the cable from the temperature blend door crank arm.

11. Remove the clip attaching the center register bracket to the plenum, and rotate the bracket up to the right.

12. Disconnect the vacuum harness at the multiple connector near the floor duct.

13. Disconnect the white vacuum hose from the vacuum motor.

14. Remove the two screws attaching the passenger's side air duct to the plenum. It may be necessary to remove the two screws which attach the lower panel door vacuum motor to the mounting bracket to gain access.

15. Remove the one plastic fastener retain-

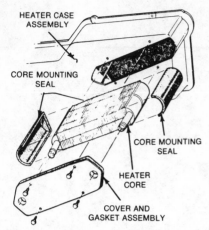

HEATER CASE ASSEMBLY

CORE MOUNTING SEAL

CORE MOUNTING SEAL

HEATER CORE

COVER AND GASKET ASSEMBLY

Heater core removal—typical of a non-air conditioned car

ing the floor air distribution duct to the left end of the plenum, and remove the duct.

16. Remove the two nuts from the lower flange of the plenum.

17. Move the plenum rearward and rotate the top of the plenum down and out from under the instrument panel.

18. Once the plenum is removed, remove the heater core cover and remove the heater core.

19. Installation is the reverse of removal.

Air Conditioned Cars

BLOWER MOTOR REMOVAL AND INSTALLATION

1968 Models

1. Take off the protective cover from the engine firewall. Disconnect the negative battery cable.

2. Take out the mounting plate-to-evaporator housing attaching screws.

3. Disconnect the motor wires.

4. Lift out the motor assembly.

5. Reverse above procedure to install.

1969–72 Models

1. Remove the battery.

2. Remove the right front wheel.

3. Remove the vacuum tank bolts and fender apron bolts.

4. Move the fender apron inboard.

5. Remove the blower motor attaching screws and vent hose.

6. Pry upward on the hood hings and remove the blower.

7. Reverse the above procedure to install.

1973 and Later Models

The procedure is the same as that outlined for 1973–77 non-air conditioned cars.

HEATER CORE REMOVAL AND INSTALLATION

1968 Models

1. Drain the cooling system and raise the front of the vehicle.

2. Remove the right front wheel and tire.

3. To gain access to the core, remove the two upper bolts and the bolts around the wheel well retaining the inner fender apron. Pull the apron down and block it in this position.

4. Disconnect the heater hoses.

5. Remove the water valve retaining screws and position the valve to one side.

6. Remove the core housing-to-dash retaining screws and the core housing from the car.

7. Remove the core from the housing by removing the retaining screws and separating the housing halves.

8. Reverse the above procedure to install, taking care to seal the housing halves together.

1969–72 Models

1. Drain the cooling system.

2. Remove the carburetor air cleaner.

3. Remove the two screws retaining the vacuum manifold to the dash. Disconnect the vacuum hoses as necessary, taking note of their placement, and move the manifold to one side of the heater core cover.

4. Disconnect the heater hoses.

5. Remove the seven attaching screws and the heater core cover.

6. Remove the heater core and pad from the housing.

7. Reverse above procedure to install.

1973–78 Models

1. Drain the cooling system.

2. Disconnect the heater hoses at the heater core tubes.

3. Remove the seven screws which retain the core cover plate to the core housing and lift off the plate.

4. Pull the heater core and mounting gasket up out of the case. Remove the core mounting gasket.

5. Reverse the above procedure to install, taking care to ensure that the core and gasket seat firmly forward of the core retention spring in the case. Fill the cooling system with the recommended mixture of water and antifreeze (coolant).

1979 and Later Models

The procedure is the same as that outlined for 1979 and later non-air conditioned cars. On models with Automatic Temperature Control, various vacuum hoses and wiring harness must

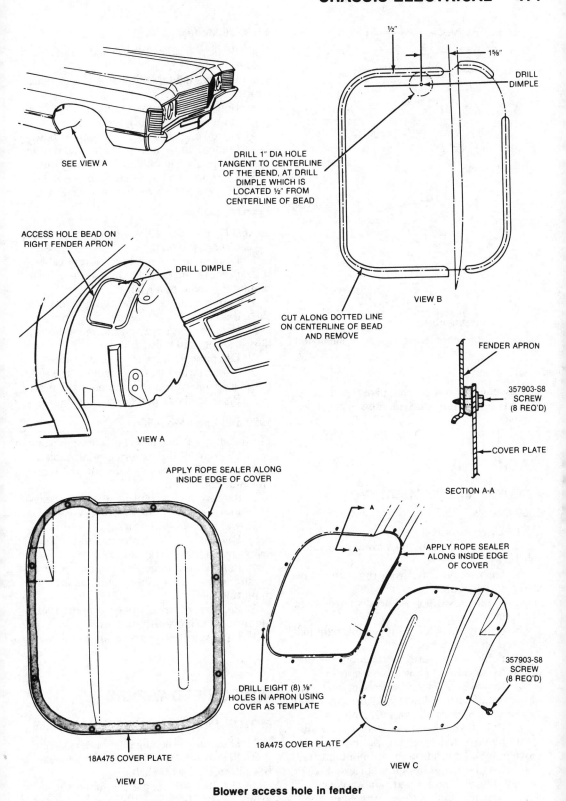

SEE VIEW A

½″

1⅝″

DRILL DIMPLE

DRILL 1″ DIA HOLE
TANGENT TO CENTERLINE
OF THE BEND, AT DRILL
DIMPLE WHICH IS
LOCATED ½″ FROM
CENTERLINE OF BEAD

VIEW B

ACCESS HOLE BEAD ON
RIGHT FENDER APRON

DRILL DIMPLE

CUT ALONG DOTTED LINE
ON CENTERLINE OF BEAD
AND REMOVE

VIEW A

FENDER APRON

357903-S8
SCREW
(8 REQ'D)

COVER PLATE

SECTION A-A

APPLY ROPE SEALER ALONG
INSIDE EDGE OF COVER

A

A

APPLY ROPE SEALER
ALONG INSIDE EDGE
OF COVER

357903-S8
SCREW
(8 REQ'D)

DRILL EIGHT (8) ⅛″
HOLES IN APRON USING
COVER AS TEMPLATE

18A475 COVER PLATE

VIEW C

18A475 COVER PLATE

VIEW D

Blower access hole in fender

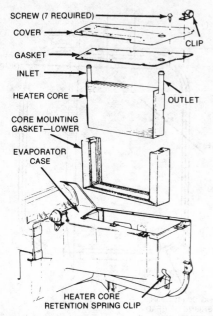

SCREW (7 REQUIRED)
COVER
CLIP
GASKET
INLET
HEATER CORE
OUTLET
CORE MOUNTING
GASKET—LOWER
EVAPORATOR
CASE
HEATER CORE
RETENTION SPRING CLIP

Typical heater core removal—air conditioned cars

be disconnected after the panel pad is removed and before the plenum can be removed.

RADIO

REMOVAL AND INSTALLATION

1968 Models

1. Disconnect battery.
2. Remove the moldings from wind shield pillars.
3. Unsnap moldings from right-side of instrument panel pad.
4. Remove two pop off access cover from cluster area.
5. Remove four screws attaching right half of pad to instrument panel.
6. Remove two screws attaching left side of pad to instrument panel above cluster.
7. Remove one screw attaching each end of instrument panel lower pad to upper pad and remove upper pad from vehicle.
8. Pull all knobs from radio control shafts.
9. Remove ten retaining buttons and remove lens and mask from instrument cluster.
10. Remove two screws from blackout cover at right of speedometer and remove cover.
11. Remove four screws attaching radio front plate to instrument cluster.
12. Pull radio out and disconnect leads.
13. Reverse procedure to install radio.

1969–70 Models

1. Remove radio knobs and wiper and washer knobs.
2. Remove lighter and pull off heater switch knobs.
3. Remove ten screws retaining instrument panel trim cover assembly and remove.
4. Remove lower rear radio support bolt.
5. Remove three nuts retaining radio in instrument panel and pull radio half-way out.
6. Disconnect all leads and remove radio.
7. Reverse procedure to install radio.

1971–79 Models

NOTE: *For the 1979 all-electronic radio, perform step 6 first.*
1. Disconnect the negative battery cable.
2. Remove the radio knobs and the nuts retaining the radio cover bezel.
3. Remove the bezel and the nut retaining the fader control to the bezal.
4. Remove the upper and lower radio support brackets and bolts.
5. Disconnect all leads from the radio.
6. Remove the two nuts retaining the radio to the instrument panel and remove the radio.
7. Reverse above procedure to install.

1980 and Later Models

For the all-electronic radio perform step 6 first.
1. Disconnect the battery ground cable.
2. Remove the radio knobs and the screws attaching the bezel.
3. Remove the radio plate attaching screws.
4. Pull the radio out to disengage it from the lower rear support bracket.
5. Disconnect the antenna and speaker leads and remove the radio.
6. Remove the radio to mounting plate retaining nuts and washers and remove the mounting plate.
7. Remove the rear upper support retaining nut and remove the support.
8. Reverse the steps to install the radio.

WINDSHIELD WIPERS

MOTOR REMOVAL AND INSTALLATION

1. Disconnect the negative battery cable.
2. Remove the wiper arm and blade assemblies from the pivots shafts.
3. On 1968–70 models, remove the cowl grille. On 1971–72 and 1977 models, remove the left side cowl grille.
4. Disconnect the wiper links at the wiper output pin by removing the retaining clip.

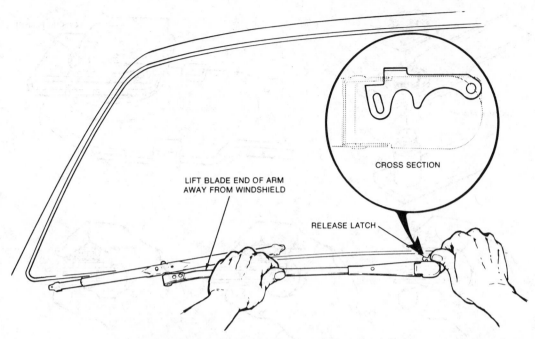

CROSS SECTION

LIFT BLADE END OF ARM
AWAY FROM WINDSHIELD

RELEASE LATCH

Installation of arm and blade assembly to pivot shaft

5. Disconnect the wire leads from the motor.

6. On 1968 models, remove the motor and bracket attaching bolts from the engine side of the firewall and remove the motor from the car. On 1969–78 models, remove the motor attaching bolts from under the dash and remove the motor. On 1979 and later models,

remove the motor attaching bolts from the dash panel extension.

7. Reverse above procedure to install.

NOTE: *Before installing the wiper arms and blades, operate the wiper motor to ensure that the pivot shafts are in the Park position when the arms and blades are installed.*

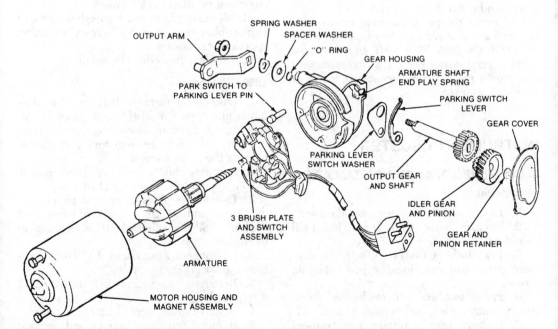

OUTPUT ARM

SPRING WASHER
SPACER WASHER

"O" RING

GEAR HOUSING

ARMATURE SHAFT
END PLAY SPRING

PARK SWITCH TO
PARKING LEVER PIN

PARKING SWITCH
LEVER

GEAR COVER

PARKING LEVER
SWITCH WASHER

OUTPUT GEAR
AND SHAFT

3 BRUSH PLATE
AND SWITCH
ASSEMBLY

IDLER GEAR
AND PINION

GEAR AND
PINION RETAINER

ARMATURE

MOTOR HOUSING AND
MAGNET ASSEMBLY

Wiper motor disassembled

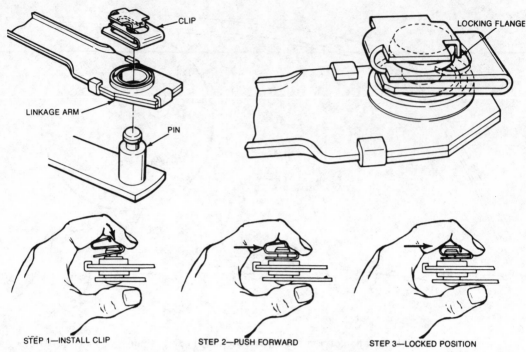

STEP 1—INSTALL CLIP STEP 2—PUSH FORWARD STEP 3—LOCKED POSITION

Installation of wiper arm connecting clips

WIPER LINKAGE REMOVAL AND INSTALLATION

1. Disconnect the battery ground cable.
2. Remove the wiper arms and blades from the pivots as an assembly.
3. Remove the cowl grille from the car.
4. Disconnect the linkage arm from the drive arm by removing the clip.
5. Remove the pivot attaching screws from the cowl and remove the pivot from the cowl.
NOTE: *On 1969–72 models, to remove the left wiper transmission, it is first necessary to loosen the attaching screws on the right wiper arm pivot.*

INSTRUMENT CLUSTER

CLUSTER REMOVAL AND INSTALLATION

1968 Models

1. Disconnect the battery ground cable.
2. Remove right and left windshield mouldings.
3. Pry moulding from right-side of instrument panel pad covering the pad retaining screws.
4. Pry off two access covers located above the speedometer lens and on underside of pad.
5. Remove screws retaining instrument panel pad, and remove pad.
6. Remove radio knobs.

7. Remove button clips retaining instrument cluster mask and lens, and remove mask and lens.
8. Disconnect speedometer cable.
9. Remove screws retaining instrument panel lower pad and remove pad.
10. Remove screws from clock retainer and clock and position clock forward.
11. Remove plate under speedometer and two rubber spacers and screws retaining speedometer assembly.
12. Reverse procedure to install.

1969–72 Models

1. Disconnect negative battery cable. Remove upper part of instrument panel by removing screws along lower edge, two screws in each of the defroster registers, and disconnecting the radio speaker.
2. Remove cluster opening finish panels from each side of instrument cluster.
3. Disconnect plugs to printed circuit, radio, heater and A/C fan, windshield wipers and washers, and any other electrical connection to cluster.
4. Disconnect heater and A/C control cables and speedometer cable.
5. Remove all knobs from instrument panel if required.
6. Remove instrument cluster trim cover.
7. Remove mounting screws and remove cluster.
8. Reverse procedure to install.

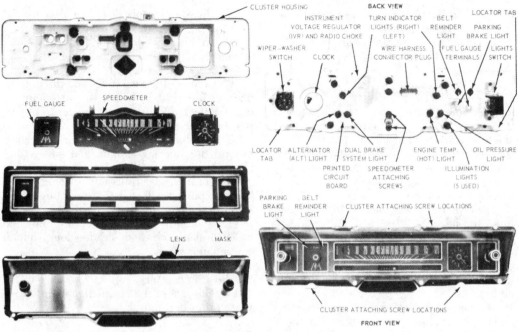

Instrument cluster—1969–72

1973–79 Models

1. Disconnect the negative battery cable.
2. Remove the steering column cover.
3. Disconnect the speedometer cable and the wire plugs to the printed circuit.

4. Remove the cluster trim cover.
5. Remove the screw attaching the transmission selector lever indicator cable to the column.
6. Remove the instrument cluster retaining

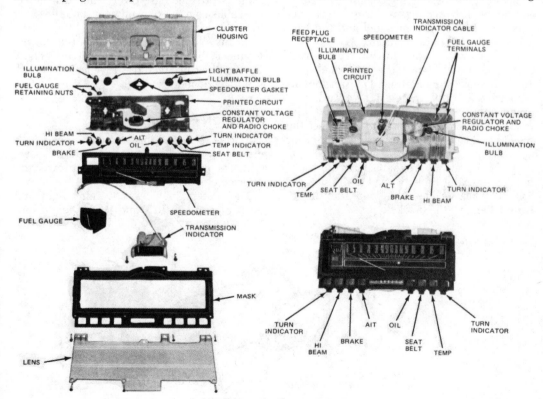

Instrument cluster—1973–77

screws and lift the cluster from the instrument panel.

7. Reverse the above procedure to install, taking care to ensure that the selector pointer is aligned.

1980 and Later Non-Electronic Cluster

1. Disconnect the negative battery cable.
2. Disconnect the speedometer cable (refer to the following section for instructions).
3. Remove the instrument cluster trim cover attaching screws and the lower two steering column cover attaching screws. Remove the trim covers.
4. Remove the lower half of the steering column shroud.
5. Remove the screw attaching the transmission selector indicator bracket to the steering column. Unfasten the cable loop from the retainer on the shift lever. Remove the column bracket.
6. Remove the cluster attaching screws. Disconnect the cluster feed plug and remove the cluster.
7. Reverse the procedure for installation. Be sure to lubricate the speedometer drive head. Adjust the selector indicator if necessary.

1980 and Later Electronic Cluster

1. Disconnect the negative battery cable.
2. Remove the steering column trim cover and lower instrument panel trim cover. Remove the keyboard trim panel and the trim panel on the left of the column.
3. Remove the instrument cluster trim cover screws and remove the trim panel.
4. Remove the instrument cluster mounting screws and pull the cluster forward. Disconnect the feed plugs and the ground wire from the back of the cluster. Disconnect the speedometer cable (see following section for details).
5. Remove the screw attaching the transmission indicator cable bracket to the steering column. Unfasten the cable loop from the retainer. Remove the bracket.

6. Unfasten the plastic clamp from around the steering column. Remove the cluster.
7. To install the cluster: Apply a small amount of silicone lubricant into the drive hole of the speedometer head.
8. Connect the feed plugs and the ground wire to the cluster. Install the speedometer cable. Attach the instrument cluster to the instrument panel.
9. Install the plastic indicator cable clamp around the steering column and engage the clamp locator pin in the column tube.
10. Place the transmission selector in the "Drive" position. Install the mounting screw into the retainer but do not tighten.
11. Rotate the plastic cable clamp until the indicator flag covers *both* location dots. Tighten the retainer screw.
12. Move the selector through all positions. Readjust if necessary.
13. The rest of the installation is in the reverse order of removal.

Speedometer Cable Core
REMOVAL AND INSTALLATION

1. Reach up behind the cluster and disconnect the cable by depressing the quick disconnect tab and pulling the cable away.
2. Remove the cable from its casing. If the cable is broken, raise the car and disconnect the cable from the transmission. Pull the cable from the casing.
3. Install the new cable into the casing. Connect the transmission (if disconnected). Engage the cable with the drive head and push it until the tab locks.

Seatbelt System

All 1974–75 Ford vehicles are equipped with the Federally-required starter interlock system. The purpose of this system is to force the wearing of seat belts.

The system includes a warning light and buzzer (as in late 1972 and 1973), weight sen-

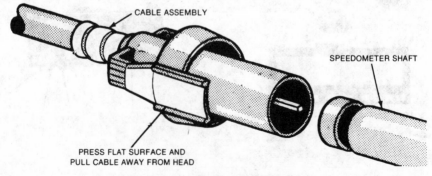

CABLE ASSEMBLY

SPEEDOMETER SHAFT

PRESS FLAT SURFACE AND
PULL CABLE AWAY FROM HEAD

Speedometer cable quick disconnect

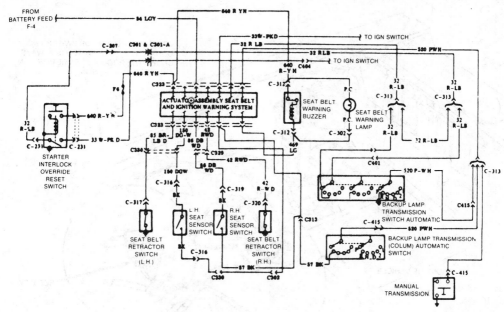

Seat belt/starter interlock system circuit

sors in the front seats, switches in the outboard front seat belt retractors, and an electronic control module. The center front is tied into the warning light and buzzer system, but not into the starter interlock.

The electronic control module requires that the driver and right front passenger first sit down, then pull out their seat belts. If this is not done, the starter will not operate, but the light and buzzer will. The sequence must be followed each time the engine is started unless the driver and passenger have remained seated and buckled. If the seat belts have been pulled out and left buckled, the engine will not start. The switches in the retractors must be cycled for each start. If the belts are released after the start, the light and buzzer will operate.

If the system should fail, preventing starting, the interlock by-pass switch under the hood can be used. This switch permits one start without interference from the interlock system. This by-pass switch can also be used for servicing purposes.

TROUBLESHOOTING

If the starter will not crank or the warning buzzer will not shut off, perform the following checks:

Problem: Front seat occupant sits on a prebuckled seat belt.

Solution: Unbuckle the prebuckled belt, fully retract, extract, and then rebuckle the belt.

Problem: The front seat occupants are buckled, but the starter will not crank.

Solution: The unoccupied seat sensor switch stuck closed before the seat was occupied. Reset the unoccupied seat sensor switches by applying and then releasing 50 lbs or more of weight to the seat directly over the seat sensor switches.

Problem: Starter will not crank with a heavy parcel on the front seat.

Solution: Buckle the seat belt around the parcel somewhere else in the car. Unbuckle the seat belt when the parcel is removed from the front seat.

Problem: Starter will not crank due to starter interlock system component failure.

Solution: An emergency starter interlock override switch is located under the hood on the fender apron. Depress the red push button on the switch and release it. This will allow one complete cycle of the ignition key from Off to Start and back to Off. Do not tape the button down as this will result in deactivation of the override feature.

LIGHTING

Headlights

REMOVAL AND INSTALLATION

1. Remove the headlight door mounting screws and the headlight door.

2. Remove the three screws that hold the headlight retainer to the adjusting ring, and remove the retainer.

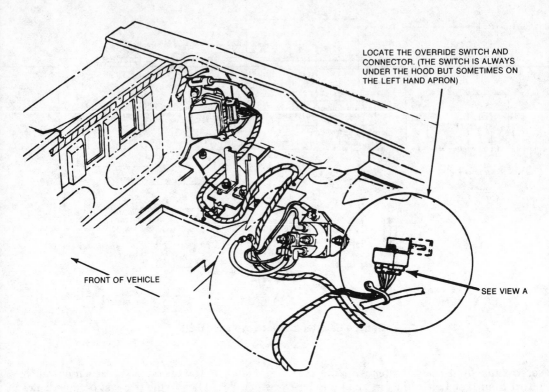

LOCATE THE OVERRIDE SWITCH AND CONNECTOR. (THE SWITCH IS ALWAYS UNDER THE HOOD BUT SOMETIMES ON THE LEFT HAND APRON)

FRONT OF VEHICLE

SEE VIEW A

CAUTION: Set the parking brake and remove the ignition key before any rework is performed. (If the no. 640 circuit is accidentally spliced into the no. 32 or no. 33 circuits, the car will start in gear)

1. Cut the no. 32 and no. 33 circuits
2. On the wiring harness end, splice the no. 32 and no. 33 circuits together. Use a B9A-14487-A butt connector on a 16 to 18 gage wire or a B9A-14487-B connector on a 10 to 14 gage wire
3. Tape the complete splice to water proof the connection
4. Reattach the connector to the override switch to prevent rattling
5. Test the rework by setting the car brakes, buckle up the seat belt and turn the key to on. If the starter cranks in the on position and in any gear the wires have been crossed. (Recheck the rework)
6. The buzzer function can be deleted by removing the buzzer from the connector and taping the connector to the harness to prevent rattling

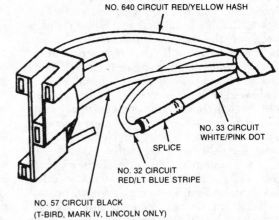

NO. 640 CIRCUIT RED/YELLOW HASH

NO. 33 CIRCUIT WHITE/PINK DOT

SPLICE

NO. 32 CIRCUIT RED/LT BLUE STRIPE

NO. 57 CIRCUIT BLACK (T-BIRD, MARK IV, LINCOLN ONLY)

VIEW A

7. The sequential seat belt warning light feature can be deleted by removing the bulb from its socket. This can only be done on previously sold vehicles. The light cannot be disconnected on a new and unsold car even if the purchaser so requests

NOTE: If the no. 32 and no. 33 circuit terminals contain two wires, cut and splice all wires from the no. 32 and no. 33 circuits into one butt connector.

Disconnecting the seat belt/starter interlock system

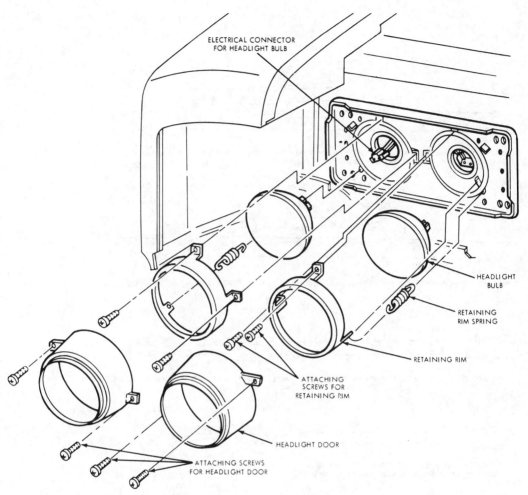

Typical headlight seal beam replacement

3. Pull the headlight forward and disconnect the wire plug. Remove the headlight.

4. Attach a new headlight to the wiring plug.

5. Install the new light in the housing and replace the retainer ring.

6. Reinstall the headlight door.

Fuses and Flashers

The fuses and flashers are located under the instrument panel on all models.

CIRCUIT PROTECTION

Fuse Link

The fuse link is a short length of insulated wire contained in the alternator wiring harness, between the alternator and the starter relay. The fuse link is several wire gauge sizes smaller than the other wires in the harness. If a booster battery is connected incorrectly to the car battery or if some component of the charging system is shorted to ground, the fuse link melts and protects the alternator. The fuse link is attached to the starter relay. The insulation on

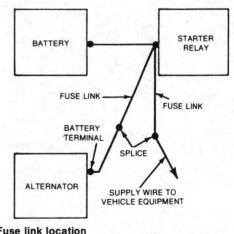

Fuse link location

REMOVE EXISTING VINYL TUBE SHIELDING
REINSTALL OVER FUSE LINK BEFORE CRIMPING
FUSE LINK TO WIRE ENDS

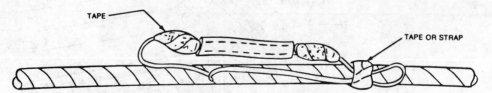

TAPE

TAPE OR STRAP

TYPICAL REPAIR USING THE SPECIAL #17 GA. (9.00" LONG-YELLOW) FUSE LINK REQUIRED FOR THE AIR/COND.
CIRCUITS (2) #687E and #261A LOCATED IN THE ENGINE COMPARTMENT

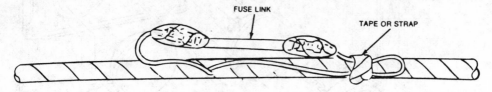

FUSE LINK

TAPE OR STRAP

TYPICAL REPAIR FOR ANY IN-LINE FUSE LINK USING THE SPECIFIED GAUGE FUSE LINK FOR THE SPECIFIC CIRCUIT

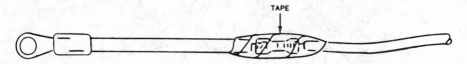

TAPE

TYPICAL REPAIR USING THE EYELET TERMINAL FUSE LINK OF THE SPECIFIED GAUGE FOR ATTACHMENT TO A CIRCUIT WIRE END

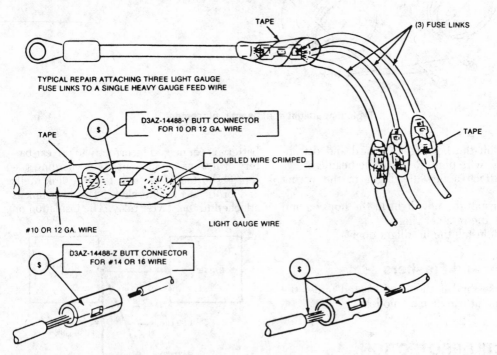

TAPE

(3) FUSE LINKS

TAPE

TYPICAL REPAIR ATTACHING THREE LIGHT GAUGE
FUSE LINKS TO A SINGLE HEAVY GAUGE FEED WIRE

TAPE

D3AZ-14488-Y BUTT CONNECTOR
FOR 10 OR 12 GA. WIRE

DOUBLED WIRE CRIMPED

#10 OR 12 GA. WIRE

LIGHT GAUGE WIRE

D3AZ-14488-Z BUTT CONNECTOR
FOR #14 OR 16 WIRE

FUSIBLE LINK REPAIR PROCEDURE

General fuse link repair procedure

the wire reads: FUSE LINK. A melted fuse link can usually be identified by cracked or bubbled insulation. If it is difficult to determine if the fuse link is melted, connect a test light to both ends of the wire. If the fuse link is not melted, the test light will light showing that an open circuit does not exist in the wire.

FUSE LINK REPLACEMENT

Fuse links originally installed in your car are black on 1970–71 models and the color of the circuit being protected on 1972 and later models. Service replacements are green or black, depending on usage. Black service replacements are used with cars using 38 and 42 amp alternators, and green service replacements on cars using 55 or 61 amp alternators. All 1972 and later models use color coded flags molded on the wire or on the terminal insulator to identify the wire gauge of the link. Color identification is as follows: Red-18 gauge wire, orange-16 gauge wire, green-14 gauge wire, blue-20 gauge wire.

1. Disconnect the negative battery cable.
2. Disconnect the eyelet of the fuse link from the starter relay.
3. Cut the other end of the fuse link from the wiring harness at the splice.

4. Connect the eyelet end of a new fuse link to the starter relay.
NOTE: *Use only an original equipment type fuse link. Under no conditions should standard wire be substituted.*
5. Splice the open end of the new fuse link into the wiring harness.
6. Solder the splice with rosin-core solder and wrap the splice with electrical tape. This splice must be soldered.
7. Connect the negative battery cable.
8. Start the engine, to check to see that the new connections complete the circuit.

WIRING DIAGRAMS

Wiring diagrams have been left out of this book. As cars have become more complex, and available with longer and longer option lists, wiring diagrams have grown in size and complexity also. It has become virtually impossible to provide a readable reproduction in a reasonable number of pages. Information on ordering wiring diagrams from the vehicle manufacturer can be found in the owners manual.

Clutch and Transmission

6

MANUAL TRANSMISSION

A 3-speed manual transmission is standard equipment on 1968–71 models. All forward gears are fully synchronized, helical-cut and in constant mesh. A column-mounted shifter is used with this transmission. On 1972 and later models, the 3-speed manual transmission is no longer available.

A 4-speed manual transmission is available as an option on 1968 models using the 390 and 428 V8 engines, and on 1969 models equipped with the 429 V8. This heavy-duty unit is also synchronized in all forware gears. On 1970 and later models, the 4 speed transmission is no longer available. This transmission used a floor-mounted shifter.

MANUAL TRANSMISSION LINKAGE ADJUSTMENT

Column Shift

1. Place the gearshift lever in the Neutral position.

2. Loosen the two gearshift adjustment nuts on the shift linkage.

3. Insert a $^3/_{16}$ in. alignment tool through the First and Reverse lever, the Second and Third gear shift lever, and the two holes in the lower casing. An alignment tool can be fabricated from $^3/_{16}$ in. rod bent to an L shape. The extension that is to be inserted into the levers should be 1 in. in length from the elbow.

4. Manipulate the levers so that the alignment tool will move freely through the alignment holes.

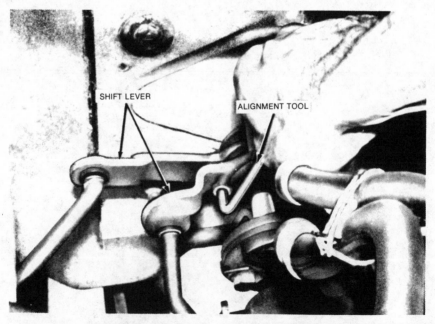

Column-mounted gearshift linkage adjustment

5. Tighten the two gearshift rod adjustment nuts.

6. Remove the tool and check linkage operation.

Floor Shift

1. Place the gearshift lever in Neutral position, then raise car on a hoist.

2. Insert a ¼ in. rod into the alignment holes of the shift levers.

3. If the holes are not in exact alignment, check for bent connecting rods or loose lever locknuts at the rod ends. Make replacements or repairs, then adjust as follows.

4. Loosen the three rod-to-lever retaining locknuts and move the levers until the ¼ in. gauge rod will enter the alignment holes. Be sure that the transmission shift levers are in Neutral, and the Reverse shifter lever is in the Neutral detent.

5. Install shift rods and torque locknuts to 18–23 ft. lbs.

6. Remove the ¼ in. gauge rod.

7. Operate the shift levers to assure correct shifting.

8. Lower the car and road-test.

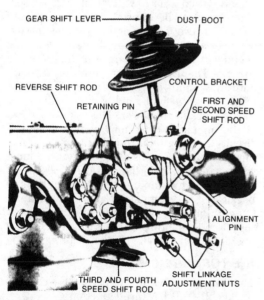

GEAR SHIFT LEVER — **DUST BOOT**

REVERSE SHIFT ROD

RETAINING PIN

CONTROL BRACKET

FIRST AND SECOND SPEED SHIFT ROD

ALIGNMENT PIN

THIRD AND FOURTH SPEED SHIFT ROD

SHIFT LINKAGE ADJUSTMENT NUTS

Floor-mounted gearshift linkage adjustment

TRANSMISSION AND CLUTCH REMOVAL AND INSTALLATION

1. Raise the vehicle on a hoist, or safely support on jackstands.

2. Disconnect the driveshaft from the rear U-joint flange and slide the front yoke from the transmission.

3. Insert a cap or rag in the transmission extension housing to prevent fluid leakage.

4. Disconnect the speedometer cable and

shifter linkage from the transmission. On models with a four-speed transmission, remove the shifter mounting bracket from the extension housing.

5. On models with a three-speed transmission, disconnect the transmission mount from the crossmember. If equipped with a four-speed transmission, remove the front parking brake cable from the crossmember and remove the crossmember from the car.

6. Remove the bolts which mount the transmission to the bellhousing. On 429 V8s, the upper left-hand transmission attaching bolt is a seal bolt. Carefully note its location so that it may be returned to its original position.

7. Move the transmission rearward until the input shaft clears the bellhousing and lower it from the car.

8. Disconnect the clutch release lever return spring.

9. If equipped with a one-piece aluminum bellhousing, remove the starter and remove the bellhousing from the engine. If equipped with a cast iron bellhousing, remove only the inspection cover from the bottom of the bellhousing.

10. Loosen the six pressure plate attaching bolts evenly to release spring pressure, and remove the clutch assembly from the car.

11. To install, position clutch assembly on flywheel and install each pressure plate attaching bolt finger-tight.

CLUTCH ARBOR   **CLUTCH DISC**

PRESSURE PLATE

Aligning clutch disc

12. Insert a transmission pilot shaft or other suitable tool to align the clutch disc with the flywheel and alternately tighten the pressure plate attaching bolts until the plate is secured to the flywheel.

13. Reverse above procedure to install transmission and driveshaft.

CLUTCH

The clutch is a system of parts which, when engaged, connects the engine to the transmission. When the clutch is disengaged (clutch pedal pushed in), the turning motion of the engine crankshaft is separated from the transmission. Since the engine does not produce enough torque at idle to turn the rear wheels and start the car in motion, it is necessary to gradually connect the engine to the rest of the drive train to prevent the engine from stalling on acceleration. It is also much easier to shift the gears within a manual transmission when engine power is disconnected from the transmission.

When the clutch pedal is depressed, a cable attached to the clutch pedal pulls on the clutch release lever. This causes the clutch release bearing, which is attached to the clutch release lever, to press against the release fingers of the pressure plate. This removes the spring pressure of the pressure plate from the clutch disc. Since it was this pressure which was holding the clutch disc against the engine flywheel, the clutch can now move away from the flywheel. If engine power is to be transmitted to the rest of the power train, the clutch must be firmly held against the flywheel (which is attached to, and turns with, the crankshaft). By depressing the clutch pedal you allow the clutch disc to move away from the flywheel, thus isolating engine power from the rest of the drive train.

The following engine displacement/clutch disc diameter chart will prove useful the next time the clutch needs replacement:

Engine	Disc Diameter (in.)
240 Six	9.5
302 V8	10.0
240, 302 Heavy-Duty	11.0
351, 390, 400 V8	11.0
429 V8	11.5

CLUTCH PEDAL FREE TRAVEL ADJUSTMENT

1. Disconnect the clutch return spring from the release lever.

2. Loosen the release lever adjusting nut and locknut, 2 or 3 turns.

3. Move the clutch release lever rearward until the throwout bearing can be felt to lightly contact the pressure plate fingers.

4. Adjust the rod length until the rod seats in the pocket in the release lever.

5. Insert a feeler gauge of specified thickness between the adjusting nut and swivel sleeve. Tighten the nut against the feeler gauge. Correct feeler gauge thicknesses are: 1968–0.206 in., 1969–0.194 in.

6. Tighten the locknut against the adjusting nut, being careful not to disturb the adjustment.

7. Connect the clutch return spring.

8. Make a final check with the engine running at 3,000 rpm, and transmission in Neutral. Under this condition, centrifugal weights on release fingers may reduce the clearance. Readjust, if necessary, to obtain at least ½ in. free-play while maintaining the 3,000 rpm to prevent fingers contacting release bearing. This is important.

AUTOMATIC TRANSMISSION

Understanding Automatic Transmissions

The automatic transmission allows engine torque and power to be transmitted to the rear wheels within a narrow range of engine operating speeds. The transmission will allow the engine to turn fast enough to produce plenty of power and torque at very low speeds, while keeping it at a sensible rpm at high vehicle speeds. The transmission performs this job entirely without driver assistance. The transmission uses a light fluid as the medium for the transmission of power. This fluid also works in the operation of various hydraulic control circuits and as a lubricant. Because the transmission fluid performs all of these three functions, trouble within the unit can easily travel from one part to another. For this reason, and because of the complexity and unusual operating principles of the transmission, a very sound understanding of the basic principles of operation will simplify troubleshooting.

THE TORQUE CONVERTER

The torque converter replaces the conventional clutch. It has three functions:

1. It allows the engine to idle with the vehicle at a standstill—even with the transmission in gear.

2. It allows the transmission to shift from range to range smoothly, without requiring that the driver close the throttle during the shift.

3. It multiplies engine torque to an increasing extent as vehicle speed drops and throttle opening is increased. This has the effect of making the transmission more responsive and reduces the amount of shifting required.

The torque converter is a metal case which

is shaped like a sphere that has been flattened on opposite sides. It is bolted to the rear end of the engine's crankshaft. Generally, the entire metal case rotates at engine speed and serves as the engine's flywheel.

The case contains three sets of blades. One set is attached directly to the case. This set forms the torus or pump. Another set is directly connected to the output shaft, and forms the turbine. The third set is mounted on a hub which, in turn, is mounted on a stationary shaft through a one-way clutch. This third set is known as the stator.

A pump, which is driven by the converter hub at engine speed, keeps the torque converter full of transmission fluid at all times. Fluid flows continuously through the unit to provide cooling.

Under low-speed acceleration, the torque converter functions as follows:

The torus is turning faster than the turbine. It picks up fluid at the center of the converter and, through centrifugal force, slings it outward. Since the outer edge of the converter moves faster than the portions at the center, the fluid picks up speed.

The fluid then enters the outer edge of the turbine blades. It then travels back toward the center of the converter case along the turbine blades. In impinging upon the turbine blades, the fluid loses the energy picked up in the torus.

If the fluid were now to immediately be returned directly into the torus, both halves of the converter would have to turn at approximately the same speed at all times, and torque input and output would both be the same.

In flowing through the torus and turbine, the fluid picks up two types of flow, or flow in two separate directions. It flows through the turbine blades, and it spins with the engine. The stator, whose blades are stationary when the vehicle is being accelerated at low speeds, converts one type of flow into another. Instead of allowing the fluid to flow straight back into the torus, the stator's curved blades turn the fluid almost 90° toward the direction of rotation of the engine. Thus the fluid does not flow as fast toward the torus, but is already spinning when the torus picks it up. This has the effect of allowing the torus to turn much faster than the turbine. This difference in speed may be compared to the difference in speed between the smaller and larger gears in any gear train. The result is that engine power output is higher, and engine torque is multiplied.

As the speed of the turbine increases, the fluid spins faster and faster in the direction of engine rotation. As a result, the ability of the stator to redirect the fluid flow is reduced.

Under cruising conditions, the stator is eventually forced to rotate on its one-way clutch in the direction of engine rotation. Under these conditions, the torque converter begins to behave almost like a solid shaft, with the torus and turbine speeds being almost equal.

THE PLANETARY GEARBOX

The ability of the torque converter to multiply engine torque is limited. Also, the unit tends to be more efficient when the turbine is rotating at relatively high speeds. Therefore, the planetary gearbox is used to carry the power output of the turbine to the driveshaft.

Planetary gears function very similarly to conventional transmission gears. However, their construction is different in that three elements make up one gear system, and in that all three elements are different from one another. The three elements are: an outer gear that is shaped like a hoop, with teeth cut into the inner surface; a sun gear, mounted on a shaft and located at the very center of the outer gear; and a set of three planet gears, held by pins in a ring-like planet carrier and meshing with both the sun gear and the outer gear. Either the outer gear or the sun gear may be held stationary, providing more than one possible torque multiplication factor for each set of gears. Also, if all three gears are forced to rotate at the same speed, the gearset forms, in effect, a solid shaft.

Most modern automatics use the planetary gears to provide either a single reduction ratio of about 1.8:1, or two reduction gears: a low of about 2.5:1, and an intermediate of about 1.5:1. Bands and clutches are used to hold various portions of the gearsets to the transmission case or to the shaft on which they are mounted. Shifting is accomplished, then, by changing the portion of each planetary gearset which is held to the transmission case or to the shaft.

THE SERVOS AND ACCUMULATORS

The servos are hydraulic pistons and cylinders. They resemble the hydraulic actuators used on many familiar machines, such as bulldozers. Hydraulic fluid enters the cylinder, under pressure, and forces the piston to move to engage the band or clutches.

The accumulators are used to cushion the engagement of the servos. The transmission fluid must pass through the accumulator on the way to the servo. The accumulator housing contains a thin piston which is sprung away from the discharge passage of the accumulator. When fluid passes through the accumulator on the way to the servo, it must move the piston against spring pressure, and this action smooths out the action of the servo.

THE HYDRAULIC CONTROL SYSTEM

The hydraulic pressure used to operate the servos comes from the main transmission oil pump. This fluid is channeled to the various servos through the shift valves. There is generally a manual shift valve which is operated by the transmission selector lever and an automatic shift valve for each automatic upshift the transmission provides: i.e., two-speed automatics have a low-high shift valve, while three-speeds will have a 1–2 valve, and a 2–3 valve.

There are two pressures which effect the operation of these valves. One is the governor pressure which is affected by vehicle speed. The other is the modulator pressure which is affected by intake manifold vacuum or throttle position. Governor pressure rises with an increase in vehicle speed, and modulator pressure rises as the throttle is opened wider. By responding to these two pressures, the shift valves cause the upshift points to be delayed with increased throttle opening to make the best use of the engine's power output.

Most transmissions also make use of an auxiliary circuit for downshifting. This circuit may be actuated by the throttle linkage or the vacuum line which actuates the modulator, or by a cable or solenoid. It applies pressure to a special downshift surface on the shift valve or valves.

The transmission modulator also governs the line pressure, used to actuate the servos. In this way, the clutches and bands will be actuated with a force matching the torque output of the engine.

TRANSMISSION APPLICATION

The body style of the car and the size of the engine usually determine which transmission is installed.

The "conventional" automatic transmission used from 1968 is a dual-range, three-speed, aluminum cased unit. The C4 automatic is installed in six-cylinder and most small V8 applications. The medium-duty FMX automatic is installed with most mid-sized V8s. A similar medium-duty CW automatic transmission was installed in 1974 and 1975 cars using a 2.75:1 rear axle ratio and the 400 cu. in. engine. Larger engine equipped cars, or ones with a trailer-towing option are equipped with the heavy-duty C6 automatic transmission.

In 1980 a new "Automatic Overdrive" transmission was introduced. The Automatic Overdrive featured a fourth speed that is automat-

ically engaged. The new transmission combines the convenience of automatic shifting with two fuel-saving features; an overdrive gear ratio and a mechanical "no-slip" feature. The Automatic Overdrive Transmission is covered in this chapter after the "conventional" automatic transmissions.

Fluid Recommendations

Year	Type	Fluid
1968–76	All	F
1977–79	C4	F
1977–79	C6	CJ
1980–83	All	CJ

PAN REMOVAL AND FLUID DRAINING

When filling a completely dry (no fluid) transmission and converter, install five quarts of transmission fluid (see fluid recommendations) and then start the engine. Shift the selector lever through all gear positions briefly and set at Park position. Check the fluid level and add enough fluid to raise the level to between the marks on the dipstick. Do not overfill the transmission.

The procedure for a partial drain and refill of the transmission fluid is as follows:

1. Raise the car on a hoist or jack stands.

2. Place a drain pan under the transmission pan.

NOTE: *On some models of the C4 transmission, the fluid is drained by disconnecting the filler tube from the transmission fluid pan.*

3. Loosen the pan attaching bolts to allow the fluid to drain.

4. When the fluid has stopped draining to level of the pan flange, remove the mounting bolts starting at the rear and along both sides of the pan, allowing the pan to drop and drain gradually.

5. When all the transmission fluid has drained, remove the pan and the fluid filter and clean them.

CAUTION: *When removing the filter on C4 transmissions, be careful not to lose the throttle pressure limit valve and spring when separating the filter from the valve body. If the valve and spring drop out—the valve is installed, large end first; the spring fits over the valve shaft.*

6. After completing the transmission repairs of adjustments, install the fluid filter screen, a new pan gasket, and the pan on the transmission. Tighten the pan attaching bolts on C4 and C6 transmissions to 12–16 ft. lbs.

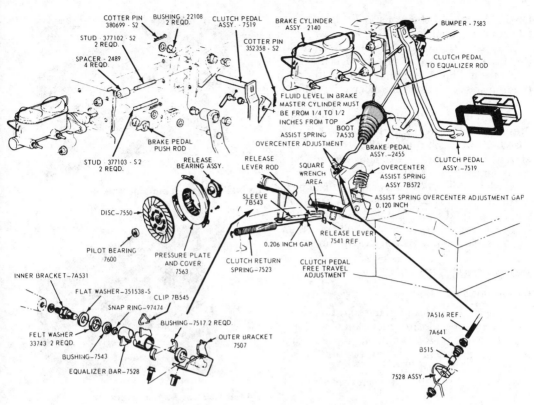

Clutch pedal and linkage adjustment—1968

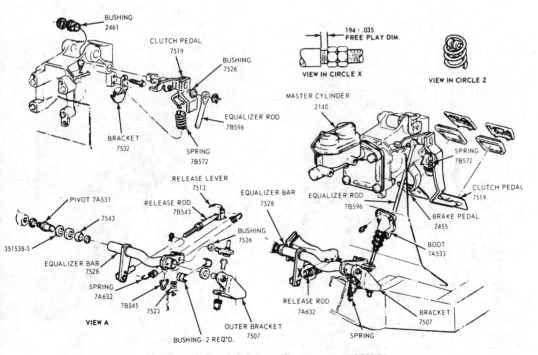

Clutch pedal and linkage adjustments—1969–71

On FMX and CW transmissions, tighten the pan attaching bolts to 10–13 ft. lbs.

7. Install three quarts of transmission fluid (see fluid recommendations) through the filler tube. If the filler tube was removed to drain the transmission, install the filler tube using a new O-ring.

8. Start and run the engine for a few minutes at low idle speed and then at the fast idle speed (about 1,200 rpm) until the normal operating temperature is reached. Do not race the engine.

9. Move the selector lever through all gear positions and place it at the Park position. Check the fluid level, and add fluid until the level is between the "add" and "full" marks on the dipstick. Do not overfill the transmission.

BAND ADJUSTMENTS

C4 Intermediate Band

1. Clean all the dirt from the adjusting screw and remove and discard the locknut.

2. Install a new locknut on the adjusting screw using a torque wrench, tighten the adjusting screw to 10 ft. lbs.

3. Back off the adjusting screw *exactly* 1¾ *turns*.

4. Hold the adjusting screw steady and tighten the locknut to the proper torque.

C4 Low-Reverse Band

1. Clean all dirt from around the band adjusting screw, and remove and discard the locknut.

2. Install a new locknut of the adjusting screw. Using a torque wrench, tighten the adjusting screw to 10 ft. lbs.

3. Back off the adjusting screw *exactly three full turns*.

4. Hold the adjusting screw steady and tighten the locknut to the proper torque.

TOOL—T59P-77370-B

C4 intermediate band adjustment

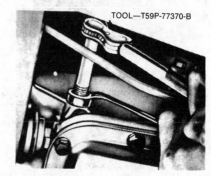

TOOL—T59P-77370-B

C4 low-Reverse band adjustment

C6 Intermediate Band Adjustment

1. Raise the car on a hoist or place it on jack stands.

2. Clean the threads of the intermediate band adjusting screw.

3. Loosen the adjustment screw locknut.

4. Tighten the adjusting screw to 10 ft. lbs. and back the screw off *exactly 1½ turns* Tighten the adjusting screw locknut.

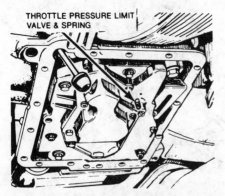

THROTTLE PRESSURE LIMIT VALVE & SPRING

C4 throttle limit valve and spring. They are held in place by the transmission oil filter. The valve is installed with the large end towards the valve body, the spring fits over the valve stem

TOOL—T59P-77370-B

C6 intermediate band adjustment

FMX, CW Front Band Adjustment

1. Drain the transmission fluid and remove the oil pan, fluid filter screen, and clip.

2. Clean the pan and filter screen and remove the old gasket.

3. Loosen the front servo adjusting screw locknut.

4. Pull back the actuating rod and insert a ¼ in. spacer bar between the adjusting screw and the servo piston stem. Tighten the adjusting screw to 10 in. lbs. torque. Remove the spacer bar and tighten the adjusting screw *an additional ¾ turn*. Hold the adjusting screw fast and tighten the locknut securely (20–25 ft. lbs.).

5. Install the transmission fluid filter screen and clip. Install pan with a new pan gasket.

6. Refill the transmission to the mark on the dipstick. Start the engine, run for a few minutes, shift the selector lever through all positions, and place it in Park. Recheck the fluid level and add fluid if necessary.

FMX, CW Rear Band Adjustments

On certain cars with a console floor shift, the entire console shift lever and linkage will have to be removed to gain access to the rear band external adjusting screw.

1. Locate the external rear band adjusting screw on transmission case, clean all dirt from the threads, and coat the threads with light oil.

NOTE: *The adjusting screw is located on the upper right-side of the transmission case. Access is often through a hole in the front floor to the right of center under the carpet.*

2. Loosen the locknut on the rear band external adjusting screw.

3. Using a torque wrench tighten the adjusting screw to 10 ft. lbs. torque. If the adjusting screw is tighter than 10 ft. lbs. torque, loosen the adjusting screw and retighten to the proper torque.

4. Back off the adjusting screw *exactly 1½ turns*. Hold the adjusting screw steady while tightening the locknut to the proper torque (35–40 ft. lbs.).

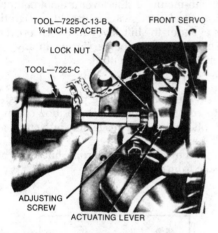

FMX front band adjustment

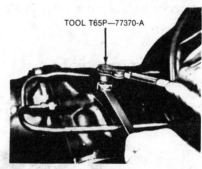

FMX, CW rear band adjustment

CW front band adjustment

NEUTRAL START SWITCH ADJUSTMENT

1968–71 Column Shift

1. With manual linkage properly adjusted, try to engage starter in each position on quadrant. Starter should engage only in Neutral or Park position.

2. Place shift lever in Neutral detent.

3. Disconnect start switch wires at plug connector. Disconnect vacuum hoses, if any. Remove screws securing neutral start switch to steering column and remove switch. Remove actuator lever along with Type III switches.

4. With switch wires facing up, move actuator lever fully to the left and insert gauge

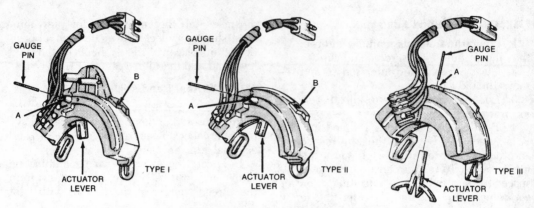

Neutral start switch adjustment—column shift

pin (No. 43 drill) into gauge pin hole at point A. See accompanying figure. On Type III switch, be sure gauge pin is inserted a full ½ in.

5. With pin in place, move actuator lever to right until positive stop is engaged.

6. On Type I and Type II switches, remove gauge pin and insert it at point B. On Type III switches, remove gauge pin, align two holes in switch at point A and reinstall gauge pin.

7. Reinstall switch on steering column. Be sure shift lever is engaged in Neutral detent.

8. Connect switch wires and vacuum hoses and remove gauge pin.

9. Check starter engagement as in Step 1.

1972 and Later Column Shift

1972 and later models which are equipped with a column-mounted shift lever are not equipped with neutral start switch. Instead, an ignition lock cylinder-to-shift lever interlock prevents these models from being started in any gear other than Park or Neutral.

1968–71 Console Shift

1. With manual linkage properly adjusted, try to engage starter at each position on quadrant. Starter should engage only in Neutral and Park positions.

2. Remove shift handle from shift lever, and console from vehicle.

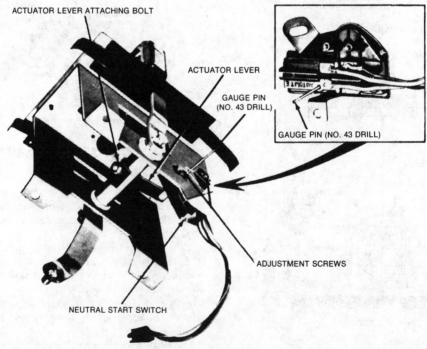

Neutral start switch adjustment—console shift

3. Loosen switch attaching screws, and move shift lever back and forward until gauge pin (No. 43 drill) can be inserted fully.

4. Place shift lever firmly against Neutral detent stop and slide switch back and forward until switch lever contacts shift lever.

5. Tighten switch attaching screws, and check starter engagement as in Step 1.

6. Reinstall console and shift linkage.

AUTOMATIC TRANSMISSION LINKAGE ADJUSTMENT

Selector Indicator

1. With engine off, loosen clamp at shift lever so shift rod is free to slide.

2. Position selector lever in D1 position (large green dot) on dual range transmissions. On select shift transmission (P R N D 2 1) position lever in D position tightly against the D stop.

3. Shift lever at transmission into D1 detent position on dual range transmissions or into D position on select shift transmissions.

NOTE: *D1 position is second from rear on all dual-range transmissions. D position is third from rear on all column shift select shift transmissions and 1968 console shift select shift transmissions. D position is fourth from rear on 1969–72 console shift select shift transmissions.*

4. Tighten the clamp retaining screw or nut. Move the selector through the ranges. Readjust if necessary.

LOCK ROD ADJUSTMENT

All 1970–71 models equipped with a floor or console-mounted selector lever incorporate a transmission lock rod to prevent the transmission selector from being moved out of the Park position when the ignition lock is in the Off position. The lock rod connects the shift tube in the steering column to the transmission manual lever. The lock rod cannot be properly adjusted until the manual linkage adjustment is correct.

1. With the transmission selector lever in

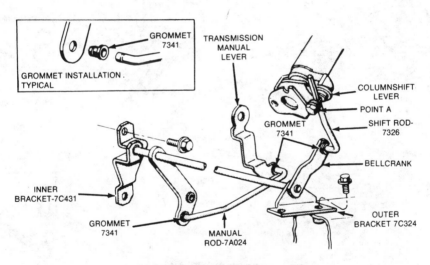

Manual linkage—1968 C6 column shift

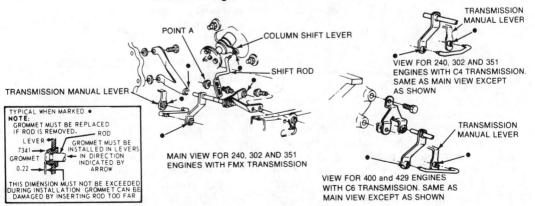

Manual linkage—1969–76 column shift

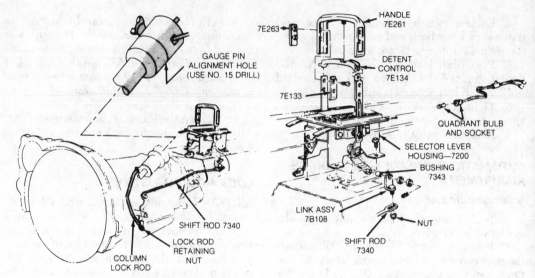

GAUGE PIN
ALIGNMENT HOLE
(USE NO. 15 DRILL)

HANDLE
7E261

7E263

DETENT
CONTROL
7E134

7E133

QUADRANT BULB
AND SOCKET

SELECTOR LEVER
HOUSING—7200

BUSHING
7343

LINK ASSY
7B108

NUT

SHIFT ROD
7340

SHIFT ROD 7340

LOCK ROD
RETAINING
NUT

COLUMN
LOCK ROD

Manual linkage—1970–71 console shift with lock rod shown, 1968–69 similar

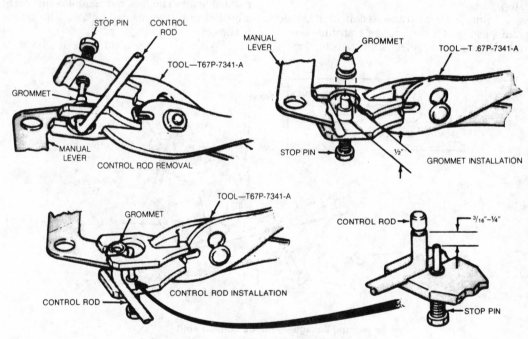

STOP PIN   CONTROL
ROD

MANUAL
LEVER

GROMMET

TOOL—T .67P-7341-A

TOOL—T67P-7341-A

GROMMET

MANUAL
LEVER

CONTROL ROD REMOVAL

STOP PIN

½"

GROMMET INSTALLATION

GROMMET

TOOL—T67P-7341-A

CONTROL ROD

³/₁₆"–¼"

CONTROL ROD

CONTROL ROD INSTALLATION

STOP PIN

Removing or installing shift linkage grommets

the Drive position, loosen the lock rod adjustment nut on the transmission manual lever.

2. Insert a .180 in. diameter rod (No. 15 drill bit) in the gauge pin hole in the steering column socket casting, it is located at the 6 o'clock position directly below the ignition lock.

3. Manipulate the pin so that the casting will not move when the pin is fully inserted.

4. Torque the lock rod adjustment nut to 10–20 ft. lbs.

5. Remove the pin and check the linkage operation.

DOWNSHIFT (THROTTLE) LINKAGE ADJUSTMENT

All Models Except Automatic Overdrive

1. With the engine off, disconnect the throttle and downshift return springs, if equipped.

2. Hold the carburetor throttle lever in the wide open position against the stop.

3. Hold the transmission downshift linkage in the full downshift position against the internal stop.

4. Turn the adjustment screw on the carburetor downshift lever to obtain 0.010–0.080 in. clearance between the screw tip and the throttle shaft lever tab.

5. Release the transmission and carburetor to their normal free positions. Install the throttle and downshift return springs, if removed.

NOTE: *AOT linkage adjustments follow in section after the AOT description.*

Automatic Overdrive Transmission

The Automatic Overdrive Transmission, introduced in 1980, features a full-mechanical overdrive fourth gear designed to reduce engine rpm and fuel consumption during highway cruising.

The design uses a split torque path in third gear (1:1 gear ratio) where 40% of the engine torque is transmitted hydraulically through the torque converter, and 60% is transmitted through "solid" connections to the driveshaft. Conventional automatic transmissions use a "fluid" coupling between input and output shafts. Thus, there is always "slip" between input and output. Slip and inefficiency is eliminated when fourth gear is reached in the Automatic Overdrive Transmission (AOT). The torque converter used with the AOT has a special blade design which reduces engine load at idle, allowing lower idle speeds and better fuel economy.

An additional feature of the AOT is the inclusion of non-adjustable bands, eliminating the need for scheduled maintenance in regular service use.

AOT THROTTLE VALVE CONTROL LINKAGE ADJUSTMENT

1. With the engine off, remove the air cleaner and make sure the fast idle cam is released—the throttle lever must be at the idle stop.

2. Turn the linkage lever adjusting screw counterclockwise until the end of the screw is flush with the face of the lever.

3. Turn the linkage adjustment screw in until there is a maximum clearance of .005 in. between the throttle lever and the end of the adjustment screw.

4. Turn the linkage lever adjusting screw clockwise three full turns. A minimum of one turn is permissible if the screw travel is limited.

5. If it is not possible to turn the adjusting screw at least one full turn, or if the initial gap of .005 in. could not be obtained, perform the linkage adjustment at the transmission.

ALTERNATE AOT THROTTLE VALVE LINKAGE ADJUSTMENT

If unable to adjust the throttle valve control linkage at the carburetor, as described above, proceed as follows.

1. At the transmission, loosen the 8 mm bolt on the throttle valve (TV) control rod sliding trunnion block. Make sure the trunnion block slides freely on the control rod.

2. Push up on the lower end of the TV control rod to insure that the carburetor linkage lever is held against the throttle lever. When the pressure is released, the control rod must stay in position.

3. Force the TV control lever on the transmission against its internal stop. While maintaining pressure tighten the trunnion block bolt. Make sure the throttle lever is at the idle stop.

AOT IDLE SPEED ADJUSTMENT

Whenever it is necessary to adjust the idle speed by more than 50 rpm either above or below the factory specifications, the adjustment screw on the linkage lever at the carburetor should also be adjusted to the following specifications:

Idle Speed Change (rpm)	Adjustment Screw Turns
50–100 increase	1½ turns out
50–100 decrease	1½ turns in
100–150 increase	2½ turns out
100–150 decrease	2½ turns in

After making any idle speed adjustments, make sure the linkage lever and throttle lever are in contact with the throttle lever at its idle stop and verify that the shift lever is in N (neutral).

Drive Train

7

REAR AXLE

Understanding Rear Axles

The rear axle is a special type of transmission that reduces the speed of the drive from the engine and transmission and divides the power to the rear wheels. Power enters the rear axle from the driveshaft via the companion flange. The flange is mounted on the drive pinion shaft. The drive pinion shaft and gear which carry the power into the differential turn at engine speed. The gear on the end of the pinion shaft drives a large ring gear the axis of rotation of which is 90° away from that of the pinion. The pinion and gear reduce the speed and multiply the power by the gear ratio of the axle, and change the direction of rotation to turn the axle shafts which drive both wheels. The rear axle gear ratio is found by dividing the number of pinion gear teeth into the number of ring gear teeth.

The ring gear drives the differential case. The case provides the two mounting points for the ends of a pinion shaft on which are mounted two pinion gears. The pinion gears drive the two side gears, one of which is located on the inner end of each axle shaft.

By driving the axle shafts through this arrangement, the differential allows the outer drive wheel to turn faster than the inner drive wheel in a turn.

The main drive pinion and the side bearings, which bear the weight of the differential case, are shimmed to provide proper bearing preload, and to position the pinion and ring gears properly.

NOTE: *The proper adjustment of the relationship of the ring and pinion gears is critical. It should be attempted only by those with extensive equipment and/or experience.*

Limited-slip differentials include clutches which tend to link each axle shaft to the differential case. Clutches may be engaged either by spring action or by pressure produced by the torque on the axles during a turn. During turning on a dry pavement, the effects of the clutches are overcome, and each wheel turns at the required speed. When slippage occurs at either wheel, however, the clutches will transmit some of the power to the wheel which has the greater amount of traction. Because of the presence of clutches, limited-slip units require a special lubricant.

Determining Axle Ratio

The drive axle of a car is said to have a certain axle ratio. This number (usually a whole number and a decimal fraction) is actually a comparison of the number of gear teeth on the ring gear and the pinion gear. For example, a 4.11 rear means that theoretically, there are 4.11 teeth on the ring gear and one tooth on the pinion gear or, put another way, the driveshaft must turn 4.11 times to turn the wheels once. Actually, on a 4.11 rear, there might be 37 teeth on the ring gear and 9 teeth on the pinion gear. By dividing the number of teeth on the pinion gear into the number of teeth on the ring gear, the numerical axle ratio (4.11) is obtained. This also provides a good method of ascertaining exactly what axle ratio one is dealing with.

Another method of determining gear ratio is to jack up and support the car so that both rear wheels are off the ground. Make a chalk mark on the rear wheel and the drive shaft. Put the transmission in neutral. Turn the rear wheel one complete turn and count the number of turns that the driveshaft makes. The number of turns that the driveshaft makes in one complete revolution of the rear wheel is an approximation of the rear axle ratio.

DRIVELINE

The driveshaft is the means by which the power from the engine and transmission (in the front of the car) is transferred to the differential and rear axles, and finally to the rear wheels.

The driveshaft assembly incorporates two universal joints—one at each end—and a slip yoke at the front end of the assembly, which fits into the back of the transmission.

All driveshafts are balanced when installed in a car. It is therefore imperative that before applying undercoating to the chassis, the driveshaft and universal joint assembly be completely covered to prevent the accidental application of undercoating to their surfaces, and the subsequent loss of balance.

Driveshaft and U-Joints

DRIVESHAFT REMOVAL

The procedure for removing the driveshaft assembly—complete with universal joint and slip yoke—is as follows:

1. Mark the relationship of the rear driveshaft yoke and the drive pinion flange of the axle. If the original yellow alignment marks are visible, there is no need for new marks. The purpose of this marking is to facilitate installation of the assembly in its exact original position, thereby maintaining proper balance.

2. Remove the four bolts or nuts which hold the rear universal joint or the circular coupling flange to the pinion flange. Wrap tape around the loose bearing caps in order to prevent them from falling off the spider.

3. Pull the driveshaft toward the rear of the vehicle until the slip yoke clears the transmission housing and the seal. Plug the hole at the rear of the transmission housing or place a container under the opening to catch any fluid which might leak.

UNIVERSAL JOINT OVERHAUL

1. Position the driveshaft assembly in a sturdy vise.

2. Remove the snap-rings which retain the bearings in the slip yoke (front only) and in the driveshaft (front and rear).

3. Using a large punch or an arbor press, drive one of the bearings in toward the center of the universal joint, which will force the opposite bearing out.

4. As each bearing is pressed or punched far enough out of the universal joint assembly that it is accessible, grip it with a pair of pliers, and pull it from the driveshaft yoke. Drive or press the spider in the opposite direction in order to make the opposite bearing accessible, and pull it free with a pair of pliers. Use this procedure to remove all bearings from both universal joints.

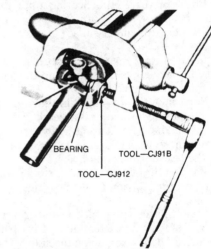

Removing the universal joint bearing

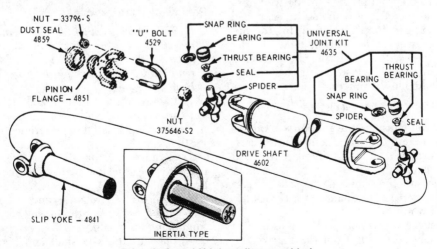

Driveshaft and U-joints disassembled

5. After removing the bearings, lift the spider from the yoke.

6. Thoroughly clean all dirt and foreign matter from the yokes on both ends of the driveshaft.

NOTE: *When installing new bearings in the yokes, it is advisable to use an arbor press. However, if this tool is not available, the bearings should be driven into position with extreme care, as a heavy jolt on the needle bearings can easily ddmage or misalign them, greatly shortening their life and hampering their efficiency.*

7. Start a new bearing into the yoke at the rear of the driveshaft.

8. Position a new spider in the rear yoke and press (or drive) the new bearing ¼ in. below the outer surface of the yoke.

9. With the bearing in position, install a new snap-ring.

10. Start a new bearing into the opposite side of the yoke.

11. Press (or drive) the bearing until the opposite bearing—which you have just installed—contacts the inner surface of the snap-ring.

12. Install a new snap-ring on the second bearing. It may be necessary to grind the surface of this second snap-ring.

13. Reposition the driveshaft in the vise, so that the front universal joint is accessible.

14. Install the new bearings, new spider, and new snap-rings in the same manner as you did for the rear universal joint.

15. Position the slip yoke on the spider. Install new bearings, nylon thrust bearings, and snap-rings.

16. Check both reassembled joints for freedom of movement. If misalignment of any part is causing a bind, a sharp rap on the side of the yoke with a brass hammer should seat the bearing needles and provide the desired freedom of movement. Care should be exercised to firmly support the shaft end during this operation, as well as to prevent blows to the bearings themselves. Under no circumstances should a driveshaft be installed in a car if there is any binding in the universal joints.

DRIVESHAFT INSTALLATION

1. Carefully inspect the rubber seal on the output shaft and the seal in end of the transmission extension housing. Replace them if they are damaged.

2. Examine the lugs on the axle pinion flange and replace the flange if the lugs are shaved or distorted.

3. Coat the yoke spline with chassis lube.

4. Remove the plug from the rear of the transmission housing.

5. Insert the yoke into the transmission housing and onto the transmission output shaft. Make sure that the yoke assembly does not bottom on the output shaft with excessive force.

6. Locate the marks which you made on the rear driveshaft yoke and the pinion flange prior to removal of the driveshaft assembly. Install the driveshaft assembly with the marks properly aligned.

7. Install the U-bolts and nuts which attach the universal joint to the pinion flange. Torque the U-bolt nuts to 8–15 ft. lbs. on models through 1978. 1979 models are attached to the rear differential flange with a circular coupling. New bolts must be used whenever the driveshaft is removed. Torque the bolts to 70–90 ft. lbs.

Rear Axle

Two basic types of rear axles are used; a removable differential carrier type and an integral carrier type which occurs in three variations; a standard type, a light duty (WER) version, and a WGY version. All WER and WGY types use C-locks on the inside end of the axle shaft to retain it, while removable carrier axles have no C-locks. To properly identify a C-lock axle, drain the lubricant, remove the rear cover and look for the C-lock on the end of the axle shaft in the differential side gear bore. All Traction-Lok (limited slip) axles are of the removable carrier type. The axle type and ratio are stamped on a plate attached to a rear housing cover bolt. Always refer to the axle tag code and ratio when ordering parts.

AXLE SHAFT REMOVAL AND INSTALLATION AND/OR BEARING REPLACEMENT

Removable Carrier Axle

NOTE: *Bearings must be pressed on and off the shaft with an arbor press. Unless you have access to one, it is inadvisable to attempt any repair work on the axle shaft and bearing assemblies.*

1. Remove the wheel, tire, and brake drum. On cars equipped with rear disc brakes, remove the caliper and disc as outlined in Chapter 9.

2. Remove the nuts holding the retainer plate to the backing plate. Disconnect the brake line.

3. Remove the retainer and install nuts, finger-tight, to prevent the brake backing plate from being dislodged.

4. Pull out the axle shaft and bearing assembly, using a slide hammer.

NOTE: *If end-play is found to be excessive, the bearing should be replaced. Shimming the bearing is not recommended as this ignores end-play of the bearing itself and could result in improper seating of the bearing.*

5. Using a chisel, nick the bearing retainer in 3 or 4 places. The retainer does not have to be cut, but merely collapsed sufficiently to allow the bearing retainer to be slid from the shaft.

6. Press off the bearing and install the new one by pressing it into position.

7. Press on the new retainer.

NOTE: *Do not attempt to press the bearing and the retainer on at the same time.*

8. Assemble the shaft and bearing in the housing, being sure that the bearing is seated properly in the housing.

9. Install the retainer, drum, wheel, and tire. Bleed the brakes. On cars equipped with rear disc brakes, install the disc and caliper as outlined in Chapter 9.

AXLE SHAFT SEAL REPLACEMENT

Removable Carrier Axle

1. Remove the axle shaft from the rear axle assembly, following the procedures previously discussed.

2. Using a two-fingered seal puller (slide hammer), remove the seal from the axle housing.

3. Thoroughly clean the recess in the rear axle housing from which the seal was removed.

4. Position a new seal on the housing and drive it into place with a seal installation tool. If this tool is not available, a wood block may be substituted.

NOTE: *Although the right and left-hand seals are identical, there are many different types of seals which have been used on Ford rear axle assemblies. It is advisable to have one of the old seals with you when you are purchasing new ones.*

5. When the seal is properly installed, install the axle shaft.

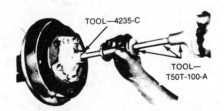

Removing the axle shaft

AXLE SHAFT, BEARING, AND SEAL REMOVAL AND INSTALLATION

Integral Carrier Type "C" Lock

1. Jack up and support the rear of the car.

2. Remove the wheels and tires from the brake drums. On cars equipped with rear disc brakes, remove the caliper and disc as outlined in Chapter 9.

3. Place a drain pan under the housing and drain the lubricant by loosening the housing cover.

4. Remove the clips securing the brake drums to the axle shaft lug nut studs and remove the drums.

5. Remove the housing cover and gasket.

6. Position jackstands under the rear frame member and lower the axle housing. This is done to give easy access to the inside of the differential.

7. Working through the opening in the differential case, remove the side gear pinion shaft lockbolt and the side gear pinion shaft.

8. Push the axle shafts inward and remove the C-locks from the inner end of the axle shafts.

9. Remove the axle shafts with a slide hammer. Be sure the seal is not damaged by the splines on the axle shaft.

10. Remove the bearing and oil seal from the housing. Two types of bearings are used on some axles, one requiring a press fit and

Removing the rear wheel bearing retaining ring

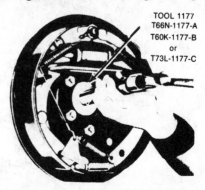

Installing the rear wheel bearing oil seal

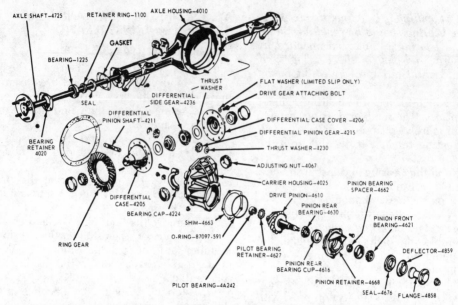

Rear axle disassembled—typical removable carrier with conventional differential

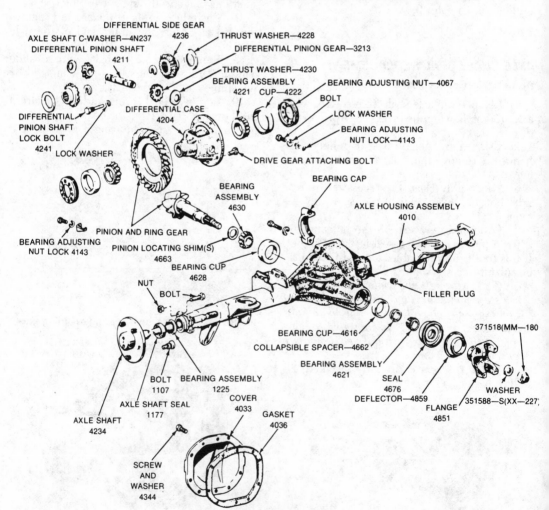

Integral carrier type rear axle assembly

Differential shaft and lockbolt—Integral type axle

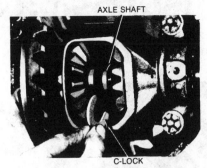

Removing "C-locks"—integral type axle

the other a loose fit. A loose fitting bearing does not necessarily indicate excessive wear.

11. Inspect the axle shaft housing and axle shafts for burrs or other irregularities. Replace any worn or damaged parts. A light yellow color on the bearing journal of the axle shaft is normal, and does not require replacement of the axle shaft. Slight pitting and wear is also normal.

12. Lightly coat the wheel bearing rollers with axle lubricant. Install the bearings in the axle housing until the bearing seats firmly against the shoulder.

13. Wipe all lubricant from the oil seal bore, before installing the seal.

14. Inspect the original seals for wear. If necessary, these may be replaced with new seals, which are prepacked with lubricant and do not require soaking.

15. Install the oil seal.

CAUTION: *Installation of the seal without the proper tool can cause distortion and seal leakage. Oil seals for the right-side are marked with green stripes and the word RIGHT. Seals for the left-side are marked yellow with the word LEFT. Do not interchange seals from side to side.*

16. Carefully slide the axle shafts into place. Be careful that you do not damage the seal with the splined end of the axle shaft. Engage the splined end of the shaft with the differential side gears.

17. Install the axle shaft C-locks on the inner end of the axle shafts and seat the C-locks in the counterbore of the differential side gears.

18. Rotate the differential pinion gears until the differential pinion shaft can be installed. Install the differential pinion shaft lockbolt.

19. Install the brake drum on the axle shaft flange. On cars equipped with rear disc brakes, install the disc and caliper as outlined in Chapter 9.

20. Install the wheel and tire on the brake drum or disc and tighten the attaching nuts.

21. Clean the gasket surface of the rear housing and install a new cover gasket and the housing cover.

22. Raise the rear axle so that it is in the running position. Add the amount of specified lubricant to bring the lubricant level to the bottom of the filler plug hole.

Suspension and Steering

FRONT SUSPENSION

Each front wheel rotates on a spindle. The spindle's upper and lower ends attach to the upper and lower ball joints which mount to an upper and lower arm respectively. Through 1978 the upper arm pivots on a bushing and shaft assembly bolted to the frame. The lower arm pivots on the No. 2 cross-member bolt. The coil spring is seated between the lower arm and the top of the spring housing on the underside of the upper arm. A shock absorber is bolted to the lower arm at the bottom and the top of the spring housing. For 1979, the front suspension was redesigned. The arm and strut assembly has been replaced by a new lower "A" arm. The upper ball joing incorporates a new low friction design, and the lower ball joint has a built-in wear indicator. A front stabilizer bar is standard.

Front Shock Absorber

REPLACEMENT

1. Remove the nut, washer, and bushing from the upper end of the shock absorber.
2. Raise the vehicle on a hoist and install jackstands under the frame rails.
3. Remove the two bolts securing the shock absorber to the lower arm and remove the shock absorber.
4. Inspect the shock absorber for leaks. Extend and compress the unit several times to check the damping action and remove any trapped air. Replace in pairs if necessary.
5. Install a new bushing and washer on the top of the shock absorber and positibn the unit inside the front spring. Install the two lower attaching bolts and torque them to 8–15 ft. lbs.
6. Remove the safety stands and lower the vehicle.

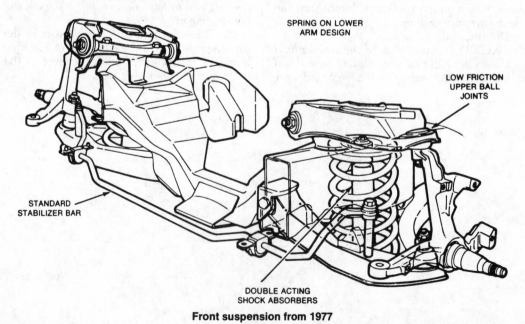

SPRING ON LOWER ARM DESIGN

LOW FRICTION UPPER BALL JOINTS

STANDARD STABILIZER BAR

DOUBLE ACTING SHOCK ABSORBERS

Front suspension from 1977

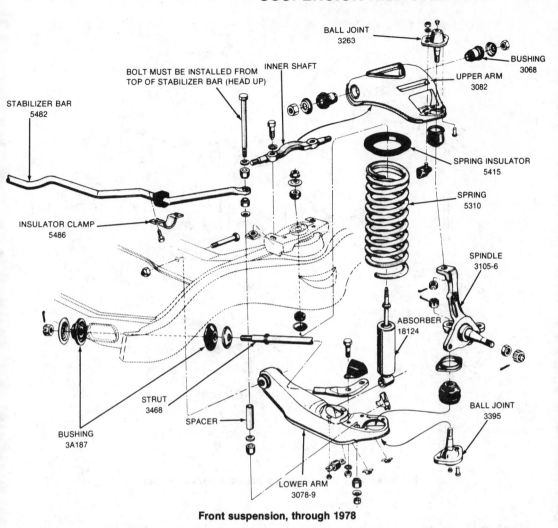

Front suspension, through 1978

7. Place a new bushing and washer on the shock absorber top stud and install the attaching nut. Torque to 22–30 ft. lbs.

Coil Spring and Lower Control Arm
REMOVAL AND INSTALLATION

Through 1978

1. Raise car and support with stands placed back of lower arms.

2. If equipped with drum type brakes, remove the wheel and brake drum as an assembly. Remove the brake backing plate attaching bolts and remove the backing plate from the spindle. Wire the assembly back out of the way.

3. If equipped with disc brakes, remove the wheel from the hub. Remove two bolts and washers which hold the caliper and brake hose bracket to the spindle. Remove the caliper from the rotor and wire it back out of the way. Then, remove the hub and rotor from the spindle.

4. Disconnect lower end of the shock absorber and push it up to the retracted position.

5. Disconnect stabilizer bar link from the lower arm.

6. Remove the cotter pins from the upper and lower ball joint stud nuts.

7. Remove two bolts and nuts holding the strut to the lower arm. (through 1978 only)

8. Loosen the lower ball joint stud nut two turns. Do not remove this nut.

9. Install spreader tool between the upper and lower ball joint studs.

10. Expand the tool until the tool exerts considerable pressure on the studs. Tap the spindle near the lower stud with a hammer to loosen the stud in the spindle. Do not loosen the stud with tool pressure only.

11. Position floor jack under the lower arm and remove the lower ball joint stud nut.

12. Lower floor jack and remove the spring and insulator.

13. Remove the A-arm-to-crossmember at-

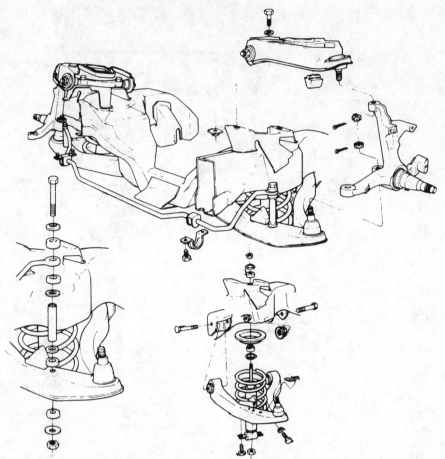

Exploded view of the front suspension, 1979 and later

taching parts, and remove the arm from the car.

14. Reverse above procedure to install. If lower control arm was replaced because of damage, check front end alignment. Torque lower arm-to-No. 2 crossmember nut to 60–90 ft. lbs. Torque the strut-to-lower arm bolts to 80–115 ft. lbs. The caliper-to-spindle bolts are torqued to 90–120 ft. lbs.

1979 and Later

1. Raise the car and support it with jackstands. Remove the tire and wheel.

2. Disconnect the stabilizer bar link from the lower arm.

3. Remove the lower shock absorber attaching bolts.

4. Remove the shock absorber upper nut and remove the shock.

5. Remove the steering center link from the pitman arm.

6. Install a spring compressor tool. Insert the securing pin through the upper ball nut and the compression rod. This pin can only be inserted one way. With the upper ball nut secured, turn the upper plate so it walks up the coil and contacts the upper spring seat. Back the nut off ½ turn.

7. Install the lower ball nut and the thrust washer on the compression rod and tighten the forcing nut until the spring is free in the seat.

8. Remove the two lower control arm pivot bolts.

9. Disengage the arm from the frame and remove the spring assembly.

10. If a new spring is being installed, mark the position of the upper and lower plates on the old spring. Also, measure the length of the spring and the amount of curvature in order to simplify the compressing and installation of the new spring.

11. Loosen the forcing nut and remove the spring from the tool.

12. Assemble the spring compressor tool on the new spring in the same position as the old spring was removed.

13. Position the spring in the lower arm.

14. Reverse the removal procedure to install.

Upper Control Arm

REPLACEMENT

1. Raise the car and support the frame with jack stands placed just behind the lower arm pivot (rear pivot on 1979 and later models). Remove the wheel.

2. Remove the cotter pin from the upper ball joint stud nut. Loosen the nut a few turns but do not remove.

3. Install a ball joint removal tool between the upper and lower ball joint studs. Expand the tool until it places the upper stud under compression. Tap the spindle near the stud with a hammer to loosen the stud.

4. Remove the tool. Raise the lower arm with a jack until pressure is relieved from the upper stud. Remove the upper stud nut.

5. Remove the upper shaft attaching bolts and the upper arm.

6. To install, position the arm to the frame, install the attaching nuts, and torque to 120–140 ft. lbs. Connect the upper stud to the spindle. Install the attaching nut, and tighten to 75 ft. lbs., then continue to tighten until the cotter pin holes align. Install a new cotter pin. Install the wheel, adjust the wheel bearings, and lower the car. Caster, camber, and toe must be adjusted after installation.

Lower Ball Joint

INSPECTION

Through 1978

1. Raise the vehicle by placing a floor jack under the lower arm or, raise the vehicle on a hoist and place a jackstand under the lower arm and lower the vehicle onto it to remove the preload from the lower ball joint.

2. Have an assistant grasp the top and bottom of the wheel and apply alternate in and out pressure to the top and bottom of the wheel.

3. Radial play of ¼ in. is acceptable measured at the inside of the wheel adjacent to the lower arm.

NOTE: *This radial play is multiplied at the outer circumference of the tire and should be measured only at the inside of the wheel.*

1979 and Later

1979 lower ball joints have built-in wear indicators. The checking surface is the round boss into which the grease fitting is threaded. If the ball joint is not worn, the checking surface should project outside the cover. If the joint is worn out, the checking surface will be flush

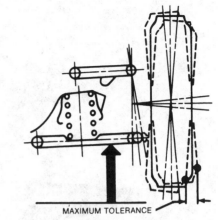

MAXIMUM TOLERANCE

Measuring lower ball joint redial play

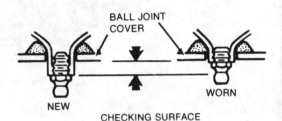

BALL JOINT COVER

NEW   WORN

CHECKING SURFACE

Lower ball joint wear indicator

with the cover. Do not jack the vehicle up to perform this check.

REPLACEMENT

NOTE: *Ford Motor Company recommends replacement of control arm and ball joint as an assembly, rather than replacement of the ball joint only. However, aftermarket replacement parts are available.*

1. Raise the vehicle on a hoist and allow the front wheels to fall to their full down position.

2. Drill a ⅛ in. hole completely through each ball joint attaching rivet.

3. Use a ⅜ in. drill in the pilot hole to drill off the head of the rivet.

4. Drive the rivets from the lower arm.

5. Place a jack under the lower arm and lower the vehicle about 6 in.

6. Remove the lower ball joint stud cotter pin and attaching nut.

7. Using a suitable tool, loosen the ball joint from the spindle and remove the ball joint from the lower arm.

8. Clean all metal burrs from the lower arm and install the new ball joint, using the service parts nuts and bolts to attach the ball joint to the lower arm. Do not attempt to rivet the ball joint again once it has been removed.

9. Check front end alignment.

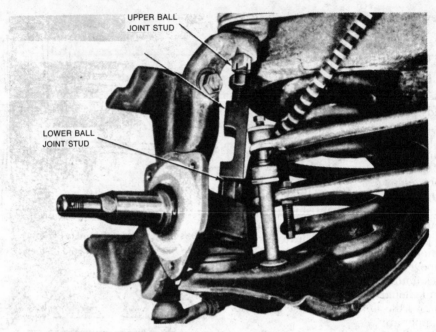

UPPER BALL
JOINT STUD

LOWER BALL
JOINT STUD

Loosening lower ball joint stud

Upper Ball Joint

INSPECTION

1. Raise the vehicle by placing a floor jack under the lower arm. Do not allow the lower arm to hang freely with the vehicle on a hoist or bumper jack.

2. Have an assistant grasp the top and bottom of the tire and move the wheel in and out.

3. As the wheel is being moved, observe the upper control arm where the spindle attaches to it. Any movement between the upper part of the spindle and the upper ball joint indicates a bad ball joint which must be replaced.

NOTE: *During this check, the lower ball joint will be unloaded and may move; this is normal and not an indication of a bad ball joint. Also, do not mistake a loose wheel bearing for a defective ball joint.*

REPLACEMENT

NOTE: *Ford Motor Company recommends replacement of control arm and ball joint as an assembly, rather than replacement of the ball joint only. However, aftermarket replacement parts are available.*

1. Raise the vehicle on a hoist and allow the front wheels to fall to their full down position.

2. Drill a ⅛ in. hole completely through each ball joint attaching rivet.

3. Using a large chisel, cut off the head of each rivet and drive them from the upper arm.

4. Place a jack under the lower arm and lower the vehicle about 6 in.

5. Remove the cotter pin and attaching nut from the ball joint stud.

6. Using a suitable tool, loosen the ball joint stud from the spindle and remove the ball joint from the upper arm.

7. Clean all metal burrs from the upper arm and install the new ball joint, using the service part nuts and bolts to attach the ball joint to the upper arm. Do not attempt to rivet the ball joint again once it has been removed.

8. Check front end alignment.

Wheel Alignment

NOTE: *The procedure for checking and adjusting front wheel alignment requires specialized equipment and professional skills. The following descriptions and adjustment procedures are for general reference only.*

Front wheel alignment is the position of the front wheels relative to each other and to the vehicle. It is determined, and must be maintained to provide safe, accurate steering with minimum tire wear. Many factors are involved in wheel alignment and adjustments are provided to return those that might change due to normal wear to their original value. The factors which determine wheel alignment are dependent on one another; therefore, when one of the factors is adjusted the others must be adjusted to compensate.

Descriptions of these and their affects on the car are provided below.

NOTE: *Do not attempt to check and adjust the front wheel alignment without first making a thorough inspection of the front suspension components.*

CAMBER

Camber angle is the number of degrees that the centerline of the wheel is inclined from the vertical. Camber reduces loading of the outer wheel bearing and improves the tire contact patch while cornering.

CASTER

Caster angle is the number of degrees that a line drawn through the steering knuckle pivots is inclined from the vertical, toward the front or rear of the car. Caster improves directional stability and decreases susceptibility to crosswinds or road surface deviations.

TOE-IN

Toe-in is the difference of the distance between the centers of the front and rear of the front wheels. It is most commonly measured in inches, but is occasionally referred to as an angle between the wheels. Toe-in is necessary to compensate for the tendency of the wheels to deflect rearward while in motion. Due to this tendency, the wheels of a vehicle, with properly adjusted toe-in, are traveling straight forward when the vehicle itself is traveling straight forward, resulting in directional stability and minimum tire wear.

Steering wheel spoke misalignment is often an indication of incorrect front end alignment. Care should be exercised when aligning the front end to maintain steering wheel spoke position. When adjusting the tie-rod ends, adjust each an equal amount (in the opposite direction) to increase or decrease toe-in. If, following toe-in adjustment, further adjustments are necessary to center the steering wheel spokes, adjust the tie-rod ends an equal amount in the same direction.

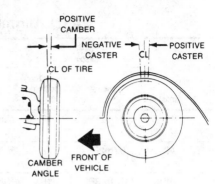

Caster and camber angles

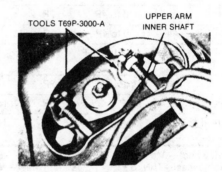

Caster and Camber adjusting tool installed

ADJUSTMENT PROCEDURES

Install Ford tool T65P-3000D (through 1978) or TP79P-3000A (from 1979), or its equivalent, on the frame rail, position the hooks around the upper control arm pivot shaft, and tighten the adjusting nuts slightly. Loosen the pivot shaft retaining bolts to permit adjustment.

To adjust caster, loosen or tighten either the front or rear adjusting nut. After adjusting caster, adjust the camber by loosening or tightening both nuts an equal amount. Tighten the shaft retaining bolts to specifications, remove the tool, and recheck the adjustments.

Adjust toe-in by loosening the clamp bolts, and turning the adjuster sleeves at the outer ends of the tie-rod. Turn the sleeves an equal amount in the opposite direction, to maintain steering wheel spoke alignment.

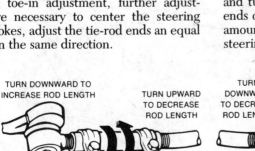
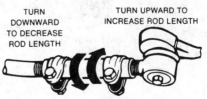

Tie-rod (toe-in) adjustments

Wheel Alignment Specifications

Year	Model	Caster		Camber		Toe-in (in.)	Steering Axis Inclin (deg)	Wheel Pivot Ratio (deg)	
		Range (deg)	Pref Setting (deg)	Range (deg)	Pref Setting (deg)			Inner Wheel	Outer Wheel
1968–69	All	0 to 2P	1P	$1/4$N to $1^1/4$P	$3/4$P	$1/8$ to $1/4$	$7^3/4$	20	$18^1/8$
1970–71	All	0 to 2P	1P	$1/4$N to $1^1/4$P	$1/2$P	$1/16$ to $5/16$	$7^3/4$	20	$19^4/25$
1972	All	1N to 3P	1P	$1/2$N to $1^1/2$P	$1/2$P	$1/16$ to $7/16$	$7^3/4$	20	$19^4/25$
1973	All	0 to 4P	2P	1N to 1P	0	$1/16$ to $7/16$	$7^3/4$	20	$18^3/4$
1974	All	0 to 4P	2P	①	②	$3/16$	$9^1/2$	20	$18^3/4$
1975	All	0 to 4P	2P	③	②	$3/16$	$9^1/2$	20	$18^3/4$
1976–77	All	$1^1/4$P to $2^3/4$P	2P	④	②	$3/16$	$9^1/2$	20	$18^3/4$
1978	All	$1^1/4$P to $2^3/4$P	2P	④	②	$1/16$ to $5/16$	9.44	20	18.69
1979	All	$2^1/4$P to $3^3/4$P	3P	$1/4$N to $1^1/4$P	$1/2$P	$1/16$ to $5/16$	11.20	20	18
1980–83	All	$2^1/4$P to $3^3/4$P	3P	$1/4$N to $1^1/4$P	$1/2$P	$1/16$ to $3/16$	10.87	20	18.51

① Left wheel—0 to 1P
Right wheel—$1/4$N to $3/4$P
② Left wheel—$1/2$P
Right wheel—$1/4$P
③ Left wheel—$3/4$N to $1^1/4$P
Right wheel—$3/4$N to $1^1/4$P

N Negative   P Positive
④ Left wheel—$1/4$N to $1^1/4$P
Right wheel—$1/2$N to 1P

REAR SUSPENSION

The rear suspension through 1978 is a coil-link design. Large, low-rate coil springs are mounted between rear axle pads and frame supports. Parallel lower arms extend forward of the spring seats to rubber frame anchor to accommodate driving and braking forces. A third link is mounted between the axle and the frame to control torque reaction forces from the rear wheels.

Lateral (side sway) motion of the rear axle is controlled by a rubber bushed rear track bar, linked laterally between the axle and frame.

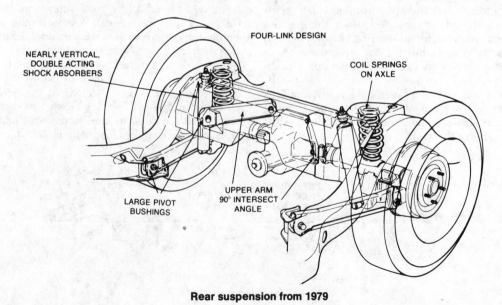

FOUR-LINK DESIGN

NEARLY VERTICAL, DOUBLE ACTING SHOCK ABSORBERS

COIL SPRINGS ON AXLE

LARGE PIVOT BUSHINGS

UPPER ARM 90° INTERSECT ANGLE

Rear suspension from 1979

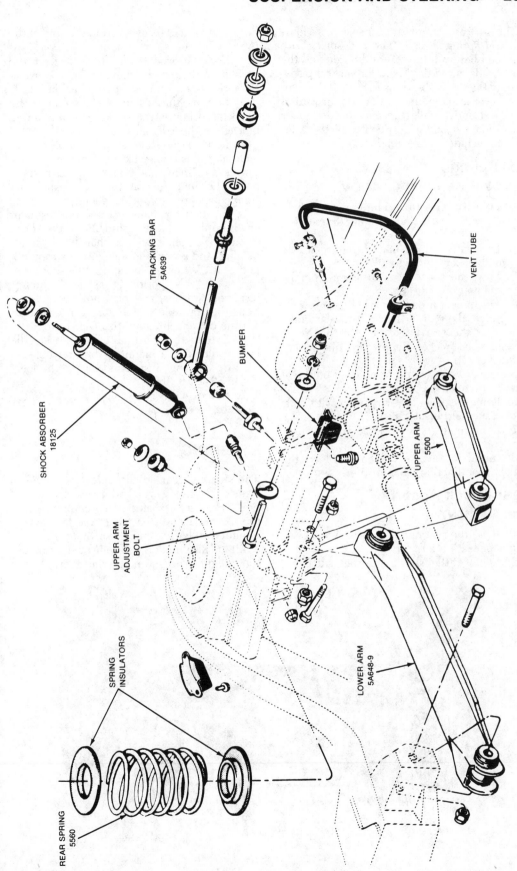

TRACKING BAR
5A639

VENT TUBE

SHOCK ABSORBER
18125

BUMPER

UPPER ARM
5500

UPPER ARM
ADJUSTMENT
BOLT

LOWER ARM
5A648-9

SPRING
INSULATORS

REAR SPRING
5560

Rear suspension through 1978

The 1979 and later rear suspension is a four-link coil spring design. The coil springs are mounted between the top of the axle and the frame pads, providing room for vertical placement of the shock absorbers in front of the axle. Two lower arms mount to the axle forward of the outer ends, while the two shorter upper arms mount near the top center of the axle, with an included angle of 90°.

Coil Springs

REMOVAL AND INSTALLATION

1. Place car on hoist and lift under rear axle housing. Place jack stands under frame side rails.
2. Disconnect track bar at the rear axle housing bracket. (through 1978).
3. Disconnect rear shock absorbers from the rear axle housing brackets.
4. Disconnect hose from axle housing vent. Disconnect the rear of the front-to-rear brake tube from the rear brake hose at the No. 4 crossmember bracket. Remove the brake hose-to-bracket clip.
5. Lower hoist with axle housing until coil springs are released.
6. Remove spring lower retainer with bolt, nut, washer and insulator.
7. Remove spring with large rubber insulator pads from car.
8. Install in reverse of above. Bleed the brakes as outlined in Chapter 9.

Rear Shock Absorber

REPLACEMENT

1. Raise the rear of the vehicle. Install jack stands beneath the frame.
2. Remove the shock absorber attaching nut, washer, and insulator from the stud at the top side of the spring upper seat. Compress the shock absorber sufficiently to clear the spring seat hole and remove the inner insulator and washer from the upper attaching stud.
3. Remove the locknut and disconnect the shock absorber lower stud at the mounting bracket on the axle housing.
4. Remove the shock absorber from the vehicle and check for leakage. If the shock absorber is in good condition, compress and expand the unit several times to expel any trapped air prior to reinstallation.
5. Position the inner washer and insulator on the upper attaching stud. Place the shock absorber in such a position that the upper attaching stud enters the hole in the spring upper seat. While maintaining the shock absorber in this position, install the outer insulator, washer, and new nut on the stud from the top side of the spring upper seat. Torque the attaching nut to 14–26 ft. lbs.
6. Extend the shock absorber. Locate the lower stud in the mounting bracket hole on the axle housing. Install and torque the locknut to 50–85 ft. lbs.
7. Remove the jack stands and lower the car. Road-test the car.

STEERING

The steering gear on all models with manual steering is the worm and recirculating ball type. The sector shaft is straddle-mounted in the cover above the gear and a housing mounted roller bearing below the gear.

All full size models with power steering use the integral type power steering gear. On this

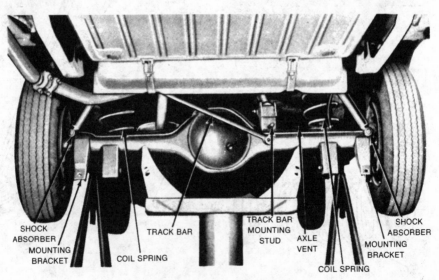

Removing the rear coil spring

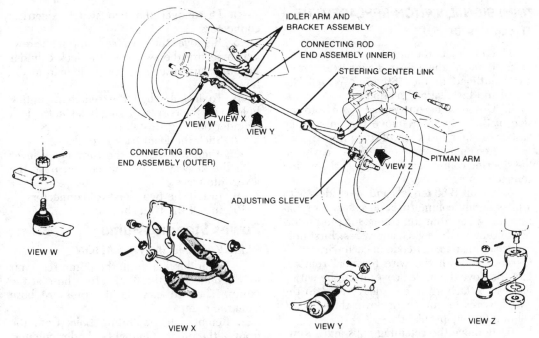

VIEW W

VIEW X

VIEW Y

VIEW Z

Manual or power steering linkage

type of steering, hydraulic assist is provided directly to the steering gear, eliminating all hoses and hardware which was previously mounted under the chassis. The most common type of steering gear used with integral power steering is the Ford torsion bar model. The torsion bar type power steering unit includes a worm and one-piece rack piston, which is meshed with the gear teeth on the steering sector shaft.

The steering linkage consists of a steering (pitman) arm, a pitman arm-to-idler arm rod, and idler arm, and tie-rods.

Steering Wheel

REMOVAL AND INSTALLATION

1. Disconnect the negative battery cable.
2. Remove the horn ring or hub cap by pushing it down and rotating it counterclockwise. Remove the retaining screws (from underside of steering wheel) and the crash pad. On 1969–70 Fords with speed control, the switch bezels must be pried up with a thin knife blade and the center trim plate removed to gain access to the crash pad retaining screws. On later models with speed control, the switches simply snap into plastic retainers inside the crash pad. Disconnect the horn and speed control wires.
3. Remove the steering wheel nut. Install a steering wheel puller on the end of the shaft and remove the wheel.

CAUTION: *The use of a knock-off type steering wheel puller or the use of a hammer*

TOOL T67L-3000-A

Steering wheel removal

on the steering shaft will damage the column bearing and, on collapsible columns, the column itself may be damaged.

4. Lubricate the steering shaft bushing with white grease. Transfer all serviceable parts to the new steering wheel.
5. With the front wheels pointing in a straight-ahead direction, and with the alignment marks on steering wheel and the steering shaft lined up, install the steering wheel and locknut.
6. Connect the horn and speed control wires and install the horn ring or hub cap. Install the crash pad and retaining screws.
7. Connect the negative battery cable.

TURN SIGNAL SWITCH REPLACEMENT
Through 1978

1. Disconnect the negative battery cable.
2. Remove the steering wheel as previously outlined in the "Steering Wheel Removal and Installation" section.
3. Unscrew the turn signal lever from the side of the column. Remove the emergency flasher retainer and knob, if so equipped.
4. Locate and remove the finish cover on the steering column and disconnect the wiring connector plugs.
5. On all 1968 models and all models with a tilt steering column it is necessary to separate the wires from the connector plug in order to remove the switch and wires. First note the location and color code of each wire, prior to removal, with the wire terminal removal tool. Remove the plastic cover from the wiring harness. Attach a piece of heavy cord to the switch wires to pull them down through the column during installation.
6. Remove the retaining clips and screws from the turn signal switch and lift the switch and wire assembly from the top of the column.
7. Tape the ends of the new switch wires together and transfer the pull cord to these wires.
8. Pull the wires down through the column with the cord and attach the new switch to the column hub.
9. If the switch wires were separated from the connector plug, press the wires into their proper location. Connect the wiring connector plugs and install the finish cover on the column.
10. Install the turn signal lever. Install the emergency flasher retainer and knob, if so equipped.
11. Install the steering wheel as outlined in the "Steering Wheel Removal and Installation" section.
12. Connect the negative battery cable and test the operation of the turn signals, horn, emergency flashers, and speed control, if so equipped.

1979 and Later

1. On standard steering columns, remove the upper extension shroud (below the steering wheel) by unsnapping the shroud from the retaining clip. On tilt columns, remove the trim shroud by removing the five self-tapping screws.
2. Use a pulling and twisting motion, while pulling straight out, to remove the turn signal switch lever.
3. Peel back the piece of foam rubber from around the switch.

4. Disconnect the two switch electrical connectors.
5. Remove the two self-tapping screws which secure the switch to the lock cylinder housing, and disengage the switch from the housing.
6. To install, align the switch mounting holes with the corresponding holes in the lock cylinder housing. Install the two screws.
7. Stick the foam back into place.
8. Align the key on the turn signal lever with the keyway in the switch and push the lever into place.
9. Install the two electrical connectors.
10. Install the trim shrouds.

Power Steering Pump
REMOVAL AND INSTALLATION

1. Drain the fluid from the pump reservoir by disconnecting the fluid return hose at the pump. Then, disconnect the pressure hose from the pump.
2. Remove the mounting bolts from the front of the pump. On eight cylinder engines, there is a nut on the rear of the pump (through 1978) which must be removed. After removal, move the pump inward to loosen the belt tension and remove the belt from the pulley. Then, remove the pump from the car.
3. To reinstall the pump, position on mounting bracket and loosely install the mounting bolts and nuts. Put the drive belt over the pulley and move the pump outward against the belt until the proper belt tension is obtained. Measure the belt tension with a belt tension gauge for the proper adjustment. Only in cases where a belt tension gauge is not available should the belt deflection method be used. If the belt deflection method is used, be sure to check with a belt tension gauge as soon as possible, since deflection method is not accurate.
4. Tighten the mounting bolts and nuts.

Ignition Lock Cylinder
Replacement
1968–69

1. Insert key and turn to Acc. position.
2. With stiff wire in hole, depress lock pin and rotate cylinder counterclockwise, then pull out cylinder.

1970 and Later

1. Disconnect the negative battery cable.
2. On cars with a fixed steering column, remove the steering wheel trim pad and the steering wheel. Insert a stiff wire into the hole located in the lock cylinder housing. On cars with a tilt steering wheel, this hole is located

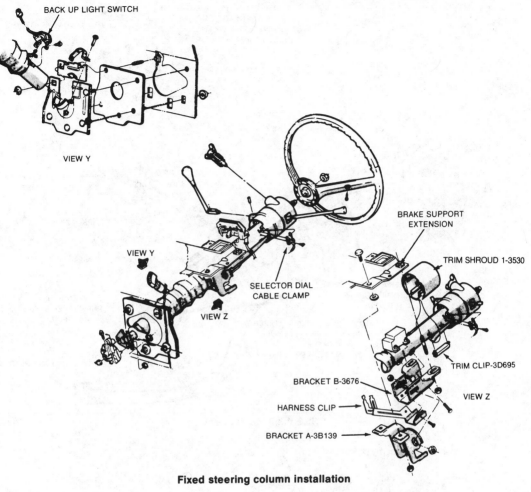

BACK UP LIGHT SWITCH

VIEW Y

VIEW Y

VIEW Z

VIEW Z

SELECTOR DIAL
CABLE CLAMP

BRAKE SUPPORT
EXTENSION

TRIM SHROUD 1-3530

TRIM CLIP-3D695

BRACKET B-3676

HARNESS CLIP

BRACKET A-3B139

Fixed steering column installation

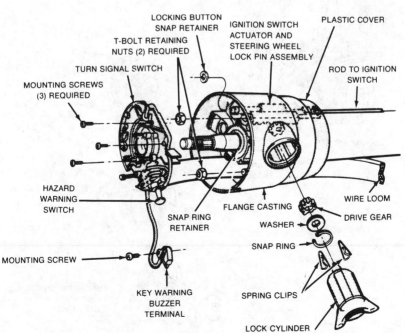

LOCKING BUTTON
SNAP RETAINER

T-BOLT RETAINING
NUTS (2) REQUIRED

TURN SIGNAL SWITCH

MOUNTING SCREWS
(3) REQUIRED

IGNITION SWITCH
ACTUATOR AND
STEERING WHEEL
LOCK PIN ASSEMBLY

PLASTIC COVER

ROD TO IGNITION
SWITCH

HAZARD
WARNING
SWITCH

SNAP RING
RETAINER

FLANGE CASTING

WIRE LOOM

DRIVE GEAR

WASHER

SNAP RING

MOUNTING SCREW

KEY WARNING
BUZZER
TERMINAL

SPRING CLIPS

LOCK CYLINDER

Fixed steering column components

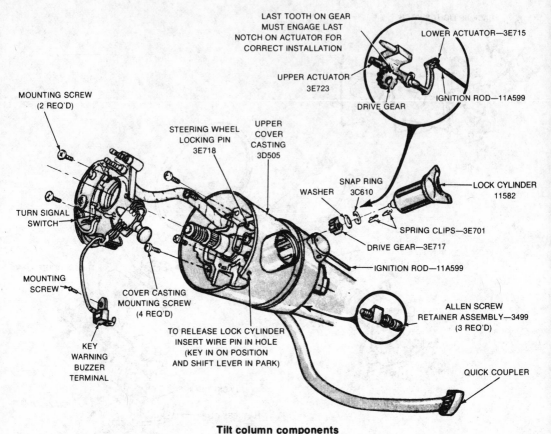

LAST TOOTH ON GEAR MUST ENGAGE LAST NOTCH ON ACTUATOR FOR CORRECT INSTALLATION

LOWER ACTUATOR—3E715

UPPER ACTUATOR 3E723

DRIVE GEAR

IGNITION ROD—11A599

MOUNTING SCREW (2 REQ'D)

STEERING WHEEL LOCKING PIN 3E718

UPPER COVER CASTING 3D505

SNAP RING 3C610

WASHER

LOCK CYLINDER 11582

TURN SIGNAL SWITCH

SPRING CLIPS—3E701

DRIVE GEAR—3E717

IGNITION ROD—11A599

MOUNTING SCREW

COVER CASTING MOUNTING SCREW (4 REQ'D)

ALLEN SCREW RETAINER ASSEMBLY—3499 (3 REQ'D)

KEY WARNING BUZZER TERMINAL

TO RELEASE LOCK CYLINDER INSERT WIRE PIN IN HOLE (KEY IN ON POSITION AND SHIFT LEVER IN PARK)

QUICK COUPLER

Tilt column components

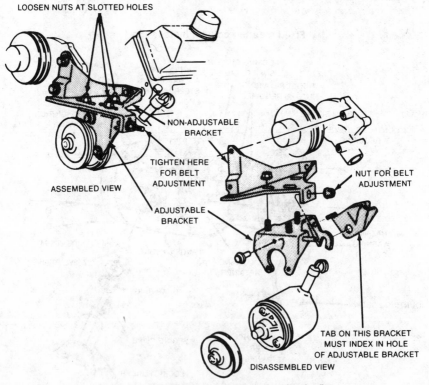

LOOSEN NUTS AT SLOTTED HOLES

NON-ADJUSTABLE BRACKET

NUT FOR BELT ADJUSTMENT

ASSEMBLED VIEW

TIGHTEN HERE FOR BELT ADJUSTMENT

ADJUSTABLE BRACKET

TAB ON THIS BRACKET MUST INDEX IN HOLE OF ADJUSTABLE BRACKET

DISASSEMBLED VIEW

Power steering pump installation (typical)

on the outside of the steering column near the emergency flasher button and it is not necessary to remove the steering wheel. On 1979 and later modular columns, remove the trim shroud, and remove the electrical connector from the key warning switch; steering wheel removal is unnecessary.

3. Place the gearshift lever in Reverse on cars with manual transmission and in Park on cars with automatic transmission, and turn the ignition key to the ON position.

4. Depress wire and remove lock cylinder and wire.

5. Insert new cylinder into housing and turn to the OFF position. This will lock the cylinder into position.

6. Reinstall steering wheel and pad if removed.

7. Connect negative battery cable.

IGNITION SWITCH REPLACEMENT

1968–69

1. Remove cylinder as above.

2. Unscrew the bezel from the ignition switch and remove switch from panel.

3. Remove insulated plug from rear of switch.

4. Install in reverse of above.

1970 through 1978

1. Disconnect the negative battery cable.

2. Remove the shrouding from the steering column, and detach and lower the steering column from the brake support bracket.

3. Disconnect the switch wiring at the multiple plug.

4. Remove the two nuts that retain the switch to the steering column.

5. On vehicles with column-mounted gearshift lever, detach the switch plunger from the switch actuator rod and remove the switch. On vehicles with console-mounted gearshift lever, remove the pin connecting the plunger to the actuator and remove the switch.

6. To reinstall the switch, place both the lock mechanism at the top of the column and the switch itself in lock position for correct adjustment. To hold the column in the lock position, place the automatic shift lever in PARK or manual shift lever in Reverse, and turn to LOCK and remove the key. New switches are held in lock by plastic shipping pins. To pin existing switches, pull the switch plunger out as far as it will go and push it back into the first detent. Insert a $3/32$ in. diameter wire in the locking hole in the top of the switch.

7. Connect the switch plunger to the switch actuator rod.

8. Position the switch on the column and install the attaching nuts. Do not tighten them.

9. Move the switch up and down to locate mid-position of rod lash, and then tighten the nuts.

10. Remove the locking pin or wire.

11. Attach the steering column to the brake support bracket and install the shrouding.

1979 and Later

1. Disconnect the negative battery cable.

2. Remove the upper shroud below the steering wheel by unsnapping the retaining clips. On the tilt column it will be necessary to remove the five attaching screws.

3. Disconnect the electrical connector from the ignition switch.

4. Drill out the bolts holding the switch to the lock cylinder using a $1/8$ in. drill bit.

5. Remove the bolts using an easy-out bolt extractor.

6. Disengage the switch from the actuator pin.

7. Adjust the new ignition switch by sliding the carrier to the Lock position. Insert a small drill bit through the switch housing and into the carrier to restrict movement of the carrier with respect to the switch housing. A new replacement comes with an adjusting pin already installed.

8. Turn the ignition key to the Lock position.

9. Install the ignition switch on the actuator pin.

10. Install new "break-off head" bolts and tighten them until the heads break off.

11. Remove the drill bit or adjusting pin.

12. Connect all electrical connections and the negative battery cable.

13. Start the car and check for proper operation of the switch.

14. Install the steering column shroud.

Tie-Rod Ends
REMOVAL AND INSTALLATION

1. Firmly apply the parking brake and place blocks behind the rear wheels.

2. Jack up the front of the car and install jackstands beneath the frame members.

3. Remove the cotter pin and castellated nut from the tie-rod end ball joint. Pull the ball joint from the socket in the spindle arm.

4. Loosen the jam nut on the tie-rod. Unscrew the tie-rod end from the tie-rod, taking care to record the number of turns needed to remove the rod end.

5. Reverse the above procedure to install, taking care to turn the tie-rod end the correct amount of turns onto the tie-rod. This is necessary to maintain proper toe-in.

Brakes

HYDRAULIC SYSTEM

All post-1966 models utilize a dual hydraulic brake circuit in accordance with Federal safety regulations. Each circuit is independent of the other, incorporating a tandem master cylinder, a pressure differential warning valve, and, on disc brake models, a proportioning valve. One circuit services the front brakes (rear of master cylinder) and the other, the rear brakes (front of master cylinder). In case of a leak or other hydraulic failure, ½ braking efficiency will be maintained. A brake system failure will decentralize the pressure differential warning valve, actuating a warning light on the dash. A proportioning valve located between the rear brake system inlet and outlet ports in the pressure differential warning valve serves to regulate the rear brake hydraulic pressure on disc brake models to prevent premature rear wheel lockup during hard braking. On models equipped with disc front/drum rear brakes, a metering valve is used to delay pressure buildup to the front discs upon initial application. The metering valve extends pad life by preventing the front discs from carrying the majority of the braking load at low operating line pressures.

Most full-sized models have been equipped with power brakes. On all drum brake equipped cars, as well as those equipped with a disc front/drum rear brake configuration, the power assist has been supplied by a manifold vacuum-operated servo, located between the master cylinder and the firewall. All models equipped with the 4 wheel disc brake system utilize a hydraulically-operated servo, also located between the master cylinder and firewall. This system, known as the hydro-boost system, is connected to the power steering pump via hydraulic hoses, using steering pump fluid pressure to supply and circulate the fluid (type ATF) to the servo.

The hydro-boost unit contains a spool valve with an open center which controls the strength of pump pressure when braking occurs. A lever assembly controls the valve's position. A boost piston provides the force necessary to operate the conventional master cylinder on the front of the booster.

A reserve of at least two assisted brake applications is supplied by a spring-loaded accumulator, which retains power steering fluid under pressure.

The brakes can be operated without assist, once the reserve is depleted.

Hydraulic System Bleeding

NOTE: *The front and rear hydraulic systems are independent. If it is known that only one system has to be bled, always bleed the brakes in a sequence that starts with the wheel cylinder farthest from the master cylinder and ends with the wheel cylinder or caliper closest to the master cylinder.*

1. Fill the master cylinder with brake fluid.
2. Install a ⅜ in. box-end wrench to the bleeder screw on the right rear wheel.

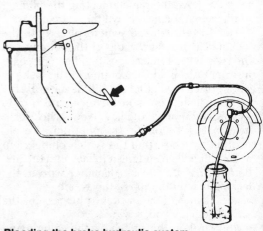

Bleeding the brake hydraulic system

3. Push a piece of small-diameter rubber tubing over the bleeder screw until it is flush against the wrench. Submerge the other end of the rubber tubing in a glass jar partially filled with clean brake fluid. Make sure the rubber tube fits on the bleeder screw snugly.

4. Have a friend apply pressure to the brake pedal. Open the bleeder screw and observe the bottle of brake fluid. If bubbles appear in the glass jar, there is air in the system. When your friend has pushed the pedal to the floor, immediately close the bleeder screw before he releases the pedal.

5. Repeat this procedure until no bubbles appear in the jar. Refill the master cylinder.

6. Repeat this procedure on the left rear, right front and left front wheels, in that order. Periodically refill the master cylinder so that it does not run dry.

7. Center the pressure differential warning valve as outlined in the "Pressure Differential Warning Valve" section.

PRESSURE DIFFERENTIAL WARNING VALVE CENTERING

Since the introduction of dual master cylinders to the hydraulic brake system, a pressure differential warning signal has been added. This signal consists of a warning light on the dashboard activated by a differential pressure switch located below the master cylinder. The signal indicates a hydraulic pressure differential between the front and rear brakes of 80–150 psi, and should warn the driver that a hydraulic failure has occurred.

After repairing and bleeding any part of the hydraulic system the warning light may remain on due to the pressure differential valve remaining in the off-center position. To centralize the valve on 1968–69 models, a pressure difference must be created in the opposite branch of the hydraulic system that was repaired or bled last.

NOTE: *Front wheel balancing of cars equipped with disc brakes may also cause a pressure differential in the front branch of the system.*

To centralize the valve:

1. Turn the ignition to either the ACC or ON position.

2. Check the fluid level in the master cylinder reservoirs. Fill to within ¼ in. of the top if necessary.

3. Depress the brake pedal firmly. The valve will centralize itself, causing the brake warning light to go out.

4. Turn the ignition off.

5. Prior to driving the vehicle, check the operation of the brakes and obtain a firm pedal.

MASTER CYLINDER REMOVAL AND INSTALLATION

Non-Power Brakes

1. Working under the dash, disconnect the master cylinder pushrod from the brake pedal. The pushrod cannot be removed from the master cylinder.

2. Disconnect the stoplight switch wires and remove the switch from the brake pedal, using care not to damage the switch.

3. Disconnect the brake lines from the master cylinder.

4. Remove the attaching screws from the firewall and remove the master cylinder from the car.

5. Reinstall in reverse of above order, leaving the brake line fittings loose at the master cylinder.

6. Fill the master cylinder, and with the brake lines loose, slowly bleed the air from the master cylinder using the foot pedal.

Power Brakes

1. Disconnect the brake lines from the master cylinder.

2. Remove the two nuts and lockwashers which attach the master cylinder to the brake booster.

3. Remove the master cylinder from the booster.

4. Reverse above procedure to reinstall.

5. Fill master cylinder and bleed entire brake system.

6. Refill master cylinder.

MASTER CYLINDER OVERHAUL

Referring to the accompanying exploded view of the dual master cylinder components, disassemble the unit as follows: Clean the exterior of the cylinder and remove the filler cover and diaphragm. Any brake fluid remaining in the cylinder should be poured out and discarded. Remove the secondary piston stop bolt from the bottom of the cylinder and remove the bleed screw, if required. With the primary piston depressed, remove the snap-ring from its retaining groove at the rear of the cylinder bore. Withdraw the pushrod and the primary piston assembly from the bore.

NOTE: *Do not remove the screw that retains the primary return spring retainer, return spring, primary cup and protector on the primary piston. The assembly is adjusted at the factory and should not be disassembled.*

Remove the secondary piston assembly.

NOTE: *Do not remove the outlet tube seats, outlet check valves and outlet check valve springs from the cylinder body.*

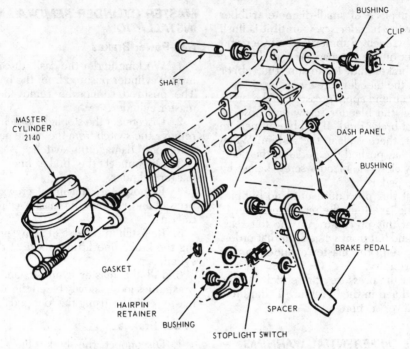

SHAFT

BUSHING

CLIP

MASTER
CYLINDER
2140

DASH PANEL

BUSHING

BRAKE PEDAL

GASKET

HAIRPIN
RETAINER

BUSHING

SPACER

STOPLIGHT SWITCH

Master cylinder installation—manual brakes

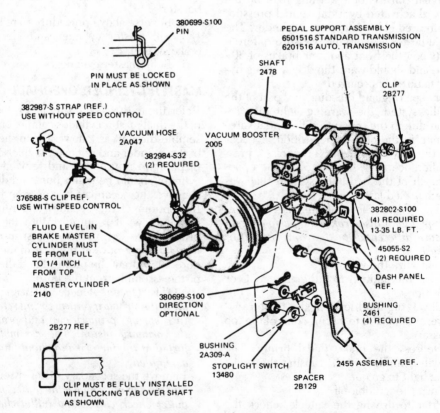

380699-S100
PIN

PIN MUST BE LOCKED
IN PLACE AS SHOWN

PEDAL SUPPORT ASSEMBLY
6501516 STANDARD TRANSMISSION
6201516 AUTO. TRANSMISSION

SHAFT
2478

CLIP
2B277

382987-S STRAP (REF.)
USE WITHOUT SPEED CONTROL

VACUUM HOSE
2A047

VACUUM BOOSTER
2005

382984-S32
(2) REQUIRED

376588-S CLIP REF.
USE WITH SPEED CONTROL

382802-S100
(4) REQUIRED
13-35 LB. FT.

FLUID LEVEL IN
BRAKE MASTER
CYLINDER MUST
BE FROM FULL
TO 1/4 INCH
FROM TOP

45055-S2
(2) REQUIRED

DASH PANEL
REF.

MASTER CYLINDER
2140

380699-S100
DIRECTION
OPTIONAL

BUSHING
2461
(4) REQUIRED

2B277 REF.

BUSHING
2A309-A

STOPLIGHT SWITCH
13480

SPACER
2B129

2455 ASSEMBLY REF.

CLIP MUST BE FULLY INSTALLED
WITH LOCKING TAB OVER SHAFT
AS SHOWN

Master cylinder installation—power brakes

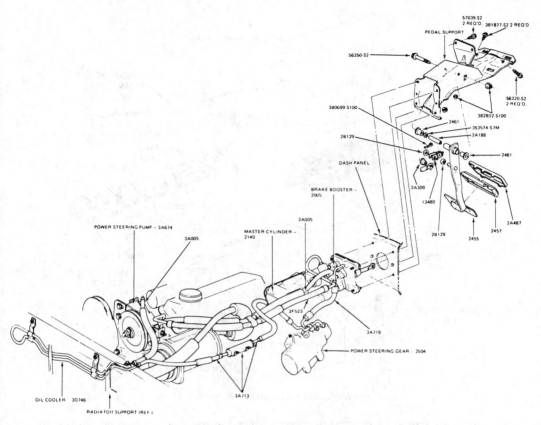

Hydro-Boost assembly and related parts

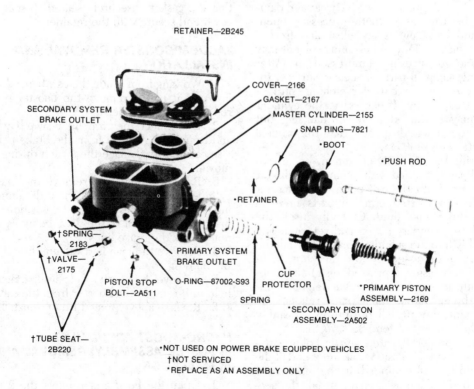

RETAINER—2B245

COVER—2166

GASKET—2167

MASTER CYLINDER—2155

SNAP RING—7821

SECONDARY SYSTEM
BRAKE OUTLET

•BOOT

•PUSH ROD

•RETAINER

†SPRING—
2183

†VALVE—
2175

PRIMARY SYSTEM
BRAKE OUTLET

CUP
PROTECTOR

•PRIMARY PISTON
ASSEMBLY—2169

PISTON STOP
BOLT—2A511

O-RING—87002-S93

SPRING

•SECONDARY PISTON
ASSEMBLY—2A502

†TUBE SEAT—
2B220

•NOT USED ON POWER BRAKE EQUIPPED VEHICLES
†NOT SERVICED
•REPLACE AS AN ASSEMBLY ONLY

Master cylinder disassembled—drum brakes

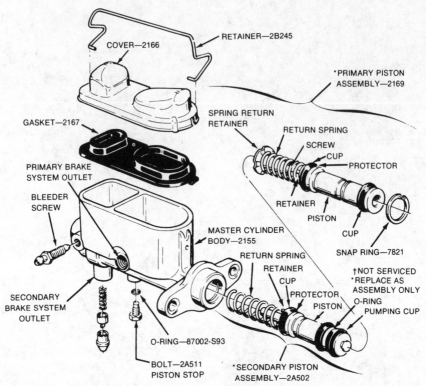

Master cylinder disassembled—disc brakes

All components should be cleaned in clean isopropyl alcohol or clean brake fluid and inspected for chipping, excessive wear and damage. Check to ensure that all recesses, openings and passageways are clear and free of foreign matter. Dirt and cleaning solvent may be removed by using compressed air. After cleaning, keep all parts on a clean surface. Inspect the cylinder bore for etching, pitting, scoring or rusting. If necessary, the cylinder bore may be honed to repair damage, but never to a diameter greater than the original diameter plus 0.003 in.

During the assembly operation, be sure to use all parts supplied with the master cylinder repair kit. With the exception of the master cylinder body, submerge all parts in extra heavy duty brake fluid. Carefully insert the complete secondary piston and return spring assembly into the cylinder bore and install the primary piston assembly into the bore. With the primary piston depressed, install the snap-ring into its groove in the cylinder bore. Install the pushrod, boot and retainer (if equipped), then install the pushrod assmbly into the primary piston. Be sure that the retainer is properly seated and is holding the pushrod securely. Position the inner end of the pushrod boot (if equipped) in the master cylinder body retaining groove. Install the secondary piston stop bolt and O-ring at the bottom of the master cylinder body. Install the bleed screw (if equipped) and position the gasket on the master cylinder filler cover. Be sure that the gasket is securely seated. Install the cover and secure with the retainer.

VACUUM BOOSTER REMOVAL AND INSTALLATION

1. Working from inside the car, beneath the instrument panel, remove the booster pushrod from the brake pedal.

2. Disconnect the stop light switch wires and remove the switch from the brake pedal. Use care not to damage the switch during removal.

3. Raise the hood and remove the master cylinder from the booster without disconnecting the brake lines. Carefully position the master cylinder out of the way, being careful not to kink the brake lines.

4. Remove the manifold vacuum hose from the booster.

5. Remove the booster to firewall attaching bolts and remove the booster from the car.

6. Reverse above procedure to reinstall.

HYDRO-BOOST ACCUMULATOR (BOOSTER ASSEMBLY) REMOVAL AND INSTALLATION

1. Open the hood and remove the 2 nuts attaching the master cylinder to the brake booster.

2. Remove the master cylinder from the hydro-boost accumulator (booster assembly).

3. Set the master cylinder aside without disturbing the hydraulic lines.

4. Disconnect the pressure, steering and return lines from the accumulator.

5. Plug the lines and ports.

6. Working below the dash, disconnect the hydro-boost pushrod from the brake pedal. To do this, disconnect the stoplight switch at the connector. Remove the hairpin retainer. Slide the spotlight switch from the brake pedal pin far enough to clear the switch outer pin hole. Remove the switch from the pin.

7. Loosen the hydro-boost attaching nuts and remove the pushrod, washers and bushing from the brake pedal pin.

8. Remove the accumulator (booster assembly).

9. Installation is the reverse of removal. Top up the power steering pump reservoir. Run the engine until all air is expelled from the system, which will escape out of the reservoir with the cap off. Then, once steering and brake assist is operational, road-test the car.

DRUM BRAKES

Drum brakes on all Fords employ single-anchor, internal-expanding, and self-adjusting brake assemblies. The automatic adjuster continuously maintains correct operating clearance between the linings and the drums by adjusting the brake in small increments in di-

rect proportion to lining wear. When applying the brakes while backing up, the linings tend to follow the rotating drum counterclockwise, thus forcing the upper end of the primary shoe against the anchor pin. Simultaneously, the wheel cylinder pushes the upper end of the secondary shoe and cable guide outward, away from the anchor pin. This movement of the secondary shoe causes the cable to pull the adjusting lever upward and against the end of the tooth on the adjusting screw starwheel. As lining wear increases, the upward travel of the adjusting lever also increases. When the linings have worn sufficiently to allow the lever to move upward far enough, it passes over the end of the tooth and engages it. Upon release

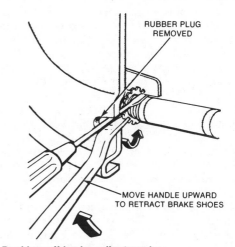

Backing off brake adjustment

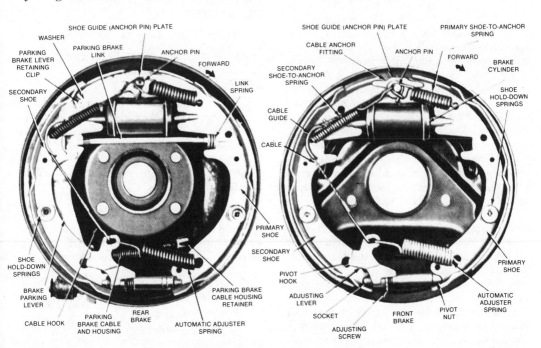

Self-adjusting drum brake assemblies

of the brakes, the adjusting spring pulls the adjuster lever downward, turning the starwheel and expanding the brakes.

DRUM BRAKE INSPECTION

1. Raise the front or rear of the car and support the car with safety stands. Make sure that the parking brake is not on.

2. If you are going to check the rear brakes, remove the lug nuts which attach the wheels to the axle shaft and remove the tires and wheels from the car. Using a pair of pliers, remove the tinnerman nuts from the wheel studs. Pull the brake drum off the axle shaft. If the brakes are adjusted too tightly to remove the drum, see Step 4. If you can remove the drum, see Step 5.

3. If you are going to check the front brakes, then the front tire, wheel and brake drum can be removed as an assembly. Remove the hub cap, then either pry the dust cover off the spindle with a prybar or pull it off with a pair of pliers. Remove the cotter pin from the spindle. Slide the nut lock off the adjusting nut, then loosen the adjusting nut until it reaches the end of the spindle. Do not remove the adjusting nut yet. Grab the tire and pull it out toward yourself, then push it back into position. This will free the outer wheel bearing from the drum hub. If the brakes are adjusted up too tightly to allow the drum to be pulled off them, go to Step 4 and loosen up the brakes, then return here. Remove the adjusting nut, washer and outer bearing from the spindle. Pull the tire, wheel, and brake drum off the spindle.

4. If the brakes are too tight to remove the drum, get under the car (make sure that you have jack stands under the car to support it) and remove the rubber plug from the bottom of the brake backing plate. Shine a flashlight into the slot in the plate. You will see the top of the adjusting screw starwheel and the adjusting lever for the automatic brake adjusting mechanism. To back off on the adjusting screw, you must first insert a small thin prybar or a piece of firm wire (coathanger wire) into the adjusting slot and push the adjusting lever away from the adjusting screw. Then, insert a brake adjusting spoon into the slot and engage the top of the starwheel. Lift up on the bottom of the adjusting spoon to force the adjusting screw starwheel downward. Repeat this operation until the brake drum is free of the brake shoes and can be pulled off.

5. Clean the brake shoes and the inside of the brake drum. There must be at least $1/16$ in. of brake lining above the heads of the brake shoe attaching rivets. The lining should not be cracked or contaminated with grease or brake fluid. If there is grease or brake fluid on the lining, it must be replaced and the source of the leak must be found and corrected. Brake fluid on the lining means leaking wheel cylinders. Grease on the brake lining means a leaking grease retainer (front wheels) or axle seal (rear brakes). If the lining is slightly glazed but otherwise in good condition, it can be cleaned up with medium sandpaper. Lift up the bottom of the wheel cylinder boots and inspect the ends of the wheel cylinders. A small amount of fluid in the end of the cylinders should be considered normal. If fluid runs out of the cylinder when the boots are lifted, however, the wheel cylinder must be rebuilt or replaced. Examine the inside of the brake drum; it should have a smooth, dull finish. If excessive brake shoe wear caused grooves to wear in the drum it must be machined or replaced. If the inside of the drum is slightly glazed, but otherwise good, it can be cleaned up with medium sandpaper.

6. If no repairs are required, install the drum and wheel. If the brake adjustment was changed to remove the drum, adjust the brakes until the drum will just fit over the brakes. After the wheel is installed it will be necessary to complete the adjustment. See "Brake Adjustment" later in this chapter. If a front wheel was removed, tighten the wheel bearing adjustment nut to 17–25 ft. lbs. while rotating the wheel. This will seat the bearing. Loosen the adjusting nut ½ turn, then retighten it to 10–15 in. lbs.

BRAKE DRUM REMOVAL AND INSTALLATION

See Steps 3 and 4 under "Drum Brakes Inspection."

BRAKE SHOE REMOVAL AND INSTALLATION

NOTE: *If you are not thoroughly familiar with the procedures involved in brake replacement, disassemble and assemble only one side at a time, leaving the other wheel intact as a reference.*

1. Remove the brake drum. See the inspection procedure.

2. Place the hollow end of a brake spring service tool (available at auto parts stores) on the brake shoe anchor pin and twist it to disengage one of the brake retracting springs. Repeat this operation to remove the other spring.

CAUTION: *Be careful the springs do not slip off the tool during removal, as they could cause personal injury.*

3. Reach behind the brake backing plate and place a finger on the end of one of the

brake hold-down spring mounting pins. Using a pair of pliers, grasp the washer on the top of the hold-down spring which corresponds to the pin that you are holding. Push down on the pliers and turn them 90° to align the slot in the washer with the head on the spring mounting pin. Remove the spring and washer and repeat this operation on the hold-down spring on the other brake shoe.

4. Place the tip of a prybar on the top of the brake adjusting screw and move the brake adjusting lever. When there is enough slack in the automatic adjuster cable, disconnect the loop on the top of the cable from the anchor. Grasp the top of each brake shoe and move it outward to disengage it from the wheel cylinder (and parking brake link on rear wheels). When the brake shoes are clear, lift them from the backing plate. Twist the shoes slightly and the automatic adjuster assembly will disassemble itself.

5. If you are working on rear brakes, grasp the end of the brake cable spring with a pair of pliers and, using the brake lever as a fulcrum, pull the end of the spring away from the lever. Disengage the cable from the brake lever.

6. The brake shoes are installed as follows: If you are working on the rear brakes, the brake cable must be connected to the secondary brake shoe before the shoe is installed on the backing plate. To do this, first transfer the parking brake lever from the old secondary shoe to the new one. This is accomplished by spreading the bottom of the horseshoe clip and disengaging the lever. Position the lever on the new secondary shoe and install the spring washer and the horseshoe clip. Close the bottom of the clip after installing it. Grasp the metal tip of the parking brake cable with a pair of pliers. Position a pair of side cutter pliers on the end of the cable coil spring and, using the pliers as a fulcrum, pull the coil spring back with the side cutters. Position the cable in the parking brake lever.

7. Apply a *light* coating of high-temperature grease to the brake shoe contact points on the backing plate. Position the primary brake shoe on the front of the backing plate and install the hold-down spring and washer over the mounting pin. Install the secondary shoe on the rear of the backing plate.

8. If working on the rear brakes, install the parking brake link between the notch in the primary brake shoe and the notch in the parking brake lever.

9. Install the automatic adjuster cable loop end on the anchor pin. Make sure that the crimped side of the loop faces the backing plate.

10. Install the return spring in the primary brake shoe and, using the tapered end of a brake spring service tool, slide the top of the spring onto the anchor pin.

CAUTION: *Be careful to make sure that the spring does not slip off the tool during installation, as it could cause injury.*

11. Install the automatic adjuster cable guide in the secondary brake shoe, making sure that the flared hole in the cable guide is inside the hole in the brake shoe. Fit the cable into the groove in the top of the cable guide.

12. Install the secondary shoe return spring through the hole in the cable guide and the brake shoe. Using the brake spring tool, slide the top of the spring onto the anchor pin.

13. Clean the threads on the adjusting screw and apply a light coating of high-temperature grease to the threads. Screw the adjuster closed, then open it one-half turn.

14. Install the adjusting screw between the brake shoes with the starwheel nearest to the secondary shoe. Make sure that the starwheel is in a position that is accessible from the adjusting slot in the backing plate.

15. Install the short hooked end of the automatic adjuster spring in the proper hole in the primary brake shoe.

16. Connect the hooked end of the automatic adjuster cable and the free end of the automatic adjuster spring in the slot in the top of the automatic adjuster lever.

17. Pull the automatic adjuster lever (the lever will pull the cable and spring with it) downward and to the left and engage the pivot hook of the lever in the hole in the secondary brake shoe.

18. Check the entire brake assembly to make sure that everything is installed properly. Make sure that the shoes engage the wheel cylinder properly and are flush on the anchor pin. Make sure that the automatic adjuster cable is flush on the anchor pin and in the slot on the back of the cable guide. Make sure that the adjusting lever rests on the adjusting screw starwheel. Pull upward on the adjusting cable until the adjusting lever is free of the starwheel, then release the cable. The adjusting lever should snap back into place on the adjusting screw starwheel and turn the wheel one tooth.

19. Expand the brake adjusting screw until the brake drum will just fit over the brake shoes.

20. Install the wheel and drum and adjust the brakes. See "Brake Adjustment."

DRUM BRAKE ADJUSTMENT

NOTE: *Drum brakes installed in Fords are self-adjusting. All that is normally required to adjust the brakes is to apply them moderately hard several times while carefully backing the car in Reverse. However, if this action proves unsatisfactory, or if it proves necessary to readjust the brakes after replacing the linings or removing the drum, the following procedure may be used.*

1. Raise the car and support it with safety stands.

2. Remove the rubber plug from the adjusting slot on the backing plate.

3. Insert a brake adjusting spoon into the slot and engage the lowest possible tooth on the starwheel. Move the end of the brake spoon downward to move the starwheel upward and expand the adjusting screw. Repeat this operation until the brakes lock the wheel.

4. Insert a small prybar or piece of firm wire (coat-hanger wire) into the adjusting slot and push the automatic adjuster lever out and free of the starwheel on the adjusting screw.

5. Holding the adjusting lever out of the way, engage the topmost tooth possible on the starwheel with a brake adjusting spoon. Move the end of the adjusting spoon upward to move the adjusting screw starwheel downward and contract the adjusting screw. Back off the adjusting screw starwheel until the wheel spins freely with the minimum of drag. Keep track of the number of turns the starwheel is backed off.

6. Repeat this operation for the other side. When backing off the brakes on the other side, the adjusting lever must be backed off the same number of turns to prevent side-to-side brake pull.

7. Repeat this operation on the other set of brakes (front or rear).

8. When all four brakes are adjusted, make several stops, while backing the car, to equalize all of the wheels.

9. Road-test the car.

WHEEL CYLINDER REMOVAL AND INSTALLATION

1. Remove the brake shoes.

2. On rear brakes, loosen the brake line on the rear of the cylinder but do not pull the line away from the cylinder or it may bend.

3. On front brakes, disconnect the metal brake line from the rubber brake hose where they join in the wheel well. Pull off the horseshoe clip that attaches the rubber brake hose to the underbody of the car. Loosen the hose at the cylinder, then turn the whole brake hose to remove it from the wheel cylinder.

4. Remove the bolts and lockwashers which attach the wheel cylinder to the backing plate and remove the cylinder.

5. Position the new wheel cylinder on the backing plate and install the cylinder attaching bolts and lockwashers.

6. Attach the metal brake line or rubber hose by reversing the procedure given in Steps 2 or 3.

7. Install the brakes.

WHEEL CYLINDER OVERHAUL

Since the travel of the pistons in the wheel cylinder changes when new brake shoes are installed, it is possible for previously good wheel cylinders to start leaking after new brakes are installed. Therefore, to save yourself the expense of having to replace new brakes which become saturated with brake fluid and the aggravation of having to take everything apart again, it is strongly recommended that wheel cylinders be rebuilt every time new brake shoes are installed. This is especially true on high-mileage cars.

1. Remove the brakes.

2. Place a bucket or old newspaper under the brake backing plate to catch the brake fluid that will run out of the wheel cylinder.

3. Remove the boots from the ends of the wheel cylinders.

4. Push one piston toward the center of the cylinder to force the opposite piston and cup out the other end of the cylinder. Reach in the open end of the cylinder and push the spring, cup, and piston out of the cylinder.

5. Remove the bleeder screw from the rear of the cylinder on the back of the backing plate.

6. Inspect the inside of the wheel cylin-

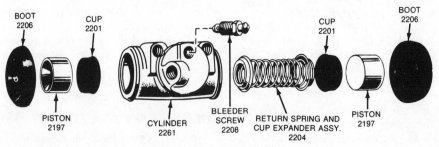

Drum brake wheel cylinder disassembled

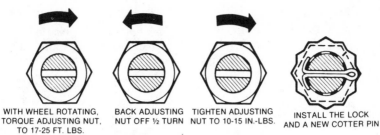

WITH WHEEL ROTATING, TORQUE ADJUSTING NUT, TO 17-25 FT. LBS.

BACK ADJUSTING NUT OFF ½ TURN

TIGHTEN ADJUSTING NUT TO 10-15 IN.-LBS.

INSTALL THE LOCK AND A NEW COTTER PIN

Front wheel bearing adjustment

der. If it is scored in any way, the cylinder must be honed with a wheel cylinder hone or fine emery paper, and finished with crocus cloth if emery paper is used. If the inside of the cylinder is excessively worn, the cylinder will have to be replaced, as only 0.003 in. of material can be removed from the cylinder walls. When honing or cleaning the wheel cylinders, keep a small amount of brake fluid in the cylinder to serve as a lubricant.

7. Clean any foreign matter from the pistons. The sides of the pistons must be smooth for the wheel cylinders to operate properly.

8. Clean the cylinder bore with alcohol and a lint-free rag. Pull the rag through the bore several times to remove all foreign matter and dry the cylinder.

9. Install the bleeder screw and the return spring in the cylinder.

10. Coat new cylinder cups with new brake fluid and install them in the cylinder. Make sure that they are square in the bore or they will leak.

11. Install the pistons in the cylinder after coating them with new brake fluid.

12. Coat the insides of the boots with new brake fluid and install them on the cylinder. Install the brakes.

Front Wheel Bearings
ADJUSTMENT

The front wheels each rotate on a set of opposed, tapered roller bearings as shown in the accompanying illustration. The grease retainer at the inside of the hub prevents lubricant from leaking into the brake drum.

Adjustment of the wheel bearings is accomplished as follows: Lift the car so that the wheel and tire are clear of the ground, then remove the grease cap and remove excess grease from the end of the spindle. Remove the cotter pin and nut lock shown in the illustration.

NOTE: *In order to prevent the brake pads from stopping the hub and rotor from seating properly, rock the rotor in and out to push the brake pads back into their bores.*

Rotate the wheel, hub, and drum assembly while tightening the adjusting nut to 17–25 ft. lbs. in order to seat the bearings. Back off the adjusting nut one half turn, then retighten the adjusting nut to 10–15 in. lbs. (*inch-pounds*). Locate the nut lock on the adjusting nut so that the castellations on the lock are lined up with the cotter pin hole in the spindle. Install a new cotter pin, bending the ends of the cotter pin around the castellated flange

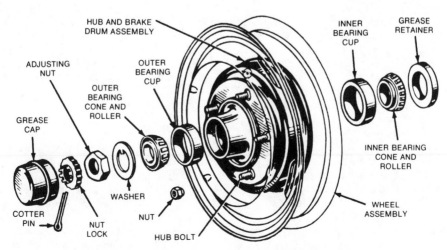

Front hub, wheel bearings and grease retainer

of the nut lock. Check the front wheel for proper rotation, then install the grease cap. If the wheel still does not rotate properly, inspect and clean or replace the wheel bearings and cups.

REMOVAL, REPACKING, AND INSTALLATION

Drum Brakes

The procedure for cleaning, repacking and adjusting front wheel bearings on vehicles equipped with self-adjusting drum brakes is as follows:

1. Taking proper safety precautions, raise the car until the wheel and tire clear the floor. Install jackstands under the lower control arms.

2. Remove the wheel cover. Remove the grease cap from the hub. Then remove the cotter pin, nut lock, adjusting nut, and flat washer from the spindle. Remove the outer bearing cone and roller assembly.

3. Pull the wheel, hub and drum assembly off the spindle. When encountering a brake drum which will not come off, disengage the adjusting lever from the adjusting screw by inserting a narrow pry bar through the adjusting hole in the carrier plate. While the lever is disengaged, back off the adjusting screw with a brake adjusting tool. The self-adjusting mechanism will not function properly if the adjusting screw is burred, chipped, or otherwise damaged in the process, so exercise extreme care.

4. Remove the grease retainer and the inner bearing cone and roller assembly from the hub.

5. Clean all grease off from the inner and outer bearing cups with solvent. Inspect the cups for pits, scratches, or excessive wear. If the cups are damaged, remove them with a drift.

6. Clean the inner and outer cone and roller assemblies with solvent and shake them dry. If the cone and roller assemblies show excessive wear or damage, replace them with the bearing cups as a unit.

7. If the new grease retainer is of leather, soak it in light engine oil for 30 minutes, prior to installation. Wipe any excess from the metal portion of the retainer. Clean the spindle and the inside of the hub with solvent to thoroughly remove all old grease.

8. Covering the spindle with a clean cloth, brush all loose dirt and dust from the brake assembly. Remove the cloth carefully so as to not get dirt on the spindle.

9. If the inner and/or outer bearing cups were removed, install the replacement cups on the hub. Be sure that the cups seat properly in the hub.

10. It is imperative that all old grease be removed from the bearings and surrounding surfaces before repacking. The new lithium-base grease is not compatible with the sodium base grease used in the past.

11. Pack the inside of the hub with wheel bearing grease. Add grease to the hub until it is flush with the inside diameter of both bearing cups. Work as much grease as possible between the rollers and cages in the cone and roller assemblies. Lubricate the cone surfaces with grease.

12. Position the inner bearing cone and roller assembly in the inner cup. If a leather grease retainer has soaked for 30 minutes, wipe all excess from the metal portion of the retainer and install. Other grease retainers require a light film of grease on the lips before installation. Using a wooden block to evenly distribute the blow of a hammer, install the retainer. Make sure that the retainer is properly seated.

13. Install the wheel, hub, and drum assembly on the wheel spindle. To prevent damage to the grease retainer and spindle threads, keep the hub centered on the spindle.

14. Install the outer bearing cone and roller assembly and the flat washer on the spindle. Install the adjusting nut.

15. Adjust the wheel bearings by tightening the adjusting nut to 17–25 ft. lbs. with the wheel rotating to seat the bearing. Then back off the adjusting nut ½ turn. Retighten the adjusting nut to 10–15 in. lbs. Install the locknut so that the castellations are aligned with the cotter pin hole. Install the cotter pin. Bend the ends of the cotter pin around the castellations of the locknut to prevent interference with the radio static collector in the grease cap. Install the grease cap.

16. Remove the adjusting hole cover from the carrier plate and, from the carrier plate side, turn the adjusting screw starwheel upward with a brake adjusting tool. Expand the brake shoes until a slight drag is felt with the drum rotating. Replace the adjusting hole cover.

17. Install the wheel cover.

Disc Brakes

1. Raise the front of the car and support it with jack stands.

2. Remove the front wheels.

NOTE: *In order to remove the rotor, the caliper and anchor plate must be removed from the car.*

3. Loosen, but do not remove, the upper anchor plate attaching bolt with a ¾ in. socket.

4. Using a ⅝ in. socket, remove the lower anchor plate attaching bolt.

NOTE: *When the caliper is removed from the car it must be wired out of the way of the rotor. Also, the brake pads will fall out of the caliper if they are not held in place when the caliper is removed. You will have to insert a small piece of wood or a folded piece of heavy cardboard between the shoes to hold them in place. Have a piece of wire and a piece of wood handy before you start the next step.*

5. Hold the caliper in place and remove the upper anchor plate attaching bolt.

6. Slide the caliper and anchor plate assembly off the rotor, inserting the block of wood between the brake pads as they become visible above the rotor.

7. When the anchor plate is clear of the rotor, wire it out of the way.

8. Remove the dust cap from the rotor hub by either prying it off with a screwdriver or pulling it off with a pair of channel-lock pliers.

9. Remove the cotter pin and the nut lock from the spindle.

10. Loosen the bearing adjusting nut until it is at the end of the spindle.

11. Grasp the rotor with a rag and pull it outward, push it inward.

12. Remove the adjusting nut and the outer bearing.

13. Remove the rotor from the spindle.

14. Place the rotor and tire on a clean, paper-covered surface with the wheel studs facing upward.

15. Working through the hole in the center of the wheel hub, tap the grease seal out of the rear of the hub with a screwdriver or drift.

NOTE: *Be careful not to damage the inner bearing while knocking out the grease seal.*

16. Remove the grease and bearing from under the rotor, and discard the grease seal.

17. Clean the inner and outer bearings and the wheel hub with a suitable solvent. Remove all old grease.

18. Thoroughly dry and wipe clean all components.

19. Clean all old grease from the spindle on the car.

20. Carefully check the bearings for any sign of scoring or other damage. If the roller bearings or bearing cages are damaged, the bearing and the corresponding bearing cup in the rotor hub must be replaced. The bearing cups must be driven out of the rotor hub to be removed. The outer bearing cup is driven out of the front of the rotor from the rear and vice versa for the inner bearing cup.

21. Whether you are reinstalling the old bearings or installing new ones, the bearings must be packed with wheel bearing grease. To do this, place a glob of grease in your left palm, then, holding one of the bearings in your right

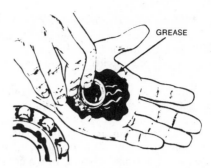

Packing the front wheel bearings

hand, drag the edge of the bearing heavily through the grease. This must be done to work as much grease as possible through the roller bearings and cage. Turn the bearing and continue to pull it through the grease until the grease is packed between the bearings and the cage all the way around the circumference of the bearing. Repeat this operation until all of the bearings are packed with grease.

22. Pack the inside of the rotor hub with a moderate amount of grease, between the bearing cups. Do not overload the hub with grease.

23. Apply a small amount of grease to the spindle.

24. Place the rotor, face down, on a protected surface and install the inner bearing.

25. Coat the lip of a new grease seal with a small amount of grease and position it on the rotor.

26. Place a block of wood on top of the grease seal and tap on the block with a hammer to install the seal. Turn the block of wood to different positions to seat it squarely in the hub.

27. Position the rotor on the spindle.

28. Install the outer bearing and washer on the spindle, inside the rotor hub.

29. Install the bearing adjusting nut and tighten it to 17–25 ft. lbs. while spinning the rotor. This will seat the bearing.

30. Back off the adjusting nut one half turn.

31. Tighten the adjusting nut to 10–15 in. lbs.

32. Install the nut lock on the adjusting nut so two of the slots align with the holes in the spindle.

33. Install a new cotter pin and bend the ends back so that they will not interfere with the dust cap.

34. Install the dust cap.

35. Install the front tires.

DISC BRAKES

Front disc brakes have been available as an option on full size models since the mid 1960s.

From 1968 to 1972 floating caliper front disc brakes were available on all models. Starting in 1973, sliding caliper front discs were made standard equipment with vacuum power assist.

Beginning with 1976 models, a 4-wheel disc brake system utilizing sliding caliper rear disc brakes is standard equipment on all station wagons and police interceptor packages, and optional on all sedans. When equipped with the 4-wheel disc brake system, brake assist is provided by a hydraulically-operated servo system known as Hydro-Boost, in lieu of the traditional vacuum-assist type. In 1979, the four wheel disc brake option was discontinued.

The rear sliding caliper assembly is similar to the one used on the front, except for the parking brake mechanism and a bigger anti-rattle spring. The parking brake lever on the caliper is cable-operated by depressing (or releasing), the parking brake pedal under the dash panel.

When the pedal is depressed, the cable rotates the parking brake lever (on the back of the caliper) and the operating shaft (inside the caliper). Three steel balls, which are located in pockets on the opposing heads of the shaft and thrust screw, roll between ramps formed in the pockets. The motion of the balls forces the thrust screw away from the shaft which, in turn, forces the piston and pad assembly against the disc to create braking action.

An automatic adjuster in the piston compensates for pad wear by moving the thrust screw.

BRAKE PAD REPLACEMENT

Floating Caliper Front Disc Brakes 1968–72

1. Raise the vehicle on a hoist and remove the front wheels.
2. Remove the lockwires from the two mounting bolts and lift the caliper away from the disc.
3. Remove the retaining clips with a pry bar and slide the outboard pad and retaining pins out of the caliper. Remove the inboard pad.
4. Slide the new inboard pad into the caliper so that the tabs are between the retaining clips and anchor plate and the backing plate lies flush against the piston.
5. Insert the outboard pad retaining pins into the outboard pad and position them in the caliper.
NOTE: *Stabilizer, insulator, pad clips, and pins should always be replaced when the disc pads are replaced.*
6. Hold the retaining pins in place (one at

a time) with a short drift pin or dowel and install the retaining clips.
7. Slide the caliper assembly over the disc and align the mounting bolt holes.
8. Install the lower bolt finger-tight. Install the upper bolt and torque to specification. Torque the lower bolt to specification. Safety-wire both bolts.
CAUTION: *Do not deviate from this procedure. The alignment of the anchor plate depends on the proper sequence of bolt installation.*
9. Check the brake fluid level and pump and brake pedal to seat the lining against the disc. Replace the wheels and rod-test the car.

Sliding Caliper Front Disc Brakes 1973–78

1. Remove approximately ⅔ of the fluid from the rear reservoir of the tandem master cylinder. Raise the vehicle, taking proper safety precautions.
2. Remove the wheel and tire assembly.
3. Remove the key retaining screw from the caliper retaining key.
4. Slide the retaining key and support spring either inward or outward from the anchor plate. To remove the key and spring, a hammer and drift may be used, taking care not to damage the key in the process.
5. Lift the caliper assembly away from the anchor plate by pushing the caliper downward against the anchor plate and rotating the upper end upward out of the anchor plate. Be careful not to stretch or twist the flexible brake hose.
6. Remove the inner shoe and lining assembly from the anchor plate. The inner shoe

CALIPER SUPPORT SPRING AND KEY

ANCHOR PLATE

Removing sliding caliper support spring and retaining key

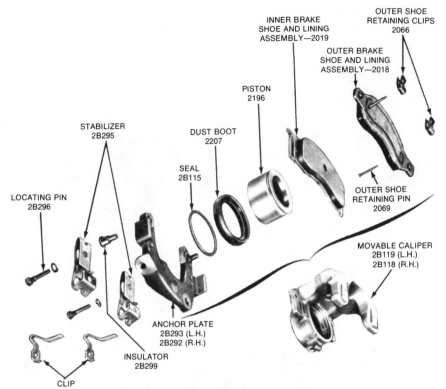

INNER BRAKE
SHOE AND LINING
ASSEMBLY—2019

OUTER SHOE
RETAINING CLIPS
2066

OUTER BRAKE
SHOE AND LINING
ASSEMBLY—2018

PISTON
2196

STABILIZER
2B295

DUST BOOT
2207

SEAL
2B115

LOCATING PIN
2B296

OUTER SHOE
RETAINING PIN
2069

MOVABLE CALIPER
2B119 (L.H.)
2B118 (R.H.)

ANCHOR PLATE
2B293 (L.H.)
2B292 (R.H.)

INSULATOR
2B299

CLIP

Floating caliper disc brake caliper disassembled

antirattle clip may become displaced at this time and should be repositioned on the anchor plate. Lightly tap on the outer shoe and lining assembly to free it from the caliper.

7. Clean the caliper, anchor plate, and disc assemblies, and inspect them for brake fluid leakage, excessive wear or signs of damage. Replace the pads, if either of them are worn to within 1/32 in. of the rivet heads.

8. To install new pads, use a 4 in. C-clamp and a block of wood 1¾ in. x 1 in. and approximately ¾ in. thick to seat the caliper hydraulic piston in its bore. This must be done in order to provide clearance for the caliper to fit over the rotor when the new linings are installed.

9. At this point, the antirattle clip should be in its place on the lower inner brake shoe support of the anchor plate with the pigtail of the clip toward the inside of the anchor plate. Position the inner brake shoe and lining assembly on the anchor plate with the pad toward the disc.

10. Install the outer brake shoe with the lower flange ends against the caliper leg abutments and the brake shoe upper flanges over the shoulders on the caliper legs. The shoe is installed correctly when its flanges fit snugly against the machined surfaces of the shoulder.

11. Remove the C-clamp used to seat the

caliper piston in its bore. The piston will remain seated.

12. Position the caliper housing lower V-groove on the anchor plate lower abutment surface.

13. Pivot the caliper housing upward toward the disc until the outer edge of the piston dust boot is about ¼ in. from the upper edge of the inboard pad.

14. In order to prevent pinching of the dust boot between the piston and the inboard pad during installation of the caliper, place a clean piece of thin cardboard between the inboard pad and the lower half of the piston dust boot.

15. Rotate the caliper housing toward the disc until a slight resistance is felt. At this point, pull the cardboard downward toward the disc centerline while rotating the caliper over the disc. Then remove the cardboard and complete the rotation of the caliper down over the disc.

16. Slide the caliper up against the upper abutment surfaces of the anchor plate and center the caliper over the lower anchor plate abutment.

17. Position the caliper support spring and key in the key slot and slide them into the opening between the lower end of the caliper and the lower anchor plate abutment until the key semicircular slot is centered over the re-

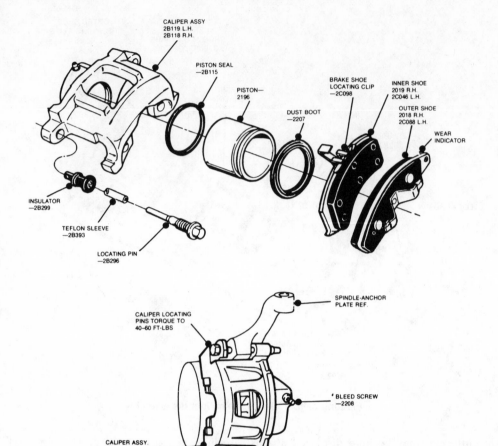

CALIPER ASSY
2B119 L.H.
2B118 R.H.

PISTON SEAL
—2B115

PISTON—
2196

DUST BOOT
—2207

BRAKE SHOE
LOCATING CLIP
—2C098

INNER SHOE
2019 R.H.
2C046 L.H.

OUTER SHOE
2018 R.H.
2C088 L.H.

WEAR
INDICATOR

INSULATOR
—2B299

TEFLON SLEEVE
—2B393

LOCATING PIN
—2B296

SPINDLE-ANCHOR
PLATE REF.

CALIPER LOCATING
PINS TORQUE TO
40–60 FT-LBS

BLEED SCREW
—2208

CALIPER ASSY.
2B119 L.H.
2B118 R.H.

ROTOR—
1K002

OUTER SHOE AND LINING
2C088 L.H.
2018 R.H.

Typical front disc brakes from 1979

taining screw threaded hole in the anchor plate.

18. Install the key retaining screw and torque to 12–16 ft. lbs.

19. Check the fluid level in the master cylinder and fill as necessary. Install the reservoir cover. Depress the brake pedal several times to properly seat the caliper and pads. Check for leakage around the caliper and flexible brake hose.

20. Install the wheel and tire assembly and torque the nuts to 70–115 ft. lbs. Install the wheel cover.

21. Lower the car. Make sure that you obtain a firm brake pedal and then road test the car for proper brake operation.

From 1979

1. Remove brake fluid from the fluid reservoir until it is half full.

2. Jack up the car and support it with safety

stands. Remove the wheel and tire assembly.

3. Remove the caliper locating pins.

4. Lift the caliper assembly from the rotor and remove the brake pads.

5. Remove and discard the plastic sleeves that are located inside the caliper locating pin insulators. These parts *must not* be reused. Also remove and discard the locating insulators. Do not reuse these parts.

6. To install new pads, use a 4 inch C-clamp and a block of wood to seat the caliper piston in its bore.

7. Install new insulators and plastic sleeves in the caliper housing.

8. Install new inner and outer brake pads. The outer pads are marked for right hand or left hand installation. Make sure they are installed correctly.

9. Reinstall the caliper. Torque the locating pins to 40–60 ft. lbs. Reinstall the wheel and tire assembly and lower the car.

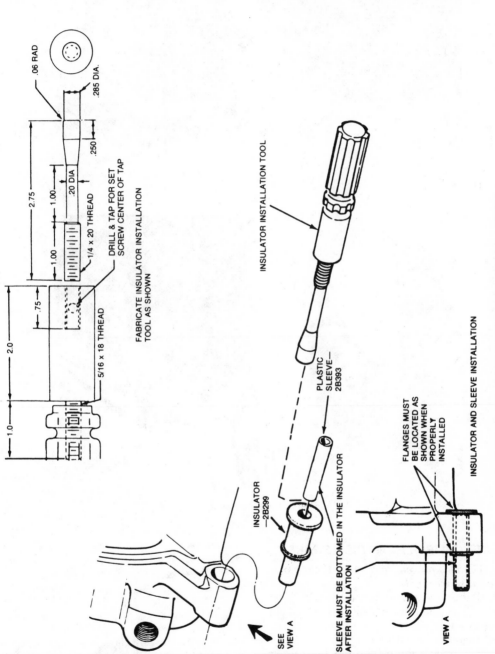

.06 RAD

.285 DIA.

.250

.20 DIA

2.75

1.00

1.00

1/4 x 20 THREAD

DRILL & TAP FOR SET
SCREW CENTER OF TAP

FABRICATE INSULATOR INSTALLATION
TOOL AS SHOWN

.75

2.0

1.0

5/16 x 18 THREAD

INSULATOR INSTALLATION TOOL

PLASTIC
SLEEVE—
2B393

INSULATOR
—2B299

SEE
VIEW A

SLEEVE MUST BE BOTTOMED IN THE INSULATOR
AFTER INSTALLATION

FLANGES MUST
BE LOCATED AS
SHOWN WHEN
PROPERLY
INSTALLED

INSULATOR AND SLEEVE INSTALLATION

VIEW A

Installing the insulator and sleeve (typical from 1979)

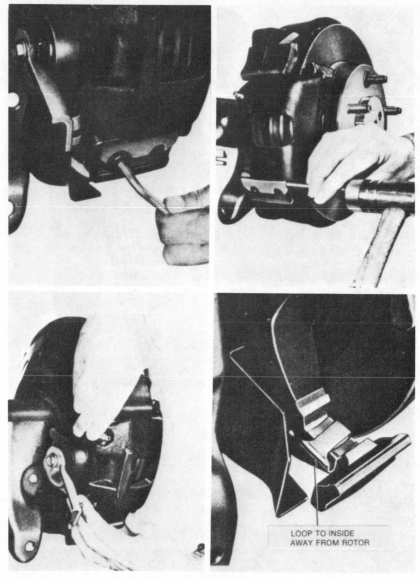

LOOP TO INSIDE
AWAY FROM ROTOR

Rear caliper removal

SLIDING CALIPER REAR DISC BRAKES

NOTE: *This procedure requires the use of a special service tool.*

1. Raise the car and support it with jackstands. Block the front wheels if they remain on the ground.

2. Remove the wheel and tire.

3. Disconnect the cable from the caliper parking brake lever. Be careful not to kink or cut the cable and return spring.

4. Unfasten the setscrew which secures the caliper key. Use a hammer and soft brass drift (if necessary) to slide the support spring and retaining key out of the anchor plate.

5. Push the caliper against the anchor plate

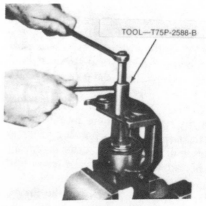

TOOL—T75P-2588-B

Bottoming the caliper piston

and rotate its upper end away from the plate. If a ridge of rust on the disc prevents caliper removal, scrape the rust away with a putty knife or similar blunt tool.

6. If the disc is rusted to the point that the caliper still can't be removed, loosen the caliper end retainer ½-turn, after removing the retaining screw and caliper parking brake lever. Also, be sure to matchmark the caliper housing and end retainer to ensure that the retainer is only given ½-turn.

CAUTION: *Turning the end retainer more than ½-turn could cause internal fluid leaks in the caliper, which would make caliper rebuilding necessary.*

7. Wire the caliper assembly out of the way to avoid stretching or kinking the brake hose.

8. Remove the inner pad assembly from the retaining clip. Tap lightly on the outer pad to free it from the caliper.

9. Mark the pads for proper installation if they are not going to be replaced. Used pads must be returned to the same side from which they were removed.

10. If the pad is worn to within ¹/₃₂ in. of any rivet head, replace all of the pads on both rear brakes. Do not replace just one pad or one set of pads; uneven braking will result.

NOTE: *Pad replacement requires the use of a special tool to bottom the piston in its bore.*

11. Inspect the caliper for leaks. Clean any rust off the caliper and anchor plate sliding surfaces or inner brake pad abutment surfaces on the anchor plate.

Installation is as follows:

1. If the end retainer was loosened in order to remove the caliper, perform the following:

   a. Install the caliper on the anchor plate and secure it with the key, but do not install the pads.

   b. Tighten the retainer end to 75–95 ft. lbs.

   c. Install the caliper parking brake lever

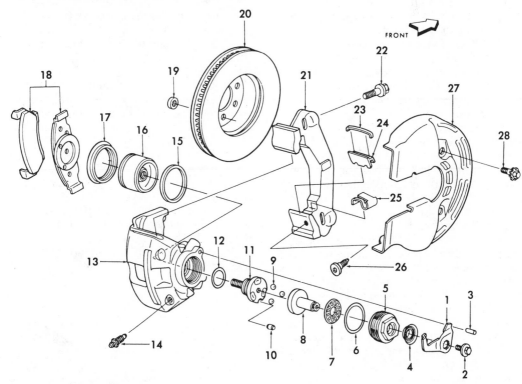

1. Parking brake actuating lever	11. Parking brake thrust screw	21. Anchor plate
2. Lever retaining bolt	12. Seal	22. Retaining bolt
3. Pin	13. Caliper housing	23. Caliper support spring
4. Retainer seal	14. Bleeder screw	24. Caliper retaining key
5. Parking brake end retainer	15. Piston seal	25. Anti-rattle clip
6. Seal	16. Piston and adjuster assembly	26. Retaining screw
7. Thrust bearing	17. Boot	27. Anti-splash shield
8. Parking brake operating shaft	18. Brake pad assemblies	28. Retaining bolt
9. Ball bearing	19. Grommet	
10. Pin	20. Disc rotor	

Rear sliding caliper assembly

with the arm pointing rearward and down. This allows the cable to pass under the axle.

d. Tighten the lever retaining screw to 16–22 ft. lbs. Check for free rotation of the lever.

e. Remove the caliper.

2. The following special steps must be performed if new pads are being installed:

a. Remove the disc and install the caliper less the pads. Use only the key to retain the caliper.

b. Seat the special tool firmly against the piston by holding the shaft rotating the tool handle.

c. Loosen the handle ¼-turn. Hold the handle and rotate the tool shaft clockwise until the caliper piston bottoms (it will continue to turn after it bottoms).

d. Rotate the handle until the piston is firmly seated.

e. Remove the caliper and install the disc.

3. Confirm that the brake pad antirattle clip is correctly positioned in the lower inner brake pad support, the clip loop should face the inside of the anchor plate.

4. Fit the inner pad assembly on the anchor plate, with the lining facing the disc.

5. Install the outer brake pad with its lower flanges against the caliper leg abutments and its upper flanges against the machined shoulder surfaces.

6. Lubricate the caliper and anchor plate sliding surfaces with special brake lubricant. Keep the lubricant off the pad and disc.

7. Position the caliper housing lower groove against the anchor plate lower abutment surfaces. Rotate the housing until it is completely over the disc. Be careful not to damage the dust boot.

8. Slide the caliper outward until the inner pad is seated firmly against the disc. Measure the outer pad-to-disc clearance. It should be ¹/₁₆ in. or less. If it is more, adjust the piston *outward* with the special tool (See step 2). Each ¼-turn of the piston is about ¹/₁₆ in. of piston movement.

CAUTION: *If piston clearance is more than ¹/₁₆ in., the adjuster may pull out of the piston when the service brakes are applied, causing adjuster failure.*

9. Center the caliper over the lower anchor plate abutment, while holding it over the upper abutment.

10. Install the retaining spring and key in the keyway and slide them into the opening at the lower end of the caliper and anchor plate abutment. Center the semi-circular slot in the key over the anchor plate setscrew hole. Tighten the setscrew to 12–16 ft. lbs.

11. Attach the parking brake cable to the lower lever end.

12. If the caliper was completely removed (lines disconnected), bleed the hydraulic system. Run the engine and lightly pump the service brake pedal 40 times; allow one second between brake applications. Check the parking brake for too much travel or too light operating effort. Repeat the pumping and adjust the cable if necessary.

13. Install the wheel and tire, remove the jackstand and lower the car.

14. Make sure that the service brake pedal feels firm and then road test the car. Check parking brake operation.

CALIPER REMOVAL, OVERHAUL, AND INSTALLATION

Floating Front Caliper—1968–72

1. Raise the vehicle on a hoist and remove the front wheels.

2. Disconnect and plug the brake line.

3. Remove the lockwires from the two caliper mounting bolts and remove the bolt. Lift the caliper off the disc.

4. Remove and discard the locating pin insulators. Replace all rubber parts at reassembly.

5. Remove the retaining clips with a screwdriver and slide the outboard pad and retaining pins out of the caliper. Remove the inboard pad. Loosen the bleed screw and drain the brake fluid.

6. Remove the two small bolts and caliper stabilizers.

7. Remove the inboard pad retaining clips and bolts.

8. Clean and inspect all parts, and reinstall on the anchor plate. Do not tighten the stabilizer bolts at this time.

9. Remove the piston by applying compressed air to the fluid inlet hole. Use care to

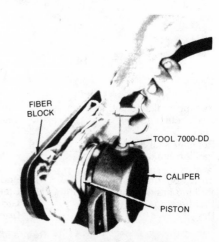

FIBER BLOCK

TOOL 7000-DD

CALIPER

PISTON

Removing the piston from the caliper

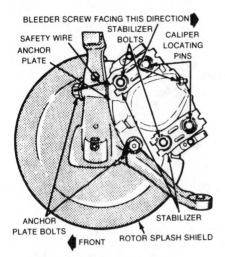

BLEEDER SCREW FACING THIS DIRECTION
STABILIZER
BOLTS
CALIPER
LOCATING
PINS
SAFETY WIRE
ANCHOR
PLATE
ANCHOR
PLATE BOLTS
STABILIZER
FRONT
ROTOR SPLASH SHIELD

Floating caliper installed—rear view

prevent the piston from popping out of control.

CAUTION: *Do not attempt to catch the piston with the hand. Use folded towels to cushion it.*

10. Remove the piston boot. Inspect the piston for scoring, pitting, or corrosion. The piston must be replaced if there is any visible damage or wear.

11. Remove the piston seal from the cylinder bore. *Do not use any metal tools for this operation.*

12. Clean the caliper with fresh brake fluid. Inspect the cylinder bore for damage or wear. Light defects can be removed by rotating crocus cloth around the bore. (Do not use any other type of abrasive.)

13. Lubricate all new rubber parts in brake fluid. Install the piston seal in the cylinder groove. Install the boot into its piston groove.

14. Install the piston, open end out, into the bore while working the boot around the outside of the piston. Make sure that the boot lip is seated in the piston groove.

15. Slide the anchor plate assembly onto the caliper housing and reinstall the locating pins. Tighten the pins to specification. Tighten the stabilizer anchor plate bolts.

16. Slide the inboard pad into the caliper so that the tabs are between the retaining clips and anchor plate and the backing plate lies flush against the piston.

17. Insert the outboard pad retaining pins into the outboard pad and position them in the caliper.

18. Hold the retaining pins in place (one at a time) with a short drift pin or dowel and install the retaining clips.

19. Slide the caliper assembly over the disc and align the mounting bolt holes.

20. Install the lower bolt finger-tight. In-

stall the upper bolt and torque to specification. Torque the lower bolt to specification. Safety-wire both bolts.

CAUTION: *Do not deviate from this procedure. The alignment of the anchor plate depends on the proper sequence of bolt installation.*

21. Connect the brake line and bleed the brakes (see "Hydraulic System Bleeding").

Sliding Front Caliper—1973–78

1. Raise the vehicle and place jackstands underneath.

2. Remove the wheel and tire assembly.

3. Disconnect the flexible brake hose from the caliper. To disconnect the hose, loosen the tube fitting which connects the end of the hose to the brake tube at its bracket on the frame. Remove the horseshoe clip from the hose and bracket, disengage the hose, and plug the end. Then unscrew the entire hose assembly from the caliper.

4. Remove the key retaining screw from the caliper retaining key.

5. Slide the retaining key and support spring either inward or outward from the anchor plate. To remove the key and spring, a hammer and drift may be used, taking care not to damage the key in the process.

6. Lift the caliper assembly away from the anchor plate by pushing the caliper downward against the anchor plate and rotating the upper end upward out of the anchor plate.

7. Remove the piston by applying compressed air to the fluid inlet port with a rubber-tipped nozzle. Place a towel or thick cloth over the piston before applying air pressure to prevent damage to the piston. If the piston is seized in the bore and cannot be forced from the caliper, lightly tap around the outside of the caliper while applying air pressure.

CAUTION: *Do not attempt to catch the piston with your hand.*

8. Remove the dust boot from the caliper assembly.

9. Remove the piston seal from the cylinder and discard it.

10. Clean all metal parts with isopropyl alcohol or a suitable non-petroleum solvent and dry them with compressed air. Be sure that there is no foreign material in the bore or component parts. Inspect the piston and bore for excessive wear or damage. Replace the piston if it is pitted, scored, or if the chrome plating is wearing off.

11. Lubricate all new rubber parts in brake fluid. Install the piston seal in the cylinder groove, being careful not to twist it. Install the dust boot by setting the flange squarely in the outer groove of the bore.

12. Coat the piston with brake fluid and in-

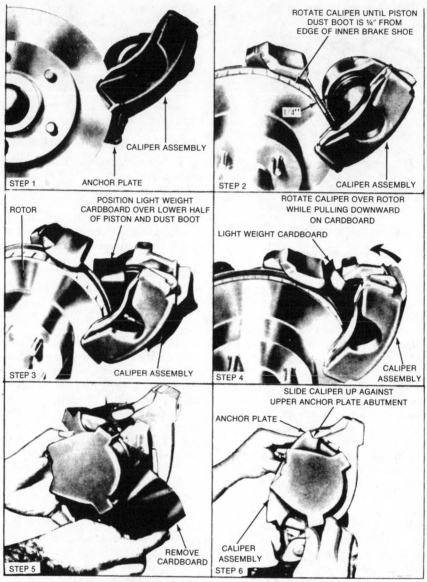

Installing sliding front caliper assembly

stall it in the bore. Work the dust boot around the outside of the piston, making sure that the boot lip is seated in the piston groove.

13. Install the caliper as outlined in Steps 12–18 in the sliding caliper "Shoe and Lining Replacement" procedure.

14. Thread the flexible brake hose and gasket onto the caliper fitting. Torque the fitting to 12–20 ft. lbs. Place the upper end of the flexible brake hose in its bracket and install the horseshoe clip. Remove the plug from the brake tube and connect the tube to the hose. Torque the tube fitting nut to 10–15 ft. lbs.

15. Bleed the brake system as outlined in the "Hydraulic System Bleeding" section.

16. Check the fluid level in the master cylinder and fill as necessary. Install the reservoir cover. Depress the brake pedal several times to properly seat the caliper and shoes. Check for leakage around the caliper and the flexible brake hose.

17. Install the wheel and tire assembly and torque the nuts to 70–115 ft. lbs. Install the wheel cover.

18. Lower the car. Make sure that you obtain a firm brake pedal and then road test the car for proper brake operation.

From 1979

1. Raise the car in the air and support it with safety stands.

2. Remove the wheel and tire assembly.

3. Disconnect the flexible brake hose from the caliper.

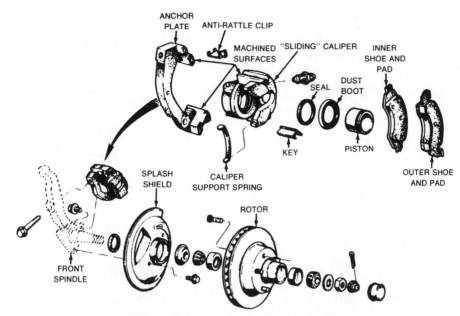

Sliding caliper front disc brake disassembled

4. Remove the caliper locating pins. Mark the left and right calipers before removal.

5. Lift the calipers from the anchor plates.

6. Installation is the reverse of removal. Torque the caliper locating pins to 40–60 ft. lbs. Torque the brake hose fitting to 20–30 ft. lbs.

NOTE: *When the hose is correctly torqued, there should be one or two fitting threads still showing at the caliper. Don't attempt to force the hose fitting flush with the caliper.*

7. Bleed the brakes.

Sliding Rear Caliper

1. Raise the car and install jackstands beneath the frame. Block the front wheels if they remain on the ground.

2. Remove the wheel and tire.

3. Disconnect and plug the rear brake pipe fitting from the hose end at the frame bracket. Unfasten the horseshoe clip from the hose fitting and separate the hose from the bracket. Unscrew the hose end fitting from the caliper.

4. Follow Steps 3–6 under "Brake Pad Removal" for rear disc brake 1976 cars.

5. Remove the caliper assembly from the car.

6. Remove the retaining screw, parking brake lever, and caliper end retainer.

7. Pull out the operating shaft, thrust bearing, and balls from the caliper.

8. Using either a magnet or tweezers, extract the thrust screw anti-rotation pin.

9. Using a ¼-in. allen key, rotate the thrust screw counterclockwise to remove it.

10. Push the piston/adjuster assembly out of its bore from behind.

NOTE: *A special tool is available to do this. Use care not to scratch the bore or press on the piston adjuster can while removing the piston.*

11. Remove and discard the following:
   a. Piston seal
   b. Boot
   c. Thrust screw O-ring seal
   d. End retainer O-ring
   e. End retainer lip seal

12. Clean all metal parts in isopropyl alcohol. Dry them with compressed air. Be sure that no foreign material remains in the caliper.

13. Inspect the caliper bores. The thrust screw bore must be smooth and show no sign of pitting.

14. If the piston is pitted, scored, or the plating worn off, replace the piston/adjuster as an assembly. The adjuster can should not be loose, high, or damaged, if it is, replace the piston/adjuster assembly. If brake adjustment is incorrect, replace the piston/adjuster assembly.

NOTE: *The piston and the adjuster must be replaced as an assembly. No attempt to repair the adjuster should be made.*

15. If in doubt about adjuster operation; check it as follows:
   a. Install the thrust screw in the piston/adjuster.
   b. Pull the two pieces apart about ¼ in. and release them.
   c. When the pieces are pulled apart, the

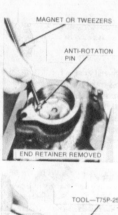

REMOVING ANTI-ROTATION PIN

END RETAINER REMOVED

REMOVING THRUST SCREW

PUSHING OUT PISTON

Disassembling rear brake caliper

brass drive ring should remain stationary, causing the nut to turn.

d. When the pieces are released, the nut should remain stationary and the drive ring rotate.

e. Replace the piston/adjuster if it fails to operate in this manner.

16. Inspect all bearing, sliding, rotating and rolling surfaces for wear, pitting or brinnelling. Replace any parts necessary. A polished appearance on ball paths or bearing surfaces is OK, as long as there is no sign of wear into the surface.

Assembly is as follows:

1. Coat a new piston seal with clean brake fluid. Seat the seal in the groove of the bore. Be sure it is not twisted.

2. Seat the flange of a new dust boot squarely in the caliper bore outer groove.

3. Coat the piston/adjuster assembly with clean brake fluid. Spread the dust boot over the piston and install the piston. Seat the dust boot in the piston/adjuster groove.

4. Lay the caliper assembly (rear of bore up) in a soft-jawed vise. Do not tighten the vise; housing distortion will result.

5. Fill the piston/adjuster assembly up to the bottom edge of thrust screw bore with clean brake fluid.

6. Install a new O-ring in the thrust screw groove, after coating it with clean brake fluid. Use a ¼ in. allen key to install the thrust screw in the piston adjuster assembly, until its top surface is flush with the bottom of the threaded bore. Align the notches on the thrust screw

with those on the caliper housing. Install the antirotation pin.

7. Install one ball in each of the three thrust screw pockets. Coat all components of the parking brake mechanism with a liberal amount of silicone grease.

8. Install the parking brake operating shaft over the balls. Coat the thrust bearing with silicone grease and fit it on the shaft.

9. Install a new lip seal and O-ring on the caliper end retainer. Coat both seals with a light film of silicone grease and install the end retainer on the caliper; tighten it to 75–90 ft. lbs. Hold the operating shaft so that it is securely seated against the parking brake mechanism during end retainer installation. If the lip seal is dislocated, reseat it.

10. Install the parking brake lever over its keyed spline, so that it points down and rearward. Torque the lever securing screw to 16–22 ft. lbs. Check the lever for freedom of movement.

11. Support the caliper and bottom the piston with the special tool as in Steps 2b through d of the "Disc Brake Pad Replacement" procedure.

12. Follow Steps 2–11 under "Brake Pad Installation" for rear disc brake 1976 cars.

13. Place a new gasket on the hose fitting and screw the fitting into the caliper port. Torque to 20–30 ft. lbs. Place the upper end of the flexible hose into its bracket and install the horseshoe clip. Do not twist or coil the brake hose. Keep the stripe on the hose straight. Unplug the pipe. Connect the hose

to the pipe and tighten the fitting to 10–15 ft. lbs.

14. Bleed the hydraulic system. Run the engine and lightly pump the brake pedal 40 times, allowing one second between pedal applications. Check the parking brake for excessive travel or too light an operating effort. Repeat the pumping and adjust the cable if necessary.

15. Install the wheel and tire. Remove the jackstands and lower the car.

16. Make sure that the brake pedal feels firm, and then road test the car. Recheck parking brake operation.

REAR DISC REMOVAL AND INSTALLATION

1. Remove the caliper assembly and wire it out of the way, unless it is to be serviced. Do not remove the anchor plate.

2. If corrosion makes identification difficult, mark the raised (not the braking) surface of the disc "RIGHT" or "LEFT" prior to removal.

3. Remove the securing nuts and take the disc off the axle shaft.

Installation is as follows:

1. If a new disc is being used, remove its protective coating with carburetor degreaser.

2. Identify the left and right discs before installation. The words "LEFT" and "RIGHT" are cast into the inner surface of the raised section of the disc. This is important, since the cooling vanes cast into the disc must face in the direction of forward rotation.

3. Install the two disc securing nuts.

4. Install the caliper.

Parking Brake
CABLE ADJUSTMENT
All Cars with Rear Drums Brakes

1. Fully release the parking brake.

2. If an axle-type hoist is available, place the transmission in Neutral and raise the vehicle. If the hoist is not available, block the front wheels, place a floor jack beneath the axle housing (following the instructions in Chapter 1), place transmission in Neutral, and raise the back of the car. It is important in all cases to raise the car by the rear axle so that the suspension does not become off-loaded thereby stretching the brake cables and giving a faulty adjustment.

NOTE: *Install jackstands beneath the frame when using a floor jack.*

3. Tighten the equalizer nut against the cable equalizer sufficiently to cause rear wheel brake drag when the wheel is turned by hand. Then, loosen the adjusting nut until the rear brakes just may be turned freely. There should be no brake drag when the cable is properly adjusted. Tighten the locknut, if so equipped, to 7–10 ft. lbs.

4. Remove the jackstands, if used, and lower the car. Check the operation of the parking brake.

Models with Rear Disc Brakes

1. Fully release the parking brake.

2. Place the transmission in Neutral. If it is necessary to raise the car to reach the adjusting nut and observe the parking brake levers, use an axle hoist or a floor jack positioned beneath the differential. This is necessary so that the rear axle remains at the curb attitude, not stretching the parking brake cables.

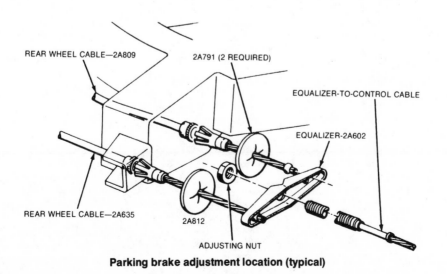

Parking brake adjustment location (typical)

Brake Specifications
All measurements given are (in.) unless noted

Year	Model	Lug Nut Torque (ft. lb.)	Master Cylinder Bore	Brake Disc		Brake Drum			Minimum Lining Thickness	
				Minimum Thickness	Maximum Run-Out	Diameter	Max Machine O/S	Max Wear Limit	Front	Rear
1968–71	All	70–115	1.000	.875	.0007	11.03	11.090	11.090	$2/32$	$2/32$
1972–75	All	70–115	1.000	1.180	.0007	11.03	11.090	11.090	$2/32$	$2/32$
1976–78	All	70–115	1.000	1.120 (front)	.003	11.03	11.090	11.090	$1/8$	$3/32$
				.895 (rear)	.003					
1979–83	All	70–115	1.000	.972	.003	11.030	11.090	11.090	$1/8$	$2/32$

NOTE: *Minimum lining thickness is as recommended by the manufacturer. Because of variations in state inspection regulations, the minimum allowable thickness may be different than recommended by the manufacturer.*

CAUTION: *If you are raising the rear of the car only, block the front wheels.*

3. Locate the adjusting nut beneath the car on the driver's side. While observing the parking brake actuating levers on the rear calipers, tighten the adjusting nut until the levers just begin to move. Then, loosen the nut sufficiently for the levers to fully return to the stop position.

4. Check the operation of the parking brake. Make sure that the actuating levers return to the stop position by attempting to pull them rearward. If the lever moves rearward, the cable adjustment is too tight, which will cause a dragging rear brake and consequent brake overheating and fade.

Troubleshooting
10

This section is designed to aid in the quick, accurate diagnosis of automotive problems. While automotive repairs can be made by many people, accurate troubleshooting is a rare skill for the amateur and professional alike.

In its simplest state, troubleshooting is an exercise in logic. It is essential to realize that an automobile is really composed of a series of systems. Some of these systems are interrelated; others are not. Automobiles operate within a framework of logical rules and physical laws, and the key to troubleshooting is a good understanding of all the automotive systems.

This section breaks the car or truck down into its component systems, allowing the problem to be isolated. The charts and diagnostic road maps list the most common problems and the most probable causes of trouble. Obviously it would be impossible to list every possible problem that could happen along with every possible cause, but it will locate MOST problems and eliminate a lot of unnecessary guesswork. The systematic format will locate problems within a given system, but, because many automotive systems are interrelated, the solution to your particular problem may be found in a number of systems on the car or truck.

USING THE TROUBLESHOOTING CHARTS

This book contains all of the specific information that the average do-it-yourself mechanic needs to repair and maintain his or her car or truck. The troubleshooting charts are designed to be used in conjunction with the specific procedures and information in the text. For instance, troubleshooting a point-type ignition system is fairly standard for all models, but you may be directed to the text to find procedures for troubleshooting an individual type of electronic ignition. You will also have to refer to the specification charts throughout the book for specifications applicable to your car or truck.

TOOLS AND EQUIPMENT

The tools illustrated in Chapter 1 (plus two more diagnostic pieces) will be adequate to troubleshoot most problems. The two other tools needed are a voltmeter and an ohmmeter. These can be purchased separately or in combination, known as a VOM meter.

In the event that other tools are required, they will be noted in the procedures.

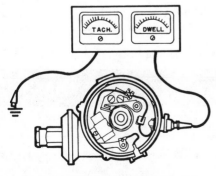

Tach-dwell hooked-up to distributor

Troubleshooting Engine Problems

See Chapters 2, 3, 4 for more information and service procedures.

Index to Systems

System	To Test	Group
Battery	Engine need not be running	1
Starting system	Engine need not be running	2
Primary electrical system	Engine need not be running	3
Secondary electrical system	Engine need not be running	4
Fuel system	Engine need not be running	5
Engine compression	Engine need not be running	6
Engine vacuum	Engine must be running	7
Secondary electrical system	Engine must be running	8
Valve train	Engine must be running	9
Exhaust system	Engine must be running	10
Cooling system	Engine must be running	11
Engine lubrication	Engine must be running	12

Index to Problems

Problem: Symptom	Begin at Specific Diagnosis, Number ____
Engine Won't Start:	
Starter doesn't turn	1.1, 2.1
Starter turns, engine doesn't	2.1
Starter turns engine very slowly	1.1, 2.4
Starter turns engine normally	3.1, 4.1
Starter turns engine very quickly	6.1
Engine fires intermittently	4.1
Engine fires consistently	5.1, 6.1
Engine Runs Poorly:	
Hard starting	3.1, 4.1, 5.1, 8.1
Rough idle	4.1, 5.1, 8.1
Stalling	3.1, 4.1, 5.1, 8.1
Engine dies at high speeds	4.1, 5.1
Hesitation (on acceleration from standing stop)	5.1, 8.1
Poor pickup	4.1, 5.1, 8.1
Lack of power	3.1, 4.1, 5.1, 8.1
Backfire through the carburetor	4.1, 8.1, 9.1
Backfire through the exhaust	4.1, 8.1, 9.1
Blue exhaust gases	6.1, 7.1
Black exhaust gases	5.1
Running on (after the ignition is shut off)	3.1, 8.1
Susceptible to moisture	4.1
Engine misfires under load	4.1, 7.1, 8.4, 9.1
Engine misfires at speed	4.1, 8.4
Engine misfires at idle	3.1, 4.1, 5.1, 7.1, 8.4

Sample Section

Test and Procedure	Results and Indications	Proceed to
4.1—Check for spark: Hold each spark plug wire approximately ¼″ from ground with gloves or a heavy, dry rag. Crank the engine and observe the spark.	→ If no spark is evident:	→ **4.2**
	→ If spark is good in some cases:	→ **4.3**
	→ If spark is good in all cases:	→ **4.6**

Specific Diagnosis

This section is arranged so that following each test, instructions are given to proceed to another, until a problem is diagnosed.

Section 1—Battery

Test and Procedure	Results and Indications	Proceed to
1.1—Inspect the battery visually for case condition (corrosion, cracks) and water level.	If case is cracked, replace battery:	**1.4**
	If the case is intact, remove corrosion with a solution of baking soda and water (**CAUTION:** *do not get the solution into the battery*), and fill with water:	**1.2**

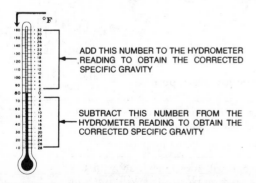

DIRT ON TOP OF BATTERY   PLUGGED VENT
CORROSION
LOOSE CABLE OR POSTS
CRACKS
LOW WATER LEVEL   **Inspect the battery case**

1.2—Check the battery cable connections: Insert a screwdriver between the battery post and the cable clamp. Turn the headlights on high beam, and observe them as the screwdriver is gently twisted to ensure good metal to metal contact.	If the lights brighten, remove and clean the clamp and post; coat the post with petroleum jelly, install and tighten the clamp:	**1.4**
	If no improvement is noted:	**1.3**

TESTING BATTERY CABLE CONNECTIONS USING A SCREWDRIVER

1.3—Test the state of charge of the battery using an individual cell tester or hydrometer.	If indicated, charge the battery. **NOTE:** *If no obvious reason exists for the low state of charge (i.e., battery age, prolonged storage), proceed to:*	**1.4**

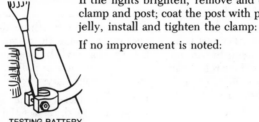

°F

ADD THIS NUMBER TO THE HYDROMETER READING TO OBTAIN THE CORRECTED SPECIFIC GRAVITY

SUBTRACT THIS NUMBER FROM THE HYDROMETER READING TO OBTAIN THE CORRECTED SPECIFIC GRAVITY

Specific Gravity (@ 80° F.)

Minimum	Battery Charge
1.260	100% Charged
1.230	75% Charged
1.200	50% Charged
1.170	25% Charged
1.140	Very Little Power Left
1.110	Completely Discharged

The effects of temperature on battery specific gravity (left) and amount of battery charge in relation to specific gravity (right)

1.4—Visually inspect battery cables for cracking, bad connection to ground, or bad connection to starter.	If necessary, tighten connections or replace the cables:	**2.1**

Section 2—Starting System
See Chapter 3 for service procedures

Test and Procedure	Results and Indications	Proceed to
Note: Tests in Group 2 are performed with coil high tension lead disconnected to prevent accidental starting.		
2.1—Test the starter motor and solenoid: Connect a jumper from the battery post of the solenoid (or relay) to the starter post of the solenoid (or relay).	If starter turns the engine normally:	2.2
	If the starter buzzes, or turns the engine very slowly:	2.4
	If no response, replace the solenoid (or relay).	3.1
	If the starter turns, but the engine doesn't, ensure that the flywheel ring gear is intact. If the gear is undamaged, replace the starter drive.	3.1
2.2—Determine whether ignition override switches are functioning properly (clutch start switch, neutral safety switch), by connecting a jumper across the switch(es), and turning the ignition switch to "start".	If starter operates, adjust or replace switch:	3.1
	If the starter doesn't operate:	2.3
2.3—Check the ignition switch "start" position: Connect a 12V test lamp or voltmeter between the starter post of the solenoid (or relay) and ground. Turn the ignition switch to the "start" position, and jiggle the key.	If the lamp doesn't light or the meter needle doesn't move when the switch is turned, check the ignition switch for loose connections, cracked insulation, or broken wires. Repair or replace as necessary:	3.1
	If the lamp flickers or needle moves when the key is jiggled, replace the ignition switch.	3.3

Checking the ignition switch "start" position

STARTER RELAY (IF EQUIPPED)

2.4—Remove and bench test the starter, according to specifications in the engine electrical section.	If the starter does not meet specifications, repair or replace as needed:	3.1
	If the starter is operating properly:	2.5
2.5—Determine whether the engine can turn freely: Remove the spark plugs, and check for water in the cylinders. Check for water on the dipstick, or oil in the radiator. Attempt to turn the engine using an 18″ flex drive and socket on the crankshaft pulley nut or bolt.	If the engine will turn freely only with the spark plugs out, and hydrostatic lock (water in the cylinders) is ruled out, check valve timing:	9.2
	If engine will not turn freely, and it is known that the clutch and transmission are free, the engine must be disassembled for further evaluation:	Chapter 3

Section 3—Primary Electrical System

Test and Procedure	Results and Indications	Proceed to
3.1—Check the ignition switch "on" position: Connect a jumper wire between the distributor side of the coil and ground, and a 12V test lamp between the switch side of the coil and ground. Remove the high tension lead from the coil. Turn the ignition switch on and jiggle the key.	If the lamp lights:	**3.2**
	If the lamp flickers when the key is jiggled, replace the ignition switch:	**3.3**
	If the lamp doesn't light, check for loose or open connections. If none are found, remove the ignition switch and check for continuity. If the switch is faulty, replace it:	**3.3**

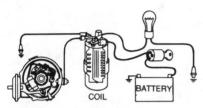

Checking the ignition switch "on" position

3.2—Check the ballast resistor or resistance wire for an open circuit, using an ohmmeter. See Chapter 3 for specific tests.	Replace the resistor or resistance wire if the resistance is zero. **NOTE:** *Some ignition systems have no ballast resistor.*	**3.3**

 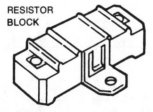

RESISTOR BLOCK

CALIBRATED RESISTANCE LEAD

Two types of resistors

3.3—On point-type ignition systems, visually inspect the breaker points for burning, pitting or excessive wear. Gray coloring of the point contact surfaces is normal. Rotate the crankshaft until the contact heel rests on a high point of the distributor cam and adjust the point gap to specifications. On electronic ignition models, remove the distributor cap and visually inspect the armature. Ensure that the armature pin is in place, and that the armature is on tight and rotates when the engine is cranked. Make sure there are no cracks, chips or rounded edges on the armature.	If the breaker points are intact, clean the contact surfaces with fine emery cloth, and adjust the point gap to specifications. If the points are worn, replace them. On electronic systems, replace any parts which appear defective. If condition persists:	**3.4**

Test and Procedure	Results and Indications	Proceed to
3.4—On point-type ignition systems, connect a dwell-meter between the distributor primary lead and ground. Crank the engine and observe the point dwell angle. On electronic ignition systems, conduct a stator (magnetic pickup assembly) test. See Chapter 3.	On point-type systems, adjust the dwell angle if necessary. **NOTE:** *Increasing the point gap decreases the dwell angle and vice-versa.*	**3.6**
	If the dwell meter shows little or no reading;	**3.5**
	On electronic ignition systems, if the stator is bad, replace the stator. If the stator is good, proceed to the other tests in Chapter 3.	

CLOSE   OPEN

NORMAL DWELL

WIDE GAP

SMALL DWELL

INSUFFICIENT DWELL

NARROW GAP

LARGE DWELL

EXCESSIVE DWELL

Dwell is a function of point gap

3.5—On the point-type ignition systems, check the condenser for short: connect an ohmeter across the condenser body and the pigtail lead.	If any reading other than infinite is noted, replace the condenser	**3.6**

OHMMETER

Checking the condenser for short

3.6—Test the coil primary resistance: On point-type ignition systems, connect an ohmmeter across the coil primary terminals, and read the resistance on the low scale. Note whether an external ballast resistor or resistance wire is used. On electronic ignition systems, test the coil primary resistance as in Chapter 3.	Point-type ignition coils utilizing ballast resistors or resistance wires should have approximately 1.0 ohms resistance. Coils with internal resistors should have approximately 4.0 ohms resistance. If values far from the above are noted, replace the coil.	**4.1**

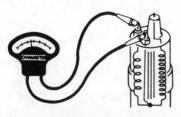

Check the coil primary resistance

Section 4—Secondary Electrical System
See Chapters 2–3 for service procedures

Test and Procedure	Results and Indications	Proceed to
4.1—Check for spark: Hold each spark plug wire approximately ¼″ from ground with gloves or a heavy, dry rag. Crank the engine, and observe the spark.	If no spark is evident:	**4.2**
	If spark is good in some cylinders:	**4.3**
	If spark is good in all cylinders:	**4.6**

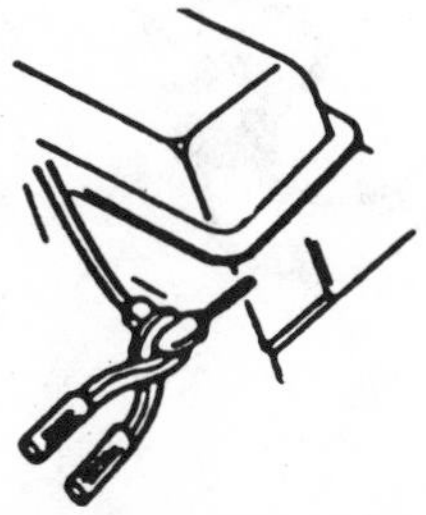

Check for spark at the plugs

Test and Procedure	Results and Indications	Proceed to
4.2—Check for spark at the coil high tension lead: Remove the coil high tension lead from the distributor and position it approximately ¼″ from ground. Crank the engine and observe spark. **CAUTION:** *This test should not be performed on engines equipped with electronic ignition.*	If the spark is good and consistent:	**4.3**
	If the spark is good but intermittent, test the primary electrical system starting at 3.3:	**3.3**
	If the spark is weak or non-existent, replace the coil high tension lead, clean and tighten all connections and retest. If no improvement is noted:	**4.4**
4.3—Visually inspect the distributor cap and rotor for burned or corroded contacts, cracks, carbon tracks, or moisture. Also check the fit of the rotor on the distributor shaft (where applicable).	If moisture is present, dry thoroughly, and retest per 4.1:	**4.1**
	If burned or excessively corroded contacts, cracks, or carbon tracks are noted, replace the defective part(s) and retest per 4.1:	**4.1**
	If the rotor and cap appear intact, or are only slightly corroded, clean the contacts thoroughly (including the cap towers and spark plug wire ends) and retest per 4.1:	
	If the spark is good in all cases:	**4.6**
	If the spark is poor in all cases:	**4.5**

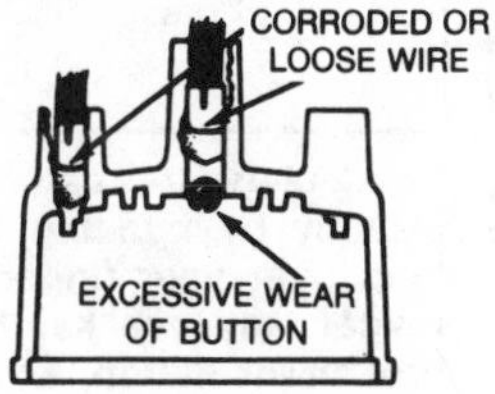

CORRODED OR LOOSE WIRE

EXCESSIVE WEAR OF BUTTON

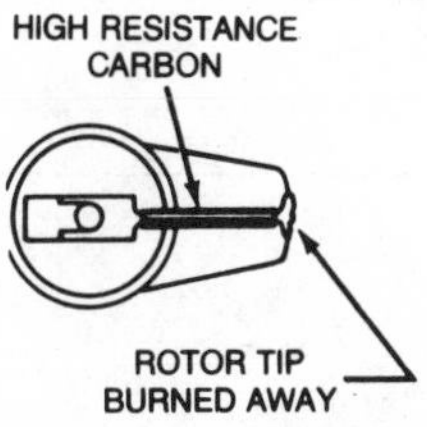

HIGH RESISTANCE CARBON

ROTOR TIP BURNED AWAY

Inspect the distributor cap and rotor

Test and Procedure	Results and Indications	Proceed to
4.4—Check the coil secondary resistance: On point-type systems connect an ohmmeter across the distributor side of the coil and the coil tower. Read the resistance on the high scale of the ohmmeter. On electronic ignition systems, see Chapter 3 for specific tests.	The resistance of a satisfactory coil should be between 4,000 and 10,000 ohms. If resistance is considerably higher (i.e., 40,000 ohms) replace the coil and retest per 4.1. **NOTE:** *This does not apply to high performance coils.*	

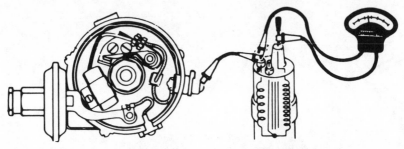

Testing the coil secondary resistance

4.5—Visually inspect the spark plug wires for cracking or brittleness. Ensure that no two wires are positioned so as to cause induction firing (adjacent and parallel). Remove each wire, one by one, and check resistance with an ohmmeter.	Replace any cracked or brittle wires. If any of the wires are defective, replace the entire set. Replace any wires with excessive resistance (over 8000 Ω per foot for suppression wire), and separate any wires that might cause induction firing.	**4.6**

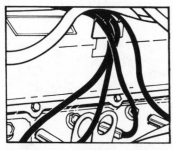

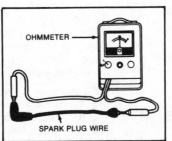

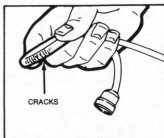

Misfiring can be the result of spark plug leads to adjacent, consecutively firing cylinders running parallel and too close together

On point-type ignition systems, check the spark plug wires as shown. On electronic ignitions, do not remove the wire from the distributor cap terminal; instead, test through the cap

Spark plug wires can be checked visually by bending them in a loop over your finger. This will reveal any cracks, burned or broken insulation. Any wire with cracked insulation should be replaced

4.6—Remove the spark plugs, noting the cylinders from which they were removed, and evaluate according to the color photos in the middle of this book.	See following.	**See following.**

Test and Procedure	Results and Indications	Proceed to
4.7—Examine the location of all the plugs.	The following diagrams illustrate some of the conditions that the location of plugs will reveal.	4.8

Two adjacent plugs are fouled in a 6-cylinder engine, 4-cylinder engine or either bank of a V-8. This is probably due to a blown head gasket between the two cylinders

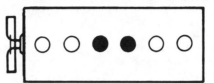

The two center plugs in a 6-cylinder engine are fouled. Raw fuel may be "boiled" out of the carburetor into the intake manifold after the engine is shut-off. Stop-start driving can also foul the center plugs, due to overly rich mixture. Proper float level, a new float needle and seat or use of an insulating spacer may help this problem

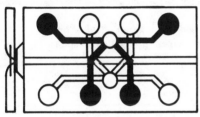

An unbalanced carburetor is indicated. Following the fuel flow on this particular design shows that the cylinders fed by the right-hand barrel are fouled from overly rich mixture, while the cylinders fed by the left-hand barrel are normal

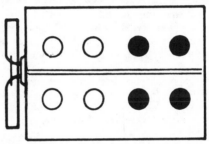

If the four rear plugs are overheated, a cooling system problem is suggested. A thorough cleaning of the cooling system may restore coolant circulation and cure the problem

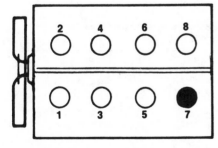

Finding one plug overheated may indicate an intake manifold leak near the affected cylinder. If the overheated plug is the second of two adjacent, consecutively firing plugs, it could be the result of ignition cross-firing. Separating the leads to these two plugs will eliminate cross-fire

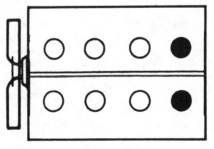

Occasionally, the two rear plugs in large, lightly used V-8's will become oil fouled. High oil consumption and smoky exhaust may also be noticed. It is probably due to plugged oil drain holes in the rear of the cylinder head, causing oil to be sucked in around the valve stems. This usually occurs in the rear cylinders first, because the engine slants that way

Test and Procedure	Results and Indications	Proceed to
4.8—Determine the static ignition timing. Using the crankshaft pulley timing marks as a guide, locate top dead center on the compression stroke of the number one cylinder.	The rotor should be pointing toward the No. 1 tower in the distributor cap, and, on electronic ignitions, the armature spoke for that cylinder should be lined up with the stator.	4.8
4.9—Check coil polarity: Connect a voltmeter negative lead to the coil high tension lead, and the positive lead to ground (**NOTE:** *Reverse the hook-up for positive ground systems*). Crank the engine momentarily. **Checking coil polarity**	If the voltmeter reads up-scale, the polarity is correct: If the voltmeter reads down-scale, reverse the coil polarity (switch the primary leads):	5.1 5.1

Section 5—Fuel System
See Chapter 4 for service procedures

Test and Procedure	Results and Indications	Proceed to
5.1—Determine that the air filter is functioning efficiently: Hold paper elements up to a strong light, and attempt to see light through the filter.	Clean permanent air filters in solvent (or manufacturer's recommendation), and allow to dry. Replace paper elements through which light cannot be seen:	5.2
5.2—Determine whether a flooding condition exists: Flooding is identified by a strong gasoline odor, and excessive gasoline present in the throttle bore(s) of the carburetor.	If flooding is not evident: If flooding is evident, permit the gasoline to dry for a few moments and restart. If flooding doesn't recur: If flooding is persistent:	5.3 5.7 5.5

If the engine floods repeatedly, check the choke butterfly flap

Test and Procedure	Results and Indications	Proceed to
5.3—Check that fuel is reaching the carburetor: Detach the fuel line at the carburetor inlet. Hold the end of the line in a cup (not styrofoam), and crank the engine.	If fuel flows smoothly: If fuel doesn't flow (**NOTE:** *Make sure that there is fuel in the tank*), or flows erratically:	5.7 5.4

Check the fuel pump by disconnecting the output line (fuel pump-to-carburetor) at the carburetor and operating the starter briefly

Test and Procedure	Results and Indications	Proceed to
5.4—Test the fuel pump: Disconnect all fuel lines from the fuel pump. Hold a finger over the input fitting, crank the engine (with electric pump, turn the ignition or pump on); and feel for suction.	If suction is evident, blow out the fuel line to the tank with low pressure compressed air until bubbling is heard from the fuel filler neck. Also blow out the carburetor fuel line (both ends disconnected):	5.7
	If no suction is evident, replace or repair the fuel pump: **NOTE:** *Repeated oil fouling of the spark plugs, or a no-start condition, could be the result of a ruptured vacuum booster pump diaphragm, through which oil or gasoline is being drawn into the intake manifold (where applicable).*	5.7
5.5—Occasionally, small specks of dirt will clog the small jets and orifices in the carburetor. With the engine cold, hold a flat piece of wood or similar material over the carburetor, where possible, and crank the engine.	If the engine starts, but runs roughly the engine is probably not run enough. If the engine won't start:	5.9
5.6—Check the needle and seat: Tap the carburetor in the area of the needle and seat.	If flooding stops, a gasoline additive (e.g., Gumout) will often cure the problem:	5.7
	If flooding continues, check the fuel pump for excessive pressure at the carburetor (according to specifications). If the pressure is normal, the needle and seat must be removed and checked, and/or the float level adjusted:	5.7
5.7—Test the accelerator pump by looking into the throttle bores while operating the throttle.	If the accelerator pump appears to be operating normally:	5.8
	If the accelerator pump is not operating, the pump must be reconditioned. Where possible, service the pump with the carburetor(s) installed on the engine. If necessary, remove the carburetor. Prior to removal:	5.8

Check for gas at the carburetor by looking down the carburetor throat while someone moves the accelerator

Test and Procedure	Results and Indications	Proceed to
5.8—Determine whether the carburetor main fuel system is functioning: Spray a commercial starting fluid into the carburetor while attempting to start the engine.	If the engine starts, runs for a few seconds, and dies:	5.9
	If the engine doesn't start:	6.1

Test and Procedure	Results and Indications	Proceed to
5.9—Uncommon fuel system malfunctions: See below:	If the problem is solved:	**6.1**
	If the problem remains, remove and recondition the carburetor.	

Condition	Indication	Test	Prevailing Weather Conditions	Remedy
Vapor lock	Engine will not restart shortly after running.	Cool the components of the fuel system until the engine starts. Vapor lock can be cured faster by draping a wet cloth over a mechanical fuel pump.	Hot to very hot	Ensure that the exhaust manifold heat control valve is operating. Check with the vehicle manufacturer for the recommended solution to vapor lock on the model in question.
Carburetor icing	Engine will not idle, stalls at low speeds.	Visually inspect the throttle plate area of the throttle bores for frost.	High humidity, 32–40° F.	Ensure that the exhaust manifold heat control valve is operating, and that the intake manifold heat riser is not blocked.
Water in the fuel	Engine sputters and stalls; may not start.	Pump a small amount of fuel into a glass jar. Allow to stand, and inspect for droplets or a layer of water.	High humidity, extreme temperature changes.	For droplets, use one or two cans of commercial gas line anti-freeze. For a layer of water, the tank must be drained, and the fuel lines blown out with compressed air.

Section 6—Engine Compression
See Chapter 3 for service procedures

6.1—Test engine compression: Remove all spark plugs. Block the throttle wide open. Insert a compression gauge into a spark plug port, crank the engine to obtain the maximum reading, and record.	If compression is within limits on all cylinders:	**7.1**
	If gauge reading is extremely low on all cylinders:	**6.2**
	If gauge reading is low on one or two cylinders: (If gauge readings are identical and low on two or more adjacent cylinders, the head gasket must be replaced.)	**6.2**

Checking compression

6.2—Test engine compression (wet): Squirt approximately 30 cc. of engine oil into each cylinder, and retest per 6.1.	If the readings improve, worn or cracked rings or broken pistons are indicated:	**See Chapter 3**
	If the readings do not improve, burned or excessively carboned valves or a jumped timing chain are indicated:	**7.1**
	NOTE: *A jumped timing chain is often indicated by difficult cranking.*	

CHILTON'S
AUTO BODY REPAIR TIPS

EASY STEP-BY-STEP TIPS FROM PROS

Tools and Materials • Step-by-Step Illustrated Procedures
How To Repair Dents, Scratches and Rust Holes
Spray Painting and Refinishing Tips

With a little practice, basic body repair procedures can be mastered by any do-it-yourself mechanic. The step-by-step repairs shown here can be applied to almost any type of auto body repair.

TOOLS & MATERIALS

You may already have basic tools, such as hammers and electric drills. Other tools unique to body repair — body hammers, grinding attachments, sanding blocks, dent puller, half-round plastic file and plastic spreaders — are relatively inexpensive and can be obtained wherever auto parts or auto body repair parts are sold. Portable air compressors and paint spray guns can be purchased or rented.

Auto Body Repair Kits

The best and most often used products are available to the do-it-yourselfer in kit form, from major manufacturers of auto body repair products. The same manufacturers also merchandise the individual products for use by pros.

Kits are available to make a wide variety of repairs, including holes, dents and scratches and fiberglass, and offer the advantage of buying the materials you'll need for the job. There is little waste or chance of materials going bad from not being used. Many kits may also contain basic body-working tools such as body files, sanding blocks and spreaders. Check the contents of the kit before buying your tools.

BODY REPAIR TIPS

Safety

Many of the products associated with auto body repair and refinishing contain toxic chemicals. Read all labels before opening containers and store them in a safe place and manner.

• Wear eye protection (safety goggles) when using power tools or when performing any operation that involves the removal of any type of material.

• Wear lung protection (disposable mask or respirator) when grinding, sanding or painting.

Sanding

1 Sand off paint before using a dent puller. When using a non-adhesive sanding disc, cover the back of the disc with an overlapping layer or two of masking tape and trim the edges. The disc will last considerably longer.

2 Use the circular motion of the sanding disc to grind *into* the edge of the repair. Grinding or sanding away from the jagged edge will only tear the sandpaper.

3 Use the palm of your hand flat on the panel to detect high and low spots. Do not use your fingertips. Slide your hand slowly back and forth.

WORKING WITH BODY FILLER

Mixing The Filler

Cleanliness and proper mixing and application are extremely important. Use a clean piece of plastic or glass or a disposable artist's palette to mix body filler.

1 Allow plenty of time and follow directions. No useful purpose will be served by adding more hardener to make it cure (set-up) faster. Less hardener means more curing time, but the mixture dries harder; more hardener means less curing time but a softer mixture.

2 Both the hardener and the filler should be thoroughly kneaded or stirred before mixing. Hardener should be a solid paste and dispense like thin toothpaste. Body filler should be smooth, and free of lumps or thick spots.

Getting the proper amount of hardener in the filler is the trickiest part of preparing the filler. Use the same amount of hardener in cold or warm weather. For contour filler (thick coats), a bead of hardener twice the diameter of the filler is about right. There's about a 5% margin on either side, but, if in doubt use less hardener.

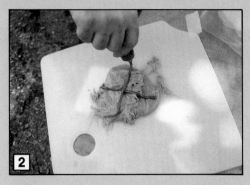

3 Mix the body filler and hardener by wiping across the mixing surface, picking the mixture up and wiping it again. Colder weather requires longer mixing times. Do not mix in a circular motion; this will trap air bubbles which will become holes in the cured filler.

Applying The Filler

1 For best results, filler should not be applied over 1/4" thick.

Apply the filler in several coats. Build it up to above the level of the repair surface so that it can be sanded or grated down.

The first coat of filler must be pressed on with a firm wiping motion.

Apply the filler in one direction only. Working the filler back and forth will either pull it off the metal or trap air bubbles.

REPAIRING DENTS

Before you start, take a few minutes to study the damaged area. Try to visualize the shape of the panel before it was damaged. If the damage is on the left fender, look at the right fender and use it as a guide. If there is access to the panel from behind, you can reshape it with a body hammer. If not, you'll have to use a dent puller. Go slowly and work the metal a little at a time. Get the panel as straight as possible before applying filler.

1 This dent is typical of one that can be pulled out or hammered out from behind. Remove the headlight cover, headlight assembly and turn signal housing.

2 Drill a series of holes ½ the size of the end of the dent puller along the stress line. Make some trial pulls and assess the results. If necessary, drill more holes and try again. Do not hurry.

3 If possible, use a body hammer and block to shape the metal back to its original contours. Get the metal back as close to its original shape as possible. Don't depend on body filler to fill dents.

4 Using an 80-grit grinding disc on an electric drill, grind the paint from the surrounding area down to bare metal. Use a new grinding pad to prevent heat buildup that will warp metal.

5 The area should look like this when you're finished grinding. Knock the drill holes in and tape over small openings to keep plastic filler out.

6 Mix the body filler (see Body Repair Tips). Spread the body filler evenly over the entire area (see Body Repair Tips). Be sure to cover the area completely.

7 Let the body filler dry until the surface can just be scratched with your fingernail. Knock the high spots from the body filler with a body file ("Cheesegrater"). Check frequently with the palm of your hand for high and low spots.

8 Check to be sure that trim pieces that will be installed later will fit exactly. Sand the area with 40-grit paper.

9 If you wind up with low spots, you may have to apply another layer of filler.

10 Knock the high spots off with 40-grit paper. When you are satisfied with the contours of the repair, apply a thin coat of filler to cover pin holes and scratches.

11 Block sand the area with 40-grit paper to a smooth finish. Pay particular attention to body lines and ridges that must be well-defined.

12 Sand the area with 400 paper and then finish with a scuff pad. The finished repair is ready for priming and painting (see Painting Tips).

Materials and photos courtesy of Ritt Jones Auto Body, Prospect Park, PA.

REPAIRING RUST HOLES

There are many ways to repair rust holes. The fiberglass cloth kit shown here is one of the most cost efficient for the owner because it provides a strong repair that resists cracking and moisture and is relatively easy to use. It can be used on large and small holes (with or without backing) and can be applied over contoured areas. Remember, however, that short of replacing an entire panel, no repair is a guarantee that the rust will not return.

1 Remove any trim that will be in the way. Clean away all loose debris. Cut away all the rusted metal. But be sure to leave enough metal to retain the contour or body shape.

2 Grind away all traces of rust with a 24-grit grinding disc. Be sure to grind back 3-4 inches from the edge of the hole down to bare metal and be sure all traces of paint, primer and rust are removed.

3 Block sand the area with 80 or 100 grit sandpaper to get a clear, shiny surface and feathered paint edge. Tap the edges of the hole inward with a ball peen hammer.

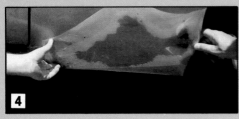

4 If you are going to use release film, cut a piece about 2-3" larger than the area you have sanded. Place the film over the repair and mark the sanded area on the film. Avoid any unnecessary wrinkling of the film.

5 Cut 2 pieces of fiberglass matte to match the shape of the repair. One piece should be about 1" smaller than the sanded area and the second piece should be 1" smaller than the first. Mix enough filler and hardener to saturate the fiberglass material (see Body Repair Tips).

6 Lay the release sheet on a flat surface and spread an even layer of filler, large enough to cover the repair. Lay the smaller piece of fiberglass cloth in the center of the sheet and spread another layer of filler over the fiberglass cloth. Repeat the operation for the larger piece of cloth.

7 Place the repair material over the repair area, with the release film facing outward. Use a spreader and work from the center outward to smooth the material, following the body contours. Be sure to remove all air bubbles.

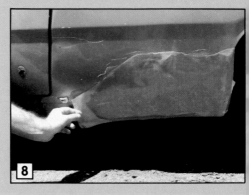

8 Wait until the repair has dried tack-free and peel off the release sheet. The ideal working temperature is 60°-90° F. Cooler or warmer temperatures or high humidity may require additional curing time. Wait longer, if in doubt.

9

9 Sand and feather-edge the entire area. The initial sanding can be done with a sanding disc on an electric drill if care is used. Finish the sanding with a block sander. Low spots can be filled with body filler; this may require several applications.

10

10 When the filler can just be scratched with a fingernail, knock the high spots down with a body file and smooth the entire area with 80-grit. Feather the filled areas into the surrounding areas.

11

11 When the area is sanded smooth, mix some topcoat and hardener and apply it directly with a spreader. This will give a smooth finish and prevent the glass matte from showing through the paint.

12

12 Block sand the topcoat smooth with finishing sandpaper (200 grit), and 400 grit. The repair is ready for masking, priming and painting (see Painting Tips).

Materials and photos courtesy Marson Corporation, Chelsea, Massachusetts

PAINTING TIPS

Preparation

1 SANDING — Use a 400 or 600 grit wet or dry sandpaper. Wet-sand the area with a 1/4 sheet of sandpaper soaked in clean water. Keep the paper wet while sanding. Sand the area until the repaired area tapers into the original finish.

2 CLEANING — Wash the area to be painted thoroughly with water and a clean rag. Rinse it thoroughly and wipe the surface dry until you're sure it's completely free of dirt, dust, fingerprints, wax, detergent or other foreign matter.

3 MASKING — Protect any areas you don't want to overspray by covering them with masking tape and newspaper. Be careful not get fingerprints on the area to be painted.

4 PRIMING — All exposed metal should be primed before painting. Primer protects the metal and provides an excellent surface for paint adhesion. When the primer is dry, wet-sand the area again with 600 grit wet-sandpaper. Clean the area again after sanding.

4

Painting Techniques

P aint applied from either a spray gun or a spray can (for small areas) will provide good results. Experiment on an old piece of metal to get the right combination before you begin painting.

SPRAYING VISCOSITY (SPRAY GUN ONLY) — Paint should be thinned to spraying viscosity according to the directions on the can. Use only the recommended thinner or reducer and the same amount of reduction regardless of temperature.

AIR PRESSURE (SPRAY GUN ONLY) — This is extremely important. Be sure you are using the proper recommended pressure.

TEMPERATURE — The surface to be painted should be approximately the same temperature as the surrounding air. Applying warm paint to a cold surface, or vice versa, will completely upset the paint characteristics.

THICKNESS — Spray with smooth strokes. In general, the thicker the coat of paint, the longer the drying time. Apply several thin coats about 30 seconds apart. The paint should remain wet long enough to flow out and no longer; heavier coats will only produce sags or wrinkles. Spray a light (fog) coat, followed by heavier color coats.

DISTANCE — The ideal spraying distance is 8″-12″ from the gun or can to the surface. Shorter distances will produce ripples, while greater distances will result in orange peel, dry film and poor color match and loss of material due to overspray.

OVERLAPPING — The gun or can should be kept at right angles to the surface at all times. Work to a wet edge at an even speed, using a 50% overlap and direct the center of the spray at the lower or nearest edge of the previous stroke.

RUBBING OUT (BLENDING) FRESH PAINT — Let the paint dry thoroughly. Runs or imperfections can be sanded out, primed and repainted.

Don't be in too big a hurry to remove the masking. This only produces paint ridges. When the finish has dried for at least a week, apply a small amount of fine grade rubbing compound with a clean, wet cloth. Use lots of water and blend the new paint with the surrounding area.

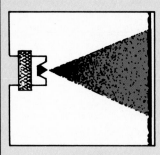

WRONG

Thin coat. Stroke too fast, not enough overlap, gun too far away.

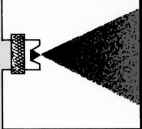

CORRECT

Medium coat. Proper distance, good stroke, proper overlap.

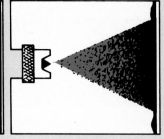

WRONG

Heavy coat. Stroke too slow, too much overlap, gun too close.

Section 7—Engine Vacuum
See Chapter 3 for service procedures

Test and Procedure	Results and Indications	Proceed to
7.1—Attach a vacuum gauge to the intake manifold beyond the throttle plate. Start the engine, and observe the action of the needle over the range of engine speeds.	See below.	**See below**

INDICATION: normal engine in good condition

Proceed to: 8.1

Normal engine
Gauge reading: steady, from 17–22 in./Hg.

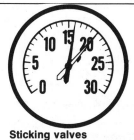

INDICATION: sticking valves or ignition miss

Proceed to: 9.1, 8.3

Sticking valves
Gauge reading: intermittent fluctuation at idle

INDICATION: late ignition or valve timing, low compression, stuck throttle valve, leaking carburetor or manifold gasket

Proceed to: 6.1

Incorrect valve timing
Gauge reading: low (10–15 in./Hg) but steady

INDICATION: improper carburetor adjustment or minor intake leak.

Proceed to: 7.2

Carburetor requires adjustment
Gauge reading: drifting needle

INDICATION: ignition miss, blown cylinder head gasket, leaking valve or weak valve spring

Proceed to: 8.3, 6.1

Blown head gasket
Gauge reading: needle fluctuates as engine speed increases

INDICATION: burnt valve or faulty valve clearance. Needle will fall when defective valve operates

Proceed to: 9.1

Burnt or leaking valves
Gauge reading: steady needle, but drops regularly

INDICATION: choked muffler, excessive back pressure in system

Proceed to: 10.1

Clogged exhaust system
Gauge reading: gradual drop in reading at idle

INDICATION: worn valve guides

Proceed to: 9.1

Worn valve guides
Gauge reading: needle vibrates excessively at idle, but steadies as engine speed increases

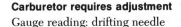

White pointer = steady gauge hand   Black pointer = fluctuating gauge hand

Test and Procedure	Results and Indications	Proceed to
7.2—Attach a vacuum gauge per 7.1, and test for an intake manifold leak. Squirt a small amount of oil around the intake manifold gaskets, carburetor gaskets, plugs and fittings. Observe the action of the vacuum gauge.	If the reading improves, replace the indicated gasket, or seal the indicated fitting or plug: If the reading remains low:	**8.1** **7.3**
7.3—Test all vacuum hoses and accessories for leaks as described in 7.2. Also check the carburetor body (dashpots, automatic choke mechanism, throttle shafts) for leaks in the same manner.	If the reading improves, service or replace the offending part(s): If the reading remains low:	**8.1** **6.1**

Section 8—Secondary Electrical System
See Chapter 2 for service procedures

Test and Procedure	Results and Indications	Proceed. to
8.1—Remove the distributor cap and check to make sure that the rotor turns when the engine is cranked. Visually inspect the distributor components.	Clean, tighten or replace any components which appear defective.	**8.2**
8.2—Connect a timing light (per manufacturer's recommendation) and check the dynamic ignition timing. Disconnect and plug the vacuum hose(s) to the distributor if specified, start the engine, and observe the timing marks at the specified engine speed.	If the timing is not correct, adjust to specifications by rotating the distributor in the engine: (Advance timing by rotating distributor opposite normal direction of rotor rotation, retard timing by rotating distributor in same direction as rotor rotation.)	**8.3**
8.3—Check the operation of the distributor advance mechanism(s): To test the mechanical advance, disconnect the vacuum lines from the distributor advance unit and observe the timing marks with a timing light as the engine speed is increased from idle. If the mark moves smoothly, without hesitation, it may be assumed that the mechanical advance is functioning properly. To test vacuum advance and/or retard systems, alternately crimp and release the vacuum line, and observe the timing mark for movement. If movement is noted, the system is operating.	If the systems are functioning: If the systems are not functioning, remove the distributor, and test on a distributor tester:	**8.4** **8.4**
8.4—Locate an ignition miss: With the engine running, remove each spark plug wire, one at a time, until one is found that doesn't cause the engine to roughen and slow down.	When the missing cylinder is identified:	**4.1**

Section 9—Valve Train
See Chapter 3 for service procedures

Test and Procedure	Results and Indications	Proceed to
9.1—Evaluate the valve train: Remove the valve cover, and ensure that the valves are adjusted to specifications. A mechanic's stethoscope may be used to aid in the diagnosis of the valve train. By pushing the probe on or near push rods or rockers, valve noise often can be isolated. A timing light also may be used to diagnose valve problems. Connect the light according to manufacturer's recommendations, and start the engine. Vary the firing moment of the light by increasing the engine speed (and therefore the ignition advance), and moving the trigger from cylinder to cylinder. Observe the movement of each valve.	Sticking valves or erratic valve train motion can be observed with the timing light. The cylinder head must be disassembled for repairs.	**See Chapter 3**
9.2—Check the valve timing: Locate top dead center of the No. 1 piston, and install a degree wheel or tape on the crankshaft pulley or damper with zero corresponding to an index mark on the engine. Rotate the crankshaft in its direction of rotation, and observe the opening of the No. 1 cylinder intake valve. The opening should correspond with the correct mark on the degree wheel according to specifications.	If the timing is not correct, the timing cover must be removed for further investigation.	**See Chapter 3**

Section 10—Exhaust System

Test and Procedure	Results and Indications	Proceed to
10.1—Determine whether the exhaust manifold heat control valve is operating: Operate the valve by hand to determine whether it is free to move. If the valve is free, run the engine to operating temperature and observe the action of the valve, to ensure that it is opening.	If the valve sticks, spray it with a suitable solvent, open and close the valve to free it, and retest. If the valve functions properly:	10.2
	If the valve does not free, or does not operate, replace the valve:	10.2
10.2—Ensure that there are no exhaust restrictions: Visually inspect the exhaust system for kinks, dents, or crushing. Also note that gases are flowing freely from the tailpipe at all engine speeds, indicating no restriction in the muffler or resonator.	Replace any damaged portion of the system:	11.1

Section 11—Cooling System
See Chapter 3 for service procedures

Test and Procedure	Results and Indications	Proceed to
11.1—Visually inspect the fan belt for glazing, cracks, and fraying, and replace if necessary. Tighten the belt so that the longest span has approximately ½″ play at its midpoint under thumb pressure (see Chapter 1).	Replace or tighten the fan belt as necessary:	11.2

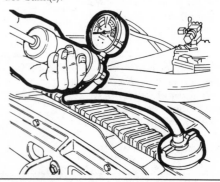

Checking belt tension

Test and Procedure	Results and Indications	Proceed to
11.2—Check the fluid level of the cooling system.	If full or slightly low, fill as necessary:	11.5
	If extremely low:	11.3
11.3—Visually inspect the external portions of the cooling system (radiator, radiator hoses, thermostat elbow, water pump seals, heater hoses, etc.) for leaks. If none are found, pressurize the cooling system to 14–15 psi.	If cooling system holds the pressure:	11.5
	If cooling system loses pressure rapidly, reinspect external parts of the system for leaks under pressure. If none are found, check dipstick for coolant in crankcase. If no coolant is present, but pressure loss continues:	11.4
	If coolant is evident in crankcase, remove cylinder head(s), and check gasket(s). If gaskets are intact, block and cylinder head(s) should be checked for cracks or holes.	
	If the gasket(s) is blown, replace, and purge the crankcase of coolant:	12.6
	NOTE: *Occasionally, due to atmospheric and driving conditions, condensation of water can occur in the crankcase. This causes the oil to appear milky white. To remedy, run the engine until hot, and change the oil and oil filter.*	
11.4—Check for combustion leaks into the cooling system: Pressurize the cooling system as above. Start the engine, and observe the pressure gauge. If the needle fluctuates, remove each spark plug wire, one at a time, noting which cylinder(s) reduce or eliminate the fluctuation.	Cylinders which reduce or eliminate the fluctuation, when the spark plug wire is removed, are leaking into the cooling system. Replace the head gasket on the affected cylinder bank(s).	

Pressurizing the cooling system

Test and Procedure	Results and Indications	Proceed to
11.5—Check the radiator pressure cap: Attach a radiator pressure tester to the radiator cap (wet the seal prior to installation). Quickly pump up the pressure, noting the point at which the cap releases.	If the cap releases within ± 1 psi of the specified rating, it is operating properly:	**11.6**
	If the cap releases at more than ± 1 psi of the specified rating, it should be replaced:	**11.6**

Checking radiator pressure cap

Test and Procedure	Results and Indications	Proceed to
11.6—Test the thermostat: Start the engine cold, remove the radiator cap, and insert a thermometer into the radiator. Allow the engine to idle. After a short while, there will be a sudden, rapid increase in coolant temperature. The temperature at which this sharp rise stops is the thermostat opening temperature.	If the thermostat opens at or about the specified temperature:	**11.7**
	If the temperature doesn't increase: (If the temperature increases slowly and gradually, replace the thermostat.)	**11.7**
11.7—Check the water pump: Remove the thermostat elbow and the thermostat, disconnect the coil high tension lead (to prevent starting), and crank the engine momentarily.	If coolant flows, replace the thermostat and retest per 11.6:	**11.6**
	If coolant doesn't flow, reverse flush the cooling system to alleviate any blockage that might exist. If system is not blocked, and coolant will not flow, replace the water pump.	

Section 12—Lubrication
See Chapter 3 for service procedures

Test and Procedure	Results and Indications	Proceed to
12.1—Check the oil pressure gauge or warning light: If the gauge shows low pressure, or the light is on for no obvious reason, remove the oil pressure sender. Install an accurate oil pressure gauge and run the engine momentarily.	If oil pressure builds normally, run engine for a few moments to determine that it is functioning normally, and replace the sender.	—
	If the pressure remains low:	**12.2**
	If the pressure surges:	**12.3**
	If the oil pressure is zero:	**12.3**
12.2—Visually inspect the oil: If the oil is watery or very thin, milky, or foamy, replace the oil and oil filter.	If the oil is normal:	**12.3**
	If after replacing oil the pressure remains low:	**12.3**
	If after replacing oil the pressure becomes normal:	—

Test and Procedure	Results and Indications	Proceed to
12.3—Inspect the oil pressure relief valve and spring, to ensure that it is not sticking or stuck. Remove and thoroughly clean the valve, spring, and the valve body.	If the oil pressure improves: If no improvement is noted:	— **12.4**
12.4—Check to ensure that the oil pump is not cavitating (sucking air instead of oil): See that the crankcase is neither over nor underfull, and that the pickup in the sump is in the proper position and free from sludge.	Fill or drain the crankcase to the proper capacity, and clean the pickup screen in solvent if necessary. If no improvement is noted:	**12.5**
12.5—Inspect the oil pump drive and the oil pump:	If the pump drive or the oil pump appear to be defective, service as necessary and retest per 12.1: If the pump drive and pump appear to be operating normally, the engine should be disassembled to determine where blockage exists:	**12.1** **See Chapter 3**
12.6—Purge the engine of ethylene glycol coolant: Completely drain the crankcase and the oil filter. Obtain a commercial butyl cellosolve base solvent, designated for this purpose, and follow the instructions precisely. Following this, install a new oil filter and refill the crankcase with the proper weight oil. The next oil and filter change should follow shortly thereafter (1000 miles).		

TROUBLESHOOTING EMISSION CONTROL SYSTEMS

See Chapter 4 for procedures applicable to individual emission control systems used on specific combinations of engine/transmission/model.

TROUBLESHOOTING THE CARBURETOR
See Chapter 4 for service procedures

Carburetor problems cannot be effectively isolated unless all other engine systems (particularly ignition and emission) are functioning properly and the engine is properly tuned.

Condition	Possible Cause
Engine cranks, but does not start	1. Improper starting procedure 2. No fuel in tank 3. Clogged fuel line or filter 4. Defective fuel pump 5. Choke valve not closing properly 6. Engine flooded 7. Choke valve not unloading 8. Throttle linkage not making full travel 9. Stuck needle or float 10. Leaking float needle or seat 11. Improper float adjustment
Engine stalls	1. Improperly adjusted idle speed or mixture **Engine hot** 2. Improperly adjusted dashpot 3. Defective or improperly adjusted solenoid 4. Incorrect fuel level in fuel bowl 5. Fuel pump pressure too high 6. Leaking float needle seat 7. Secondary throttle valve stuck open 8. Air or fuel leaks 9. Idle air bleeds plugged or missing 10. Idle passages plugged **Engine Cold** 11. Incorrectly adjusted choke 12. Improperly adjusted fast idle speed 13. Air leaks 14. Plugged idle or idle air passages 15. Stuck choke valve or binding linkage 16. Stuck secondary throttle valves 17. Engine flooding—high fuel level 18. Leaking or misaligned float
Engine hesitates on acceleration	1. Clogged fuel filter 2. Leaking fuel pump diaphragm 3. Low fuel pump pressure 4. Secondary throttle valves stuck, bent or misadjusted 5. Sticking or binding air valve 6. Defective accelerator pump 7. Vacuum leaks 8. Clogged air filter 9. Incorrect choke adjustment (engine cold)
Engine feels sluggish or flat on acceleration	1. Improperly adjusted idle speed or mixture 2. Clogged fuel filter 3. Defective accelerator pump 4. Dirty, plugged or incorrect main metering jets 5. Bent or sticking main metering rods 6. Sticking throttle valves 7. Stuck heat riser 8. Binding or stuck air valve 9. Dirty, plugged or incorrect secondary jets 10. Bent or sticking secondary metering rods. 11. Throttle body or manifold heat passages plugged 12. Improperly adjusted choke or choke vacuum break.
Carburetor floods	1. Defective fuel pump. Pressure too high. 2. Stuck choke valve 3. Dirty, worn or damaged float or needle valve/seat 4. Incorrect float/fuel level 5. Leaking float bowl

Condition	Possible Cause
Engine idles roughly and stalls	1. Incorrect idle speed 2. Clogged fuel filter 3. Dirt in fuel system or carburetor 4. Loose carburetor screws or attaching bolts 5. Broken carburetor gaskets 6. Air leaks 7. Dirty carburetor 8. Worn idle mixture needles 9. Throttle valves stuck open 10. Incorrectly adjusted float or fuel level 11. Clogged air filter
Engine runs unevenly or surges	1. Defective fuel pump 2. Dirty or clogged fuel filter 3. Plugged, loose or incorrect main metering jets or rods 4. Air leaks 5. Bent or sticking main metering rods 6. Stuck power piston 7. Incorrect float adjustment 8. Incorrect idle speed or mixture 9. Dirty or plugged idle system passages 10. Hard, brittle or broken gaskets 11. Loose attaching or mounting screws 12. Stuck or misaligned secondary throttle valves
Poor fuel economy	1. Poor driving habits 2. Stuck choke valve 3. Binding choke linkage 4. Stuck heat riser 5. Incorrect idle mixture 6. Defective accelerator pump 7. Air leaks 8. Plugged, loose or incorrect main metering jets 9. Improperly adjusted float or fuel level 10. Bent, misaligned or fuel-clogged float 11. Leaking float needle seat 12. Fuel leak 13. Accelerator pump discharge ball not seating properly 14. Incorrect main jets
Engine lacks high speed performance or power	1. Incorrect throttle linkage adjustment 2. Stuck or binding power piston 3. Defective accelerator pump 4. Air leaks 5. Incorrect float setting or fuel level 6. Dirty, plugged, worn or incorrect main metering jets or rods 7. Binding or sticking air valve 8. Brittle or cracked gaskets 9. Bent, incorrect or improperly adjusted secondary metering rods 10. Clogged fuel filter 11. Clogged air filter 12. Defective fuel pump

TROUBLESHOOTING FUEL INJECTION PROBLEMS

Each fuel injection system has its own unique components and test procedures, for which it is impossible to generalize. Refer to Chapter 4 of this Repair & Tune-Up Guide for specific test and repair procedures, if the vehicle is equipped with fuel injection.

TROUBLESHOOTING ELECTRICAL PROBLEMS

See Chapter 5 for service procedures

For any electrical system to operate, it must make a complete circuit. This simply means that the power flow from the battery must make a complete circle. When an electrical component is operating, power flows from the battery to the component, passes through the component causing it to perform its function (lighting a light bulb), and then returns to the battery through the ground of the circuit. This ground is usually (but not always) the metal part of the car or truck on which the electrical component is mounted.

Perhaps the easiest way to visualize this is to think of connecting a light bulb with two wires attached to it to the battery. If one of the two wires attached to the light bulb were attached to the negative post of the battery and the other were attached to the positive post of the battery, you would have a complete circuit. Current from the battery would flow to the light bulb, causing it to light, and return to the negative post of the battery.

The normal automotive circuit differs from this simple example in two ways. First, instead of having a return wire from the bulb to the battery, the light bulb returns the current to the battery through the chassis of the vehicle. Since the negative battery cable is attached to the chassis and the chassis is made of electrically conductive metal, the chassis of the vehicle can serve as a ground wire to complete the circuit. Secondly, most automotive circuits contain switches to turn components on and off as required.

Every complete circuit from a power source must include a component which is using the power from the power source. If you were to disconnect the light bulb from the wires and touch the two wires together (don't do this) the power supply wire to the component would be grounded before the normal ground connection for the circuit.

Because grounding a wire from a power source makes a complete circuit—less the required component to use the power—this phenomenon is called a short circuit. Common causes are: broken insulation (exposing the metal wire to a metal part of the car or truck), or a shorted switch.

Some electrical components which require a large amount of current to operate also have a relay in their circuit. Since these circuits carry a large amount of current, the thickness of the wire in the circuit (gauge size) is also greater. If this large wire were connected from the component to the control switch on the instrument panel, and then back to the component, a voltage drop would occur in the circuit. To prevent this potential drop in voltage, an electromagnetic switch (relay) is used. The large wires in the circuit are connected from the battery to one side of the relay, and from the opposite side of the relay to the component. The relay is normally open, preventing current from passing through the circuit. An additional, smaller, wire is connected from the relay to the control switch for the circuit. When the control switch is turned on, it grounds the smaller wire from the relay and completes the circuit. This closes the relay and allows current to flow from the battery to the component. The horn, headlight, and starter circuits are three which use relays.

It is possible for larger surges of current to pass through the electrical system of your car or truck. If this surge of current were to reach an electrical component, it could burn it out. To prevent this, fuses, circuit breakers or fusible links are connected into the current supply wires of most of the major electrical systems. When an electrical current of excessive power passes through the component's fuse, the fuse blows out and breaks the circuit, saving the component from destruction.

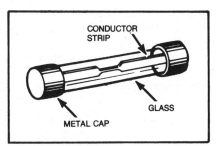

Typical automotive fuse

A circuit breaker is basically a self-repairing fuse. The circuit breaker opens the circuit the same way a fuse does. However, when either the short is removed from the circuit or the surge subsides, the circuit breaker resets itself and does not have to be replaced as a fuse does.

A fuse link is a wire that acts as a fuse. It is normally connected between the starter relay and the main wiring harness. This connection is usually under the hood. The fuse link (if installed) protects all the

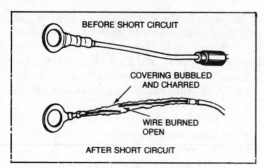

Most fusible links show a charred, melted insulation when they burn out

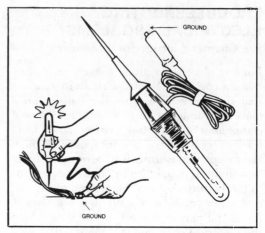

The test light will show the presence of current when touched to a hot wire and grounded at the other end

chassis electrical components, and is the probable cause of trouble when none of the electrical components function, unless the battery is disconnected or dead.

Electrical problems generally fall into one of three areas:

1. The component that is not functioning is not receiving current.

2. The component itself is not functioning.

3. The component is not properly grounded.

The electrical system can be checked with a test light and a jumper wire. A test light is a device that looks like a pointed screwdriver with a wire attached to it and has a light bulb in its handle. A jumper wire is a piece of insulated wire with an alligator clip attached to each end.

If a component is not working, you must follow a systematic plan to determine which of the three causes is the villain.

1. Turn on the switch that controls the inoperable component.

2. Disconnect the power supply wire from the component.

3. Attach the ground wire on the test light to a good metal ground.

4. Touch the probe end of the test light to the end of the power supply wire that was disconnected from the component. If the component is receiving current, the test light will go on.

NOTE: *Some components work only when the ignition switch is turned on.*

If the test light does not go on, then the problem is in the circuit between the battery and the component. This includes all the switches, fuses, and relays in the system. Follow the wire that runs back to the battery. The problem is an open circuit between the

battery and the component. If the fuse is blown and, when replaced, immediately blows again, there is a short circuit in the system which must be located and repaired. If there is a switch in the system, bypass it with a jumper wire. This is done by connecting one end of the jumper wire to the power supply wire into the switch and the other end of the jumper wire to the wire coming out of the switch. If the test light lights with the jumper wire installed, the switch or whatever was bypassed is defective.

NOTE: *Never substitute the jumper wire for the component, since it is required to use the power from the power source.*

5. If the bulb in the test light goes on, then the current is getting to the component that is not working. This eliminates the first of the three possible causes. Connect the power supply wire and connect a jumper wire from the component to a good metal ground. Do this with the switch which controls the component turned on, and also the ignition switch turned on if it is required for the component to work. If the component works with the jumper wire installed, then it has a bad ground. This is usually caused by the metal area on which the component mounts to the chassis being coated with some type of foreign matter.

6. If neither test located the source of the trouble, then the component itself is defective. Remember that for any electrical system to work, all connections must be clean and tight.

Troubleshooting Basic Turn Signal and Flasher Problems
See Chapter 5 for service procedures

Most problems in the turn signals or flasher system can be reduced to defective flashers or bulbs, which are easily replaced. Occasionally, the turn signal switch will prove defective.

F = Front   R = Rear   ● = Lights off   ○ = Lights on

Condition		Possible Cause
Turn signals light, but do not flash	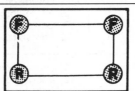	Defective flasher
No turn signals light on either side	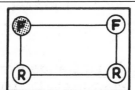	Blown fuse. Replace if defective. Defective flasher. Check by substitution. Open circuit, short circuit or poor ground.
Both turn signals on one side don't work	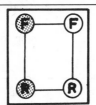	Bad bulbs. Bad ground in both (or either) housings.
One turn signal light on one side doesn't work	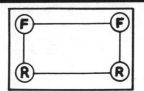	Defective bulb. Corrosion in socket. Clean contacts. Poor ground at socket.
Turn signal flashes too fast or too slowly	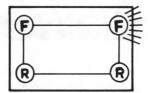	Check any bulb on the side flashing too fast. A heavy-duty bulb is probably installed in place of a regular bulb. Check the bulb flashing too slowly. A standard bulb was probably installed in place of a heavy-duty bulb. Loose connections or corrosion at the bulb socket.
Indicator lights don't work in either direction		Check if the turn signals are working. Check the dash indicator lights. Check the flasher by substitution.
One indicator light doesn't light		On systems with one dash indicator: See if the lights work on the same side. Often the filaments have been reversed in systems combining stoplights with taillights and turn signals. Check the flasher by substitution. On systems with two indicators: Check the bulbs on the same side. Check the indicator light bulb. Check the flasher by substitution.

Troubleshooting Lighting Problems
See Chapter 5 for service procedures

Condition	Possible Cause
One or more lights don't work, but others do	1. Defective bulb(s) 2. Blown fuse(s) 3. Dirty fuse clips or light sockets 4. Poor ground circuit
Lights burn out quickly	1. Incorrect voltage regulator setting or defective regulator 2. Poor battery/alternator connections
Lights go dim	1. Low/discharged battery 2. Alternator not charging 3. Corroded sockets or connections 4. Low voltage output
Lights flicker	1. Loose connection 2. Poor ground. (Run ground wire from light housing to frame) 3. Circuit breaker operating (short circuit)
Lights "flare"—Some flare is normal on acceleration—If excessive, see "Lights Burn Out Quickly"	High voltage setting
Lights glare—approaching drivers are blinded	1. Lights adjusted too high 2. Rear springs or shocks sagging 3. Rear tires soft

Troubleshooting Dash Gauge Problems
Most problems can be traced to a defective sending unit or faulty wiring. Occasionally, the gauge itself is at fault. See Chapter 5 for service procedures.

Condition	Possible Cause
COOLANT TEMPERATURE GAUGE	
Gauge reads erratically or not at all	1. Loose or dirty connections 2. Defective sending unit. 3. Defective gauge. To test a bi-metal gauge, remove the wire from the sending unit. Ground the wire for an instant. If the gauge registers, replace the sending unit. To test a magnetic gauge, disconnect the wire at the sending unit. With ignition ON gauge should register COLD. Ground the wire; gauge should register HOT.
AMMETER GAUGE—TURN HEADLIGHTS ON (DO NOT START ENGINE). NOTE REACTION	
Ammeter shows charge Ammeter shows discharge Ammeter does not move	1. Connections reversed on gauge 2. Ammeter is OK 3. Loose connections or faulty wiring 4. Defective gauge

Condition	Possible Cause

OIL PRESSURE GAUGE

Gauge does not register or is inaccurate	1. On mechanical gauge, Bourdon tube may be bent or kinked. 2. Low oil pressure. Remove sending unit. Idle the engine briefly. If no oil flows from sending unit hole, problem is in engine. 3. Defective gauge. Remove the wire from the sending unit and ground it for an instant with the ignition ON. A good gauge will go to the top of the scale. 4. Defective wiring. Check the wiring to the gauge. If it's OK and the gauge doesn't register when grounded, replace the gauge. 5. Defective sending unit.

ALL GAUGES

All gauges do not operate	1. Blown fuse 2. Defective instrument regulator
All gauges read low or erratically All gauges pegged	3. Defective or dirty instrument voltage regulator 4. Loss of ground between instrument voltage regulator and frame 5. Defective instrument regulator

WARNING LIGHTS

Light(s) do not come on when ignition is ON, but engine is not started	1. Defective bulb 2. Defective wire 3. Defective sending unit. Disconnect the wire from the sending unit and ground it. Replace the sending unit if the light comes on with the ignition ON.
Light comes on with engine running	4. Problem in individual system 5. Defective sending unit

Troubleshooting Clutch Problems

It is false economy to replace individual clutch components. The pressure plate, clutch plate and throwout bearing should be replaced as a set, and the flywheel face inspected, whenever the clutch is overhauled. See Chapter 6 for service procedures.

Condition	Possible Cause
Clutch chatter	1. Grease on driven plate (disc) facing 2. Binding clutch linkage or cable 3. Loose, damaged facings on driven plate (disc) 4. Engine mounts loose 5. Incorrect height adjustment of pressure plate release levers 6. Clutch housing or housing to transmission adapter misalignment 7. Loose driven plate hub
Clutch grabbing	1. Oil, grease on driven plate (disc) facing 2. Broken pressure plate 3. Warped or binding driven plate. Driven plate binding on clutch shaft
Clutch slips	1. Lack of lubrication in clutch linkage or cable (linkage or cable binds, causes incomplete engagement) 2. Incorrect pedal, or linkage adjustment 3. Broken pressure plate springs 4. Weak pressure plate springs 5. Grease on driven plate facings (disc)

Troubleshooting Clutch Problems (cont.)

Condition	Possible Cause
Incomplete clutch release	1. Incorrect pedal or linkage adjustment or linkage or cable binding 2. Incorrect height adjustment on pressure plate release levers 3. Loose, broken facings on driven plate (disc) 4. Bent, dished, warped driven plate caused by overheating
Grinding, whirring grating noise when pedal is depressed	1. Worn or defective throwout bearing 2. Starter drive teeth contacting flywheel ring gear teeth. Look for milled or polished teeth on ring gear.
Squeal, howl, trumpeting noise when pedal is being released (occurs during first inch to inch and one-half of pedal travel)	Pilot bushing worn or lack of lubricant. If bushing appears OK, polish bushing with emery cloth, soak lube wick in oil, lube bushing with oil, apply film of chassis grease to clutch shaft pilot hub, reassemble. NOTE: Bushing wear may be due to misalignment of clutch housing or housing to transmission adapter
Vibration or clutch pedal pulsation with clutch disengaged (pedal fully depressed)	1. Worn or defective engine transmission mounts 2. Flywheel run out. (Flywheel run out at face not to exceed 0.005″) 3. Damaged or defective clutch components

Troubleshooting Manual Transmission Problems
See Chapter 6 for service procedures

Condition	Possible Cause
Transmission jumps out of gear	1. Misalignment of transmission case or clutch housing. 2. Worn pilot bearing in crankshaft. 3. Bent transmission shaft. 4. Worn high speed sliding gear. 5. Worn teeth or end-play in clutch shaft. 6. Insufficient spring tension on shifter rail plunger. 7. Bent or loose shifter fork. 8. Gears not engaging completely. 9. Loose or worn bearings on clutch shaft or mainshaft. 10. Worn gear teeth. 11. Worn or damaged detent balls.
Transmission sticks in gear	1. Clutch not releasing fully. 2. Burred or battered teeth on clutch shaft, or sliding sleeve. 3. Burred or battered transmission mainshaft. 4. Frozen synchronizing clutch. 5. Stuck shifter rail plunger. 6. Gearshift lever twisting and binding shifter rail. 7. Battered teeth on high speed sliding gear or on sleeve. 8. Improper lubrication, or lack of lubrication. 9. Corroded transmission parts. 10. Defective mainshaft pilot bearing. 11. Locked gear bearings will give same effect as stuck in gear.
Transmission gears will not synchronize	1. Binding pilot bearing on mainshaft, will synchronize in high gear only. 2. Clutch not releasing fully. 3. Detent spring weak or broken. 4. Weak or broken springs under balls in sliding gear sleeve. 5. Binding bearing on clutch shaft, or binding countershaft. 6. Binding pilot bearing in crankshaft. 7. Badly worn gear teeth. 8. Improper lubrication. 9. Constant mesh gear not turning freely on transmission mainshaft. Will synchronize in that gear only.

Condition	Possible Cause
Gears spinning when shifting into gear from neutral	1. Clutch not releasing fully. 2. In some cases an extremely light lubricant in transmission will cause gears to continue to spin for a short time after clutch is released. 3. Binding pilot bearing in crankshaft.
Transmission noisy in all gears	1. Insufficient lubricant, or improper lubricant. 2. Worn countergear bearings. 3. Worn or damaged main drive gear or countergear. 4. Damaged main drive gear or mainshaft bearings. 5. Worn or damaged countergear anti-lash plate.
Transmission noisy in neutral only	1. Damaged main drive gear bearing. 2. Damaged or loose mainshaft pilot bearing. 3. Worn or damaged countergear anti-lash plate. 4. Worn countergear bearings.
Transmission noisy in one gear only	1. Damaged or worn constant mesh gears. 2. Worn or damaged countergear bearings. 3. Damaged or worn synchronizer.
Transmission noisy in reverse only	1. Worn or damaged reverse idler gear or idler bushing. 2. Worn or damaged mainshaft reverse gear. 3. Worn or damaged reverse countergear. 4. Damaged shift mechanism.

TROUBLESHOOTING AUTOMATIC TRANSMISSION PROBLEMS

Keeping alert to changes in the operating characteristics of the transmission (changing shift points, noises, etc.) can prevent small problems from becoming large ones. If the problem cannot be traced to loose bolts, fluid level, misadjusted linkage, clogged filters or similar problems, you should probably seek professional service.

Transmission Fluid Indications

The appearance and odor of the transmission fluid can give valuable clues to the overall condition of the transmission. Always note the appearance of the fluid when you check the fluid level or change the fluid. Rub a small amount of fluid between your fingers to feel for grit and smell the fluid on the dipstick.

If the fluid appears:	It indicates:
Clear and red colored	Normal operation
Discolored (extremely dark red or brownish) or smells burned	Band or clutch pack failure, usually caused by an overheated transmission. Hauling very heavy loads with insufficient power or failure to change the fluid often result in overheating. Do not confuse this appearance with newer fluids that have a darker red color and a strong odor (though not a burned odor).
Foamy or aerated (light in color and full of bubbles)	1. The level is too high (gear train is churning oil) 2. An internal air leak (air is mixing with the fluid). Have the transmission checked professionally.
Solid residue in the fluid	Defective bands, clutch pack or bearings. Bits of band material or metal abrasives are clinging to the dipstick. Have the transmission checked professionally.
Varnish coating on the dipstick	The transmission fluid is overheating

TROUBLESHOOTING DRIVE AXLE PROBLEMS

First, determine when the noise is most noticeable.

Drive Noise: Produced under vehicle acceleration.

Coast Noise: Produced while coasting with a closed throttle.

Float Noise: Occurs while maintaining constant speed (just enough to keep speed constant) on a level road.

External Noise Elimination

It is advisable to make a thorough road test to determine whether the noise originates in the rear axle or whether it originates from the tires, engine, transmission, wheel bearings or road surface. Noise originating from other places cannot be corrected by servicing the rear axle.

ROAD NOISE

Brick or rough surfaced concrete roads produce noises that seem to come from the rear axle. Road noise is usually identical in Drive or Coast and driving on a different type of road will tell whether the road is the problem.

TIRE NOISE

Tire noise can be mistaken as rear axle noise, even though the tires on the front are at fault. Snow tread and mud tread tires or tires worn unevenly will frequently cause vibrations which seem to originate elsewhere; *temporarily, and for test purposes only,* inflate the tires to 40–50 lbs. This will significantly alter the noise produced by the tires, but will not alter noise from the rear axle. Noises from the rear axle will normally cease at speeds below 30 mph on coast, while tire noise will continue at lower tone as speed is decreased. The rear axle noise will usually change from drive conditions to coast conditions, while tire noise will not. Do not forget to lower the tire pressure to normal after the test is complete.

ENGINE/TRANSMISSION NOISE

Determine at what speed the noise is most pronounced, then stop in a quiet place. With the transmission in Neutral, run the engine through speeds corresponding to road speeds where the noise was noticed. Noises produced with the vehicle standing still are coming from the engine or transmission.

FRONT WHEEL BEARINGS

Front wheel bearing noises, sometimes confused with rear axle noises, will not change when comparing drive and coast conditions. While holding the speed steady, lightly apply the footbrake. This will often cause wheel bearing noise to lessen, as some of the weight is taken off the bearing. Front wheel bearings are easily checked by jacking up the wheels and spinning the wheels. Shaking the wheels will also determine if the wheel bearings are excessively loose.

REAR AXLE NOISES

Eliminating other possible sources can narrow the cause to the rear axle, which normally produces noise from worn gears or bearings. Gear noises tend to peak in a narrow speed range, while bearing noises will usually vary in pitch with engine speeds.

Noise Diagnosis

The Noise Is:	Most Probably Produced By:
1. Identical under Drive or Coast	Road surface, tires or front wheel bearings
2. Different depending on road surface	Road surface or tires
3. Lower as speed is lowered	Tires
4. Similar when standing or moving	Engine or transmission
5. A vibration	Unbalanced tires, rear wheel bearing, unbalanced driveshaft or worn U-joint
6. A knock or click about every two tire revolutions	Rear wheel bearing
7. Most pronounced on turns	Damaged differential gears
8. A steady low-pitched whirring or scraping, starting at low speeds	Damaged or worn pinion bearing
9. A chattering vibration on turns	Wrong differential lubricant or worn clutch plates (limited slip rear axle)
10. Noticed only in Drive, Coast or Float conditions	Worn ring gear and/or pinion gear

Troubleshooting Steering & Suspension Problems

Condition	Possible Cause
Hard steering (wheel is hard to turn)	1. Improper tire pressure 2. Loose or glazed pump drive belt 3. Low or incorrect fluid 4. Loose, bent or poorly lubricated front end parts 5. Improper front end alignment (excessive caster) 6. Bind in steering column or linkage 7. Kinked hydraulic hose 8. Air in hydraulic system 9. Low pump output or leaks in system 10. Obstruction in lines 11. Pump valves sticking or out of adjustment 12. Incorrect wheel alignment
Loose steering (too much play in steering wheel)	1. Loose wheel bearings 2. Faulty shocks 3. Worn linkage or suspension components 4. Loose steering gear mounting or linkage points 5. Steering mechanism worn or improperly adjusted 6. Valve spool improperly adjusted 7. Worn ball joints, tie-rod ends, etc.
Veers or wanders (pulls to one side with hands off steering wheel)	1. Improper tire pressure 2. Improper front end alignment 3. Dragging or improperly adjusted brakes 4. Bent frame 5. Improper rear end alignment 6. Faulty shocks or springs 7. Loose or bent front end components 8. Play in Pitman arm 9. Steering gear mountings loose 10. Loose wheel bearings 11. Binding Pitman arm 12. Spool valve sticking or improperly adjusted 13. Worn ball joints
Wheel oscillation or vibration transmitted through steering wheel	1. Low or uneven tire pressure 2. Loose wheel bearings 3. Improper front end alignment 4. Bent spindle 5. Worn, bent or broken front end components 6. Tires out of round or out of balance 7. Excessive lateral runout in disc brake rotor 8. Loose or bent shock absorber or strut
Noises (see also "Troubleshooting Drive Axle Problems")	1. Loose belts 2. Low fluid, air in system 3. Foreign matter in system 4. Improper lubrication 5. Interference or chafing in linkage 6. Steering gear mountings loose 7. Incorrect adjustment or wear in gear box 8. Faulty valves or wear in pump 9. Kinked hydraulic lines 10. Worn wheel bearings
Poor return of steering	1. Over-inflated tires 2. Improperly aligned front end (excessive caster) 3. Binding in steering column 4. No lubrication in front end 5. Steering gear adjusted too tight
Uneven tire wear (see "How To Read Tire Wear")	1. Incorrect tire pressure 2. Improperly aligned front end 3. Tires out-of-balance 4. Bent or worn suspension parts

HOW TO READ TIRE WEAR

The way your tires wear is a good indicator of other parts of the suspension. Abnormal wear patterns are often caused by the need for simple tire maintenance, or for front end alignment.

Excessive wear at the center of the tread indicates that the air pressure in the tire is consistently too high. The tire is riding on the center of the tread and wearing it prematurely. Occasionally, this wear pattern can result from outrageously wide tires on narrow rims. The cure for this is to replace either the tires or the wheels.

This type of wear usually results from consistent under-inflation. When a tire is under-inflated, there is too much contact with the road by the outer treads, which wear prematurely. When this type of wear occurs, and the tire pressure is known to be consistently correct, a bent or worn steering component or the need for wheel alignment could be indicated.

Feathering is a condition when the edge of each tread rib develops a slightly rounded edge on one side and a sharp edge on the other. By running your hand over the tire, you can usually feel the sharper edges before you'll be able to see them. The most common causes of feathering are incorrect toe-in setting or deteriorated bushings in the front suspension.

When an inner or outer rib wears faster than the rest of the tire, the need for wheel alignment is indicated. There is excessive camber in the front suspension, causing the wheel to lean too much putting excessive load on one side of the tire. Misalignment could also be due to sagging springs, worn ball joints, or worn control arm bushings. Be sure the vehicle is loaded the way it's normally driven when you have the wheels aligned.

Cups or scalloped dips appearing around the edge of the tread almost always indicate worn (sometimes bent) suspension parts. Adjustment of wheel alignment alone will seldom cure the problem. Any worn component that connects the wheel to the suspension can cause this type of wear. Occasionally, wheels that are out of balance will wear like this, but wheel imbalance usually shows up as bald spots between the outside edges and center of the tread.

Second-rib wear is usually found only in radial tires, and appears where the steel belts end in relation to the tread. It can be kept to a minimum by paying careful attention to tire pressure and frequently rotating the tires. This is often considered normal wear but excessive amounts indicate that the tires are too wide for the wheels.

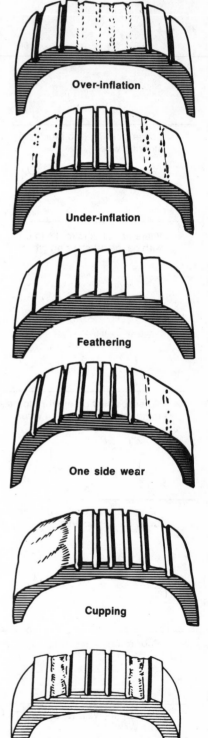

Over-inflation

Under-inflation

Feathering

One side wear

Cupping

Second-rib wear

Troubleshooting Disc Brake Problems

Condition	Possible Cause
Noise—groan—brake noise emanating when slowly releasing brakes (creep-groan)	Not detrimental to function of disc brakes—no corrective action required. (This noise may be eliminated by slightly increasing or decreasing brake pedal efforts.)
Rattle—brake noise or rattle emanating at low speeds on rough roads, (front wheels only).	1. Shoe anti-rattle spring missing or not properly positioned. 2. Excessive clearance between shoe and caliper. 3. Soft or broken caliper seals. 4. Deformed or misaligned disc. 5. Loose caliper.
Scraping	1. Mounting bolts too long. 2. Loose wheel bearings. 3. Bent, loose, or misaligned splash shield.
Front brakes heat up during driving and fail to release	1. Operator riding brake pedal. 2. Stop light switch improperly adjusted. 3. Sticking pedal linkage. 4. Frozen or seized piston. 5. Residual pressure valve in master cylinder. 6. Power brake malfunction. 7. Proportioning valve malfunction.
Leaky brake caliper	1. Damaged or worn caliper piston seal. 2. Scores or corrosion on surface of cylinder bore.
Grabbing or uneven brake action— Brakes pull to one side	1. Causes listed under "Brakes Pull". 2. Power brake malfunction. 3. Low fluid level in master cylinder. 4. Air in hydraulic system. 5. Brake fluid, oil or grease on linings. 6. Unmatched linings. 7. Distorted brake pads. 8. Frozen or seized pistons. 9. Incorrect tire pressure. 10. Front end out of alignment. 11. Broken rear spring. 12. Brake caliper pistons sticking. 13. Restricted hose or line. 14. Caliper not in proper alignment to braking disc. 15. Stuck or malfunctioning metering valve. 16. Soft or broken caliper seals. 17. Loose caliper.
Brake pedal can be depressed without braking effect	1. Air in hydraulic system or improper bleeding procedure. 2. Leak past primary cup in master cylinder. 3. Leak in system. 4. Rear brakes out of adjustment. 5. Bleeder screw open.
Excessive pedal travel	1. Air, leak, or insufficient fluid in system or caliper. 2. Warped or excessively tapered shoe and lining assembly. 3. Excessive disc runout. 4. Rear brake adjustment required. 5. Loose wheel bearing adjustment. 6. Damaged caliper piston seal. 7. Improper brake fluid (boil). 8. Power brake malfunction. 9. Weak or soft hoses.

Troubleshooting Disc Brake Problems (cont.)

Condition	Possible Cause
Brake roughness or chatter (pedal pumping)	1. Excessive thickness variation of braking disc. 2. Excessive lateral runout of braking disc. 3. Rear brake drums out-of-round. 4. Excessive front bearing clearance.
Excessive pedal effort	1. Brake fluid, oil or grease on linings. 2. Incorrect lining. 3. Frozen or seized pistons. 4. Power brake malfunction. 5. Kinked or collapsed hose or line. 6. Stuck metering valve. 7. Scored caliper or master cylinder bore. 8. Seized caliper pistons.
Brake pedal fades (pedal travel increases with foot on brake)	1. Rough master cylinder or caliper bore. 2. Loose or broken hydraulic lines/connections. 3. Air in hydraulic system. 4. Fluid level low. 5. Weak or soft hoses. 6. Inferior quality brake shoes or fluid. 7. Worn master cylinder piston cups or seals.

Troubleshooting Drum Brakes

Condition	Possible Cause
Pedal goes to floor	1. Fluid low in reservoir. 2. Air in hydraulic system. 3. Improperly adjusted brake. 4. Leaking wheel cylinders. 5. Loose or broken brake lines. 6. Leaking or worn master cylinder. 7. Excessively worn brake lining.
Spongy brake pedal	1. Air in hydraulic system. 2. Improper brake fluid (low boiling point). 3. Excessively worn or cracked brake drums. 4. Broken pedal pivot bushing.
Brakes pulling	1. Contaminated lining. 2. Front end out of alignment. 3. Incorrect brake adjustment. 4. Unmatched brake lining. 5. Brake drums out of round. 6. Brake shoes distorted. 7. Restricted brake hose or line. 8. Broken rear spring. 9. Worn brake linings. 10. Uneven lining wear. 11. Glazed brake lining. 12. Excessive brake lining dust. 13. Heat spotted brake drums. 14. Weak brake return springs. 15. Faulty automatic adjusters. 16. Low or incorrect tire pressure.

Condition	Possible Cause
Squealing brakes	1. Glazed brake lining.
	2. Saturated brake lining.
	3. Weak or broken brake shoe retaining spring.
	4. Broken or weak brake shoe return spring.
	5. Incorrect brake lining.
	6. Distorted brake shoes.
	7. Bent support plate.
	8. Dust in brakes or scored brake drums.
	9. Linings worn below limit.
	10. Uneven brake lining wear.
	11. Heat spotted brake drums.
Chirping brakes	1. Out of round drum or eccentric axle flange pilot.
Dragging brakes	1. Incorrect wheel or parking brake adjustment.
	2. Parking brakes engaged or improperly adjusted.
	3. Weak or broken brake shoe return spring.
	4. Brake pedal binding.
	5. Master cylinder cup sticking.
	6. Obstructed master cylinder relief port.
	7. Saturated brake lining.
	8. Bent or out of round brake drum.
	9. Contaminated or improper brake fluid.
	10. Sticking wheel cylinder pistons.
	11. Driver riding brake pedal.
	12. Defective proportioning valve.
	13. Insufficient brake shoe lubricant.
Hard pedal	1. Brake booster inoperative.
	2. Incorrect brake lining.
	3. Restricted brake line or hose.
	4. Frozen brake pedal linkage.
	5. Stuck wheel cylinder.
	6. Binding pedal linkage.
	7. Faulty proportioning valve.
Wheel locks	1. Contaminated brake lining.
	2. Loose or torn brake lining.
	3. Wheel cylinder cups sticking.
	4. Incorrect wheel bearing adjustment.
	5. Faulty proportioning valve.
Brakes fade (high speed)	1. Incorrect lining.
	2. Overheated brake drums.
	3. Incorrect brake fluid (low boiling temperature).
	4. Saturated brake lining.
	5. Leak in hydraulic system.
	6. Faulty automatic adjusters.
Pedal pulsates	1. Bent or out of round brake drum.
Brake chatter and shoe knock	1. Out of round brake drum.
	2. Loose support plate.
	3. Bent support plate.
	4. Distorted brake shoes.
	5. Machine grooves in contact face of brake drum (Shoe Knock).
	6. Contaminated brake lining.
	7. Missing or loose components.
	8. Incorrect lining material.
	9. Out-of-round brake drums.
	10. Heat spotted or scored brake drums.
	11. Out-of-balance wheels.

Troubleshooting Drum Brakes (cont.)

Condition	Possible Cause
Brakes do not self adjust	1. Adjuster screw frozen in thread. 2. Adjuster screw corroded at thrust washer. 3. Adjuster lever does not engage star wheel. 4. Adjuster installed on wrong wheel.
Brake light glows	1. Leak in the hydraulic system. 2. Air in the system. 3. Improperly adjusted master cylinder pushrod. 4. Uneven lining wear. 5. Failure to center combination valve or proportioning valve.

Mechanic's Data

General Conversion Table

Multiply By	To Convert	To	
		LENGTH	
2.54	Inches	Centimeters	.3937
25.4	Inches	Millimeters	.03937
30.48	Feet	Centimeters	.0328
.304	Feet	Meters	3.28
.914	Yards	Meters	1.094
1.609	Miles	Kilometers	.621
		VOLUME	
.473	Pints	Liters	2.11
.946	Quarts	Liters	1.06
3.785	Gallons	Liters	.264
.016	Cubic inches	Liters	61.02
16.39	Cubic inches	Cubic cms.	.061
28.3	Cubic feet	Liters	.0353
		MASS (Weight)	
28.35	Ounces	Grams	.035
.4536	Pounds	Kilograms	2.20
—	To obtain	From	Multiply by

Multiply By	To Convert	To	
		AREA	
.645	Square inches	Square cms.	.155
.836	Square yds.	Square meters	1.196
		FORCE	
4.448	Pounds	Newtons	.225
.138	Ft./lbs.	Kilogram/meters	7.23
1.36	Ft./lbs.	Newton-meters	.737
.112	In./lbs.	Newton-meters	8.844
		PRESSURE	
.068	Psi	Atmospheres	14.7
6.89	Psi	Kilopascals	.145
		OTHER	
1.104	Horsepower (DIN)	Horsepower (SAE)	.9861
.746	Horsepower (SAE)	Kilowatts (KW)	1.34
1.60	Mph	Km/h	.625
.425	Mpg	Km/1	2.35
—	To obtain	From	Multiply by

Tap Drill Sizes

National Coarse or U.S.S.

Screw & Tap Size	Threads Per Inch	Use Drill Number
No. 5	40	.39
No. 6	32	.36
No. 8	32	.29
No. 10	24	.25
No. 12	24	.17
1/4	20	8
5/16	18	.F
3/8	16	5/16
7/16	14	.U
1/2	13	27/64
9/16	12	31/64
5/8	11	17/32
3/4	10	21/32
7/8	9	49/64

National Coarse or U.S.S.

Screw & Tap Size	Threads Per Inch	Use Drill Number
1	8	7/8
1 1/8	7	63/64
1 1/4	7	1 7/64
1 1/2	6	1 11/32

National Fine or S.A.E.

Screw & Tap Size	Threads Per Inch	Use Drill Number
No. 5	44	.37
No. 6	40	.33
No. 8	36	.29
No. 10	32	.21

National Fine or S.A.E.

Screw & Tap Size	Threads Per Inch	Use Drill Number
No. 12	28	.15
1/4	28	3
6/16	24	1
3/8	24	.Q
7/16	20	.W
1/2	20	29/64
9/16	18	33/64
5/8	18	37/64
3/4	16	11/16
7/8	14	13/16
1 1/8	12	1 3/64
1 1/4	12	1 11/64
1 1/2	12	1 27/64

Drill Sizes In Decimal Equivalents

Inch	Decimal	Wire	mm	Inch	Decimal	Wire	mm	Inch	Decimal	Wire & Letter	mm	Inch	Decimal	Letter	mm	Inch	Decimal	mm
1/64	.0156		.39		.0730	49			.1614		4.1		.2717		6.9		.4331	11.0
	.0157		.4		.0748		1.9		.1654		4.2		.2720	I		7/16	.4375	11.11
	.0160	78			.0760	48			.1660	19			.2756		7.0		.4528	11.5
	.0165		.42		.0768		1.95		.1673		4.25		.2770	J		29/64	.4531	11.51
	.0173		.44	5/64	.0781		1.98		.1693		4.3		.2795		7.1	15/32	.4688	11.90
	.0177		.45		.0785	47			.1695	18			.2810	K			.4724	12.0
	.0180	77			.0787		2.0	11/64	.1719		4.36	9/32	.2812		7.14	31/64	.4844	12.30
	.0181		.46		.0807		2.05		.1730	17			.2835		7.2		.4921	12.5
	.0189		.48		.0810	46			.1732		4.4		.2854		7.25	1/2	.5000	12.70
	.0197		.5		.0820	45			.1770	16			.2874		7.3		.5118	13.0
	.0200	76			.0827		2.1		.1772		4.5		.2900	L		33/64	.5156	13.09
	.0210	75			.0846		2.15		.1800	15			.2913		7.4	17/32	.5312	13.49
	.0217		.55		.0860	44			.1811		4.6		.2950	M			.5315	13.5
	.0225	74			.0866		2.2		.1820	14			.2953		7.5	35/64	.5469	13.89
	.0236		.6		.0886		2.25		.1850	13		19/64	.2969		7.54		.5512	14.0
	.0240	73			.0890	43			.1850		4.7		.2992		7.6	9/16	.5625	14.28
	.0250	72			.0906		2.3		.1870		4.75		.3020	N			.5709	14.5
	.0256		.65		.0925		2.35	3/16	.1875		4.76		.3031		7.7	37/64	.5781	14.68
	.0260	71			.0935	42			.1890		4.8		.3051		7.75		.5906	15.0
	.0276		.7	3/32	.0938		2.38		.1890	12			.3071		7.8	19/32	.5938	15.08
	.0280	70			.0945		2.4		.1910	11			.3110		7.9	39/64	.6094	15.47
	.0292	69			.0960	41			.1929		4.9	5/16	.3125		7.93		.6102	15.5
	.0295		.75		.0965		2.45		.1935	10			.3150		8.0	5/8	.6250	15.87
	.0310	68			.0980	40			.1960	9			.3160	O			.6299	16.0
1/32	.0312		.79		.0981		2.5		.1969		5.0		.3189		8.1	41/64	.6406	16.27
	.0315		.8		.0995	39			.1990	8			.3228		8.2		.6496	16.5
	.0320	67			.1015	38			.2008		5.1		.3230	P		21/32	.6562	16.66
	.0330	66			.1024		2.6		.2010	7			.3248		8.25		.6693	17.0
	.0335		.85		.1040	37		13/64	.2031		5.16		.3268		8.3	43/64	.6719	17.06
	.0350	65			.1063		2.7		.2040	6		21/64	.3281		8.33	11/16	.6875	17.46
	.0354		.9		.1065	36			.2047		5.2		.3307		8.4		.6890	17.5
	.0360	64			.1083		2.75		.2055	5			.3320	Q		45/64	.7031	17.85
	.0370	63		7/64	.1094		2.77		.2067		5.25		.3346		8.5		.7087	18.0
	.0374		.95		.1100	35			.2087		5.3		.3386		8.6	23/32	.7188	18.25
	.0380	62			.1102		2.8		.2090	4			.3390	R			.7283	18.5
	.0390	61			.1110	34			.2126		5.4		.3425		8.7	47/64	.7344	18.65
	.0394		1.0		.1130	33			.2130	3		11/32	.3438		8.73		.7480	19.0
	.0400	60			.1142		2.9		.2165		5.5		.3445		8.75	3/4	.7500	19.05
	.0410	59			.1160	32		7/32	2188		5.55		.3465		8.8	49/64	.7656	19.44
	.0413		1.05		.1181		3.0		.2205		5.6		.3480	S			.7677	19.5
	.0420	58			.1200	31			.2210	2			.3504		8.9	25/32	.7812	19.84
	.0430	57			.1220		3.1		.2244		5.7		.3543		9.0		.7874	20.0
	.0433		1.1	1/8	.1250		3.17		.2264		5.75		.3580	T		51/64	.7969	20.24
	.0453		1.15		.1260		3.2		.2280	1			.3583		9.1		.8071	20.5
3/64	.0465	56			.1280		3.25		.2283		5.8	23/64	.3594		9.12	13/16	.8125	20.63
	.0469		1.19		.1285	30			.2323		5.9		.3622		9.2		.8268	21.0
	.0472		1.2		.1299		3.3		.2340	A			.3642		9.25	53/64	.8281	21.03
	.0492		1.25		.1339		3.4	15/64	.2344		5.95		.3661		9.3	27/32	.8438	21.43
	.0512		1.3		.1360	29			.2362		6.0		.3680	U			.8465	21.5
	.0520	55			.1378		3.5		.2380	B			.3701		9.4	55/64	.8594	21.82
	.0531		1.35		.1405	28			.2402		6.1		.3740		9.5		.8661	22.0
	.0550	54		9/64	.1406		3.57		.2420	C		3/8	.3750		9.52	7/8	.8750	22.22
	.0551		1.4		.1417		3.6		.2441		6.2		.3770	V			.8858	22.5
	.0571		1.45		.1440	27			.2460	D			.3780		9.6	57/64	.8906	22.62
	.0591		1.5		.1457		3.7		.2461		6.25		.3819		9.7		.9055	23.0
	.0595	53			.1470	26			.2480		6.3		.3839		9.75	29/32	.9062	23.01
	.0610		1.55		.1476		3.75	1/4	.2500	E	6.35		.3858		9.8	59/64	.9219	23.41
1/16	.0625		1.59		.1495	25			.2520		6.		.3860	W			.9252	23.5
	.0630		1.6		.1496		3.8		.2559		6.5		.3898		9.9	15/16	.9375	23.81
	.0635	52			.1520	24			.2570	F		25/64	.3906		9.92		.9449	24.0
	.0650		1.65		.1535		3.9		.2598		6.6		.3937		10.0	61/64	.9531	24.2
	.0669		1.7		.1540	23			.2610	G			.3970	X			.9646	24.5
	.0670	51		5/32	.1562		3.96		.2638		6.7		.4040	Y		31/32	.9688	24.6
	.0689		1.75		.1570	22		17/64	.2656		6.74	13/32	.4062		10.31		.9843	25.0
	.0700	50			.1575		4.0		.2657		6.75		.4130	Z		63/64	.9844	25.0
	.0709		1.8		.1590	21			.2660	H			.4134		10.5	1	1.0000	25.4
	.0728		1.85		.1610	20			.2677		6.8	27/64	.4219		10.71			

Index

Chilton's Repair & Tune-Up Guides

The complete line covers domestic cars, imports, trucks, vans, RV's and 4-wheel drive vehicles.

CODE	TITLE	CODE	TITLE
#7199	AMC 75-82; all models	#6935	GM Sub-compact 71-81 inc. Vega,
#7165	Alliance 1983		Monza, Astre, Sunbird, Starfire & Skyhawk
#7323	Aries 81-82	#6937	Granada 75-80
#7032	Arrow Pick-Up 79-81	#5905	GTO 68-73
#7193	Aspen 76-80	#5821	GTX 68-73
#5902	Audi 70-73	#7204	Honda 73-82
#7028	Audi 4000/5000 77-81	#7191	Horizon 78-82
#6337	Audi Fox 73-75	#5912	International Scout 67-73
#5807	Barracuda 65-72	#7136	Jeep CJ 1945-81
#7203	Blazer 69-82	#6739	Jeep Wagoneer, Commando, Cherokee 66-79
#5576	BMW 59-70	#6962	Jetta 1980
#6844	BMW 70-79	#7203	Jimmy 69-82
#7027	Bobcat	#7059	J-2000 1982
#7307	Buick Century/Regal 75-83	#7165	Le Car 76-83
#7045	Camaro 67-81	#7323	Le Baron 1982
#6695	Capri 70-77	#5905	Le Mans 68-73
#7195	Capri 79-82	#7055	Lynx 81-82 inc. EXP & LN-7
#7059	Cavalier 1982	#6634	Maverick 70-77
#5807	Challenger 65-72	#7198	Mazda 71-82
#7037	Challenger (Import) 71-81	#7031	Mazda RX-7 79-81
#7041	Champ 78-81	#6065	Mercedes-Benz 59-70
#6316	Charger/Coronet 71-75	#5907	Mercedes-Benz 68-73
#7162	Chevette 76-82 inc. diesel	#6809	Mercedes-Benz 74-79
#7313	Chevrolet 68-83 all full size models	#7128	Mercury 68-71 all full sized models
#7167	Chevrolet/GMC Pick-Ups 70-82	#7194	Mercury Mid-Size 71-82 inc. Continental,
#7169	Chevrolet/GMC Vans 67-82		Cougar, XR-7 & Montego
#7310	Chevrolet S-10/GMC S-15 Pick-Ups 82-83	#7173	MG 61-80
#7051	Chevy Luv 72-81 inc. 4wd	#6973	Monarch 75-80
#7056	Chevy Mid-Size 64-82 inc. El Camino,	#6542	Mustang 65-73
	Chevelle, Laguna, Malibu & Monte Carlo	#6812	Mustang II 74-78
#6841	Chevy II 62-79	#7195	Mustang 79-82
#7059	Cimarron 1982	#6841	Nova 69-79
#7049	Citation 80-81	#7049	Omega 81-82
#7037	Colt 71-81	#7191	Omni 78-82
#6634	Comet 70-77	#6575	Opel 71-75
#7194	Continental 1982	#5982	Peugeot 70-74
#6691	Corvair 60-69 inc. Turbo	#7049	Phoenix 81-82
#6576	Corvette 53-62	#7027	Pinto 71-80
#7192	Corvette 63-82	#8552	Plymouth 68-76 full sized models
#7190	Cutlass 70-82	#7168	Plymouth Vans 67-82
#6324	Dart 68-76	#5822	Porsche 69-73
#6962	Dasher 74-80	#7048	Porsche 924 & 928 77-81 inc. Turbo
#5790	Datsun 61-72	#6962	Rabbit 75-80
#7196	Datsun F10, 310, Nissan Stanza 77-82	#7323	Reliant 81-82
#7170	Datsun 200SX, 510, 610, 710, 810 73-82	#7165	Renault 75-83
#7197	Datsun 1200, 210/Nissan Sentra 73-82	#5821	Roadrunner 68-73
#7172	Datsun Z & ZX 70-82	#5988	Saab 69-75
#7050	Datsun Pick-Ups 70-81 inc. 4wd	#7041	Sapporo 78-81
#6324	Demon 68-76	#5821	Satellite 68-73
#6554	Dodge 68-77 all full sized models	#6962	Scirocco 75-80
#7323	Dodge 400 1982	#7059	Skyhawk 1982
#6486	Dodge Charger 67-70	#7049	Skylark 80-81
#7168	Dodge Vans 67-82	#7208	Subaru 70-82
#6326	Duster 68-76	#5905	Tempest 68-73
#7055	Escort 81-82 inc. EXP & LN-7	#6320	Torino 62-75
#6320	Fairlane 62-75	#5795	Toyota 66-70
#7312	Fairmont 78-83	#7043	Toyota Celica & Supra 71-81
#7042	Fiat 69-81	#7036	Toyota Corolla, Carina, Tercel, Starlet 70-81
#6846	Fiesta 78-80	#7044	Toyota Corona, Cressida, Crown, Mark II 70-81
#7046	Firebird 67-81	#7035	Toyota Pick-Ups 70-81
#7059	Firenza 1982	#5910	Triumph 69-73
#7128	Ford 68-81 all full sized models	#7162	T-1000 1982
#7140	Ford Bronco 66-81	#6326	Valiant 68-76
#6983	Ford Courier 72-80	#5796	Volkswagen 49-71
#7194	Ford Mid-Size 71-82 inc. Torino, Gran	#6837	Volkswagen 70-81
	Torino, Ranchero, Elite, LTD II & Thunder-	#7193	Volaré 76-80
	bird	#6529	Volvo 56-69
#7166	Ford Pick-Ups 65-82 inc. 4wd	#7040	Volvo 70-80
#7171	Ford Vans 61-82	#7312	Zephyr 78-83
#7165	Fuego 82-83		

Chilton's Repair & Tune-Up Guides are available at your local retailer or by mailing a check or money order for **$10.95** plus **$1.00** to cover postage and handling to:

Chilton Book Company
Dept. DM
Radnor, PA 19089

NOTE: When ordering be sure to include your name & address, book code & title.